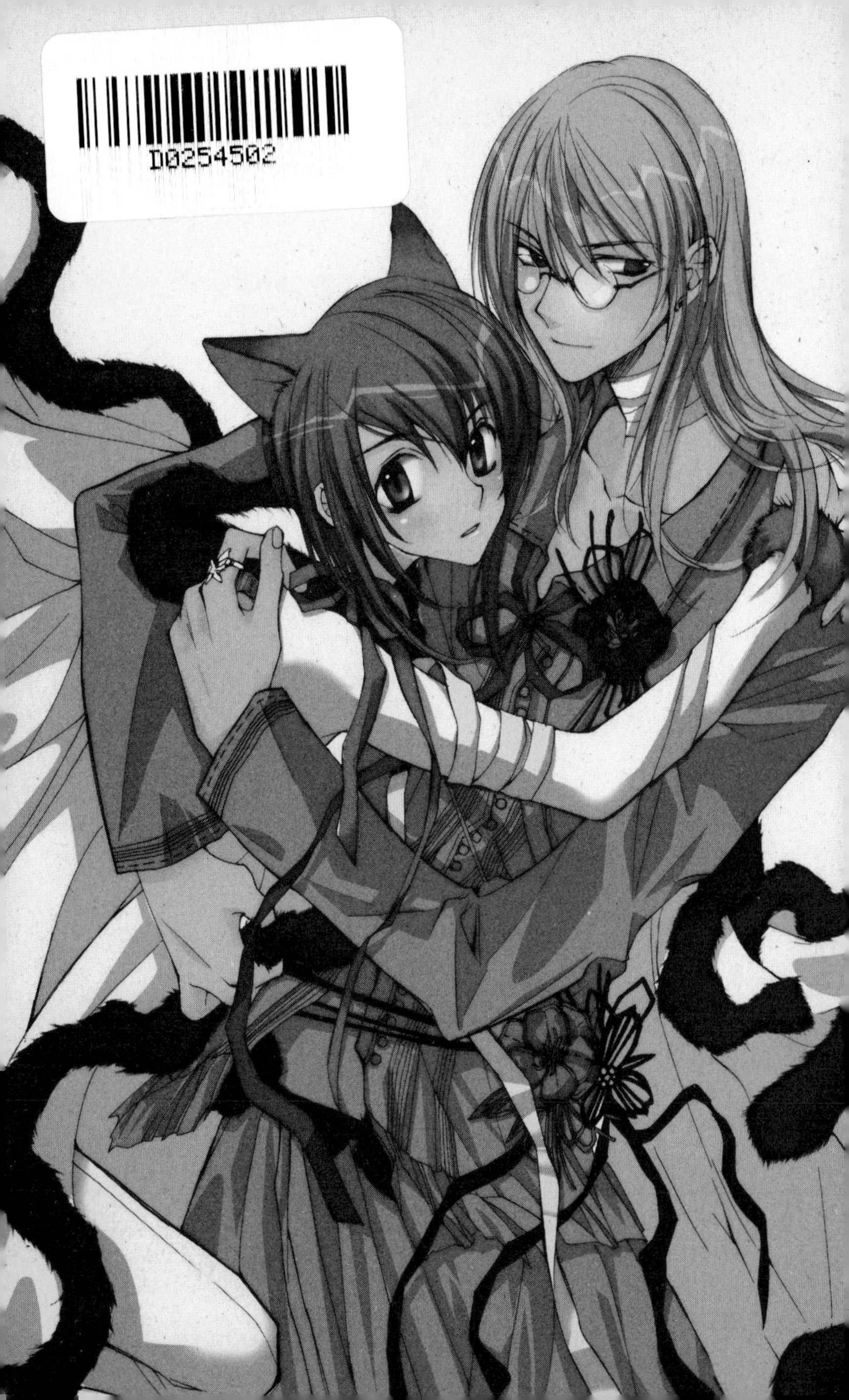

LOVELESS

UN:KOUGA_LOVELESS_2003

TABLE OF CONTENTS

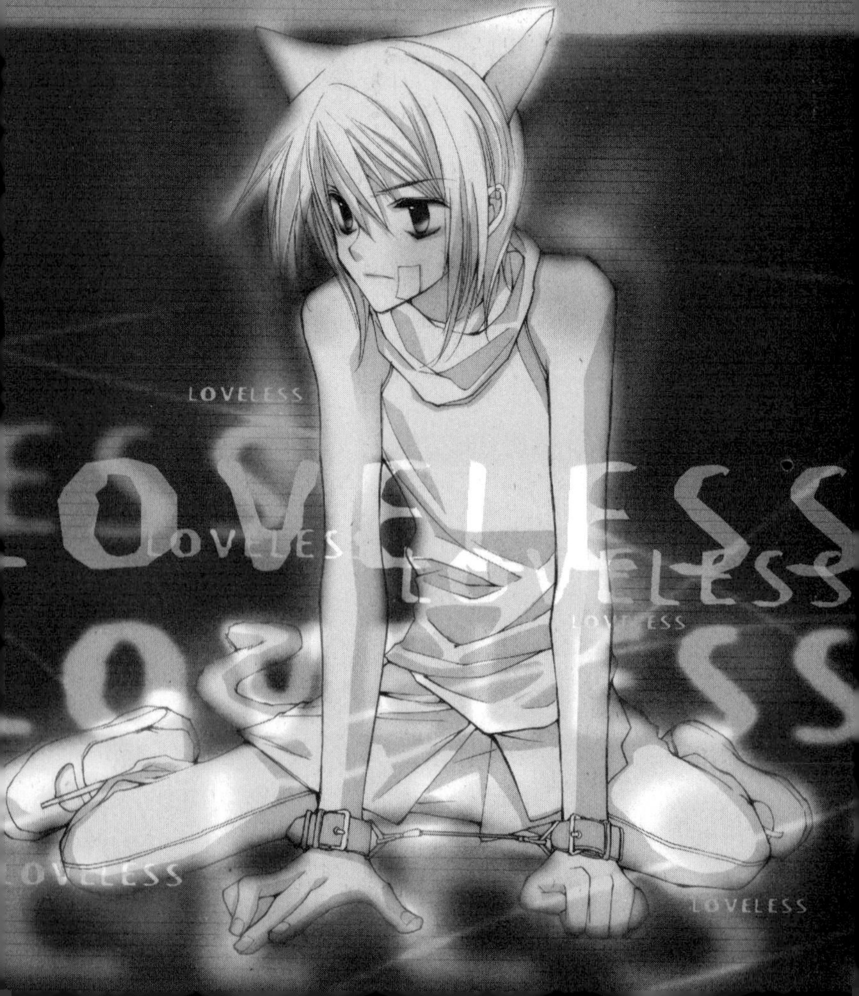
LOVELESS

Volume 2

HAMBURG // LONDON // LOS ANGELES // TOKYO

Loveless Vol. 2
Created by Yun Kouga

Translation - Ray Yoshimoto
English Adaptation - Christine Boylan
Retouch and Lettering - Fawn Lau
Cover Design - Al-Insan Lashley

Editor - Lillian Diaz-Przybyl
Digital Imaging Manager - Chris Buford
Managing Editor - Lindsey Johnston
VP of Production - Ron Klamert
Editor-In-Chief - Rob Tokar
Publisher - Mike Kiley
President and C.O.O. - John Parker
C.E.O. and Chief Creative Officer - Stuart Levy

A  Manga

TOKYOPOP Inc.
5900 Wilshire Blvd. Suite 2000
Los Angeles, CA 90036

E-mail: info@TOKYOPOP.com
Come visit us online at www.TOKYOPOP.com

ISBN:1-59816-222-5

First TOKYOPOP printing: June 2006
20 19 18 17 16 15 14 13
Printed in the USA

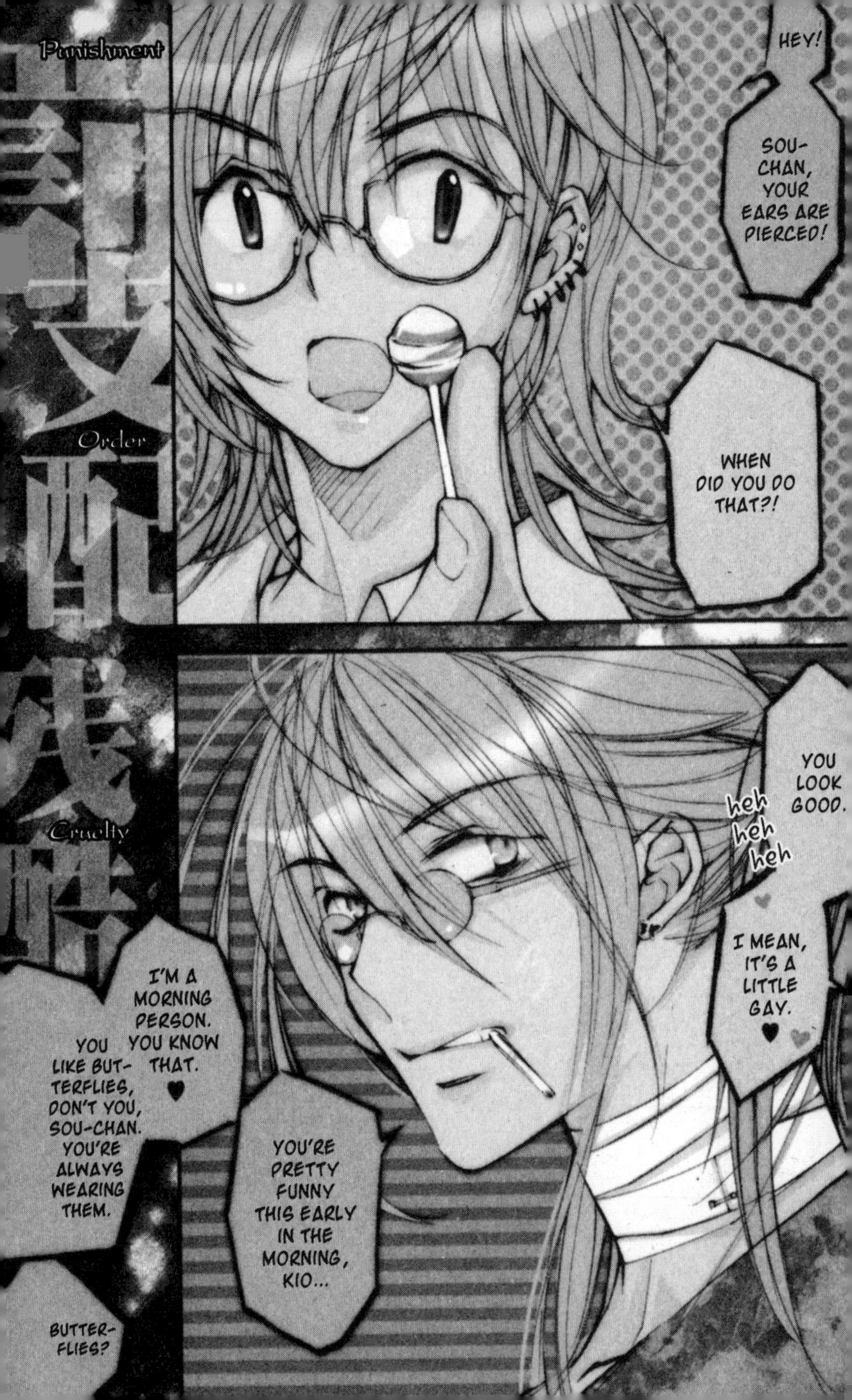
HEY!
SOU-CHAN, YOUR EARS ARE PIERCED!
WHEN DID YOU DO THAT?!
YOU LOOK GOOD.
heh heh heh
I MEAN, IT'S A LITTLE GAY.
YOU'RE PRETTY FUNNY THIS EARLY IN THE MORNING, KIO...
I'M A MORNING PERSON. YOU KNOW THAT.
YOU LIKE BUT-TERFLIES, DON'T YOU, SOU-CHAN. YOU'RE ALWAYS WEARING THEM.
BUTTER-FLIES?
Punishment
Order
Cruelty

The Volume of The Absolute Toy Master
Chapter 1

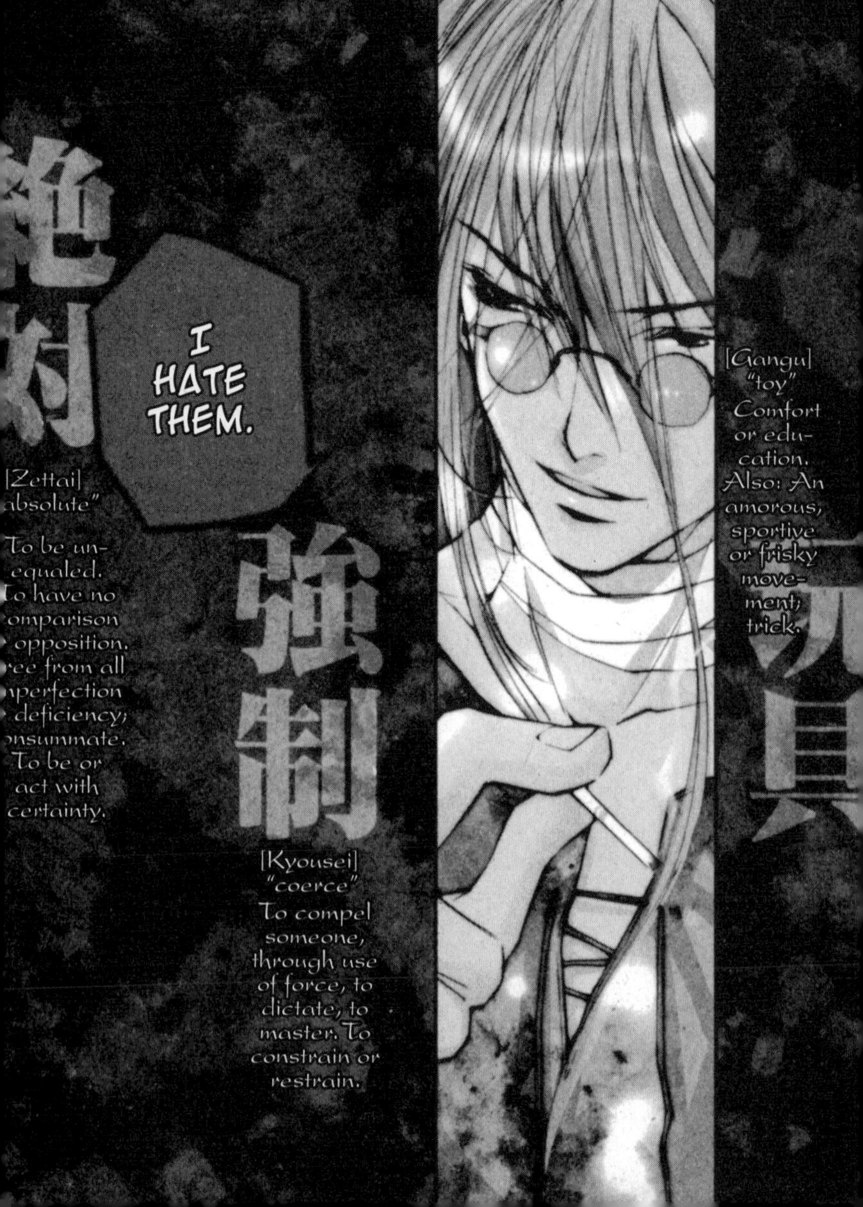
[Gangu] "toy" Comfort or education. Also: An amorous, sportive or frisky movement; trick.
I HATE THEM.
強制
[Kyousei] "coerce" To compel someone, through use of force, to dictate, to master. To constrain or restrain.
絶対
[Zettai] absolute" To be unequaled. To have no omparison opposition. ree from all nperfection deficiency; onsummate. To be or act with certainty.

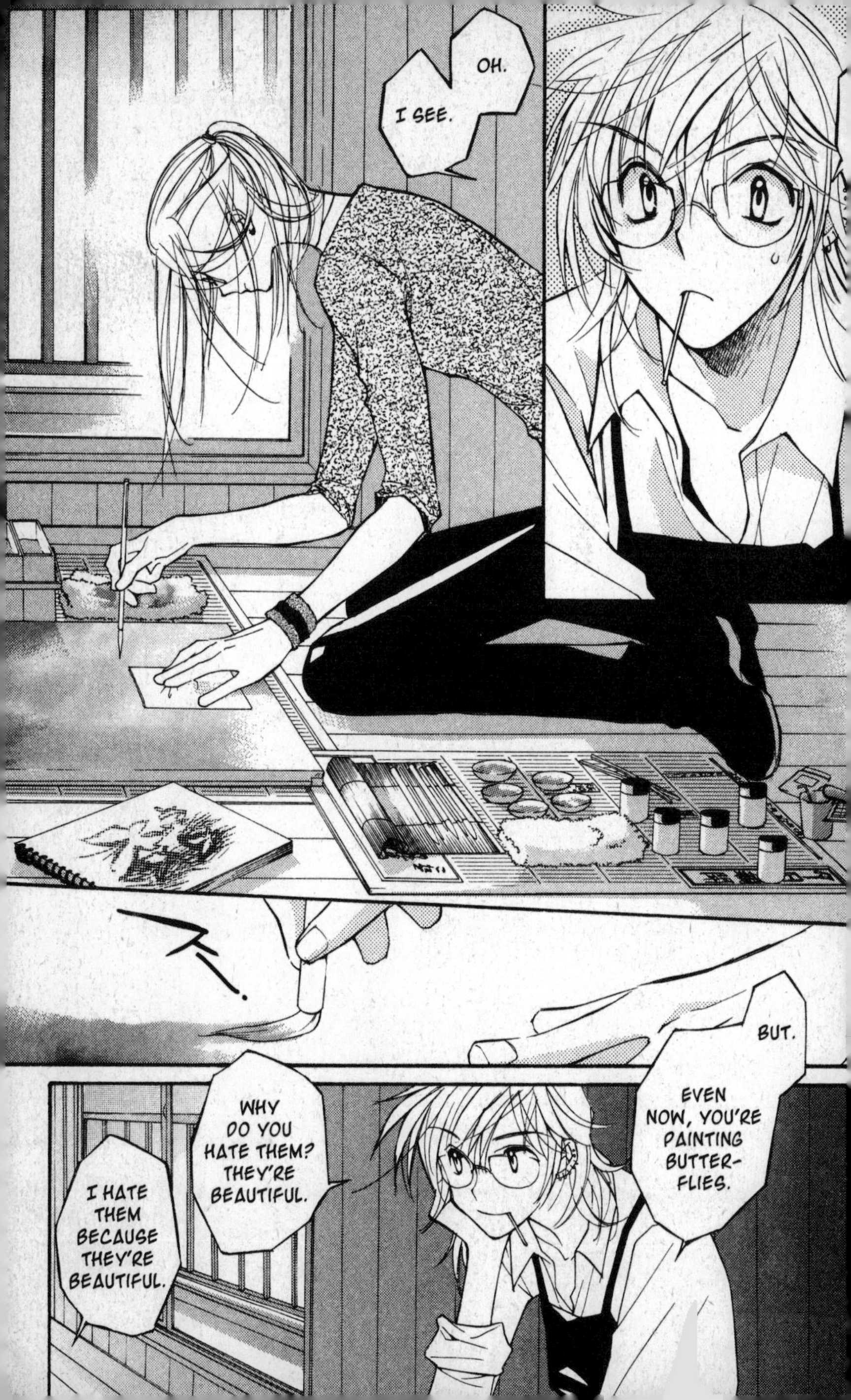
OH.
I SEE.
ス—
BUT.
EVEN NOW, YOU'RE PAINTING BUTTER-FLIES.
WHY DO YOU HATE THEM? THEY'RE BEAUTIFUL.
I HATE THEM BECAUSE THEY'RE BEAUTIFUL.

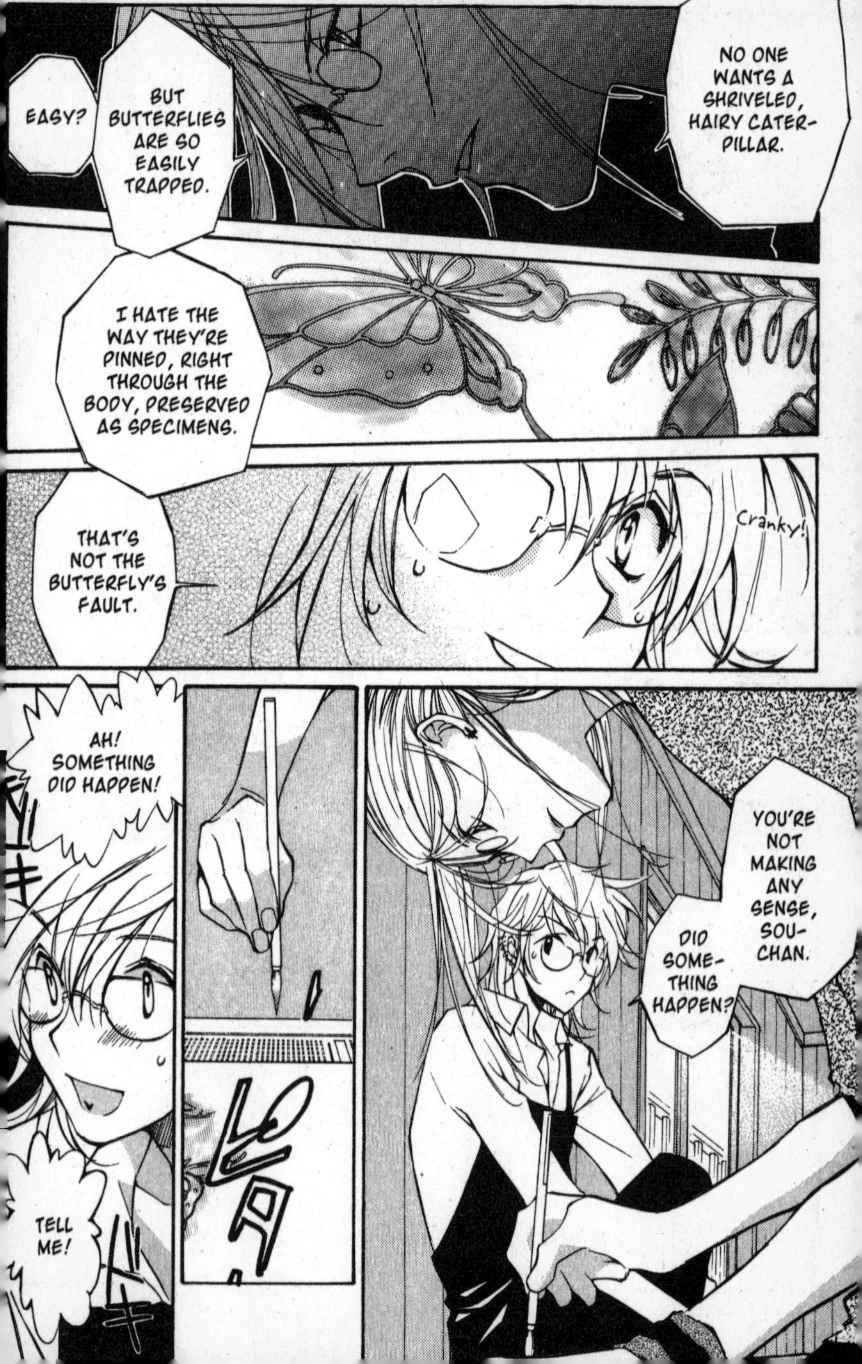
NO ONE WANTS A SHRIVELED, HAIRY CATER-PILLAR.
BUT BUTTERFLIES ARE SO EASILY TRAPPED.
EASY?
I HATE THE WAY THEY'RE PINNED, RIGHT THROUGH THE BODY, PRESERVED AS SPECIMENS.
Cranky!
THAT'S NOT THE BUTTERFLY'S FAULT.
YOU'RE NOT MAKING ANY SENSE, SOU-CHAN.
DID SOME-THING HAPPEN?
AH! SOMETHING DID HAPPEN!
TELL ME!

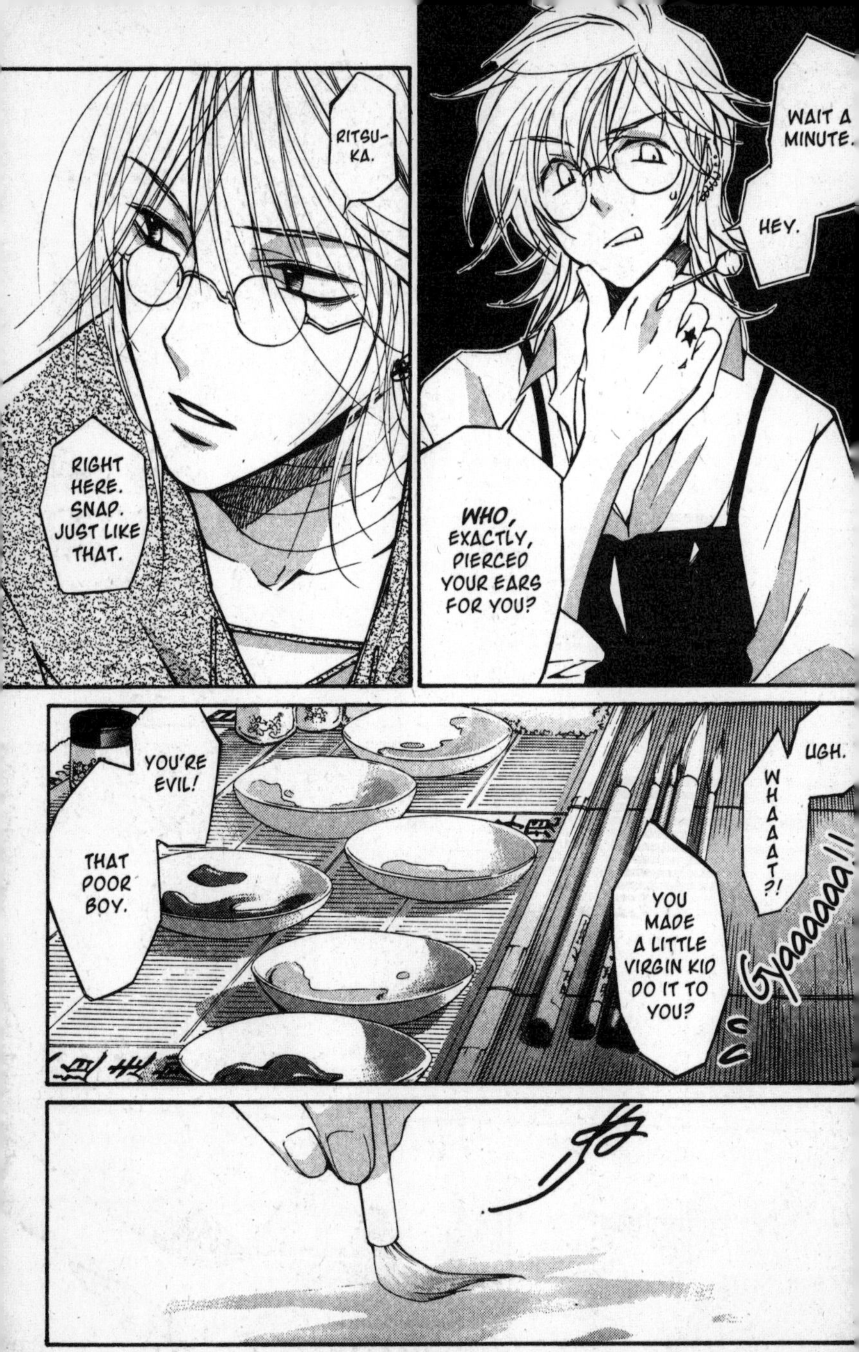
WAIT A MINUTE.
HEY.
WHO, EXACTLY, PIERCED YOUR EARS FOR YOU?
RITSU-KA.
RIGHT HERE. SNAP. JUST LIKE THAT.
UGH.
WHAAAAT?!
Gyaaaaaa!!
YOU MADE A LITTLE VIRGIN KID DO IT TO YOU?
YOU'RE EVIL!
THAT POOR BOY.

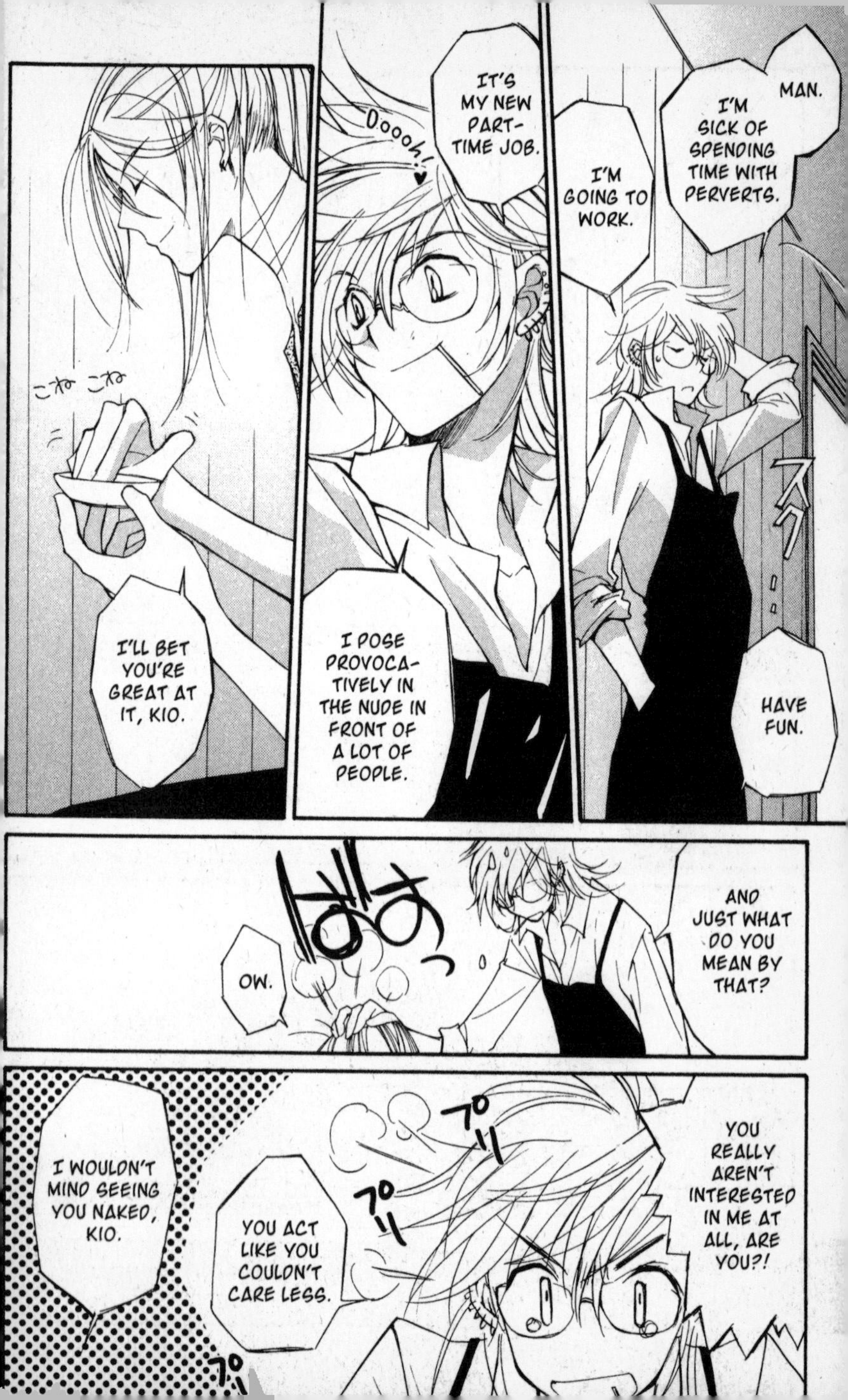
MAN.
I'M SICK OF SPENDING TIME WITH PERVERTS.
I'M GOING TO WORK.
スク
HAVE FUN.
IT'S MY NEW PART-TIME JOB.
Ooooh!♥
I POSE PROVOCATIVELY IN THE NUDE IN FRONT OF A LOT OF PEOPLE.
こね こね
I'LL BET YOU'RE GREAT AT IT, KIO.
AND JUST WHAT DO YOU MEAN BY THAT?
OW.
YOU REALLY AREN'T INTERESTED IN ME AT ALL, ARE YOU?!
YOU ACT LIKE YOU COULDN'T CARE LESS.
I WOULDN'T MIND SEEING YOU NAKED, KIO.

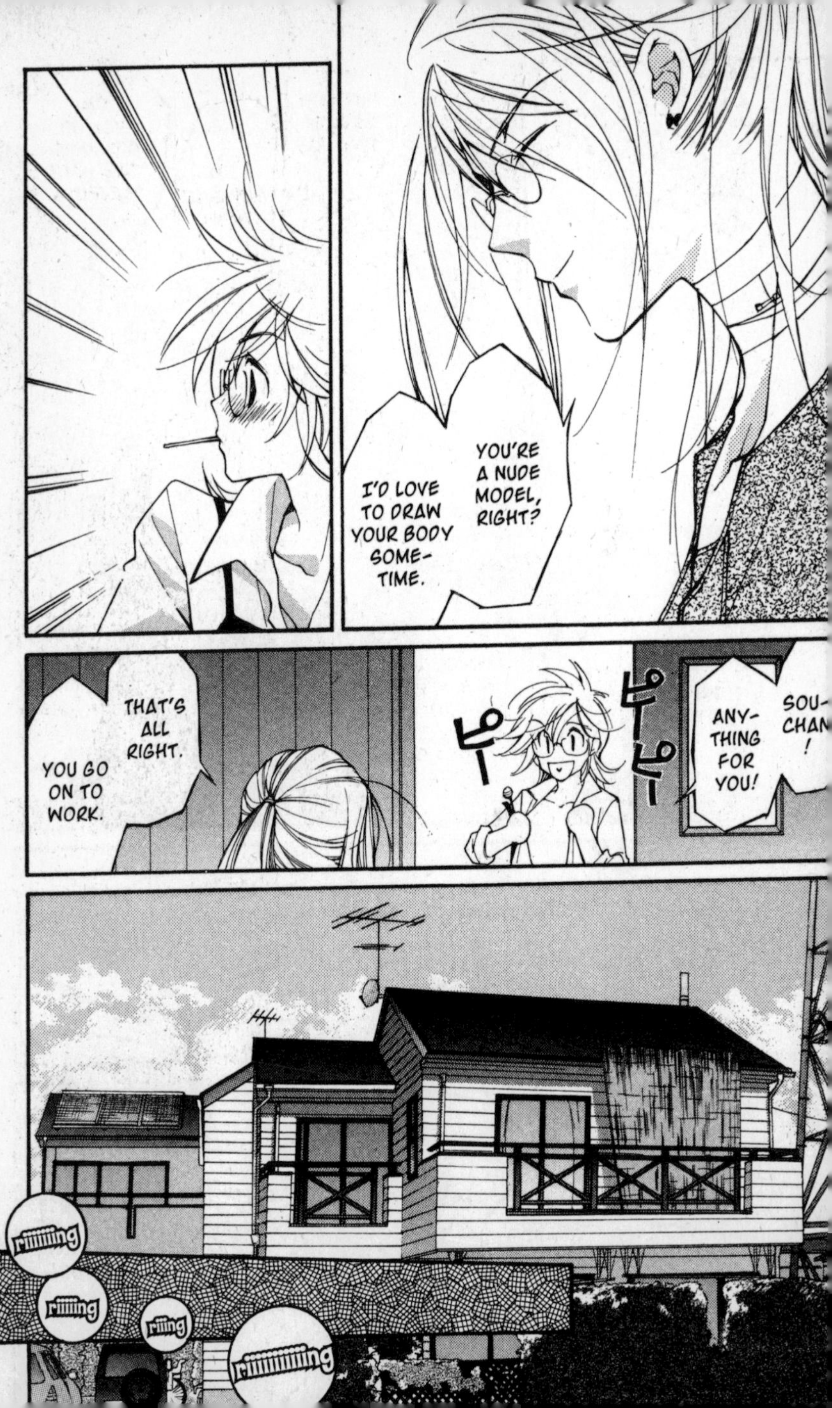
YOU'RE A NUDE MODEL, RIGHT?
I'D LOVE TO DRAW YOUR BODY SOME-TIME.
SOU-CHAN!
ANY-THING FOR YOU!
ピーピー
THAT'S ALL RIGHT.
YOU GO ON TO WORK.
riiiiiiing
riiiiing
riiing
riiiiiiiiiiing

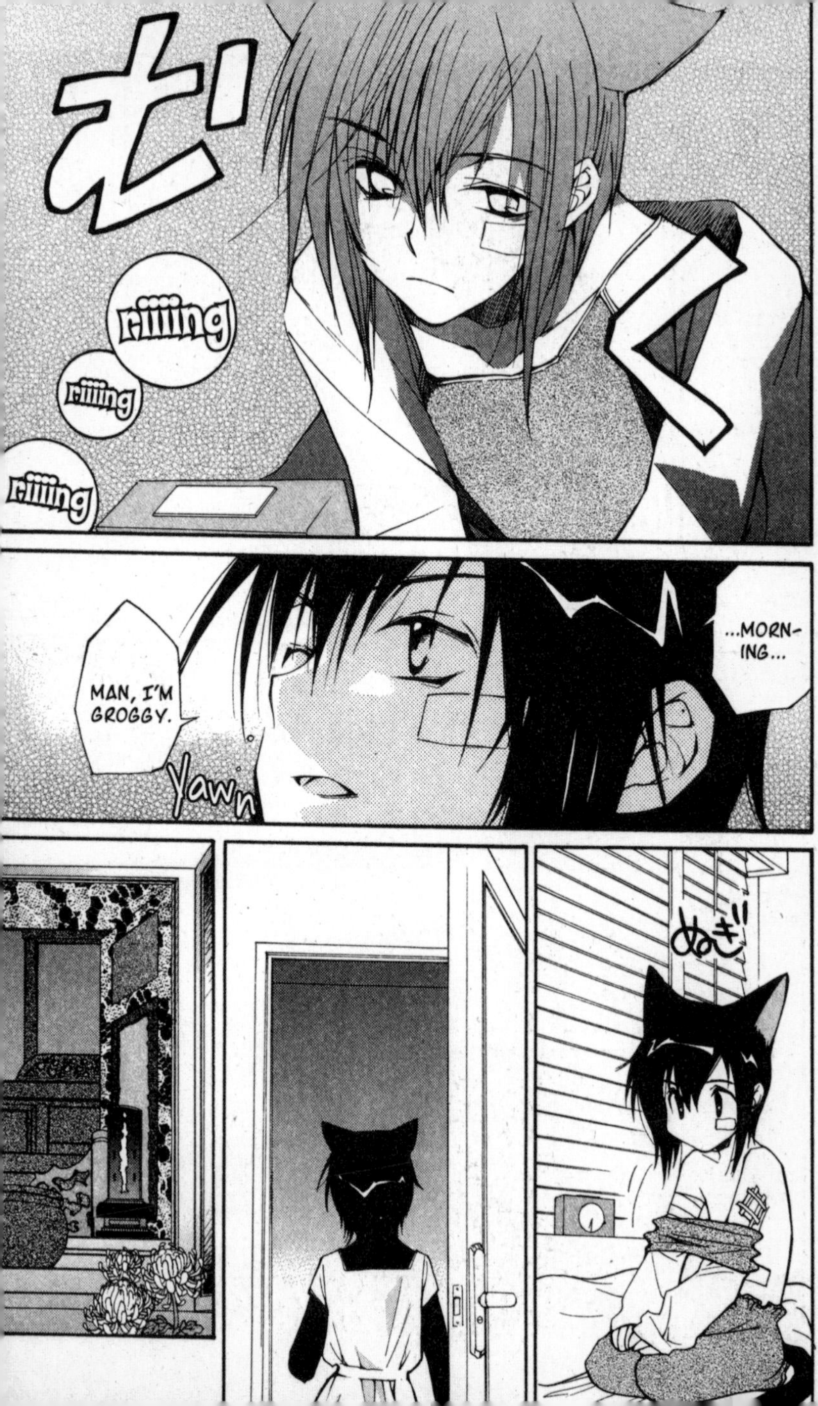
む
riiiing
riiiing
riiiing
...MORNING...
MAN, I'M GROGGY.
Yawn
ぬぎ

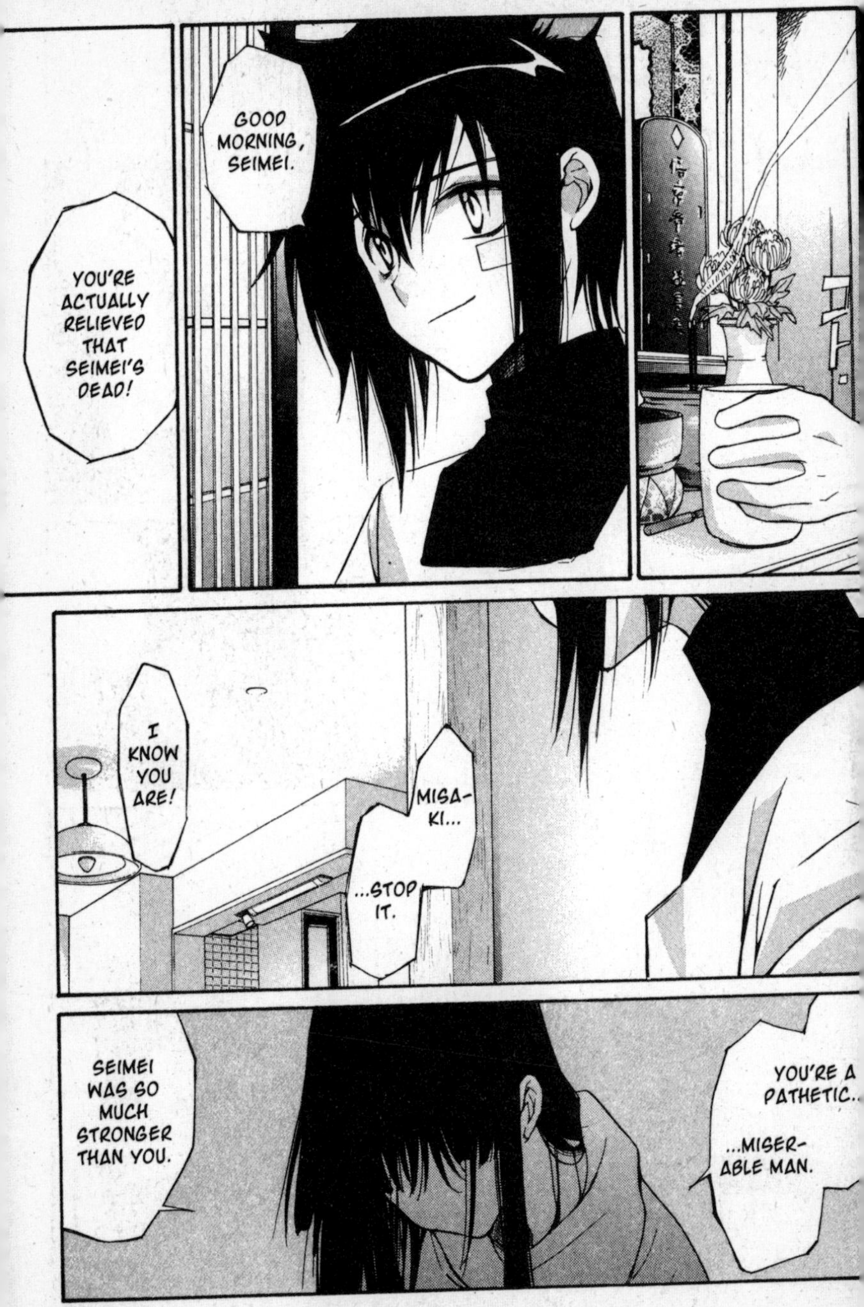
GOOD MORNING, SEIMEI.
YOU'RE ACTUALLY RELIEVED THAT SEIMEI'S DEAD!
MISA-KI...
...STOP IT.
I KNOW YOU ARE!
YOU'RE A PATHETIC...
...MISER-ABLE MAN.
SEIMEI WAS SO MUCH STRONGER THAN YOU.

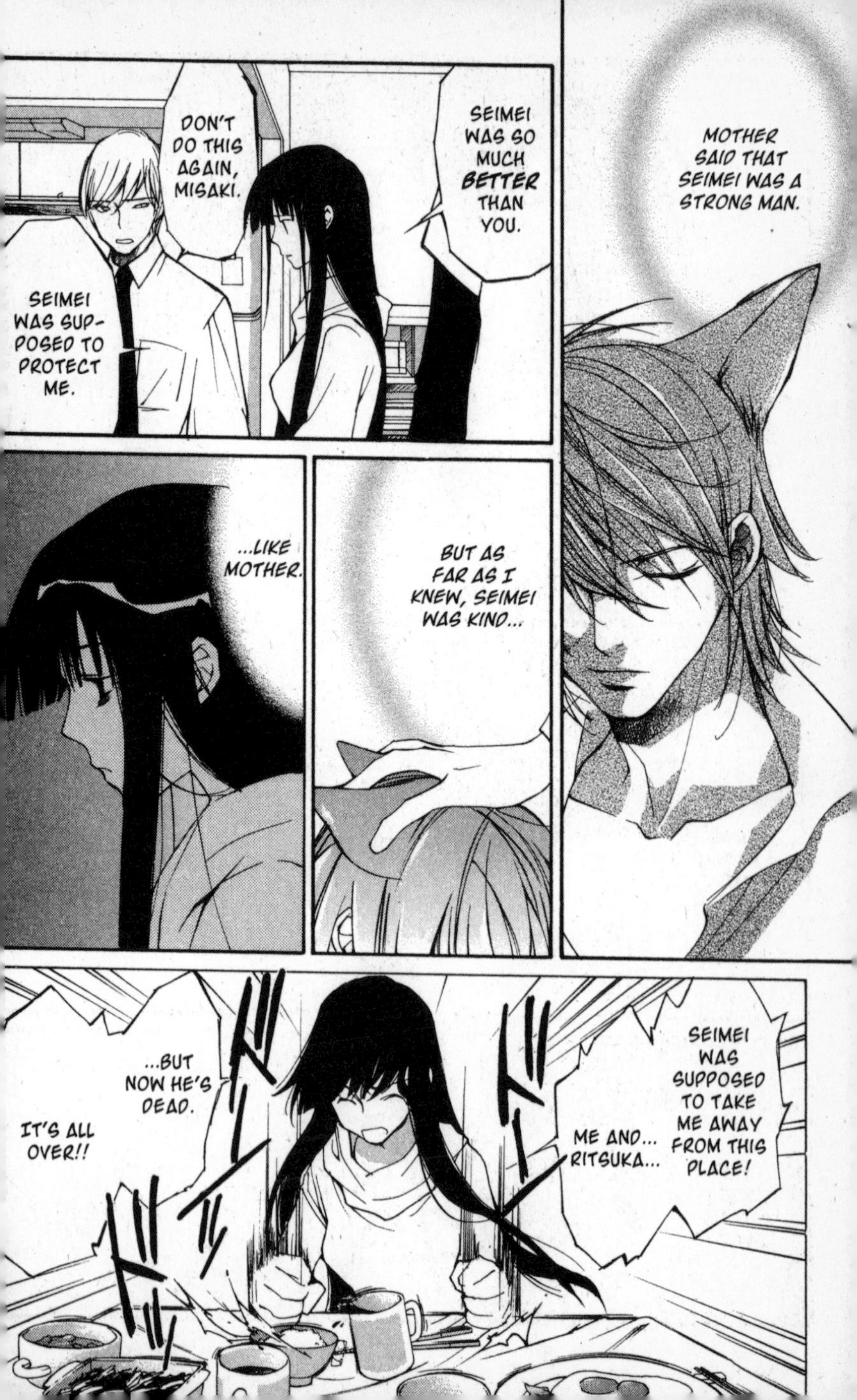
MOTHER SAID THAT SEIMEI WAS A STRONG MAN.
SEIMEI WAS SO MUCH BETTER THAN YOU.
DON'T DO THIS AGAIN, MISAKI.
SEIMEI WAS SUPPOSED TO PROTECT ME.
BUT AS FAR AS I KNEW, SEIMEI WAS KIND...
...LIKE MOTHER.
SEIMEI WAS SUPPOSED TO TAKE ME AWAY FROM THIS PLACE!
ME AND... RITSUKA...
...BUT NOW HE'S DEAD.
IT'S ALL OVER!!

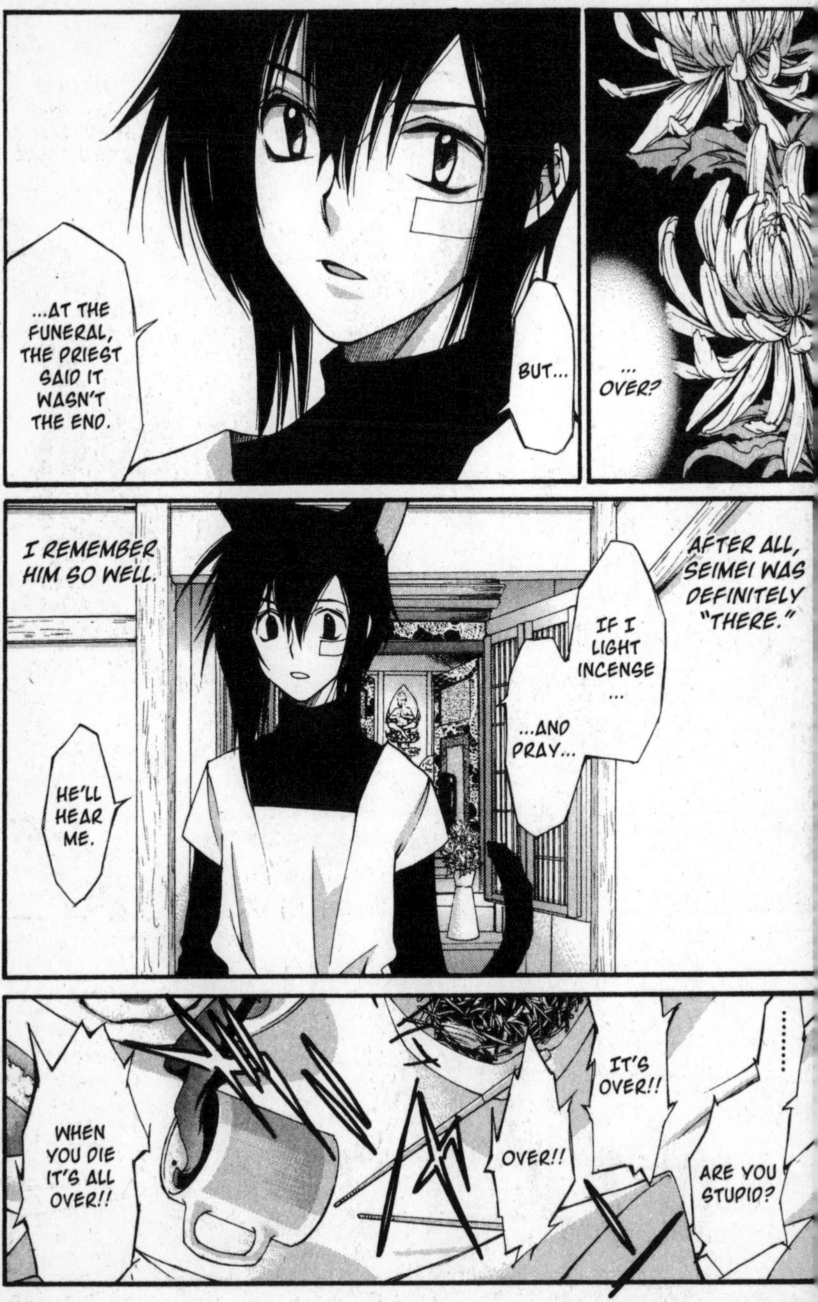

... OVER?
...AT THE FUNERAL, THE PRIEST SAID IT WASN'T THE END.
BUT...
AFTER ALL, SEIMEI WAS DEFINITELY "THERE."
I REMEMBER HIM SO WELL.
IF I LIGHT INCENSE ...
...AND PRAY...
HE'LL HEAR ME.
......
IT'S OVER!!
ARE YOU STUPID?
OVER!!
WHEN YOU DIE IT'S ALL OVER!!

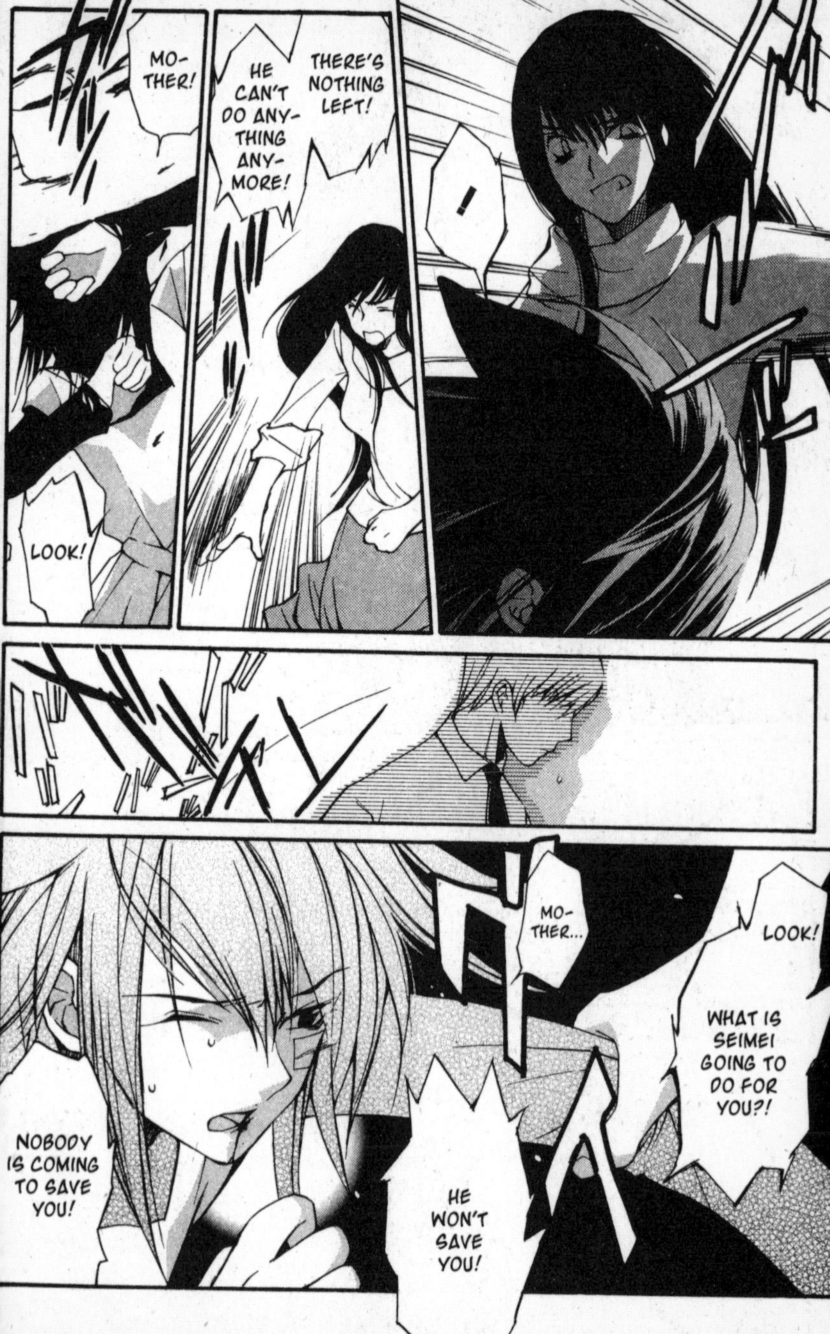
!
THERE'S NOTHING LEFT!
HE CAN'T DO ANYTHING ANYMORE!
MO-THER!
LOOK!
LOOK!
WHAT IS SEIMEI GOING TO DO FOR YOU?!
MO-THER...
HE WON'T SAVE YOU!
NOBODY IS COMING TO SAVE YOU!

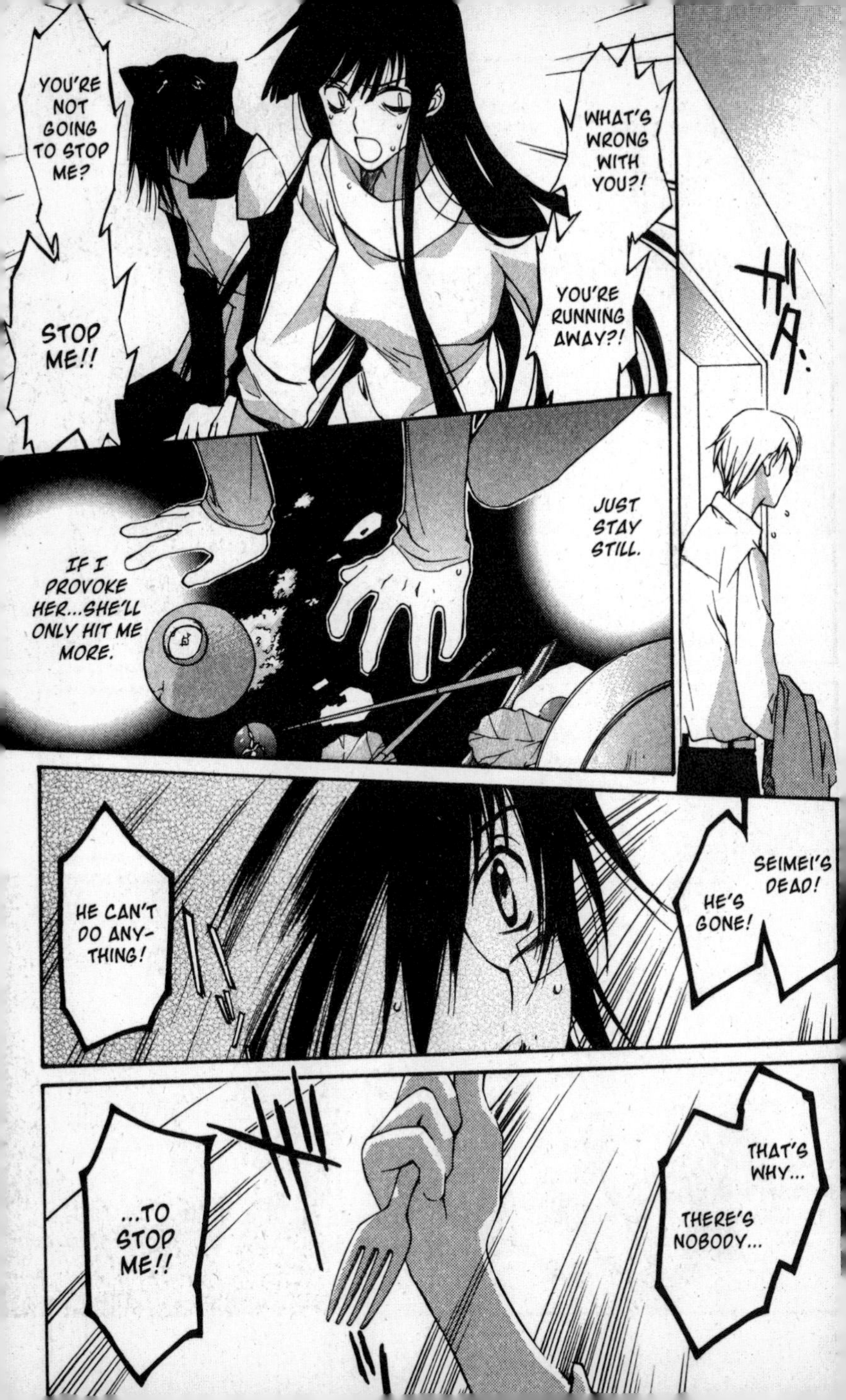
WHAT'S WRONG WITH YOU?!
YOU'RE NOT GOING TO STOP ME?
YOU'RE RUNNING AWAY?!
STOP ME!!
JUST STAY STILL.
IF I PROVOKE HER...SHE'LL ONLY HIT ME MORE.
SEIMEI'S DEAD!
HE'S GONE!
HE CAN'T DO ANY-THING!
THAT'S WHY...
THERE'S NOBODY...
...TO STOP ME!!

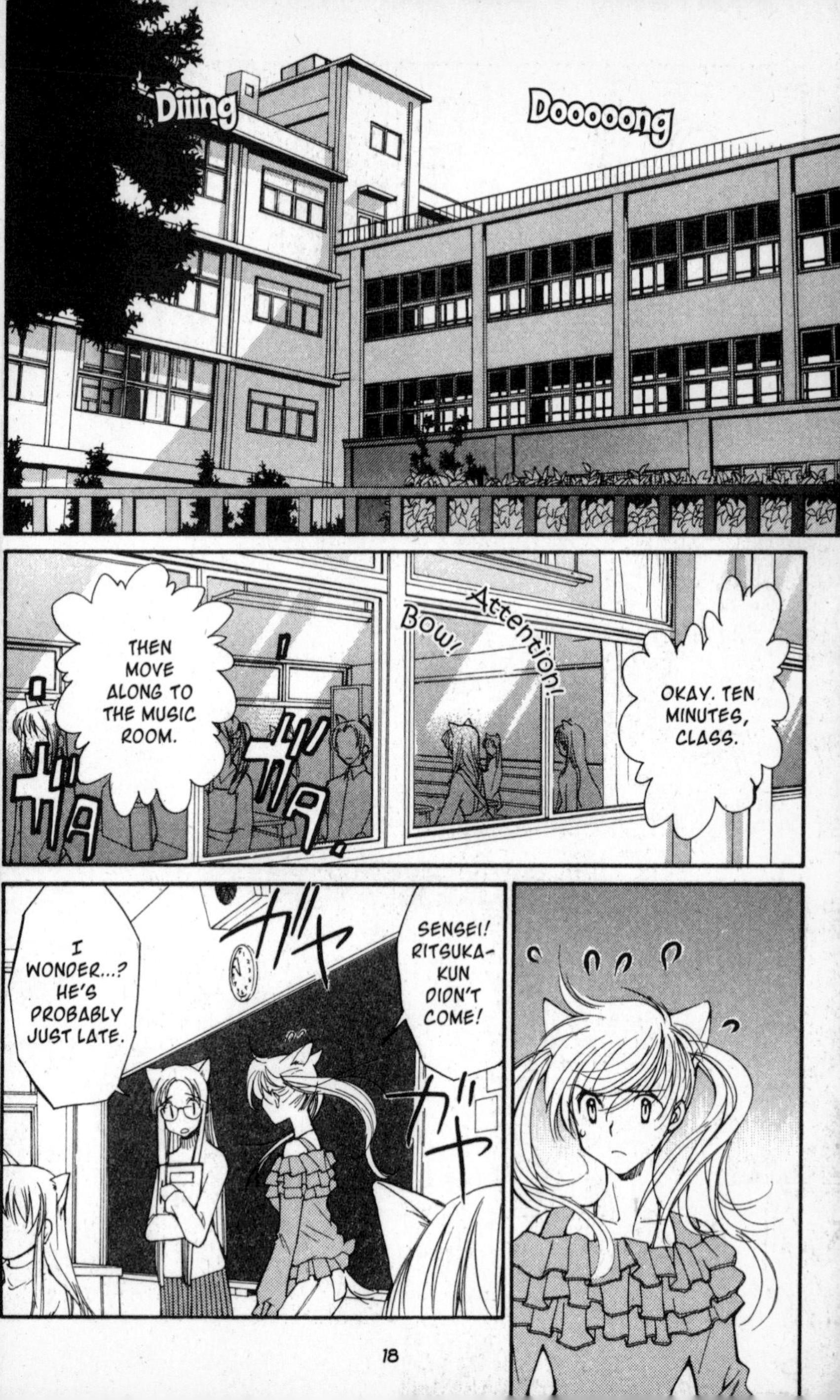
Diiing
Doooooong
OKAY. TEN MINUTES, CLASS.
Attention!
Bow!
ガタ
ガタ
THEN MOVE ALONG TO THE MUSIC ROOM.
ガヤ
SENSEI! RITSUKA-KUN DIDN'T COME!
ガヤ
I WONDER...? HE'S PROBABLY JUST LATE.

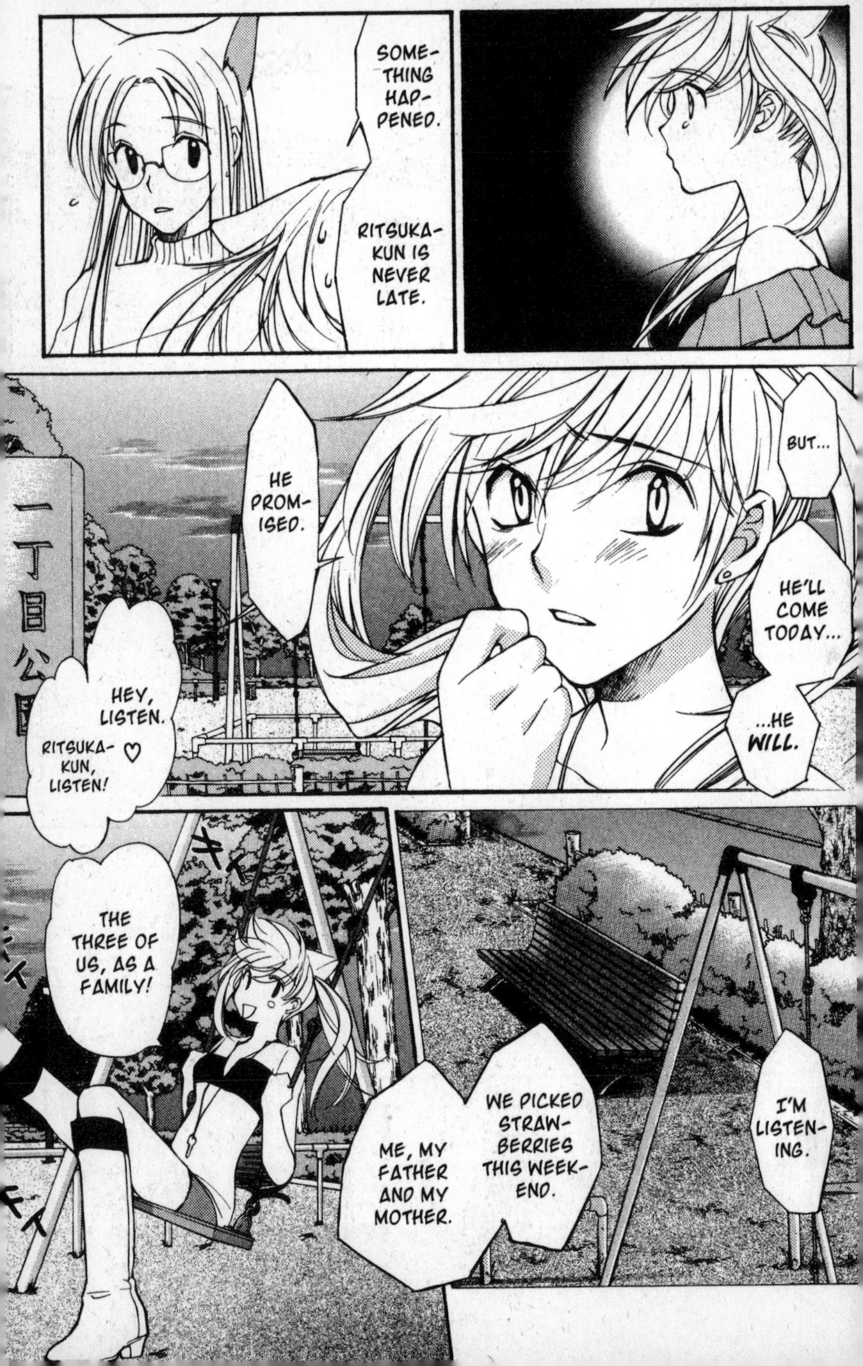
SOMETHING HAPPENED.
RITSUKA-KUN IS NEVER LATE.
BUT...
HE'LL COME TODAY...
...HE **WILL.**
HE PROMISED.
一丁目公園
HEY, LISTEN.
RITSUKA-KUN, LISTEN! ♡
I'M LISTENING.
WE PICKED STRAWBERRIES THIS WEEKEND.
ME, MY FATHER AND MY MOTHER.
THE THREE OF US, AS A FAMILY!

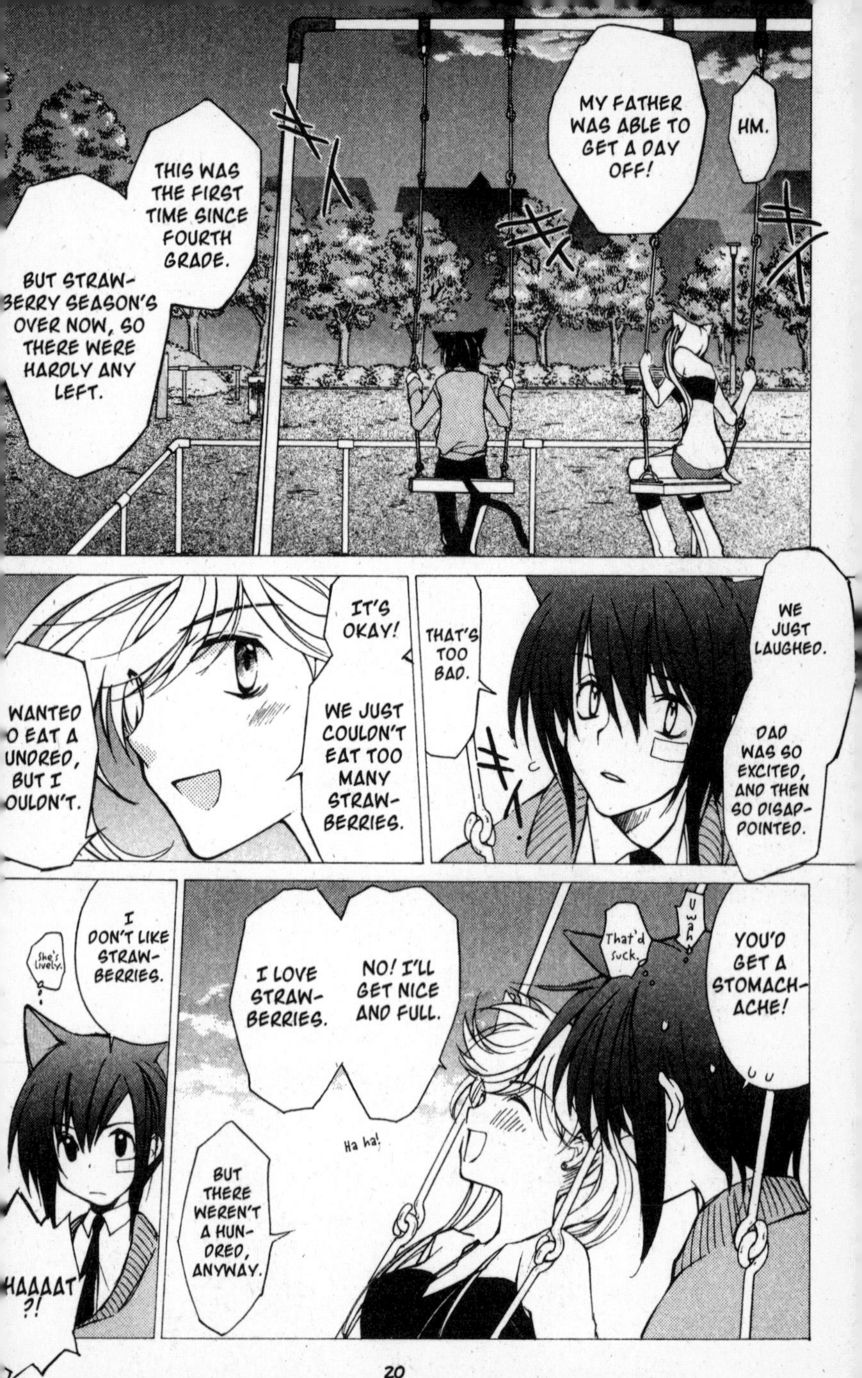
HM.
MY FATHER WAS ABLE TO GET A DAY OFF!
THIS WAS THE FIRST TIME SINCE FOURTH GRADE.
BUT STRAW-BERRY SEASON'S OVER NOW, SO THERE WERE HARDLY ANY LEFT.
WE JUST LAUGHED.
DAD WAS SO EXCITED, AND THEN SO DISAP-POINTED.
THAT'S TOO BAD.
IT'S OKAY!
WE JUST COULDN'T EAT TOO MANY STRAW-BERRIES.
WANTED O EAT A UNDRED, BUT I OULDN'T.
YOU'D GET A STOMACH-ACHE!
Uwah
That'd suck.
NO! I'LL GET NICE AND FULL.
I LOVE STRAW-BERRIES.
Ha ha!
BUT THERE WEREN'T A HUN-DRED, ANYWAY.
I DON'T LIKE STRAW-BERRIES.
She's lively.
HAAAAT ?!

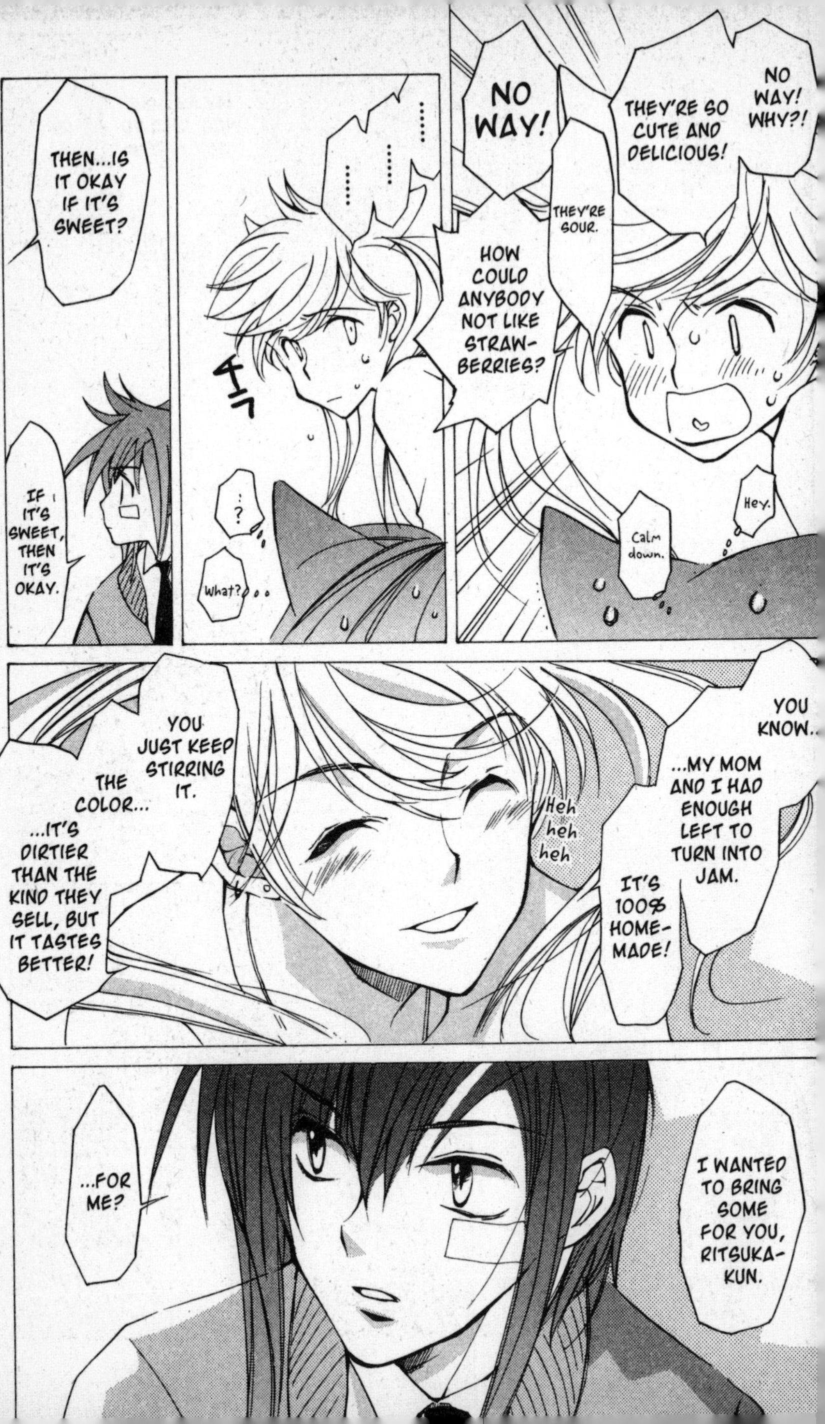
NO WAY! WHY?!
THEY'RE SO CUTE AND DELICIOUS!
NO WAY!
THEY'RE SOUR.
HOW COULD ANYBODY NOT LIKE STRAW-BERRIES?
Hey.
Calm down.
......
?
What?
THEN...IS IT OKAY IF IT'S SWEET?
IF IT'S SWEET, THEN IT'S OKAY.
YOU KNOW...
...MY MOM AND I HAD ENOUGH LEFT TO TURN INTO JAM.
IT'S 100% HOME-MADE!
Heh heh heh
YOU JUST KEEP STIRRING IT.
THE COLOR...
...IT'S DIRTIER THAN THE KIND THEY SELL, BUT IT TASTES BETTER!
I WANTED TO BRING SOME FOR YOU, RITSUKA-KUN.
...FOR ME?

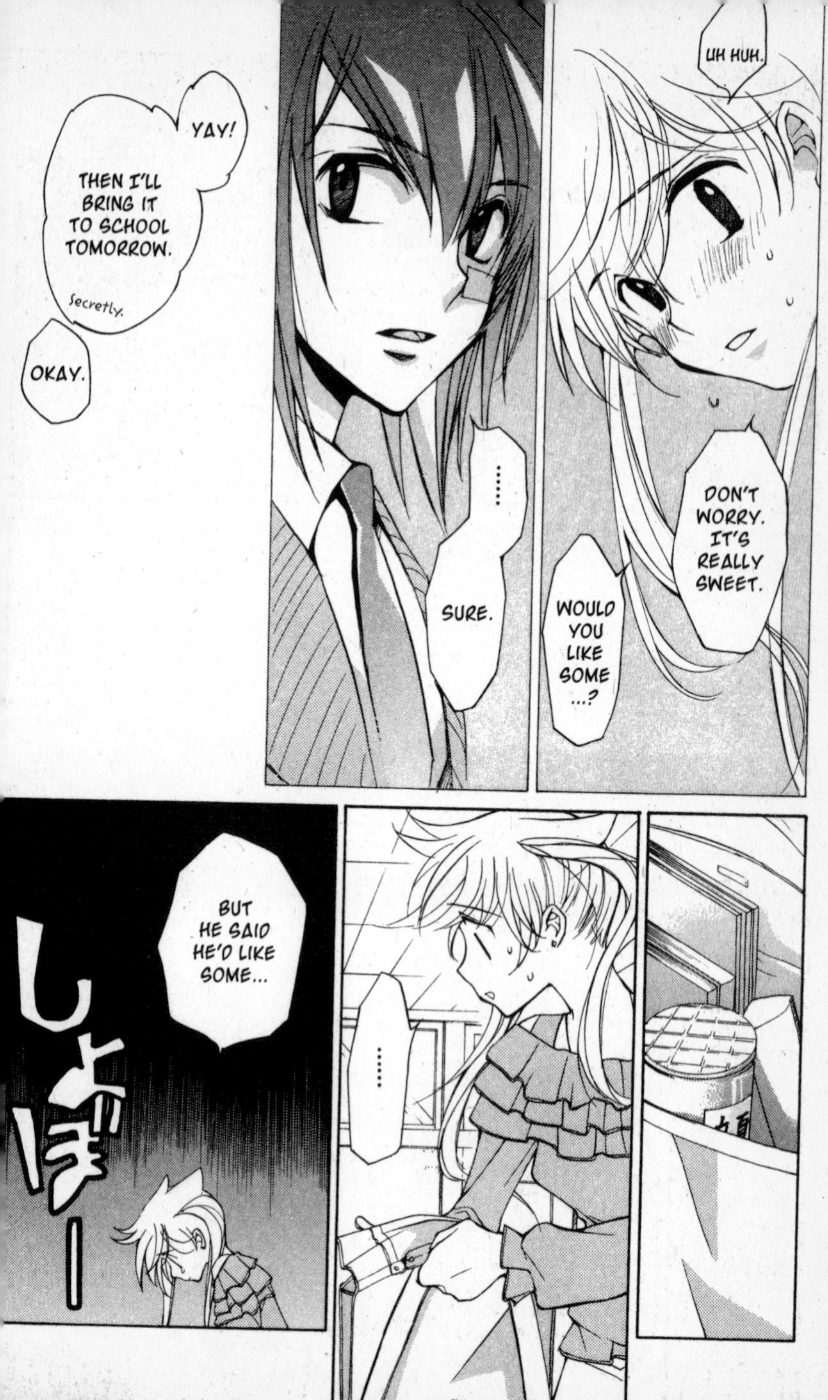
UH HUH.
DON'T WORRY. IT'S REALLY SWEET.
WOULD YOU LIKE SOME ...?
......
SURE.
YAY!
THEN I'LL BRING IT TO SCHOOL TOMORROW.
Secretly.
OKAY.
......
BUT HE SAID HE'D LIKE SOME...
しょぼー

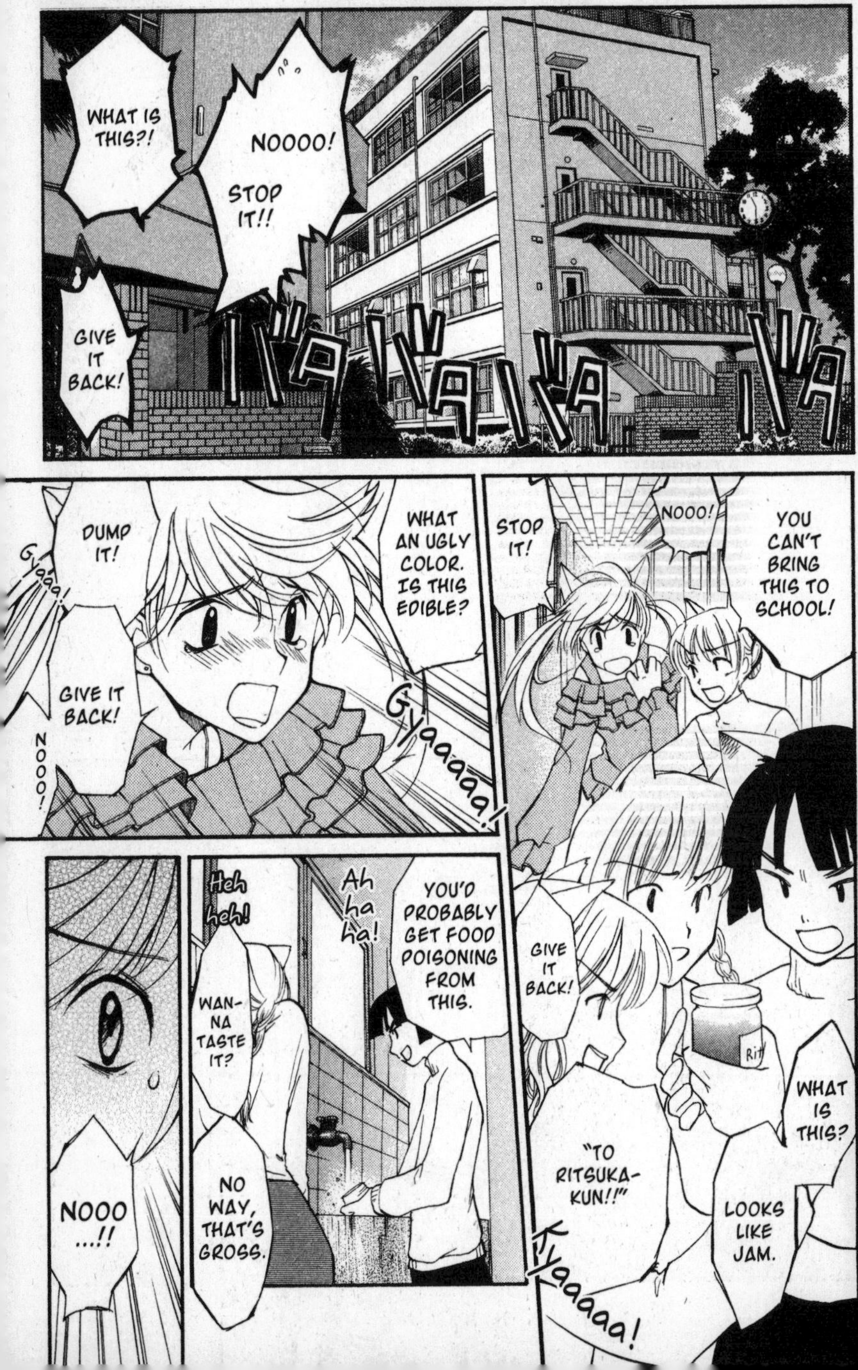
IYA
NOOOO! STOP IT!!
WHAT IS THIS?!
GIVE IT BACK!
IYA IYA
YOU CAN'T BRING THIS TO SCHOOL!
NOOO!
STOP IT!
Rit
WHAT IS THIS?
LOOKS LIKE JAM.
GIVE IT BACK!
"TO RITSUKA-KUN!!"
Kyaaaaa!
WHAT AN UGLY COLOR. IS THIS EDIBLE?
Gyaaaaa!
DUMP IT!
Gyaaa!
GIVE IT BACK!
NOOO!
YOU'D PROBABLY GET FOOD POISONING FROM THIS.
Ah ha ha!
Heh heh!
WANNA TASTE IT?
NO WAY, THAT'S GROSS.
NOOO ...!!

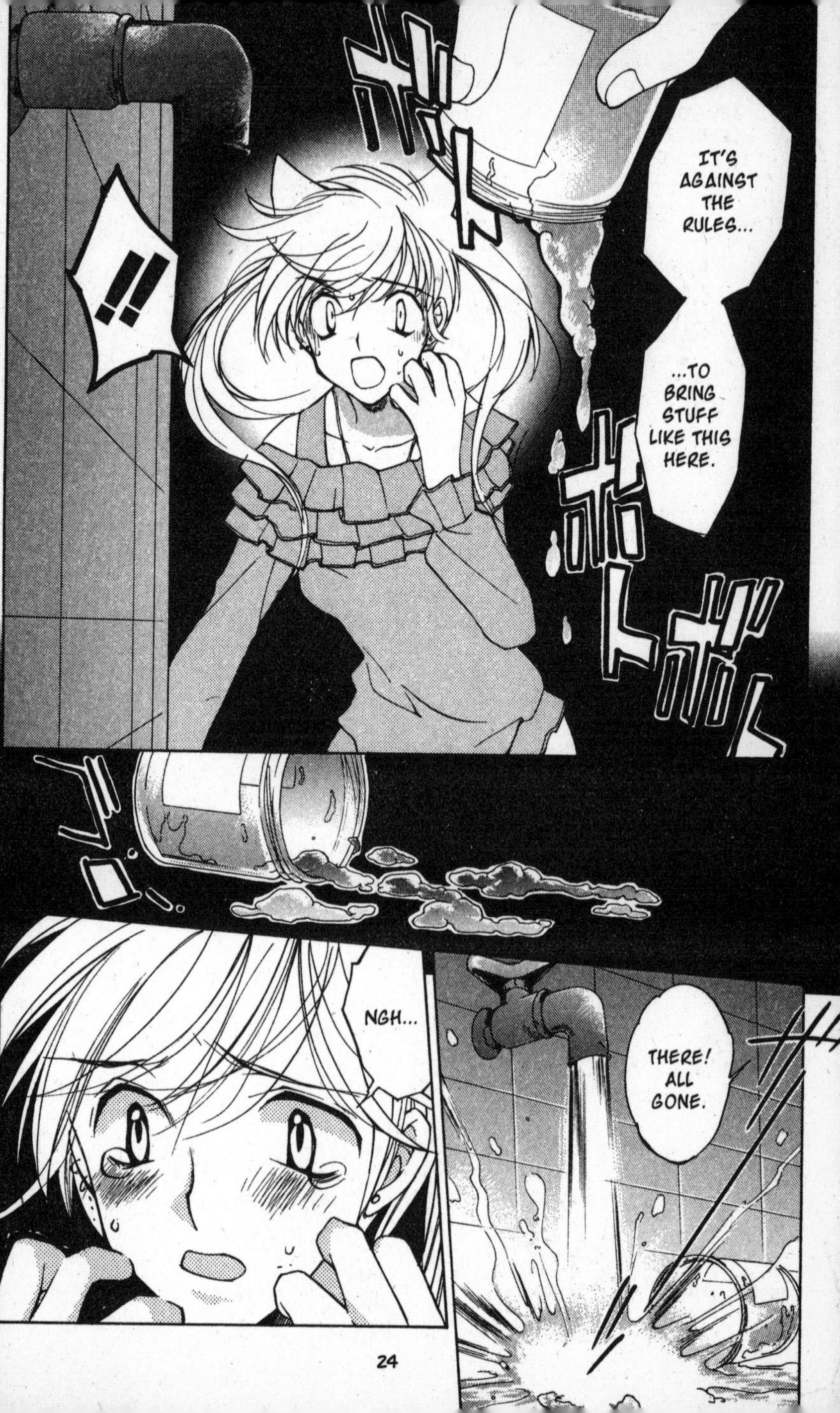

IT'S AGAINST THE RULES...
...TO BRING STUFF LIKE THIS HERE.
!!
THERE! ALL GONE.
NGH...

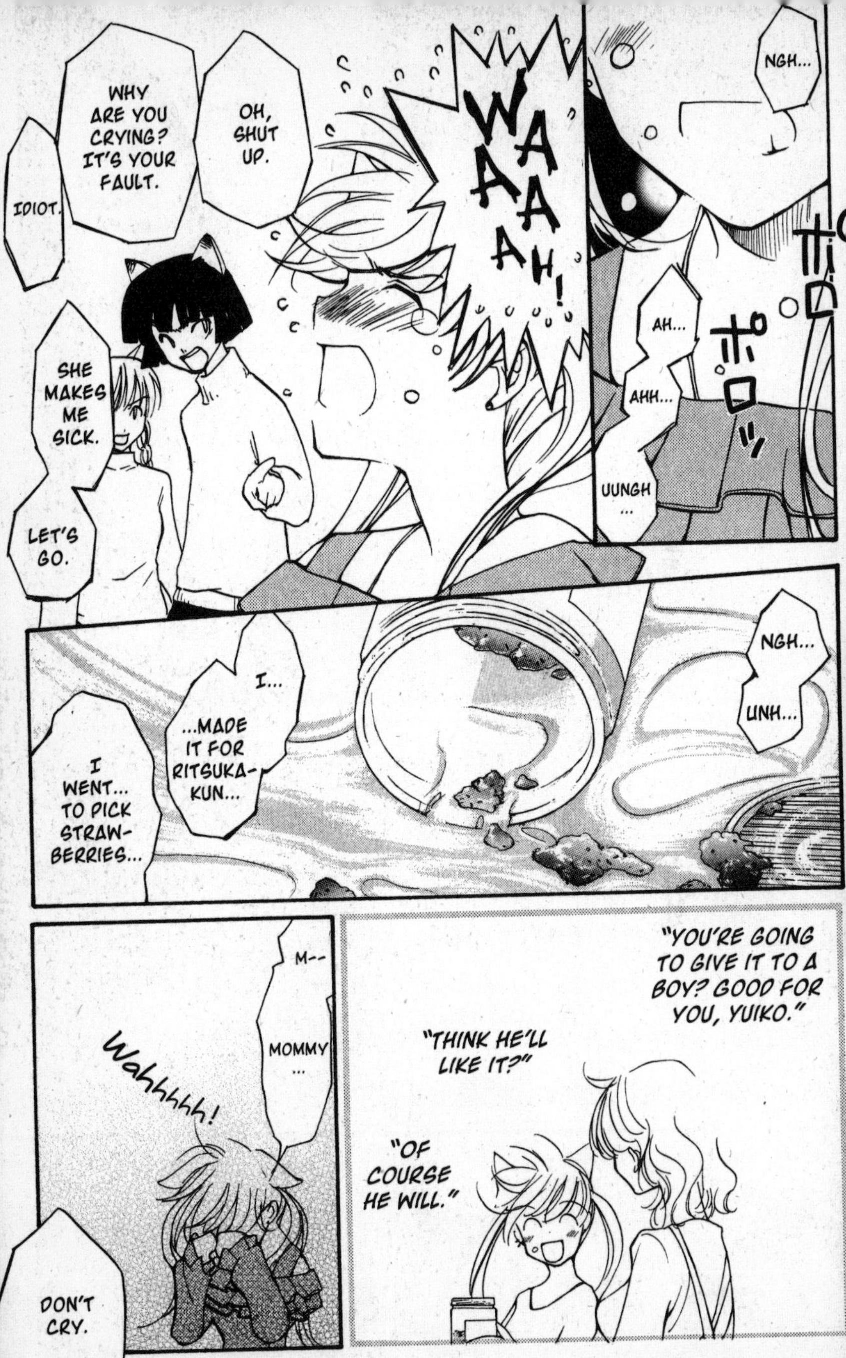
NGH...
AH...
AHH...
UUNGH...
ポロッ
WAAAAH!
OH, SHUT UP.
WHY ARE YOU CRYING? IT'S YOUR FAULT.
IDIOT.
SHE MAKES ME SICK.
LET'S GO.
NGH...
UNH...
I...
...MADE IT FOR RITSUKA-KUN...
I WENT... TO PICK STRAW-BERRIES...
"YOU'RE GOING TO GIVE IT TO A BOY? GOOD FOR YOU, YUIKO."
"THINK HE'LL LIKE IT?"
"OF COURSE HE WILL."
M--
MOMMY...
Wahhhhh!
DON'T CRY.

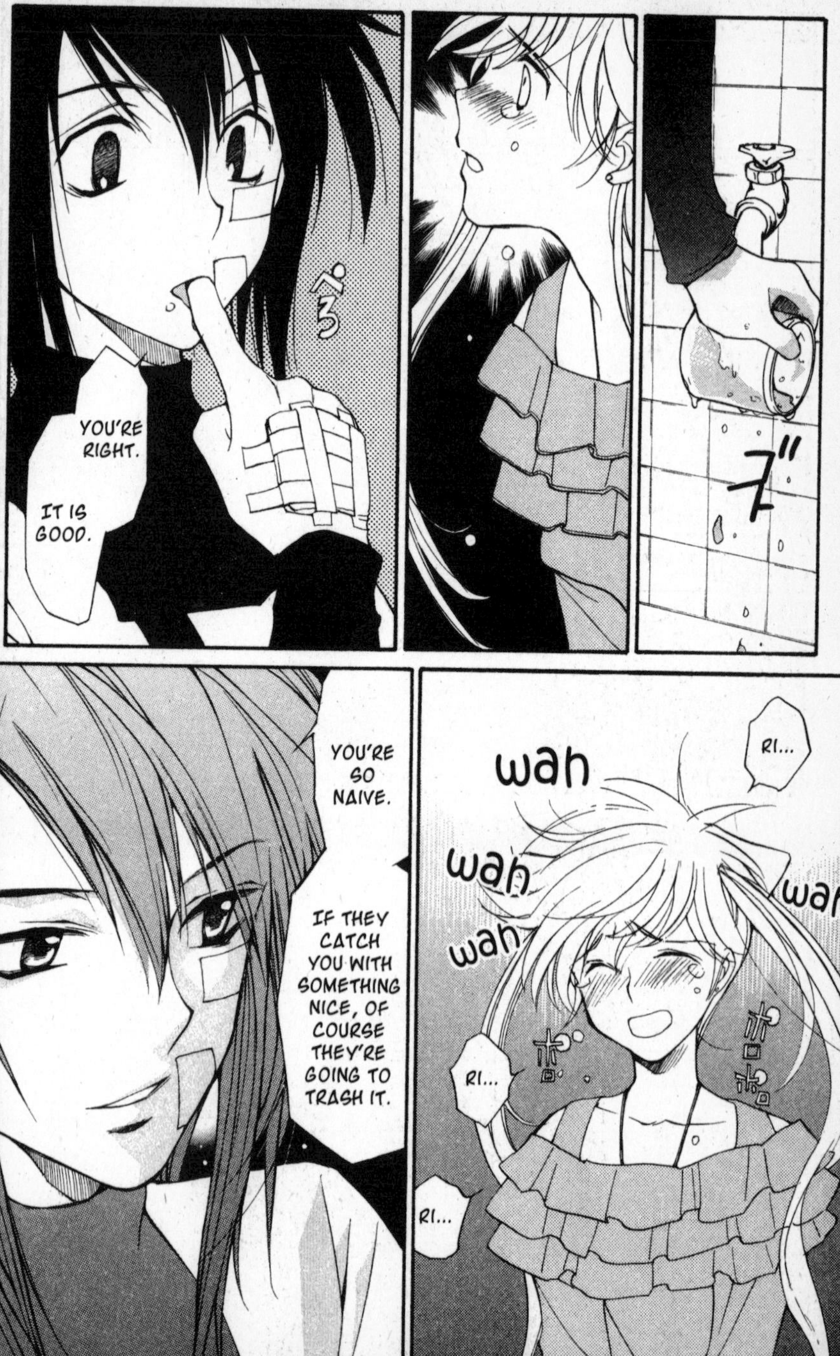
ザ
ぺろ
YOU'RE RIGHT.
IT IS GOOD.
RI...
wah
wah
wah
RI...
RI...
YOU'RE SO NAIVE.
IF THEY CATCH YOU WITH SOMETHING NICE, OF COURSE THEY'RE GOING TO TRASH IT.

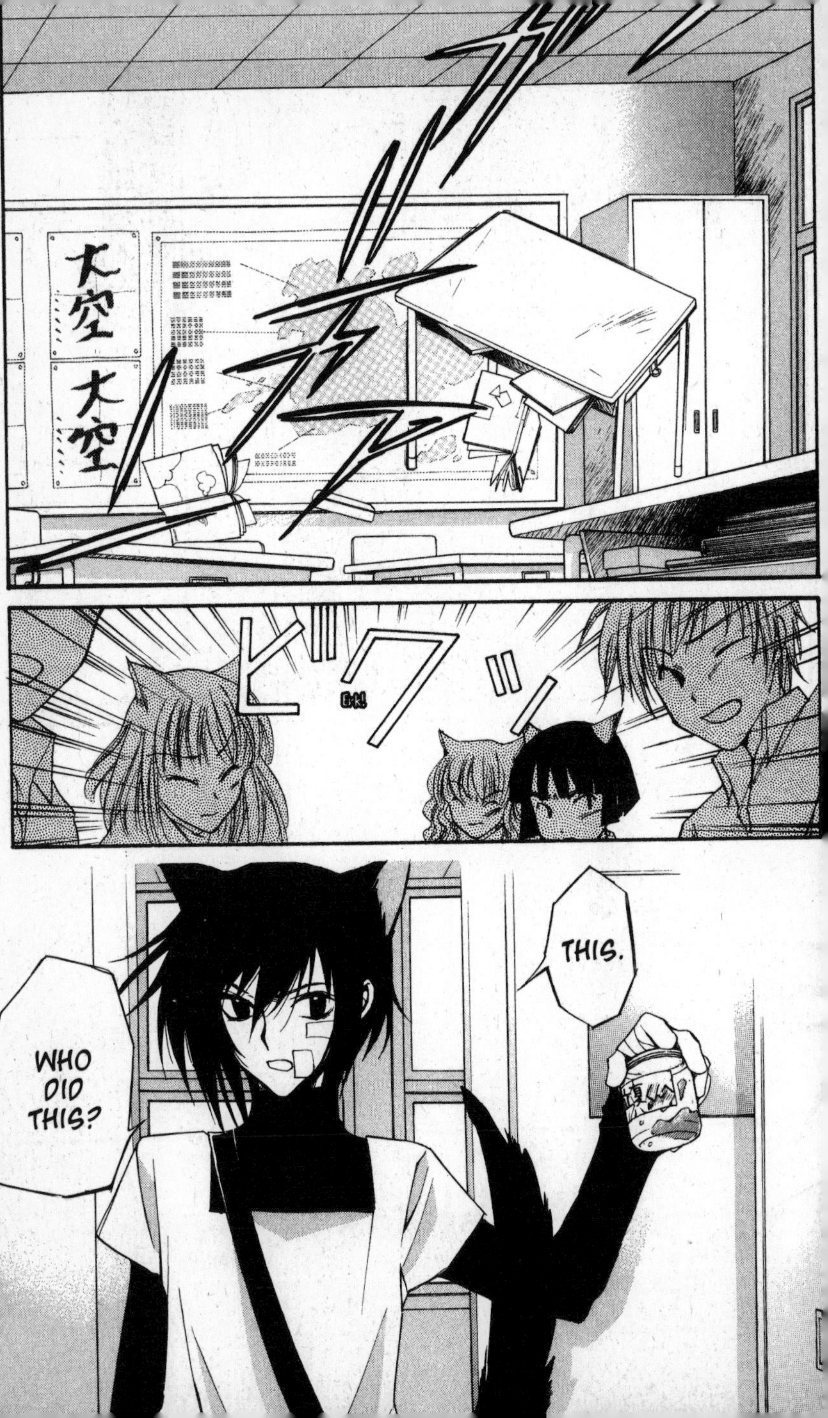
大空
大空
ビクッ
ERK!
THIS.
WHO DID THIS?

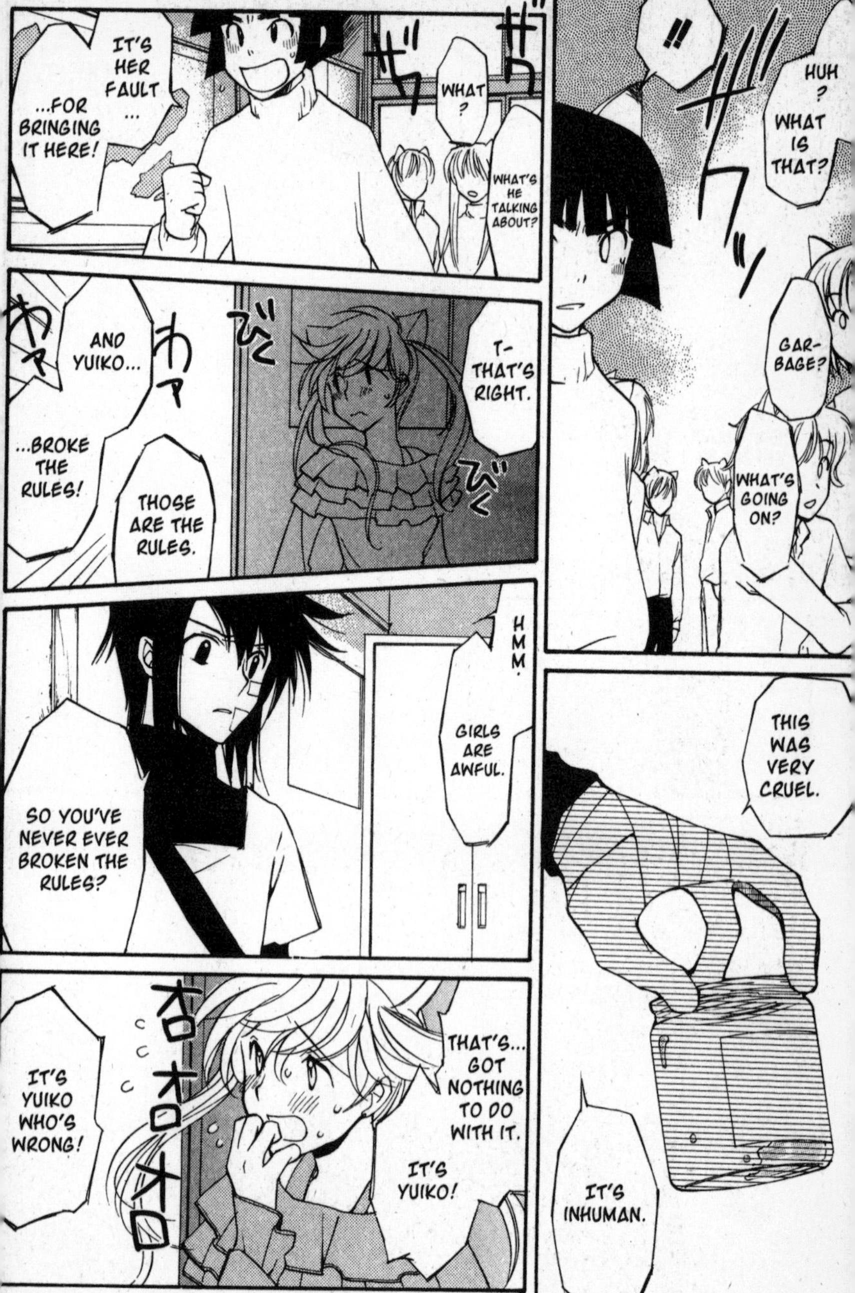
!!
ザワ ザワ
HUH? WHAT IS THAT?
GAR-BAGE?
WHAT'S GOING ON?
THIS WAS VERY CRUEL.
IT'S INHUMAN.
ザワ ザワ
WHAT?
WHAT'S HE TALKING ABOUT?
IT'S HER FAULT...
...FOR BRINGING IT HERE!
T-THAT'S RIGHT.
びく びく
わァ わァ
AND YUIKO...
...BROKE THE RULES!
THOSE ARE THE RULES.
HMM.
GIRLS ARE AWFUL.
SO YOU'VE NEVER EVER BROKEN THE RULES?
THAT'S... GOT NOTHING TO DO WITH IT.
IT'S YUIKO!
オロ オロ
IT'S YUIKO WHO'S WRONG!

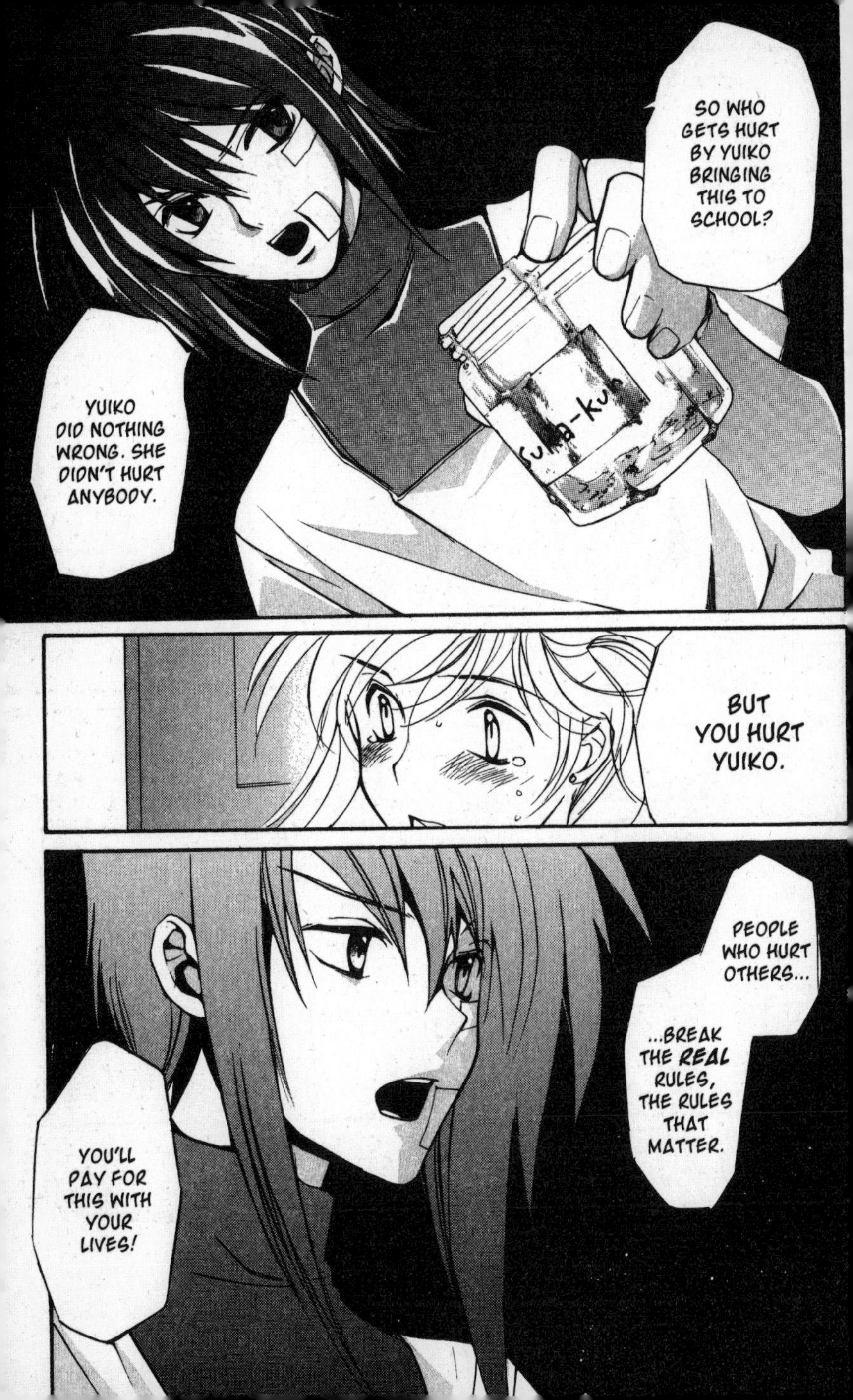
SO WHO GETS HURT BY YUIKO BRINGING THIS TO SCHOOL?
YUIKO DID NOTHING WRONG. SHE DIDN'T HURT ANYBODY.
BUT YOU HURT YUIKO.
PEOPLE WHO HURT OTHERS...
...BREAK THE *REAL* RULES, THE RULES THAT MATTER.
YOU'LL PAY FOR THIS WITH YOUR LIVES!

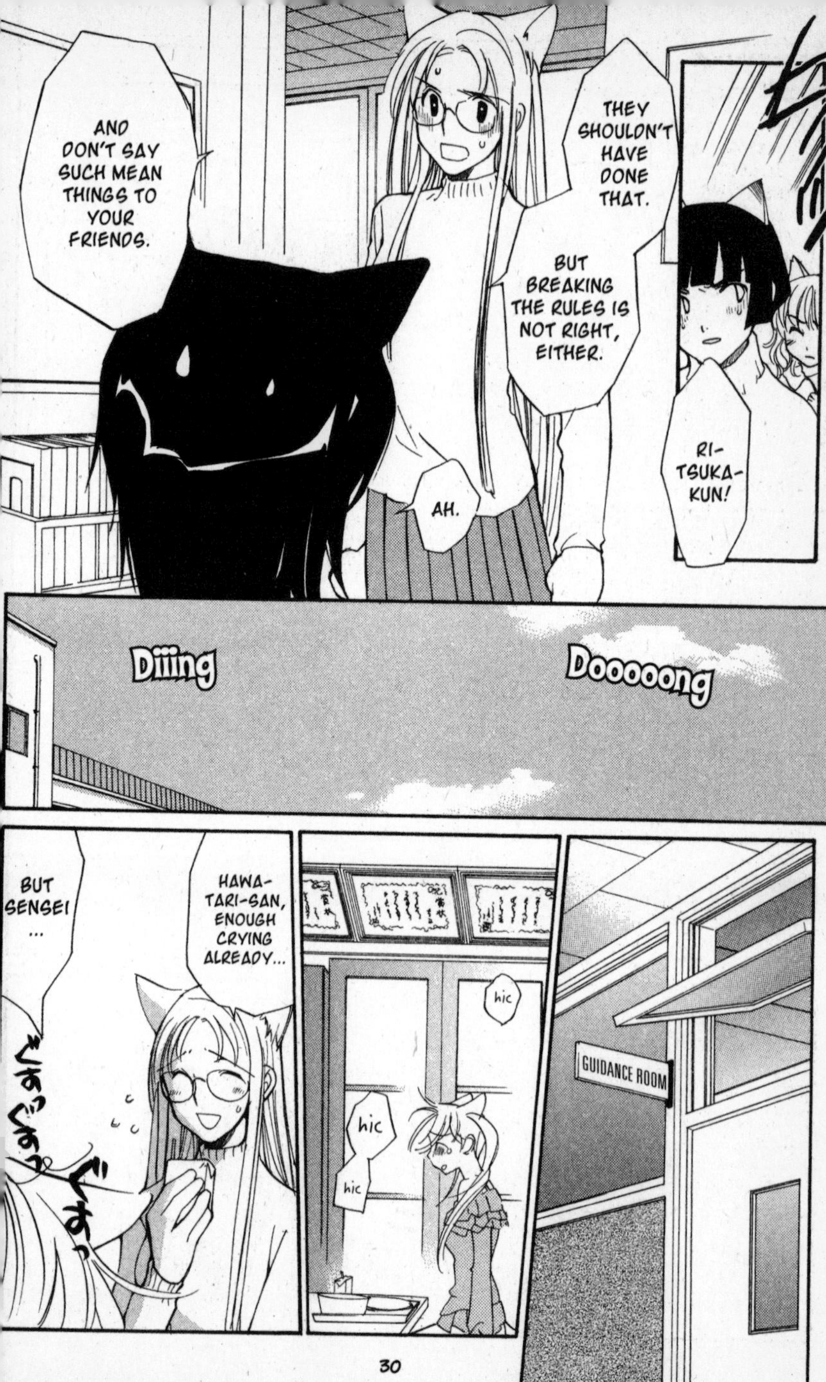
THEY SHOULDN'T HAVE DONE THAT.
BUT BREAKING THE RULES IS NOT RIGHT, EITHER.
AND DON'T SAY SUCH MEAN THINGS TO YOUR FRIENDS.
RI-TSUKA-KUN!
AH.
Diiing Doooooong
GUIDANCE ROOM
hic
hic
hic
HAWA-TARI-SAN, ENOUGH CRYING ALREADY...
BUT SENSEI ...

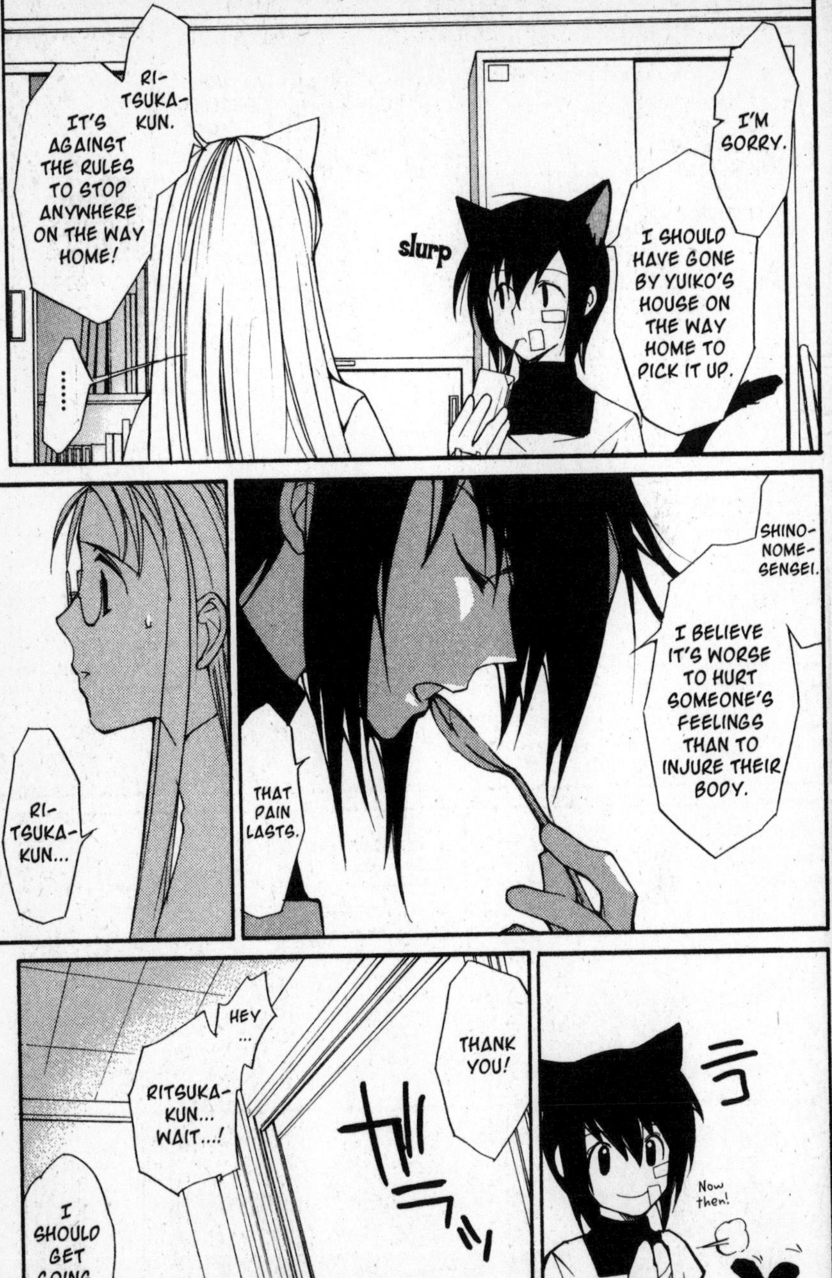
I'M SORRY.
I SHOULD HAVE GONE BY YUIKO'S HOUSE ON THE WAY HOME TO PICK IT UP.
slurp
RI-TSUKA-KUN.
IT'S AGAINST THE RULES TO STOP ANYWHERE ON THE WAY HOME!
......
SHINO-NOME-SENSEI.
I BELIEVE IT'S WORSE TO HURT SOMEONE'S FEELINGS THAN TO INJURE THEIR BODY.
THAT PAIN LASTS.
RI-TSUKA-KUN...
Now then!
THANK YOU!
HEY...
RITSUKA-KUN... WAIT...!
I SHOULD GET GOING.

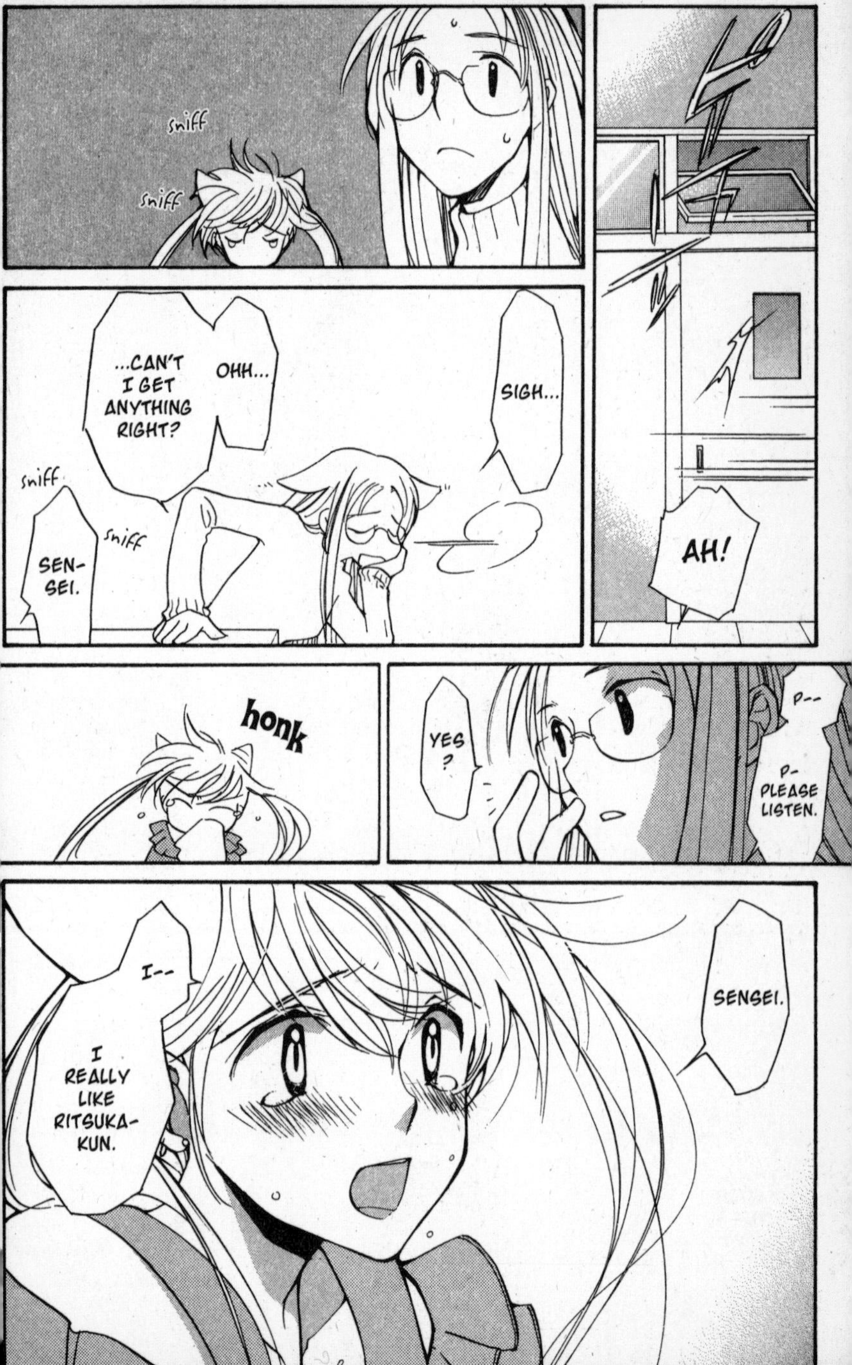
AH!
sniff
sniff
SIGH...
OHH...
...CAN'T I GET ANYTHING RIGHT?
sniff
sniff
SEN-SEI.
P--
P-PLEASE LISTEN.
YES?
honk
SENSEI.
I--
I REALLY LIKE RITSUKA-KUN.

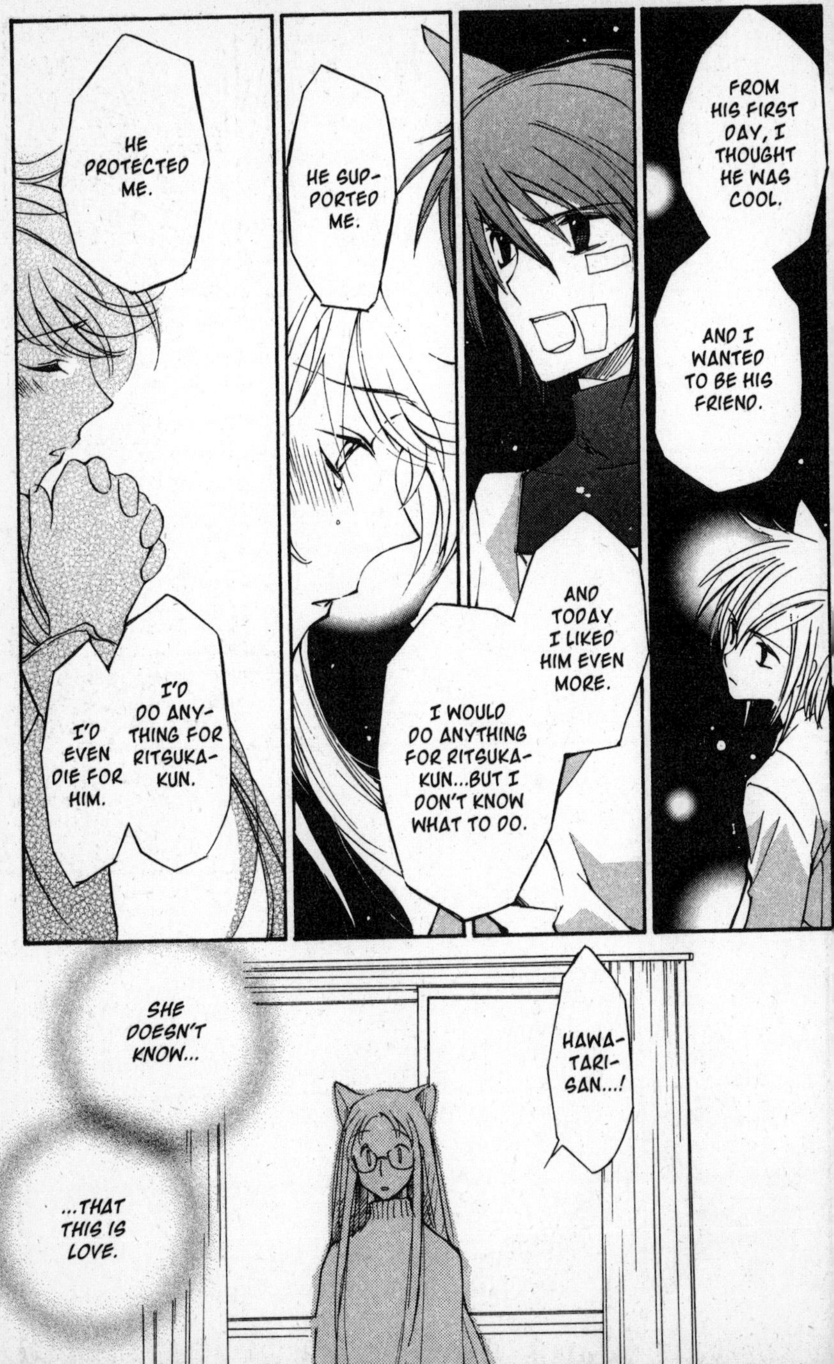
FROM HIS FIRST DAY, I THOUGHT HE WAS COOL.
AND I WANTED TO BE HIS FRIEND.
AND TODAY I LIKED HIM EVEN MORE.
I WOULD DO ANYTHING FOR RITSUKA-KUN...BUT I DON'T KNOW WHAT TO DO.
HE SUPPORTED ME.
HE PROTECTED ME.
I'D DO ANYTHING FOR RITSUKA-KUN.
I'D EVEN DIE FOR HIM.
HAWATARI-SAN...!
SHE DOESN'T KNOW...
...THAT THIS IS LOVE.

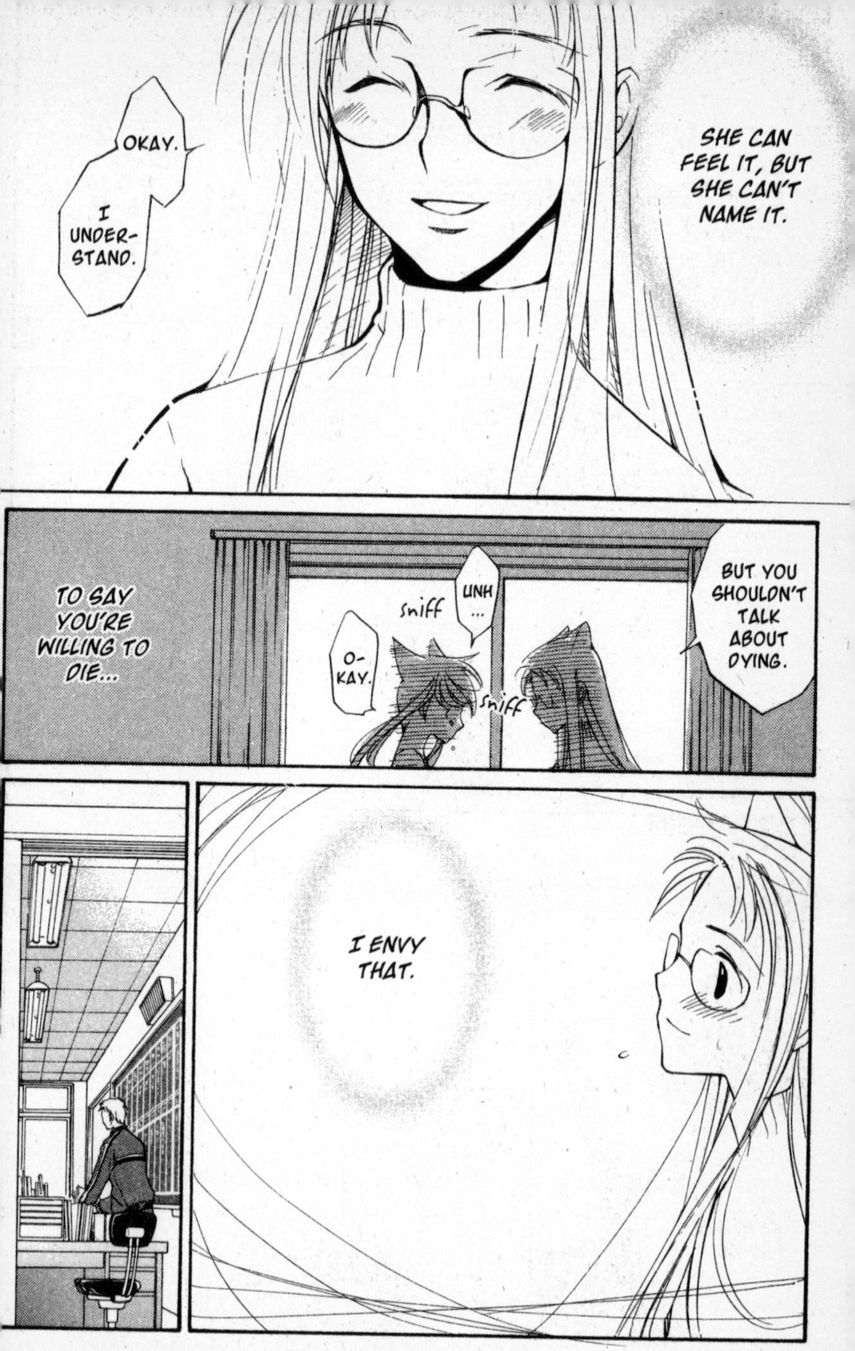
SHE CAN FEEL IT, BUT SHE CAN'T NAME IT.
OKAY.
I UNDER-STAND.
BUT YOU SHOULDN'T TALK ABOUT DYING.
UNH ...
sniff
O-KAY.
sniff
TO SAY YOU'RE WILLING TO DIE...
I ENVY THAT.

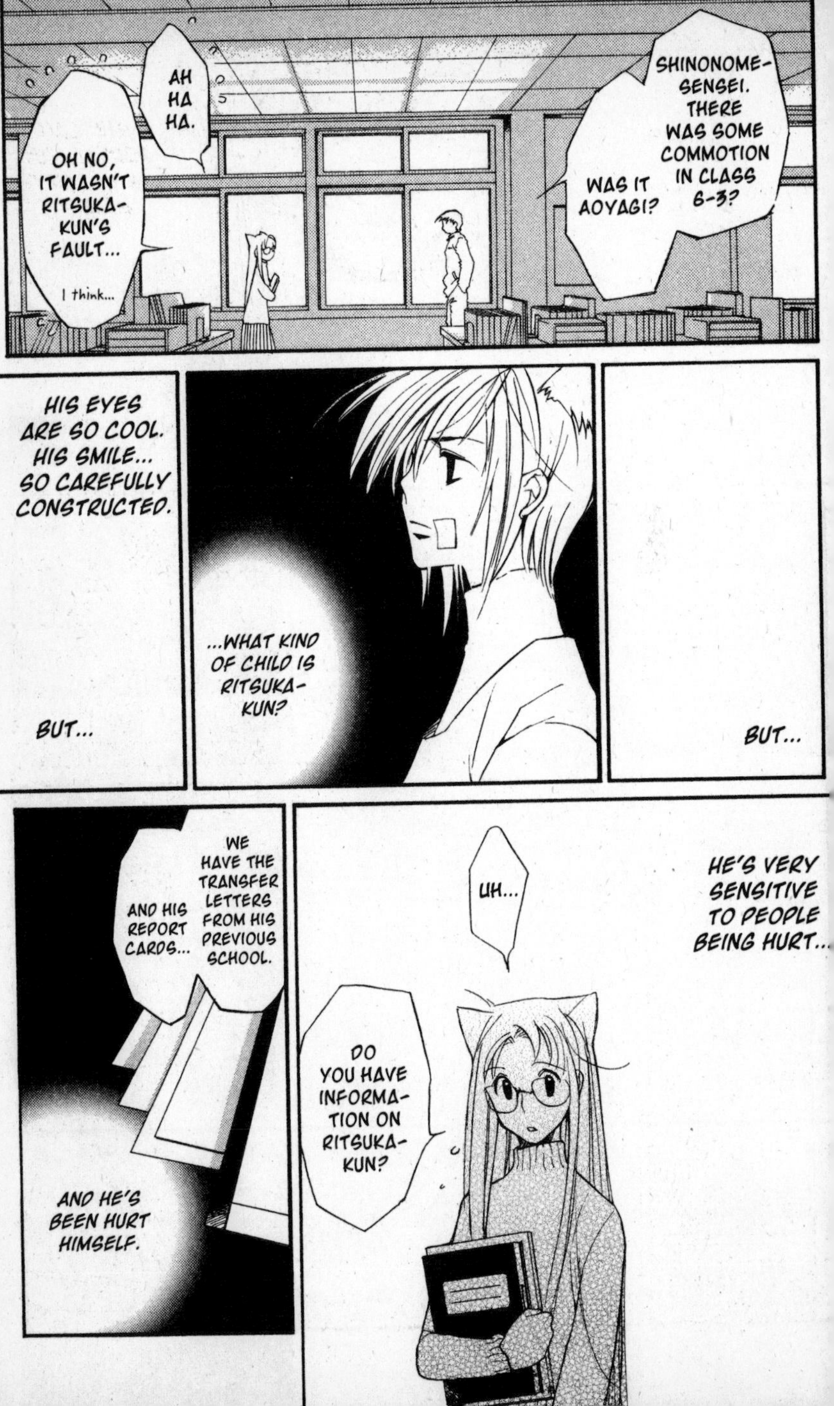

SHINONOME-SENSEI. THERE WAS SOME COMMOTION IN CLASS 6-3?
WAS IT AOYAGI?
AH HA HA.
OH NO, IT WASN'T RITSUKA-KUN'S FAULT...
I think...
BUT...
...WHAT KIND OF CHILD IS RITSUKA-KUN?
HIS EYES ARE SO COOL. HIS SMILE... SO CAREFULLY CONSTRUCTED.
BUT...
HE'S VERY SENSITIVE TO PEOPLE BEING HURT...
UH...
DO YOU HAVE INFORMATION ON RITSUKA-KUN?
WE HAVE THE TRANSFER LETTERS FROM HIS PREVIOUS SCHOOL.
AND HIS REPORT CARDS...
AND HE'S BEEN HURT HIMSELF.

HOW DID HE GET INJURED?

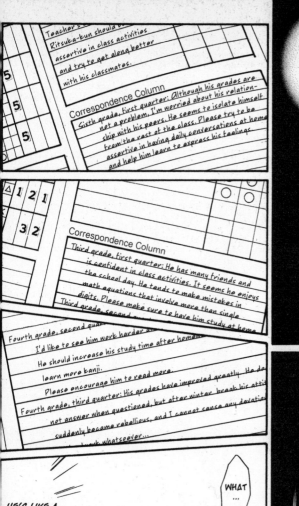

Teacher's ...
Ritsuka-bun should be...
assertive in class activities
and try to get along better
with his classmates.

Correspondence Column
Sixth grade, first quarter: Although his grades are
not a problem, I'm worried about his relationship with his peers. He seems to isolate himself
from the rest of the class. Please try to be
assertive in having daily conversations at home
and help him learn to express his feelings.

| | 1 | 2 | 1 | | | ○ | ○ |
| | 3 | 2 | | | | | |

Correspondence Column
Third grade, first quarter: He has many friends and
is confident in class activities. It seems he enjoys
the school day. He tends to make mistakes in
math equations that involve more than single
digits. Please make sure to have him study at home.
Third grade, second qu...

Fourth grade, second qua...
I'd like to see him work harder...
He should increase his study time after homew...
learn more kanji.
Please encourage him to read more.
Fourth grade, third quarter: His grades have improved greatly. He doe...
not answer when questioned, but after winter break his attit...
suddenly became rebellious, and I cannot sense any devotio...
...work whatsoever...

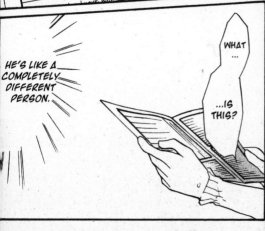

HE'S LIKE A COMPLETELY DIFFERENT PERSON.

WHAT ...
...IS THIS?

A FIGHT?

BULLYING?

...ABUSE?

36

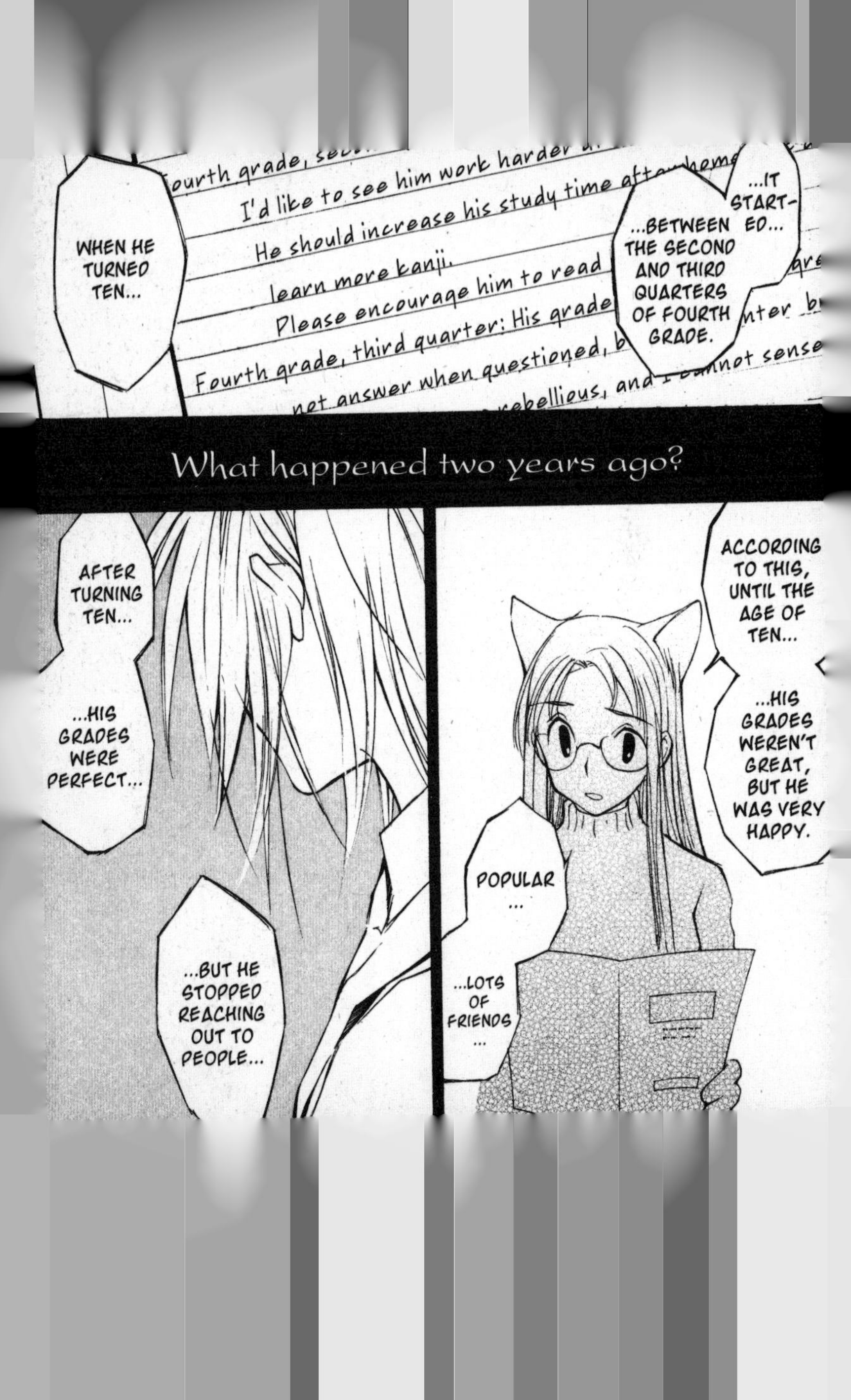

...IT STARTED...
...BETWEEN THE SECOND AND THIRD QUARTERS OF FOURTH GRADE.
WHEN HE TURNED TEN...
I'd like to see him work harder
He should increase his study time
learn more kanji.
Please encourage him to read
Fourth grade, third quarter: His grade
Fourth grade, third quarter: His grade
not answer when questioned,
rebellious, and I cannot sense
What happened two years ago?
ACCORDING TO THIS, UNTIL THE AGE OF TEN...
...HIS GRADES WEREN'T GREAT, BUT HE WAS VERY HAPPY.
POPULAR...
...LOTS OF FRIENDS...
AFTER TURNING TEN...
...HIS GRADES WERE PERFECT...
...BUT HE STOPPED REACHING OUT TO PEOPLE...

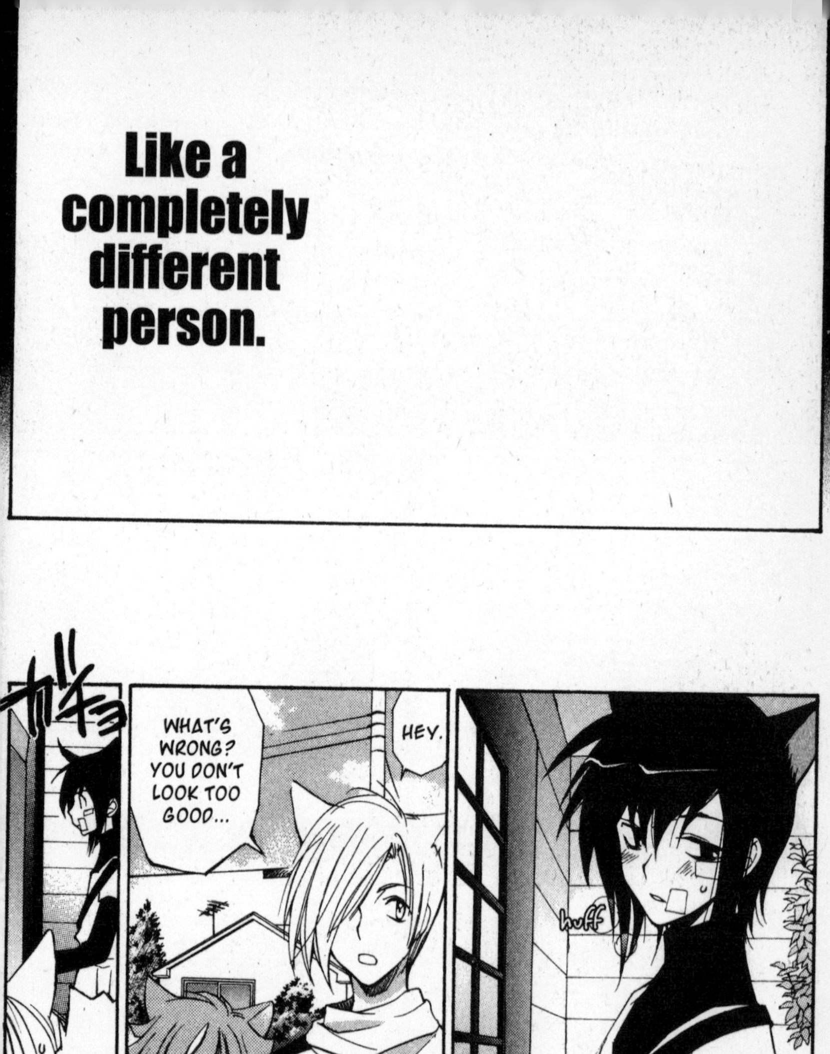
Like a completely different person.
huff
HEY.
WHAT'S WRONG? YOU DON'T LOOK TOO GOOD...
HEY! DON'T IGNORE US!
WE CAME TO TALK!

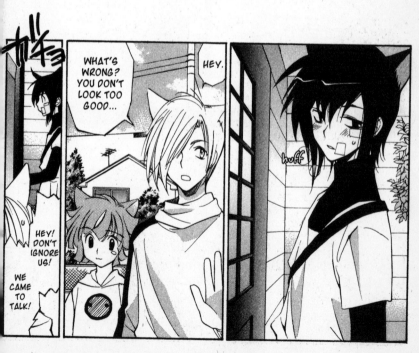

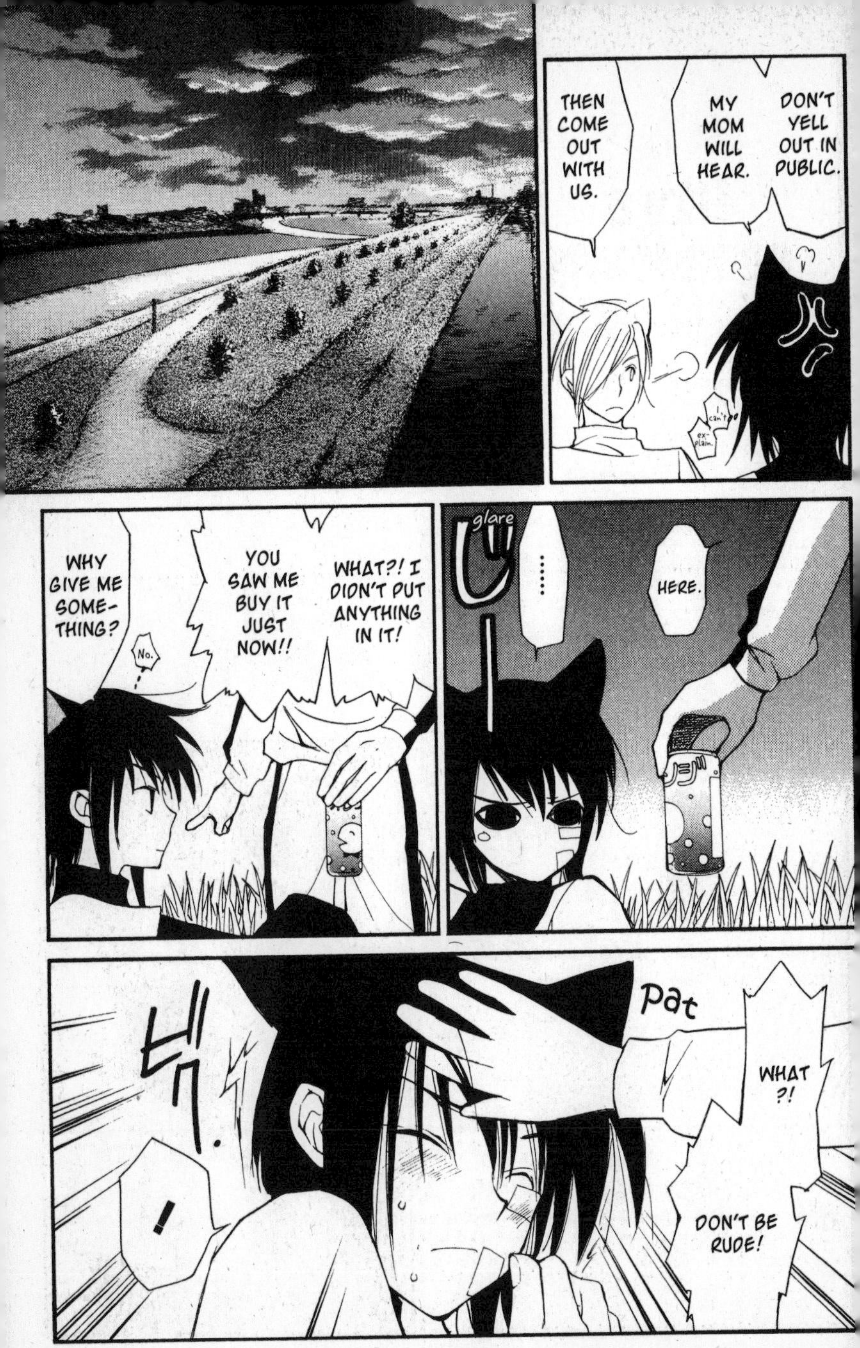
DON'T YELL OUT IN PUBLIC.
MY MOM WILL HEAR.
THEN COME OUT WITH US.
I can't ex-plain.
HERE.
glare
......
WHAT?! I DIDN'T PUT ANYTHING IN IT!
YOU SAW ME BUY IT JUST NOW!!
WHY GIVE ME SOMETHING?
No.
Pat
WHAT ?!
DON'T BE RUDE!
!

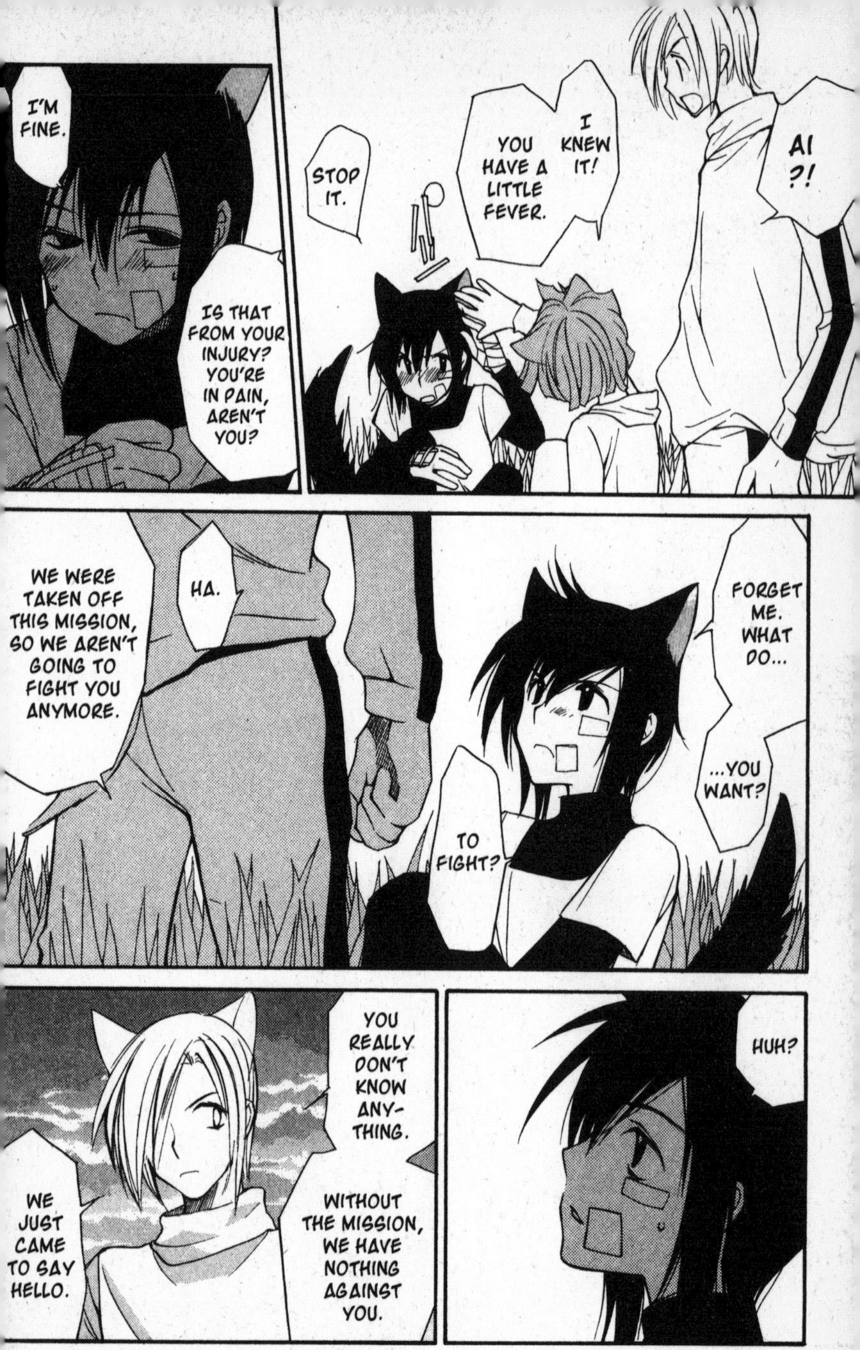
AI ?!
I KNEW IT!
YOU HAVE A LITTLE FEVER.
STOP IT.
IS THAT FROM YOUR INJURY? YOU'RE IN PAIN, AREN'T YOU?
I'M FINE.
FORGET ME. WHAT DO...
...YOU WANT?
TO FIGHT?
HA.
WE WERE TAKEN OFF THIS MISSION, SO WE AREN'T GOING TO FIGHT YOU ANYMORE.
HUH?
YOU REALLY DON'T KNOW ANY-THING.
WITHOUT THE MISSION, WE HAVE NOTHING AGAINST YOU.
WE JUST CAME TO SAY HELLO.

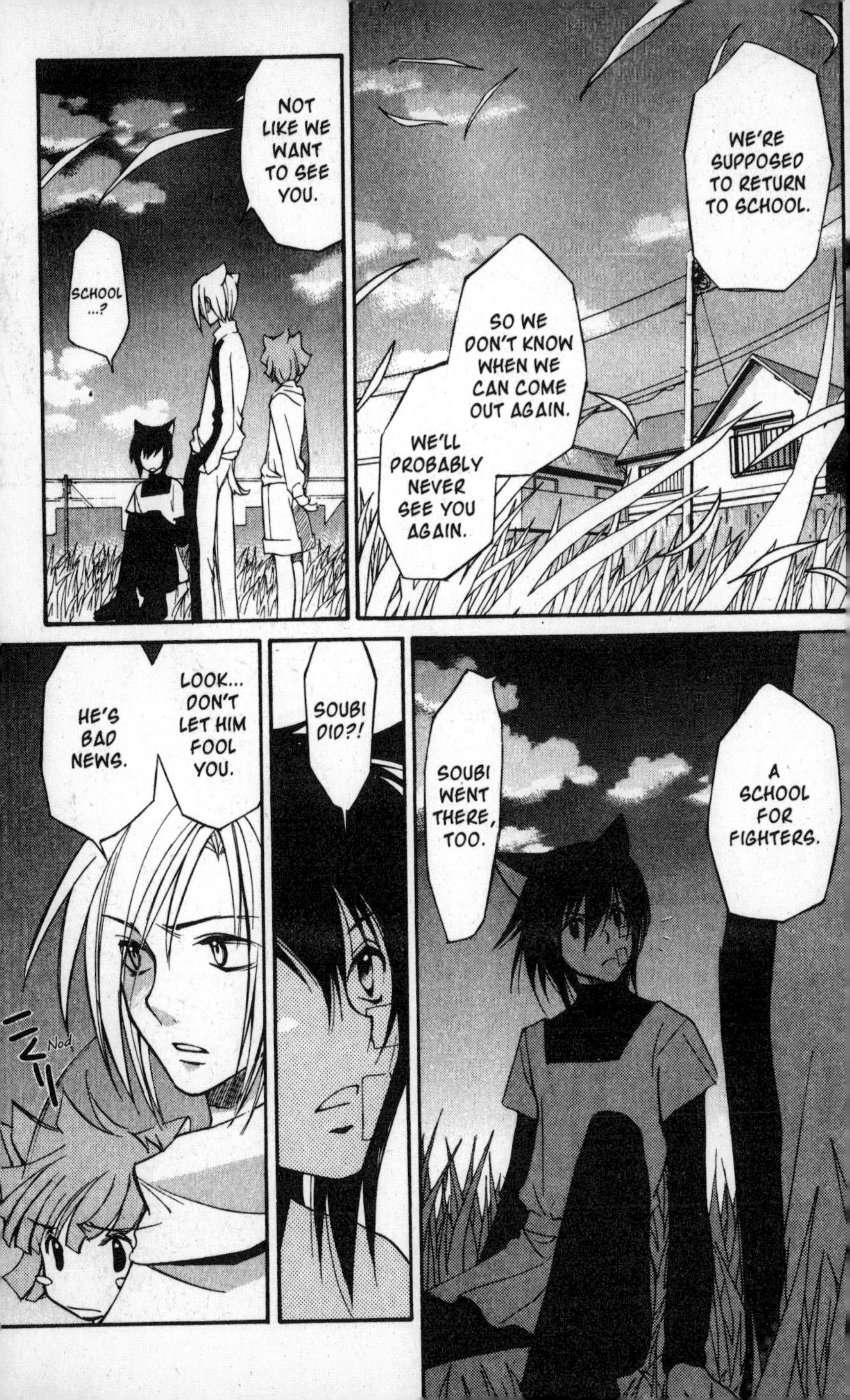
WE'RE SUPPOSED TO RETURN TO SCHOOL.
SO WE DON'T KNOW WHEN WE CAN COME OUT AGAIN.
WE'LL PROBABLY NEVER SEE YOU AGAIN.
NOT LIKE WE WANT TO SEE YOU.
SCHOOL ...?
A SCHOOL FOR FIGHTERS.
SOUBI WENT THERE, TOO.
SOUBI DID?!
LOOK... DON'T LET HIM FOOL YOU.
HE'S BAD NEWS.
Nod

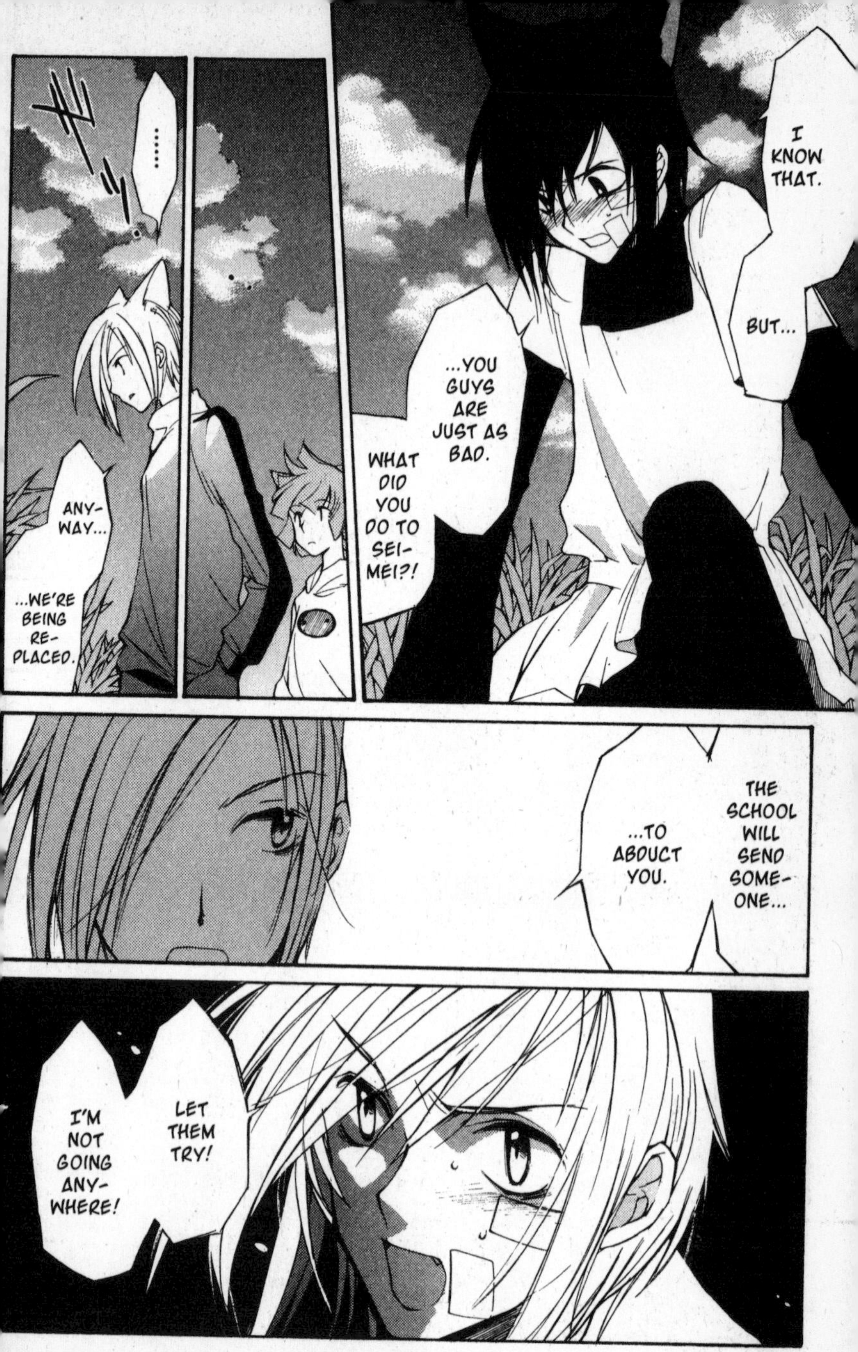
I KNOW THAT.
BUT...
...YOU GUYS ARE JUST AS BAD.
WHAT DID YOU DO TO SEI-MEI?!
......
ANY-WAY...
...WE'RE BEING RE-PLACED.
THE SCHOOL WILL SEND SOME-ONE...
...TO ABDUCT YOU.
LET THEM TRY!
I'M NOT GOING ANY-WHERE!

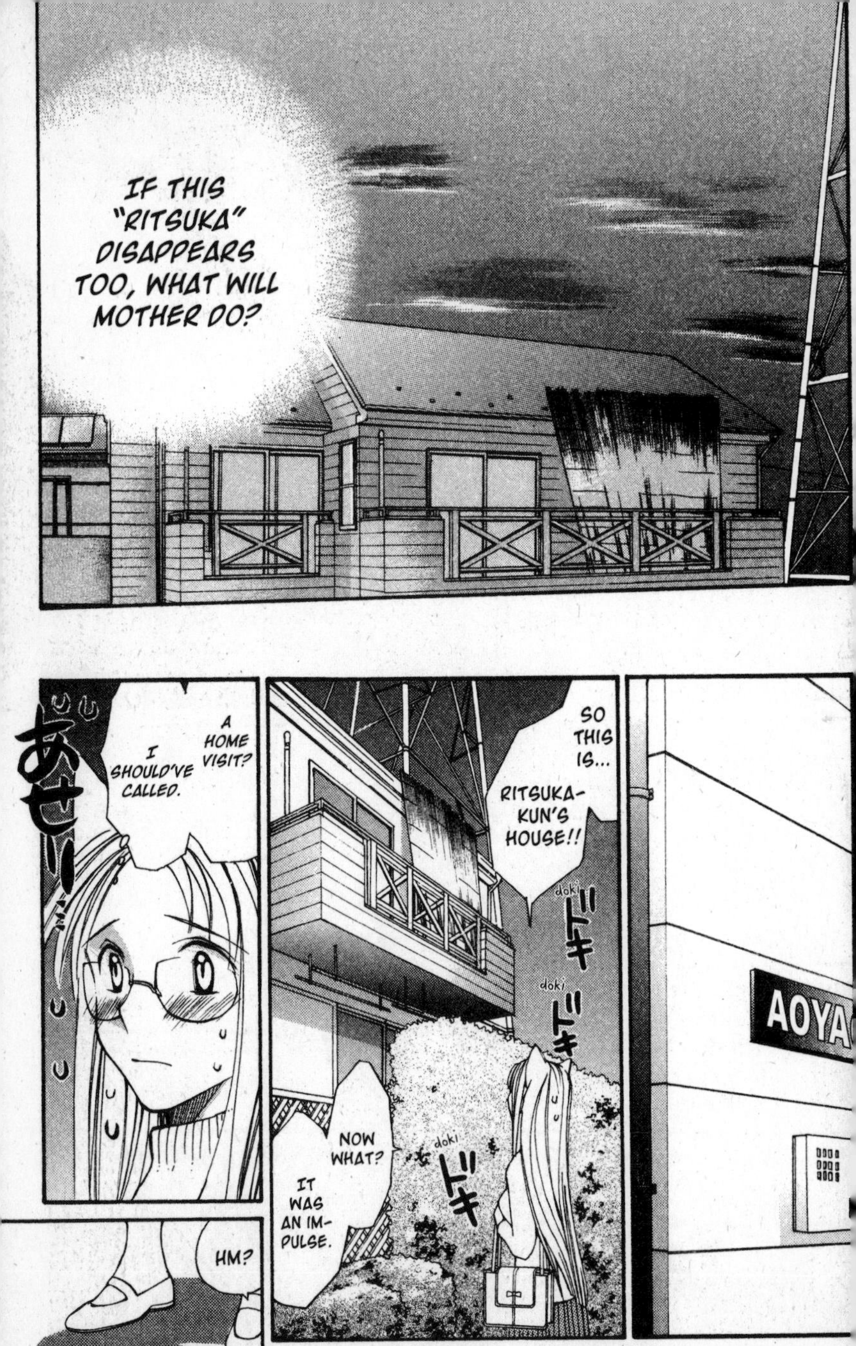
IF THIS "RITSUKA" DISAPPEARS TOO, WHAT WILL MOTHER DO?
AOYA
SO THIS IS...
RITSUKA-KUN'S HOUSE!!
doki ドキ
doki ドキ
NOW WHAT?
IT WAS AN IMPULSE.
doki ドキ
A HOME VISIT?
I SHOULD'VE CALLED.
あせー
HM?

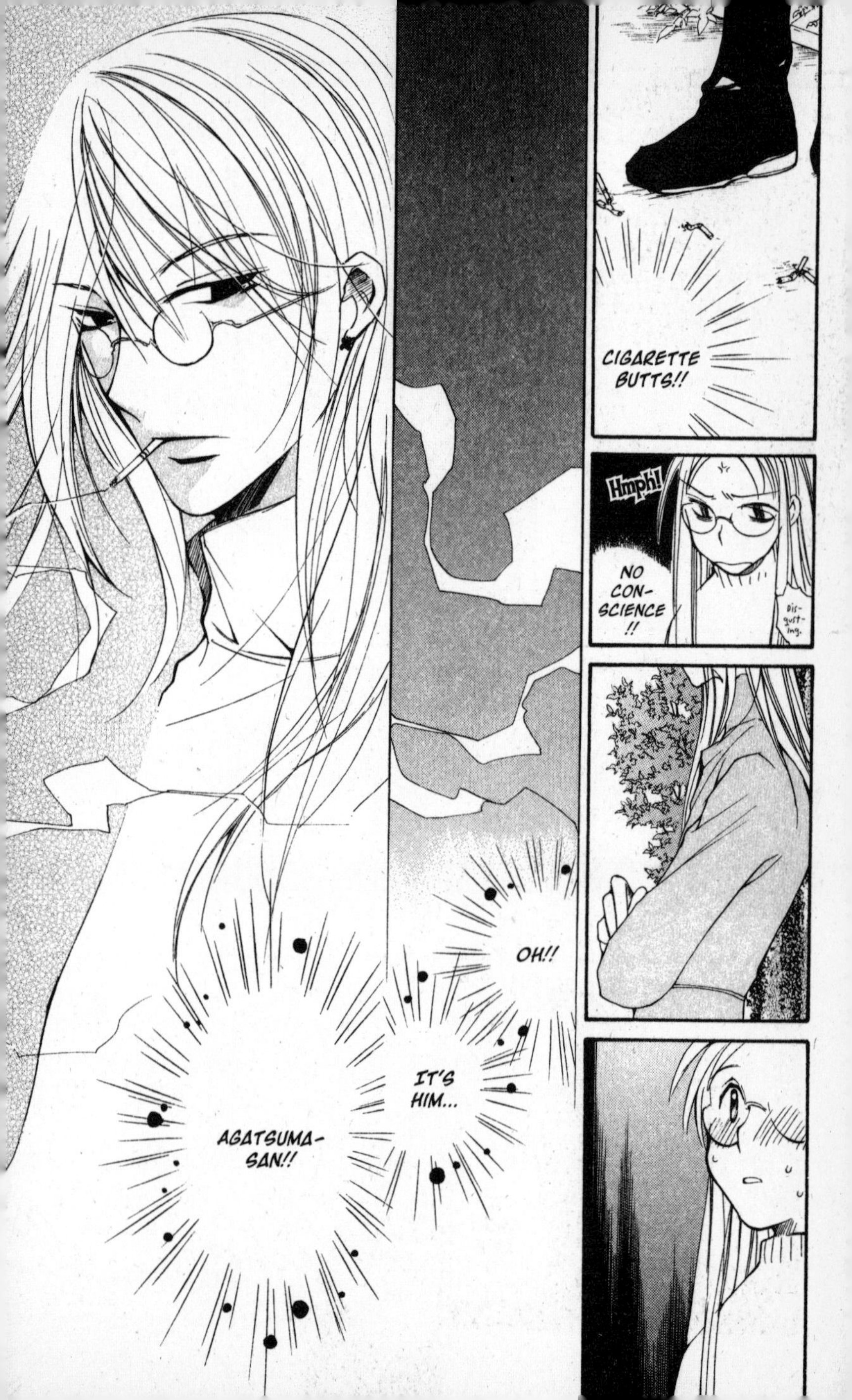
CIGARETTE BUTTS!!
Hmph!
NO CON-SCIENCE!!
Dis-gust-ing.
OH!!
IT'S HIM...
AGATSUMA-SAN!!

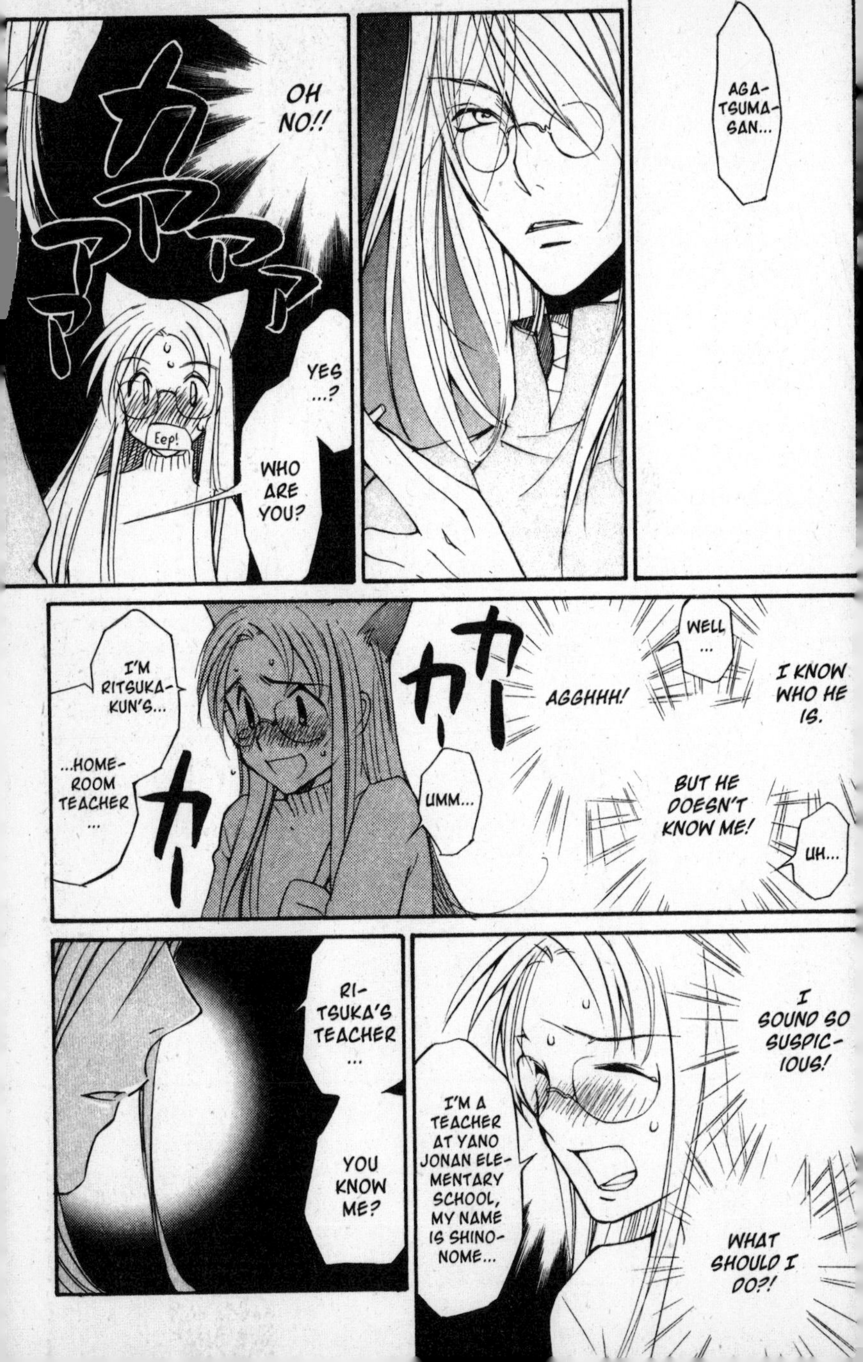
AGATSUMA-SAN...
OH NO!!
YES ...?
Eep!
WHO ARE YOU?
WELL ...
I KNOW WHO HE IS.
BUT HE DOESN'T KNOW ME!
UH...
AGGHHH!
UMM...
I'M RITSUKA-KUN'S...
...HOMEROOM TEACHER ...
I SOUND SO SUSPICIOUS!
WHAT SHOULD I DO?!
I'M A TEACHER AT YANO JONAN ELEMENTARY SCHOOL, MY NAME IS SHINONOME...
RITSUKA'S TEACHER ...
YOU KNOW ME?

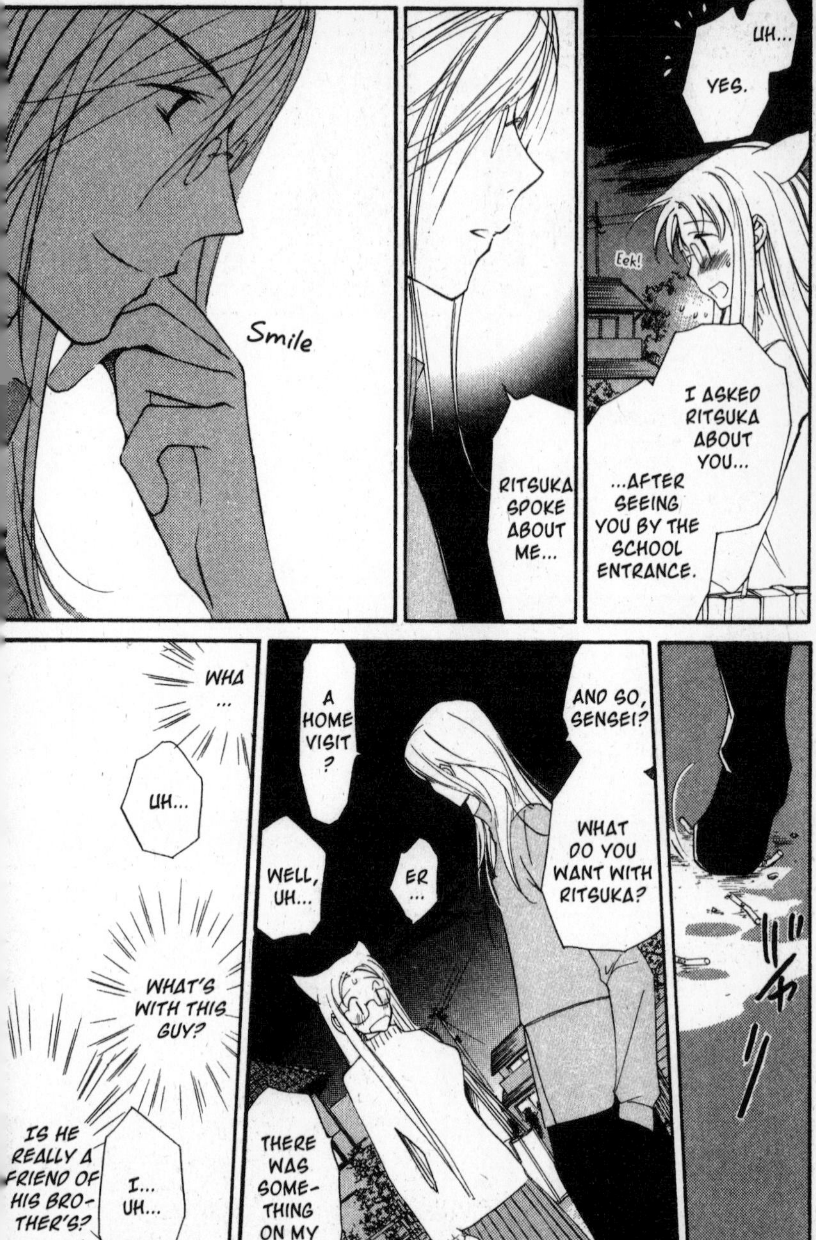

UH...
YES.
Eek!
I ASKED RITSUKA ABOUT YOU...
...AFTER SEEING YOU BY THE SCHOOL ENTRANCE.
RITSUKA SPOKE ABOUT ME...
Smile
ジャリ
AND SO, SENSEI?
WHAT DO YOU WANT WITH RITSUKA?
A HOME VISIT?
ER...
WELL, UH...
THERE WAS SOMETHING ON MY MIND...
WHA...
UH...
WHAT'S WITH THIS GUY?
I... UH...
IS HE REALLY A FRIEND OF HIS BROTHER'S?

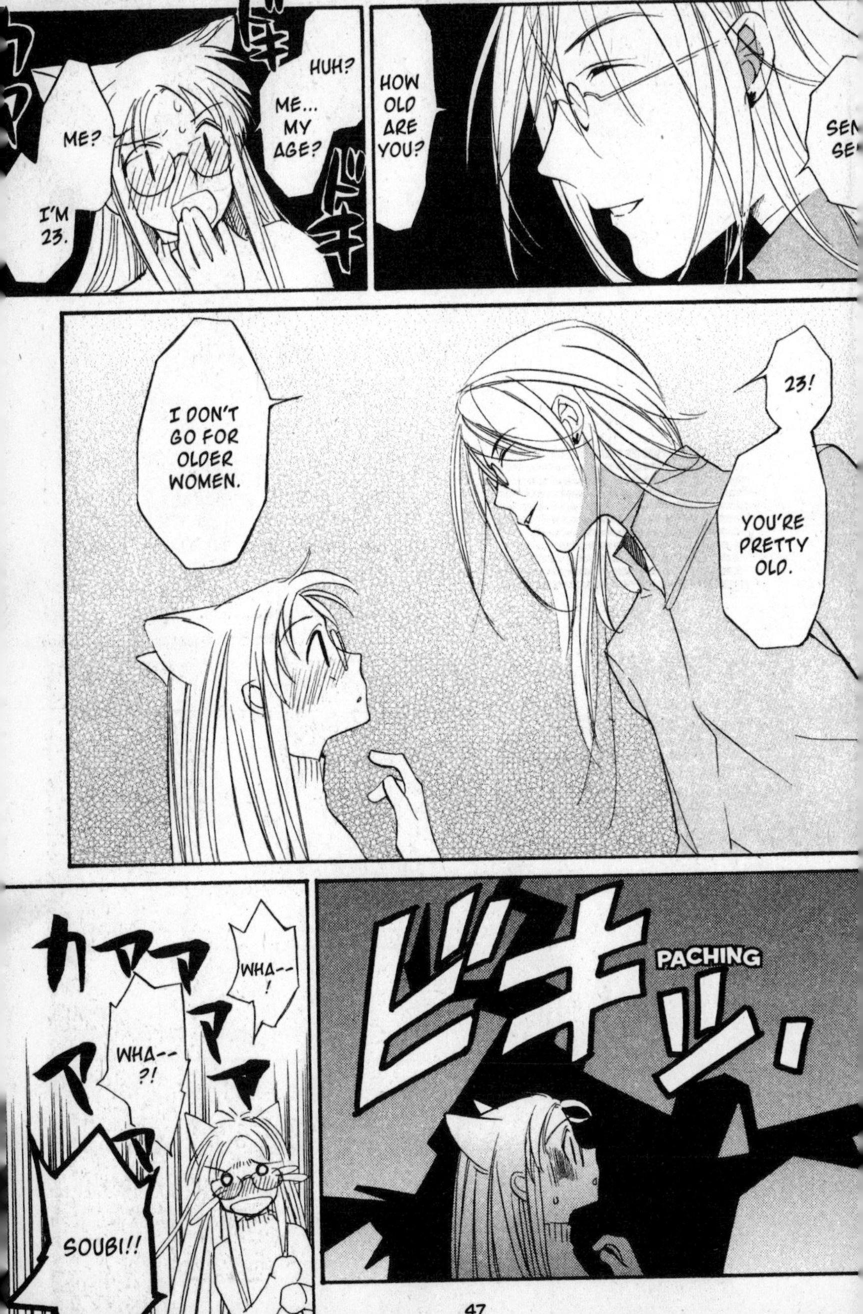
HOW OLD ARE YOU?
HUH?
ME... MY AGE?
ME?
I'M 23.
23!
YOU'RE PRETTY OLD.
I DON'T GO FOR OLDER WOMEN.
PACHING
WHA-- !
WHA-- ?!
SOUBI!!

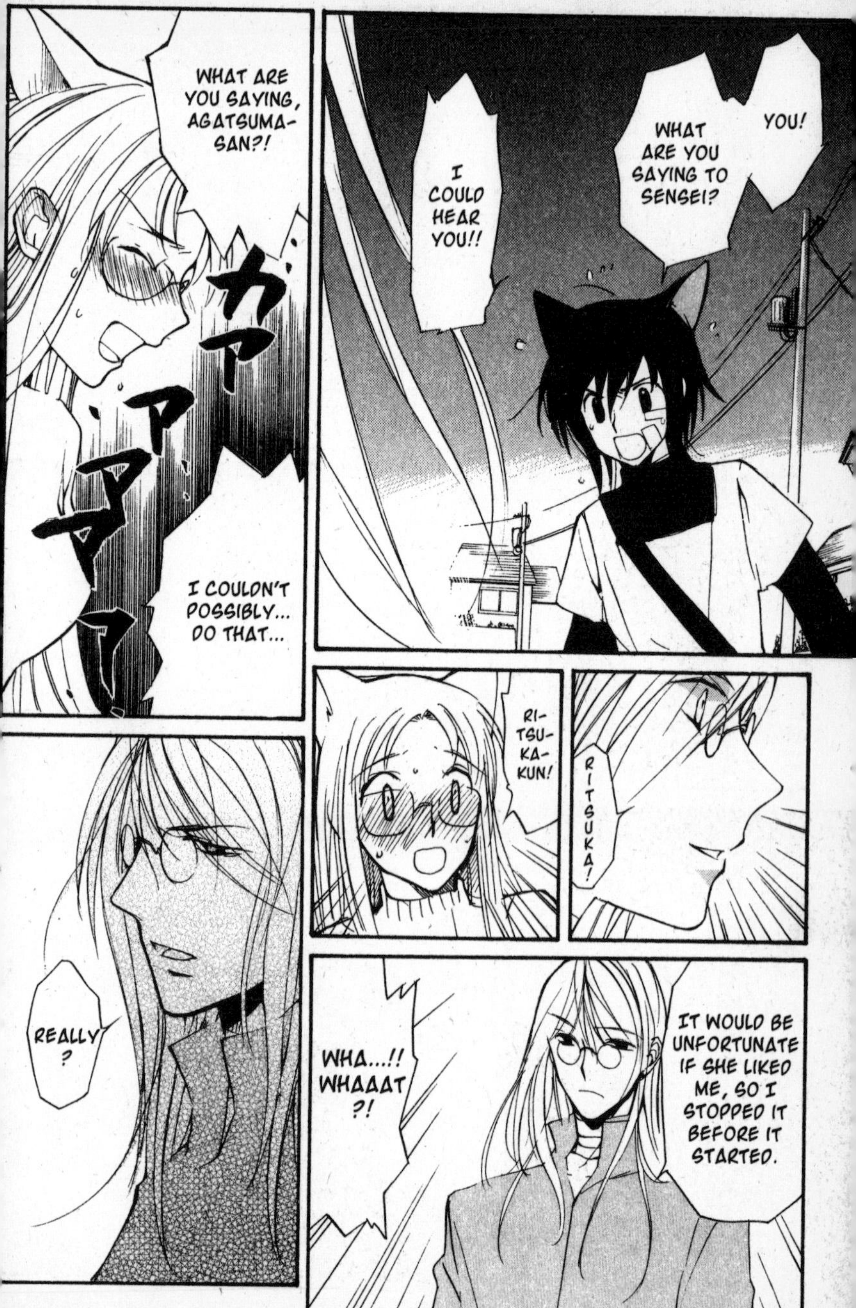
YOU!
WHAT ARE YOU SAYING TO SENSEI?
I COULD HEAR YOU!!
WHAT ARE YOU SAYING, AGATSUMA-SAN?!
I COULDN'T POSSIBLY... DO THAT...
RITSUKA!
RI-TSU-KA-KUN!
IT WOULD BE UNFORTUNATE IF SHE LIKED ME, SO I STOPPED IT BEFORE IT STARTED.
WHA...!! WHAAAT?!
REALLY?

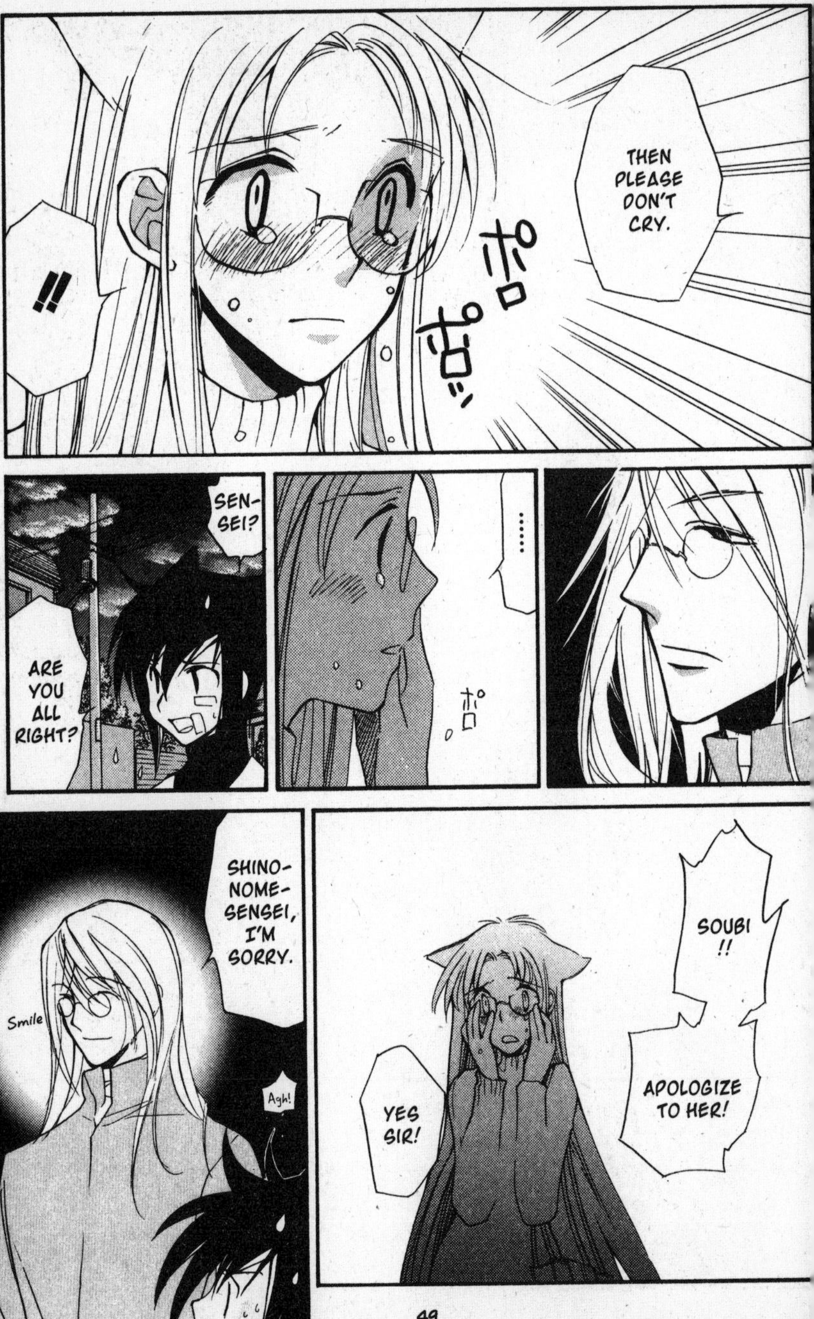
THEN PLEASE DON'T CRY.
ポロ
ポロッ
!!
......
ポロ
SEN-SEI?
ARE YOU ALL RIGHT?
SOUBI !!
APOLOGIZE TO HER!
YES SIR!
SHINO-NOME-SENSEI, I'M SORRY.
Smile
Agh!

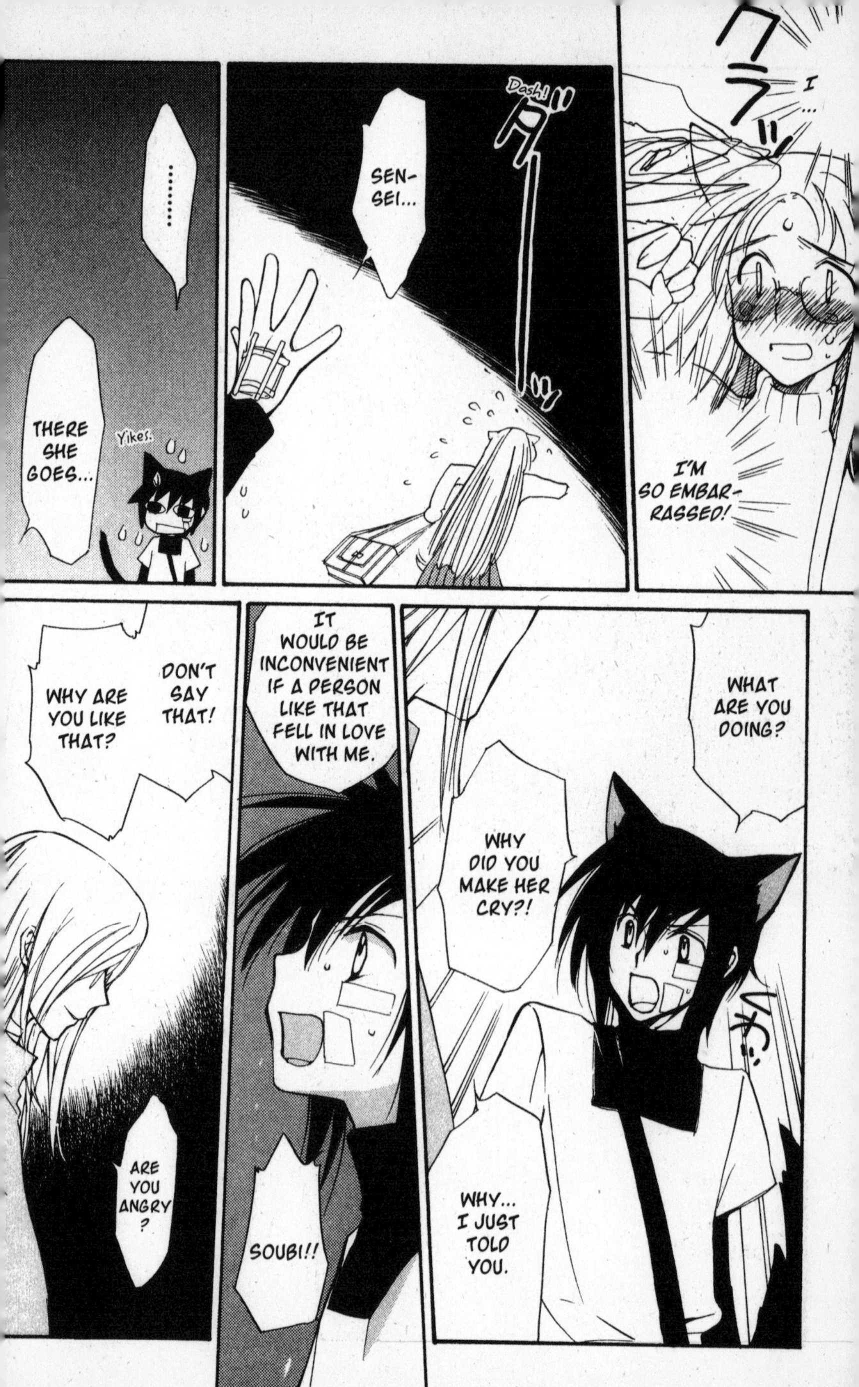
I...
I'M SO EMBARRASSED!
SEN-SEI...
Dash!
......
Yikes.
THERE SHE GOES...
WHAT ARE YOU DOING?
WHY DID YOU MAKE HER CRY?!
WHY... I JUST TOLD YOU.
IT WOULD BE INCONVENIENT IF A PERSON LIKE THAT FELL IN LOVE WITH ME.
SOUBI!!
DON'T SAY THAT!
WHY ARE YOU LIKE THAT?
ARE YOU ANGRY?

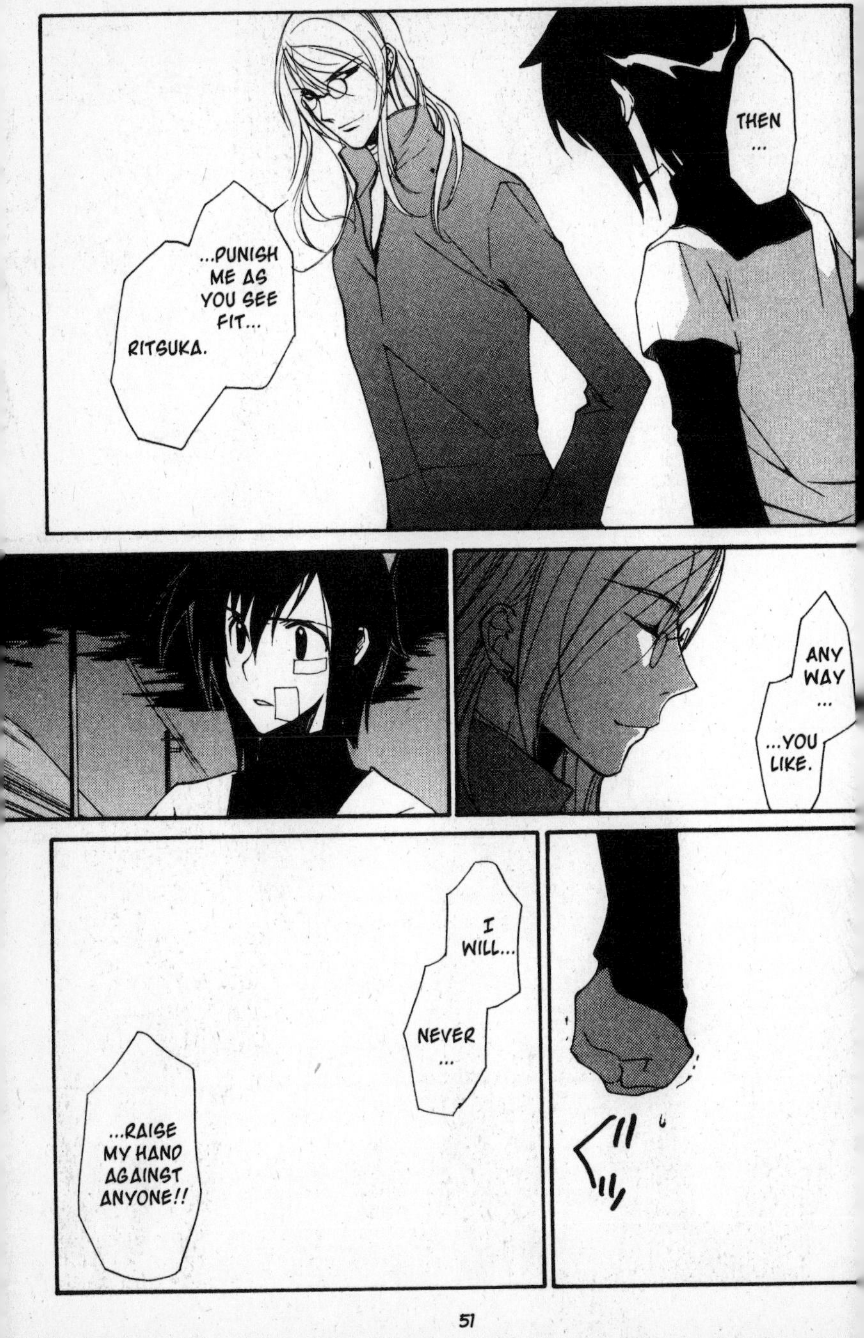
THEN ...
...PUNISH ME AS YOU SEE FIT... RITSUKA.
ANY WAY ...
...YOU LIKE.
I WILL...
NEVER ...
...RAISE MY HAND AGAINST ANYONE!!

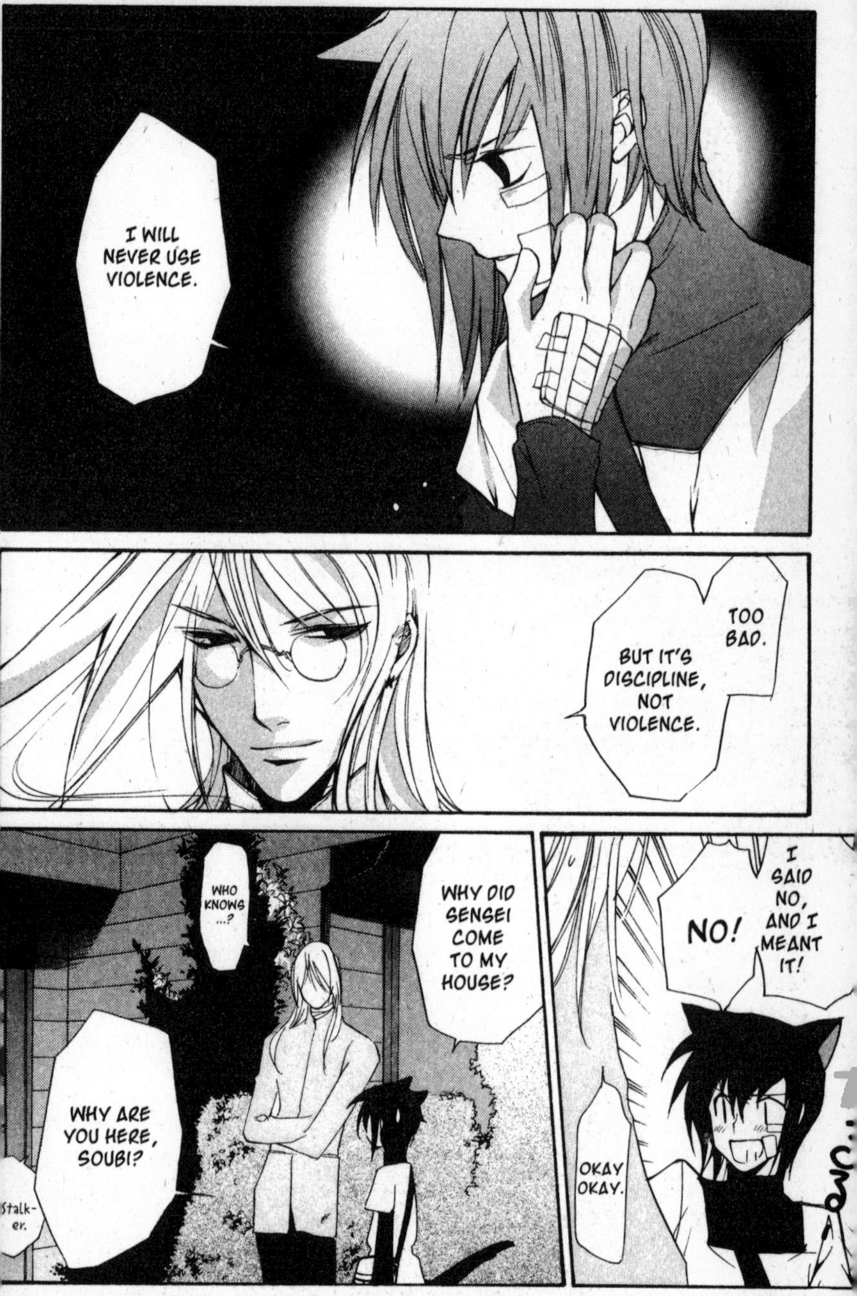
I WILL NEVER USE VIOLENCE.
TOO BAD.
BUT IT'S DISCIPLINE, NOT VIOLENCE.
I SAID NO, AND I MEANT IT!
NO!
OKAY OKAY.
WHY DID SENSEI COME TO MY HOUSE?
WHO KNOWS ...?
WHY ARE YOU HERE, SOUBI?
Stalker.

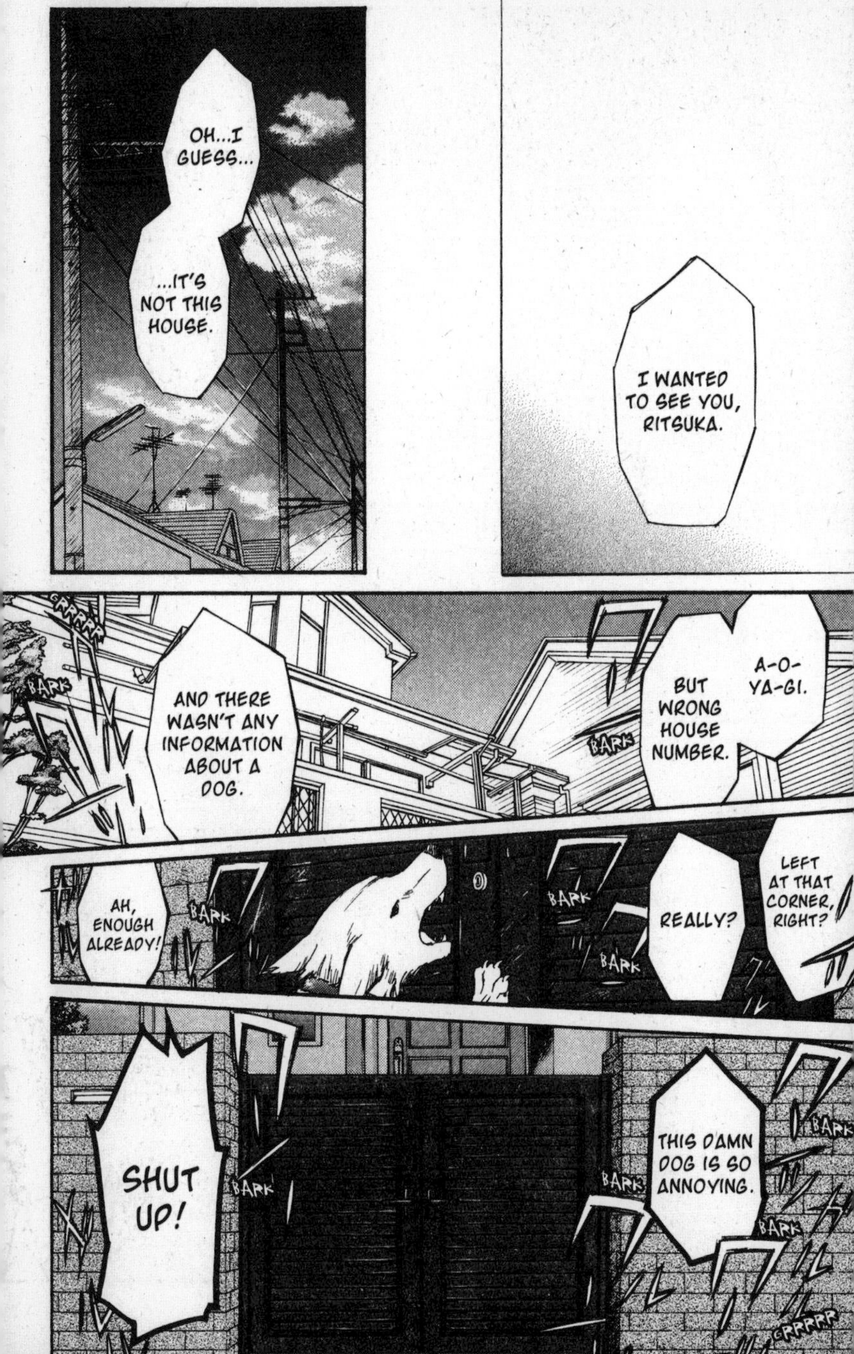
I WANTED TO SEE YOU, RITSUKA.
OH...I GUESS...
...IT'S NOT THIS HOUSE.
A-O-YA-GI.
BUT WRONG HOUSE NUMBER.
BARK
AND THERE WASN'T ANY INFORMATION ABOUT A DOG.
GRRRRRR
BARK
LEFT AT THAT CORNER, RIGHT?
REALLY?
BARK
BARK
BARK
AH, ENOUGH ALREADY!
BARK
THIS DAMN DOG IS SO ANNOYING.
BARK
BARK
GRRRRR
BARK
SHUT UP!

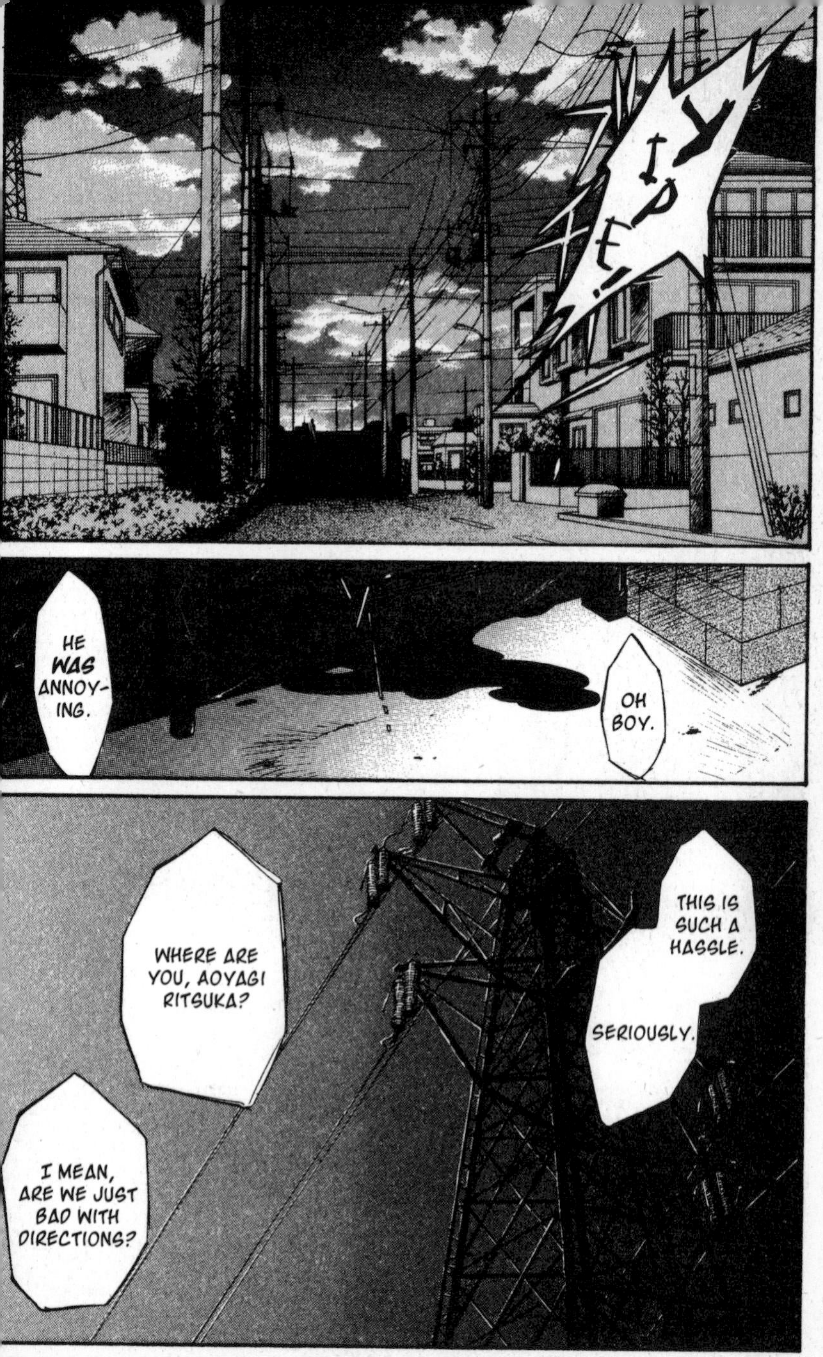
YIPE!!
OH BOY.
HE WAS ANNOYING.
THIS IS SUCH A HASSLE.
SERIOUSLY.
WHERE ARE YOU, AOYAGI RITSUKA?
I MEAN, ARE WE JUST BAD WITH DIRECTIONS?

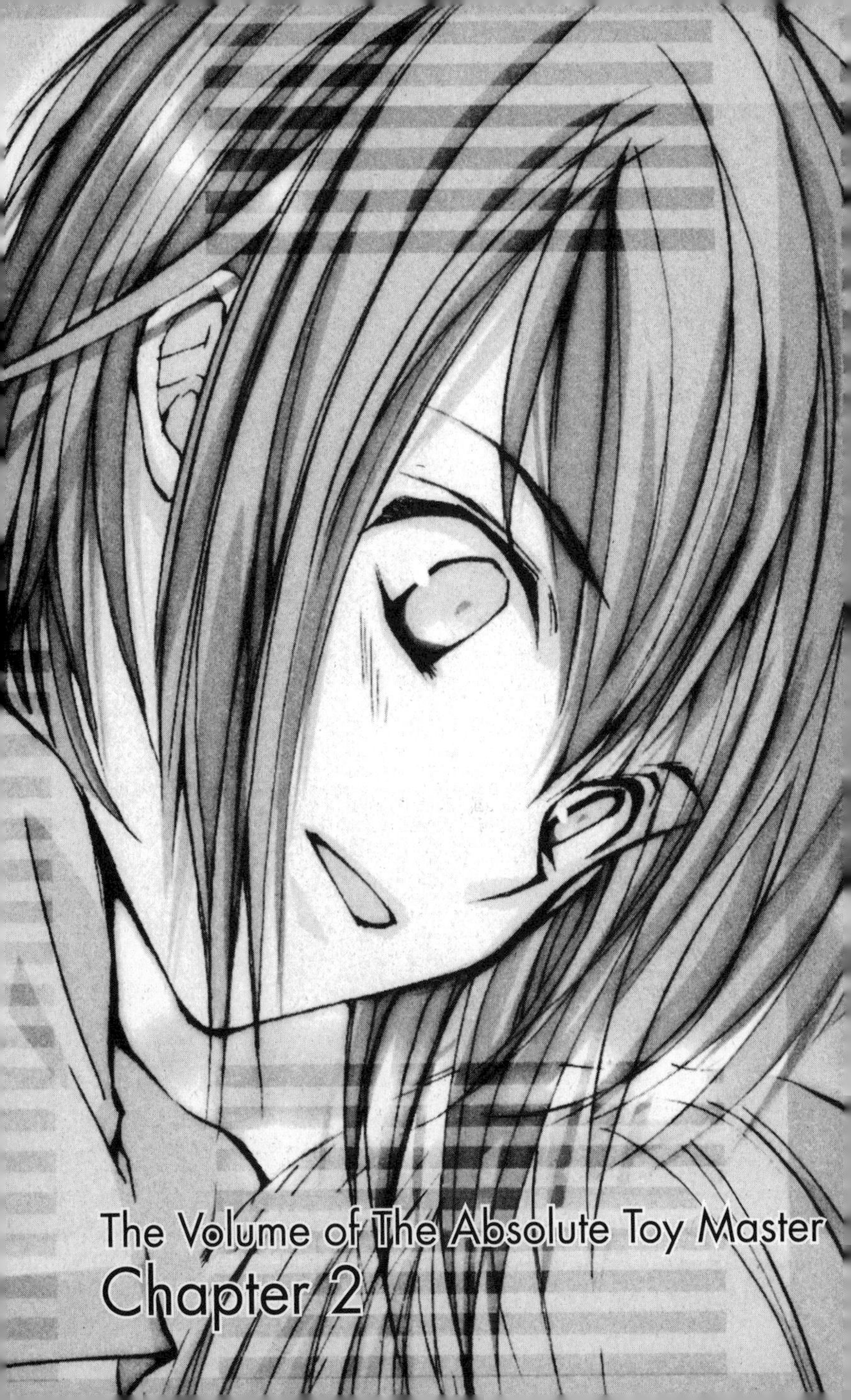
The Volume of The Absolute Toy Master
Chapter 2

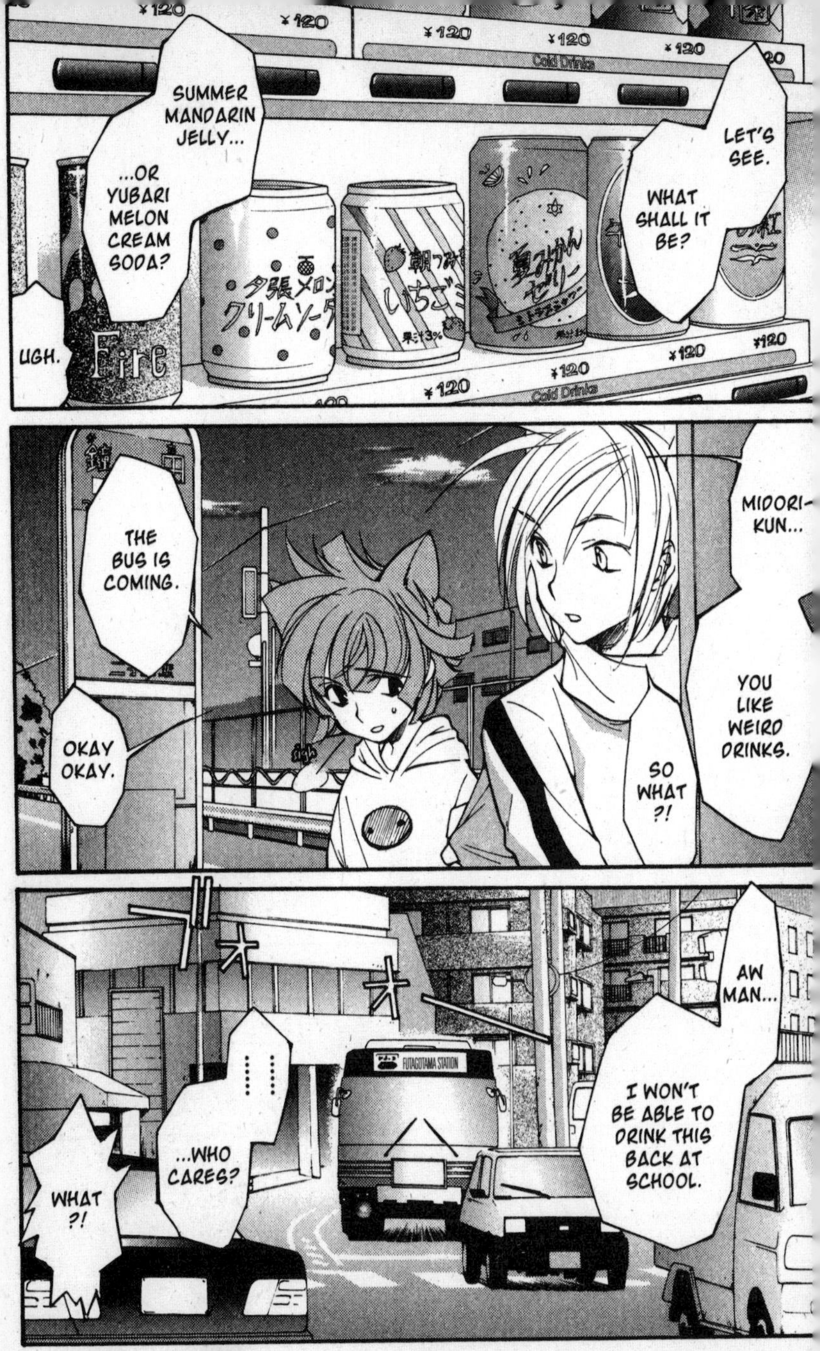
LET'S SEE.
WHAT SHALL IT BE?
SUMMER MANDARIN JELLY...
...OR YUBARI MELON CREAM SODA?
UGH.
Cold Drinks
Fire
MIDORI-KUN...
YOU LIKE WEIRD DRINKS.
SO WHAT?!
THE BUS IS COMING.
OKAY OKAY.
AW MAN...
I WON'T BE ABLE TO DRINK THIS BACK AT SCHOOL.
FUTAGOTAMA STATION
......
...WHO CARES?
WHAT?!

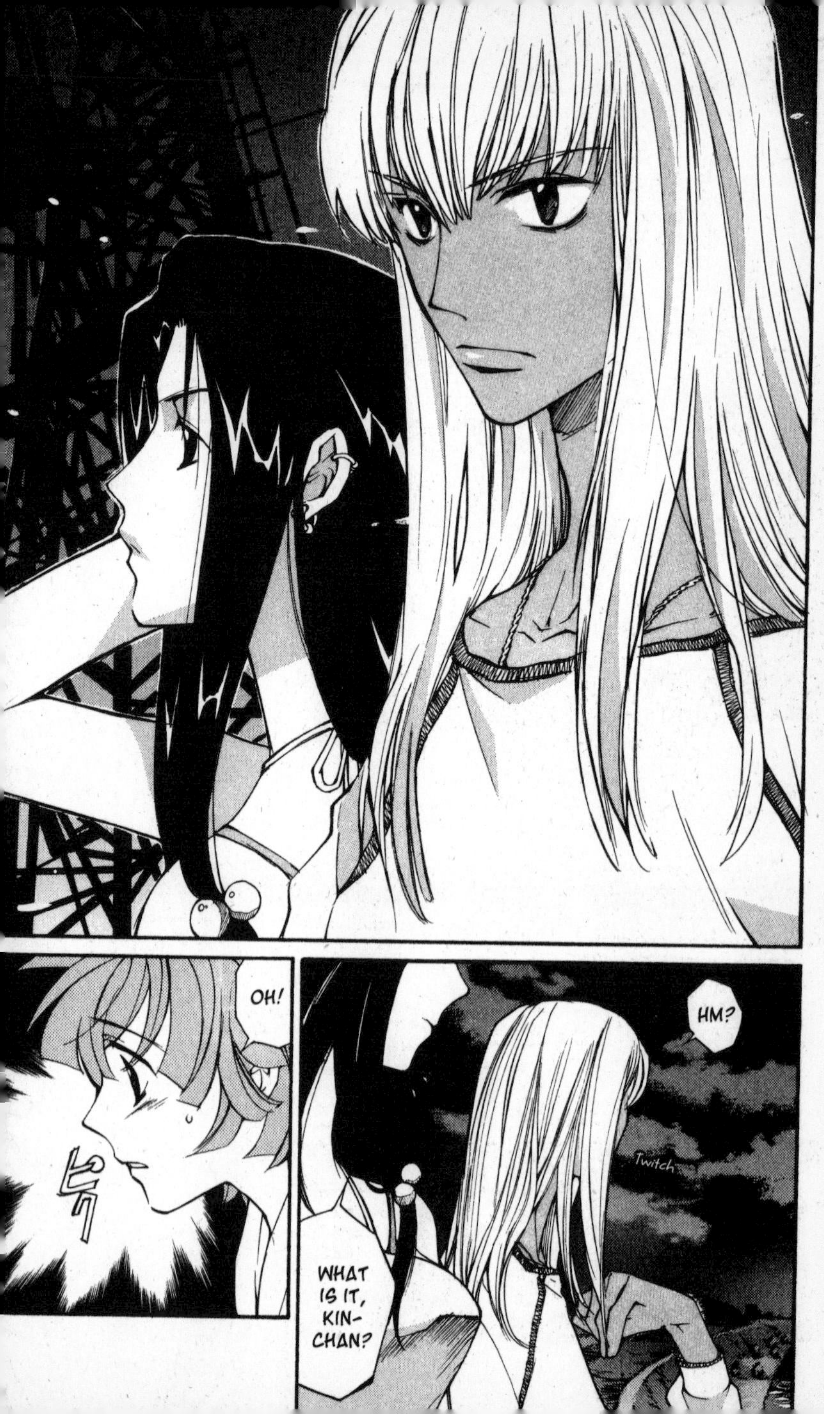
HM?
Twitch
WHAT IS IT, KIN-CHAN?
OH!

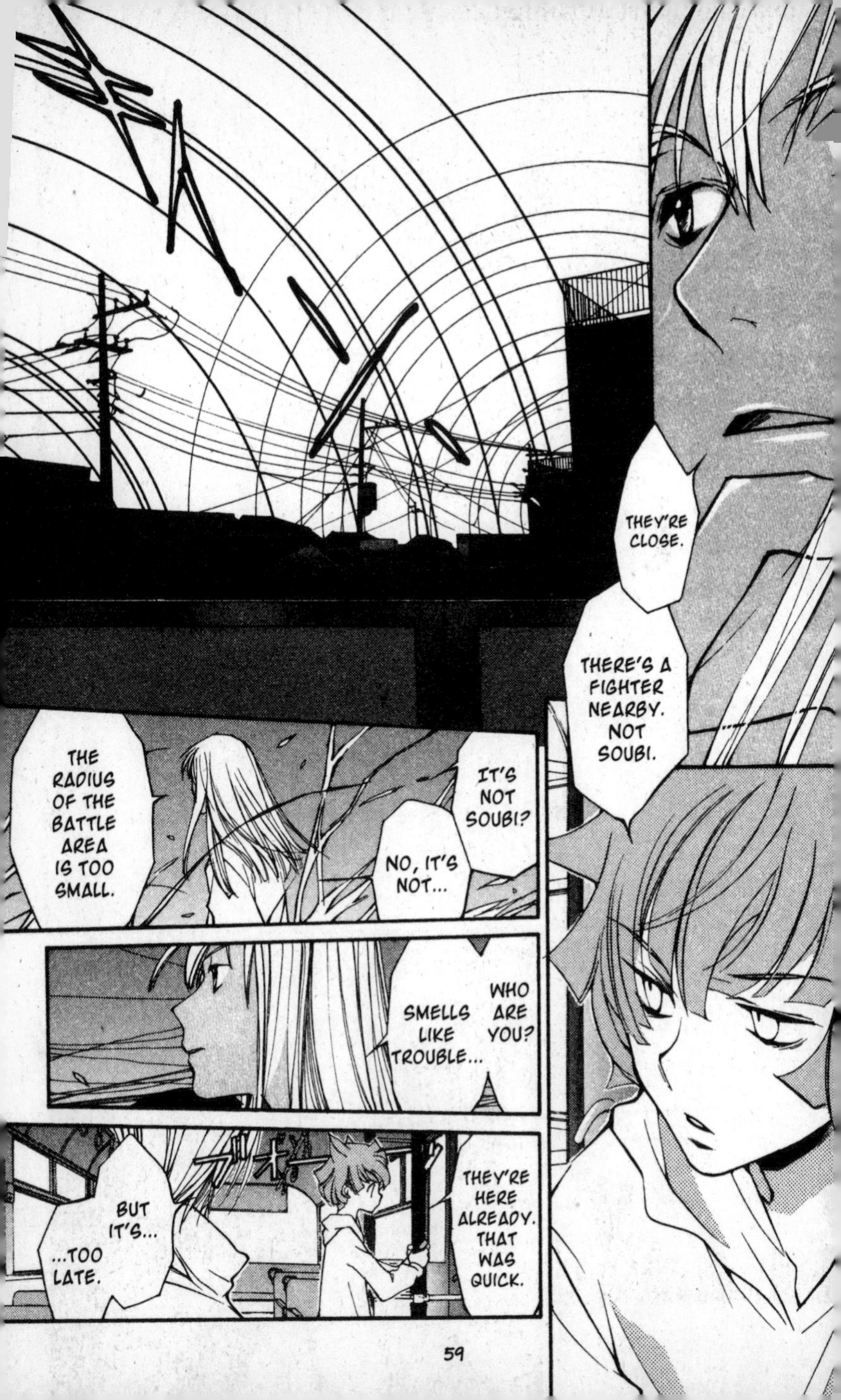
THEY'RE CLOSE.
THERE'S A FIGHTER NEARBY. NOT SOUBI.
IT'S NOT SOUBI?
NO, IT'S NOT...
THE RADIUS OF THE BATTLE AREA IS TOO SMALL.
WHO ARE YOU?
SMELLS LIKE TROUBLE...
THEY'RE HERE ALREADY. THAT WAS QUICK.
BUT IT'S...
...TOO LATE.

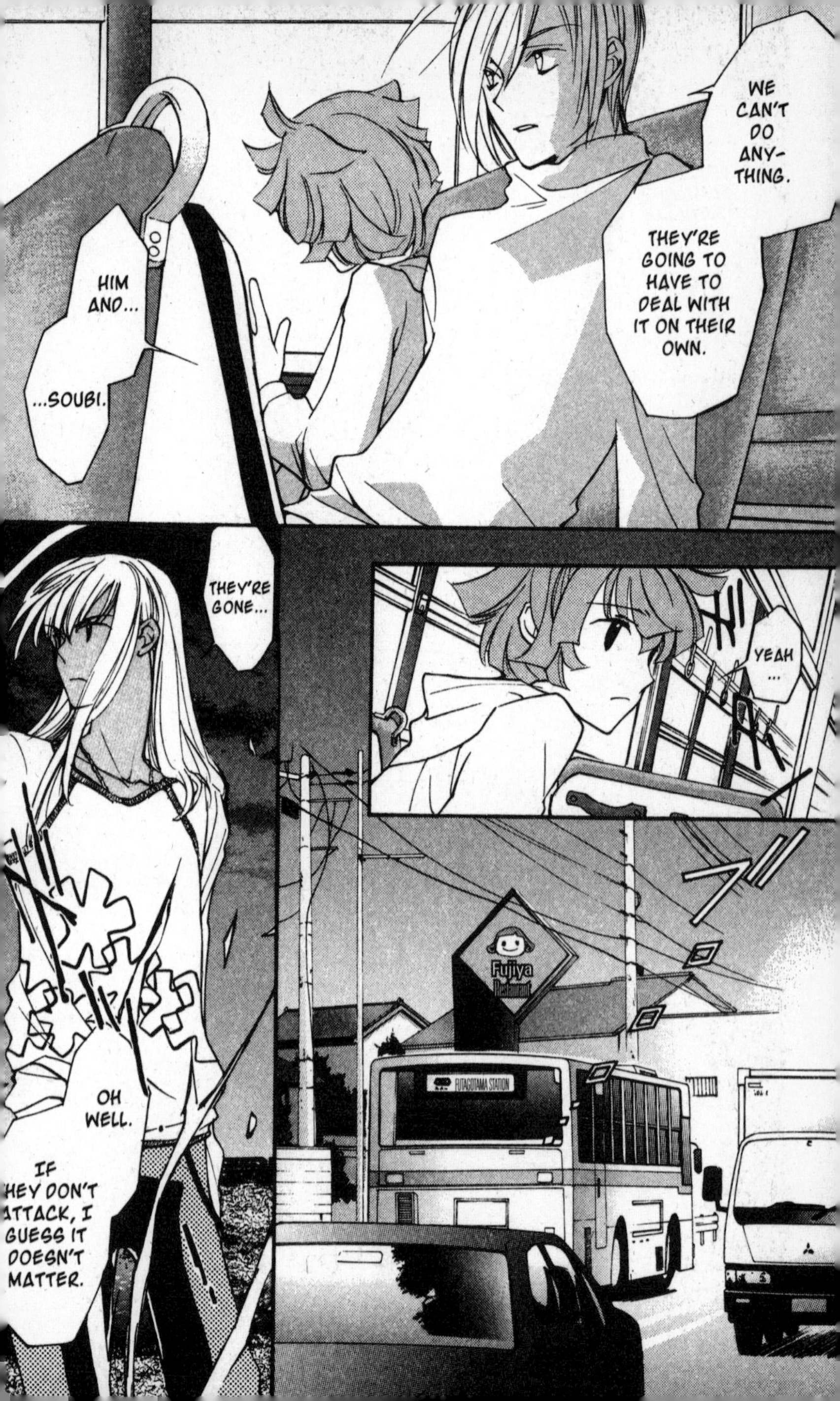
WE CAN'T DO ANY-THING.
THEY'RE GOING TO HAVE TO DEAL WITH IT ON THEIR OWN.
HIM AND...
...SOUBI.
YEAH ...
Fujiya Restaurant
FUTAGOTAMA STATION
THEY'RE GONE...
OH WELL.
IF HEY DON'T TTACK, I GUESS IT DOESN'T MATTER.

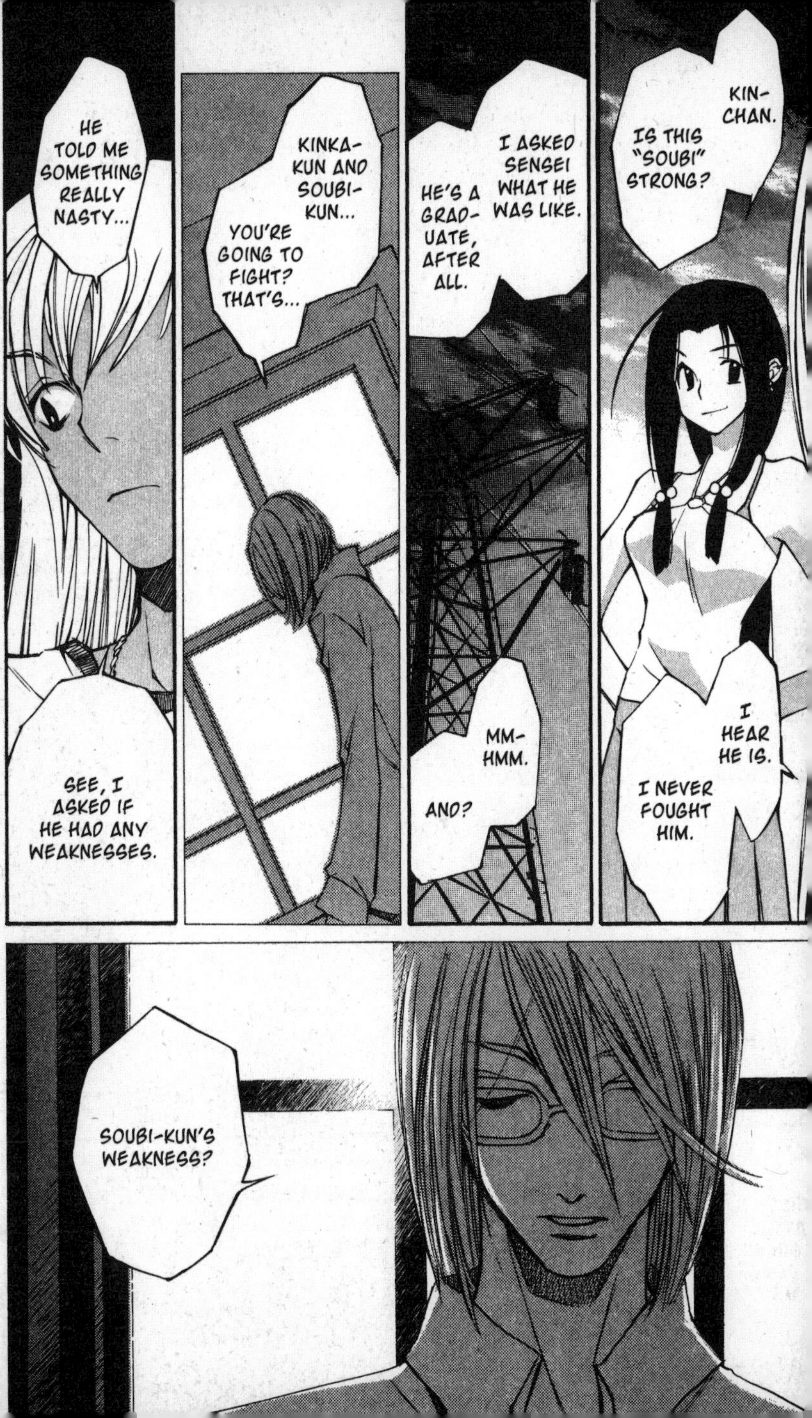
KIN-CHAN.
IS THIS "SOUBI" STRONG?
I HEAR HE IS.
I NEVER FOUGHT HIM.
I ASKED SENSEI WHAT HE WAS LIKE.
HE'S A GRADUATE, AFTER ALL.
MM-HMM.
AND?
KINKA-KUN AND SOUBI-KUN...
YOU'RE GOING TO FIGHT? THAT'S...
HE TOLD ME SOMETHING REALLY NASTY...
SEE, I ASKED IF HE HAD ANY WEAKNESSES.
SOUBI-KUN'S WEAKNESS?

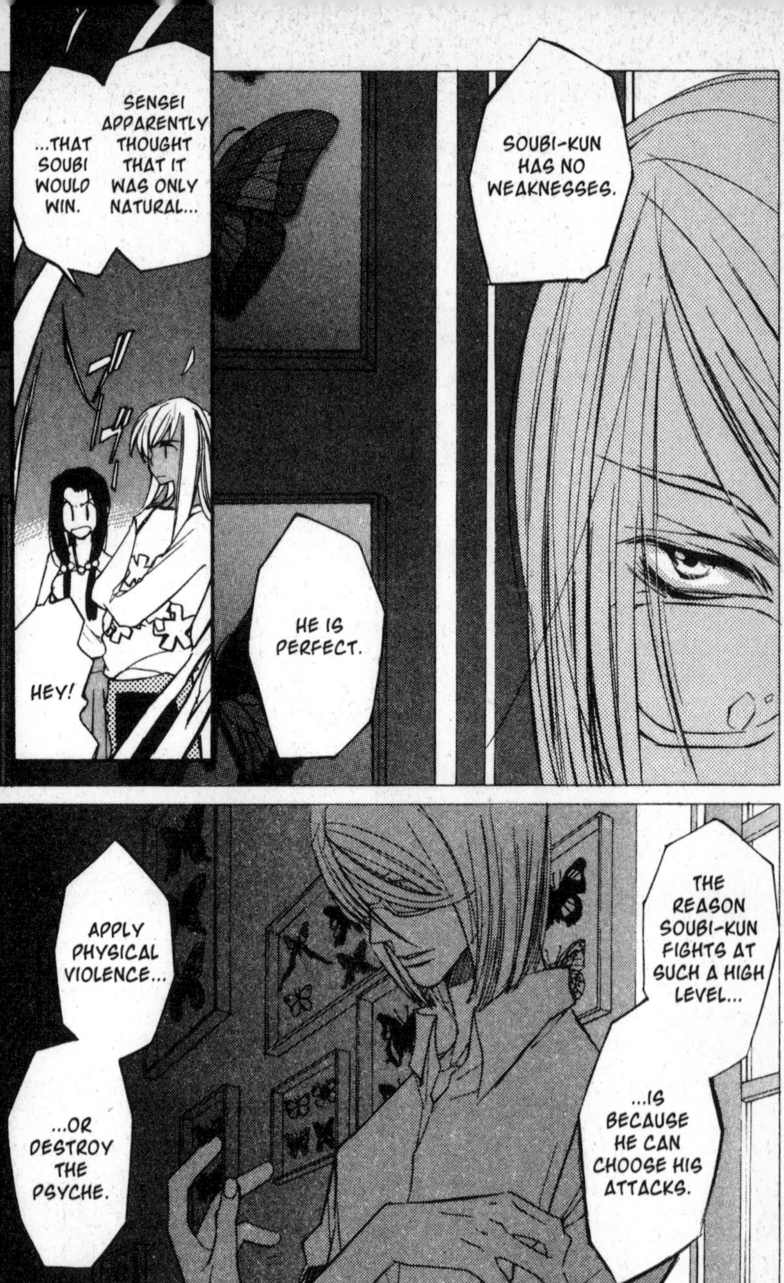
SOUBI-KUN HAS NO WEAKNESSES.
HE IS PERFECT.
SENSEI APPARENTLY THOUGHT THAT IT WAS ONLY NATURAL...
...THAT SOUBI WOULD WIN.
HEY!
THE REASON SOUBI-KUN FIGHTS AT SUCH A HIGH LEVEL...
...IS BECAUSE HE CAN CHOOSE HIS ATTACKS.
APPLY PHYSICAL VIOLENCE...
...OR DESTROY THE PSYCHE.

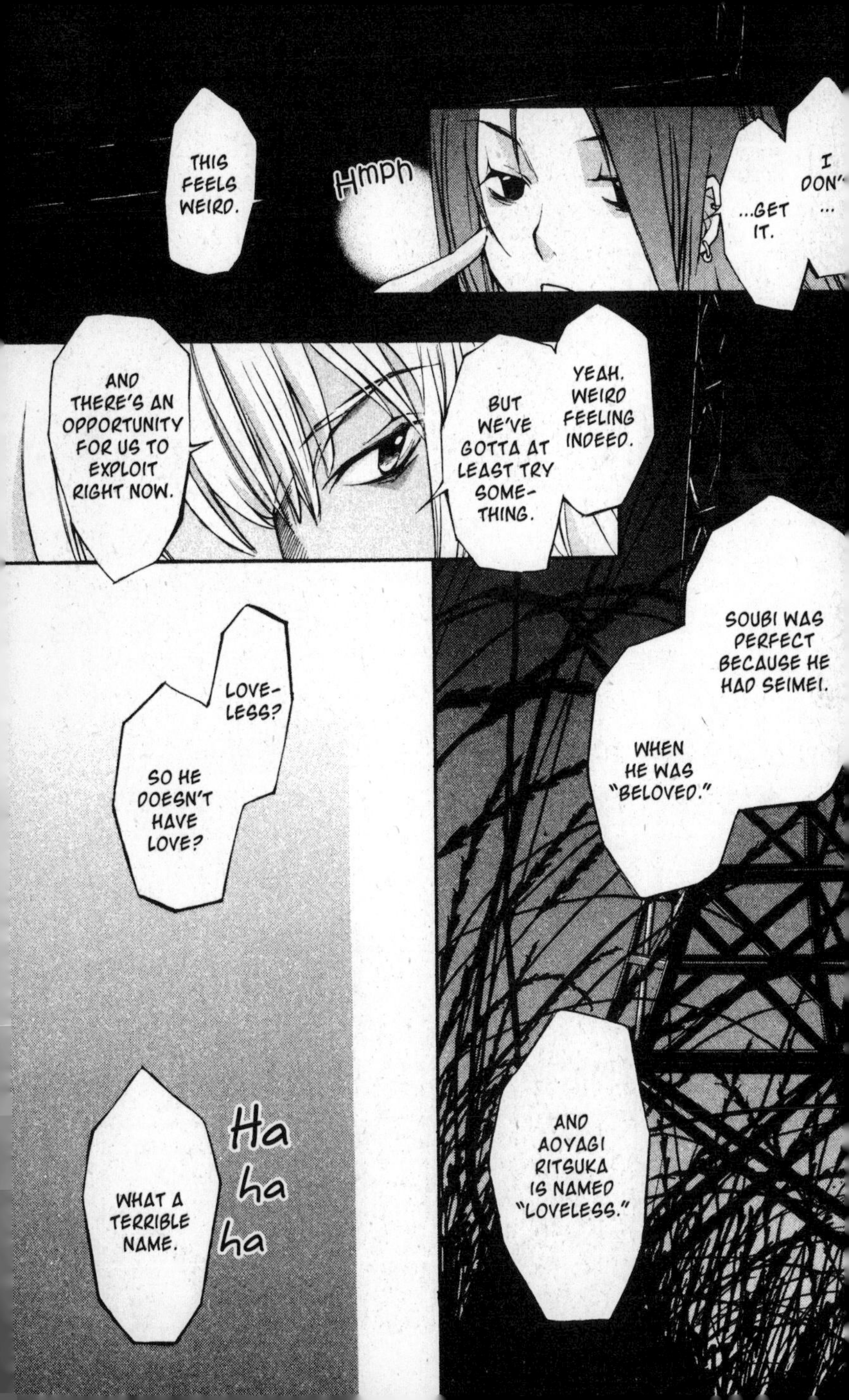
I DON' ...
...GET IT.
Hmph
THIS FEELS WEIRD.
YEAH. WEIRD FEELING INDEED.
BUT WE'VE GOTTA AT LEAST TRY SOME-THING.
AND THERE'S AN OPPORTUNITY FOR US TO EXPLOIT RIGHT NOW.
SOUBI WAS PERFECT BECAUSE HE HAD SEIMEI.
WHEN HE WAS "BELOVED."
AND AOYAGI RITSUKA IS NAMED "LOVELESS."
LOVE-LESS?
SO HE DOESN'T HAVE LOVE?
Ha ha ha
WHAT A TERRIBLE NAME.

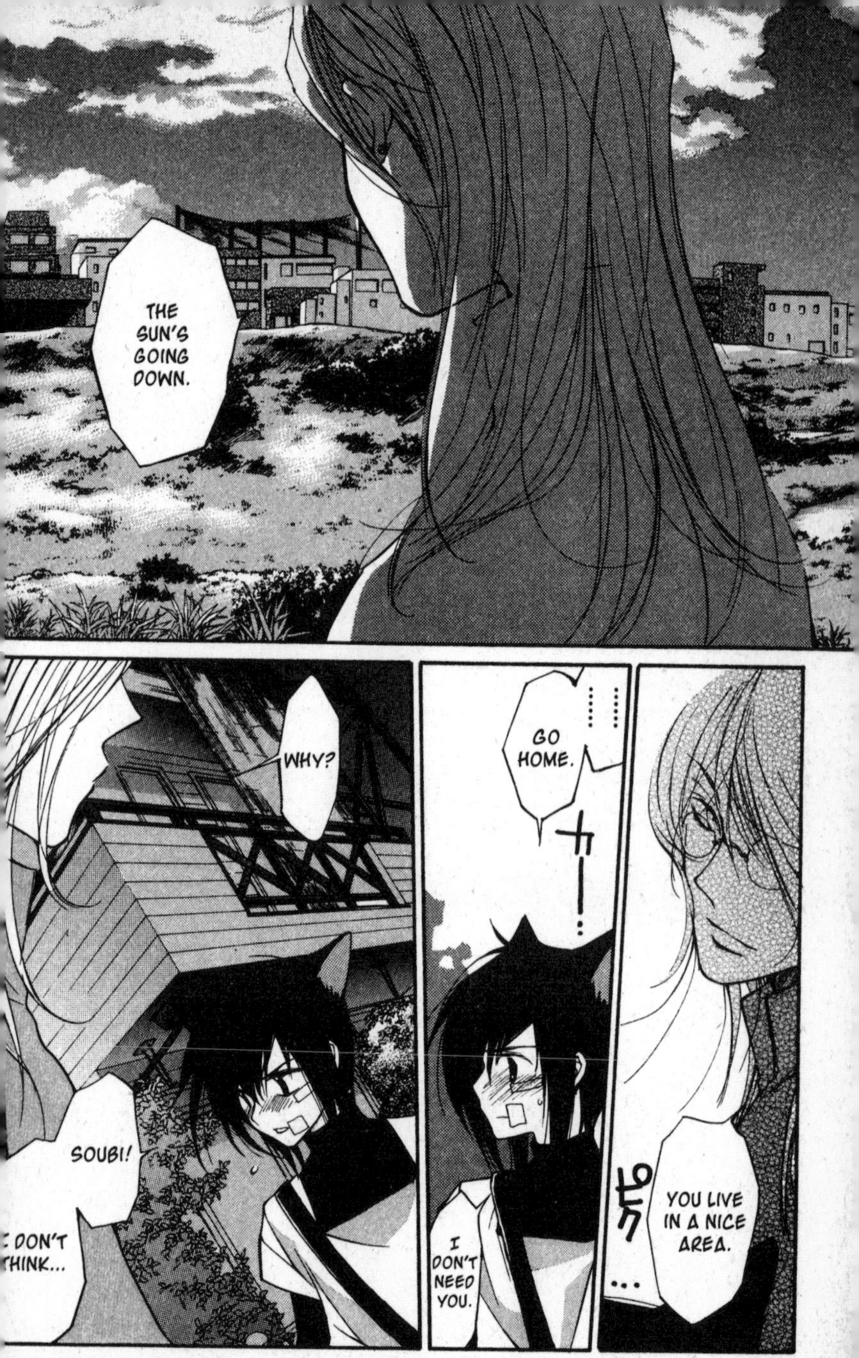
THE SUN'S GOING DOWN.
YOU LIVE IN A NICE AREA.
...
......
GO HOME.
カー
I DON'T NEED YOU.
WHY?
SOUBI!
DON'T THINK...

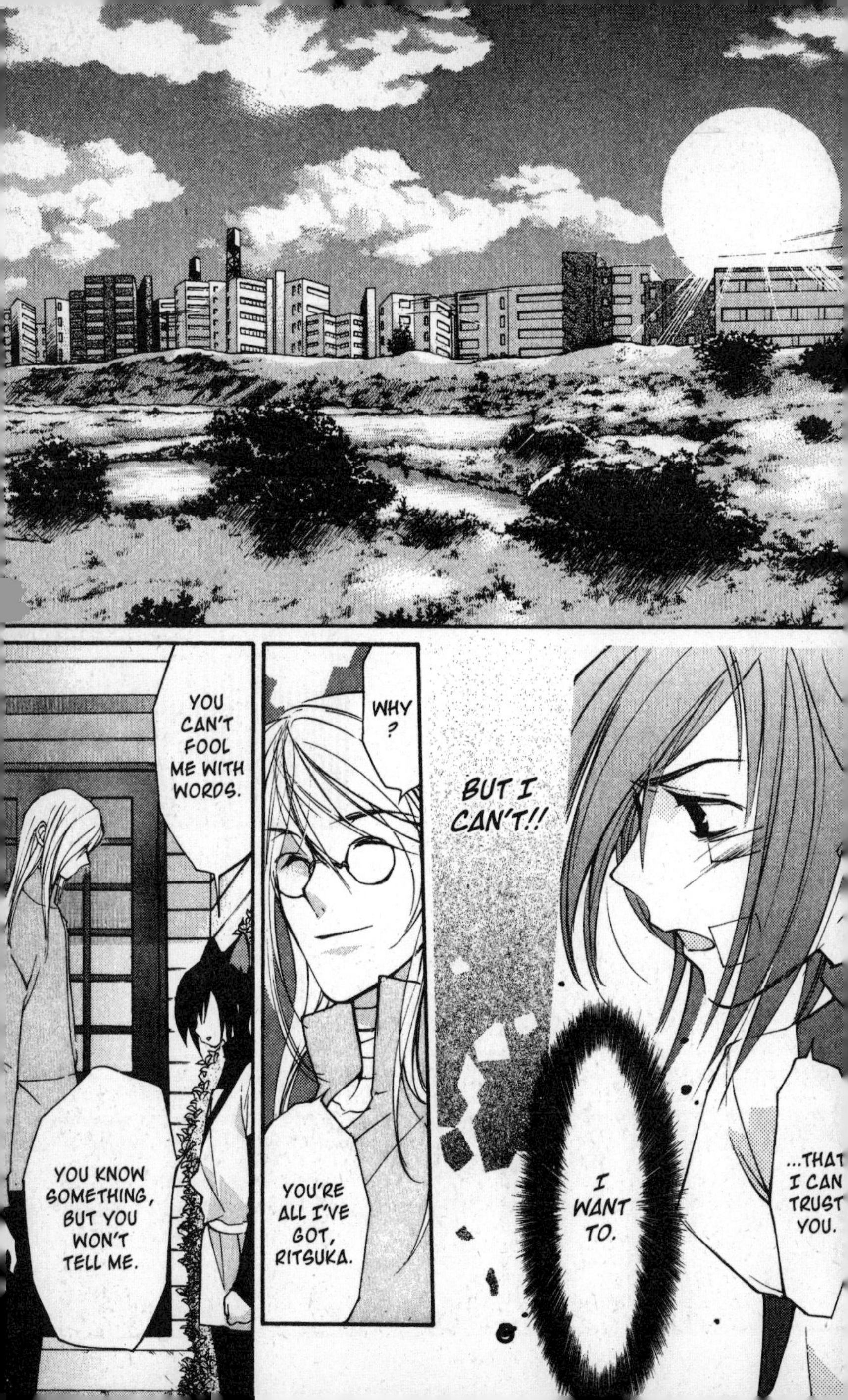
...THAT I CAN TRUST YOU.
I WANT TO.
BUT I CAN'T!!
WHY?
YOU'RE ALL I'VE GOT, RITSUKA.
YOU CAN'T FOOL ME WITH WORDS.
YOU KNOW SOMETHING, BUT YOU WON'T TELL ME.

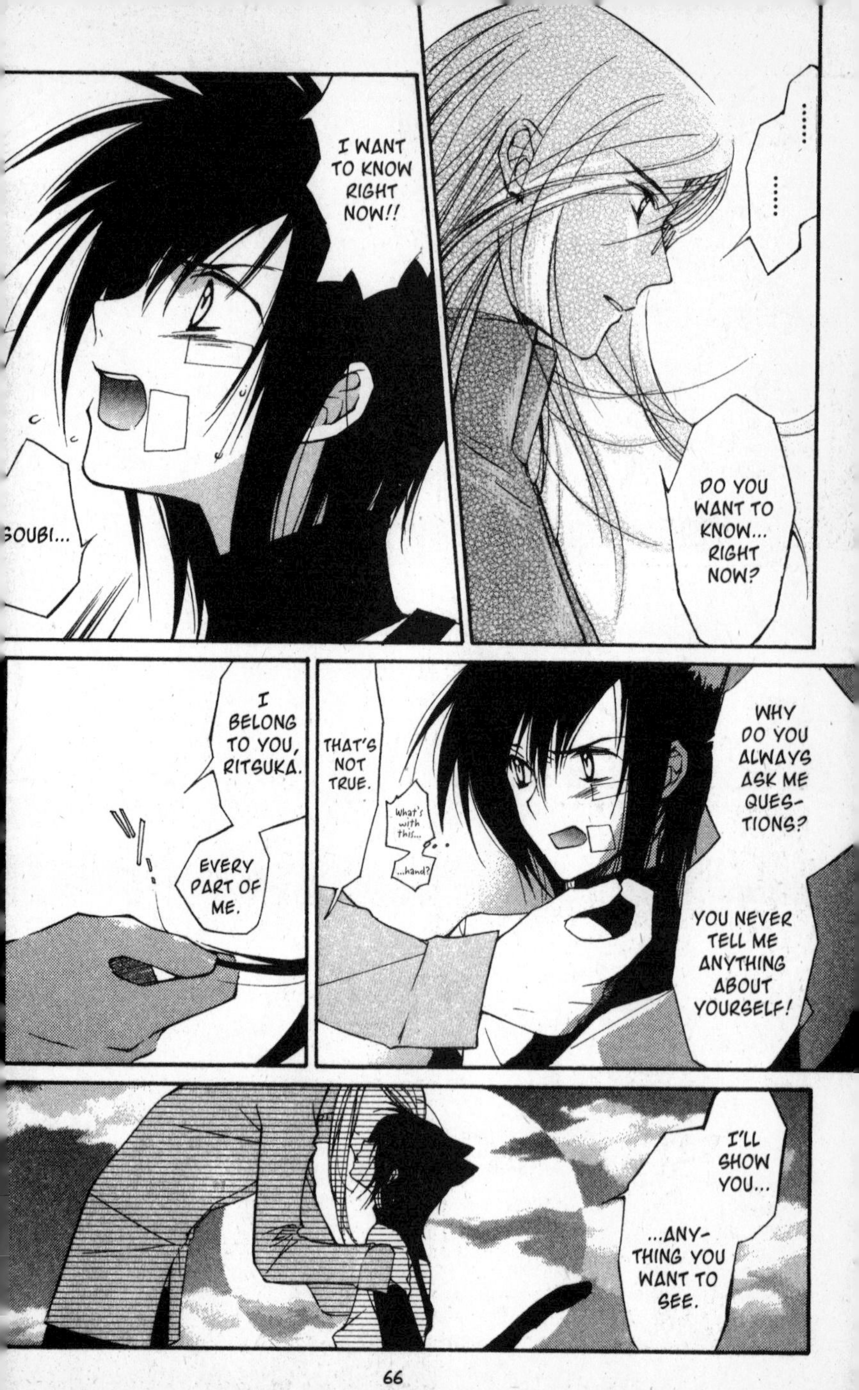
......
......
DO YOU WANT TO KNOW... RIGHT NOW?
I WANT TO KNOW RIGHT NOW!!
SOUBI...
WHY DO YOU ALWAYS ASK ME QUES-TIONS?
YOU NEVER TELL ME ANYTHING ABOUT YOURSELF!
What's with this...
...hand?
THAT'S NOT TRUE.
I BELONG TO YOU, RITSUKA.
EVERY PART OF ME.
I'LL SHOW YOU...
...ANY-THING YOU WANT TO SEE.

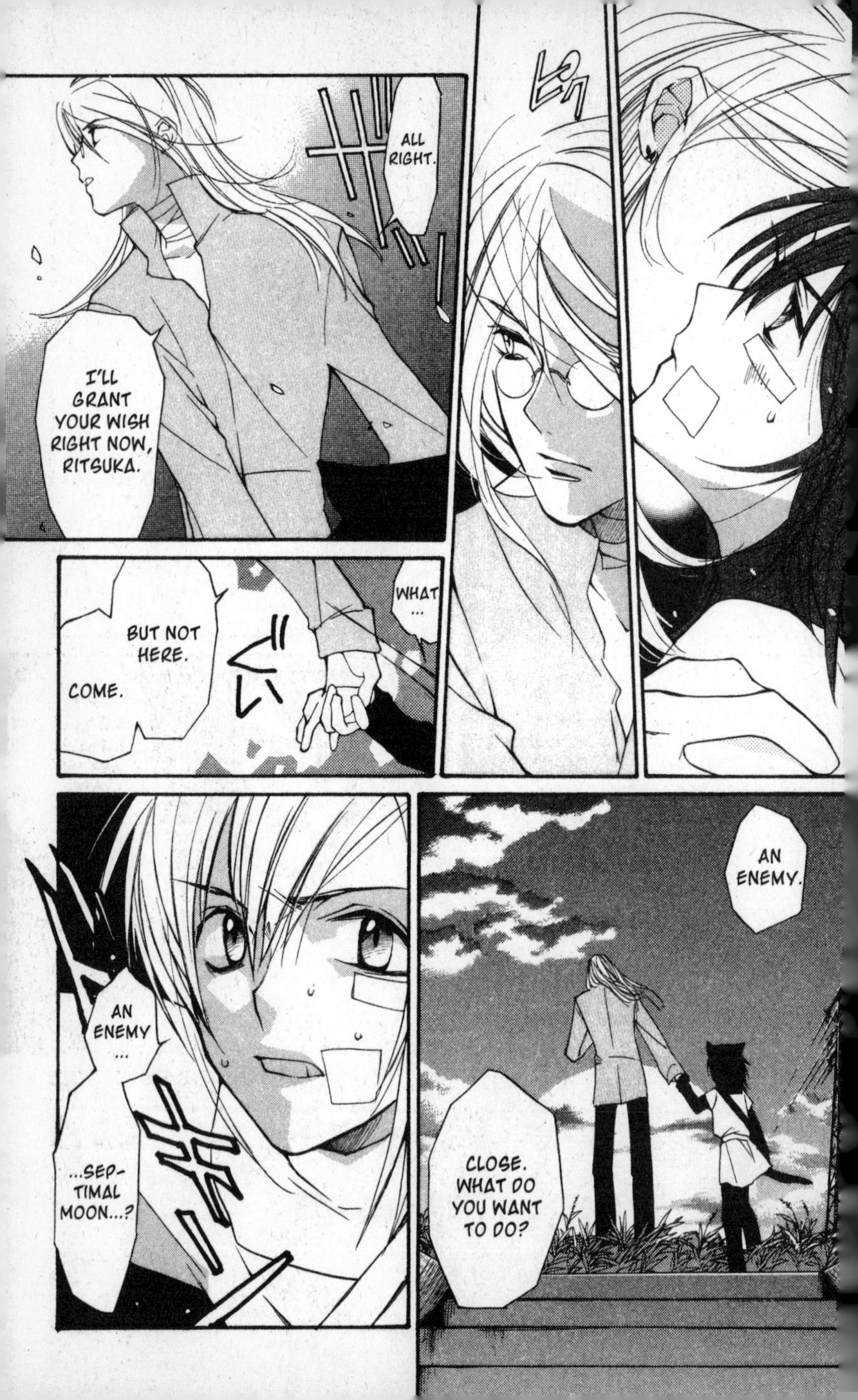
ピク
ALL RIGHT.
I'LL GRANT YOUR WISH RIGHT NOW, RITSUKA.
WHAT...
BUT NOT HERE.
COME.
AN ENEMY.
CLOSE. WHAT DO YOU WANT TO DO?
AN ENEMY...
...SEP-TIMAL MOON...?

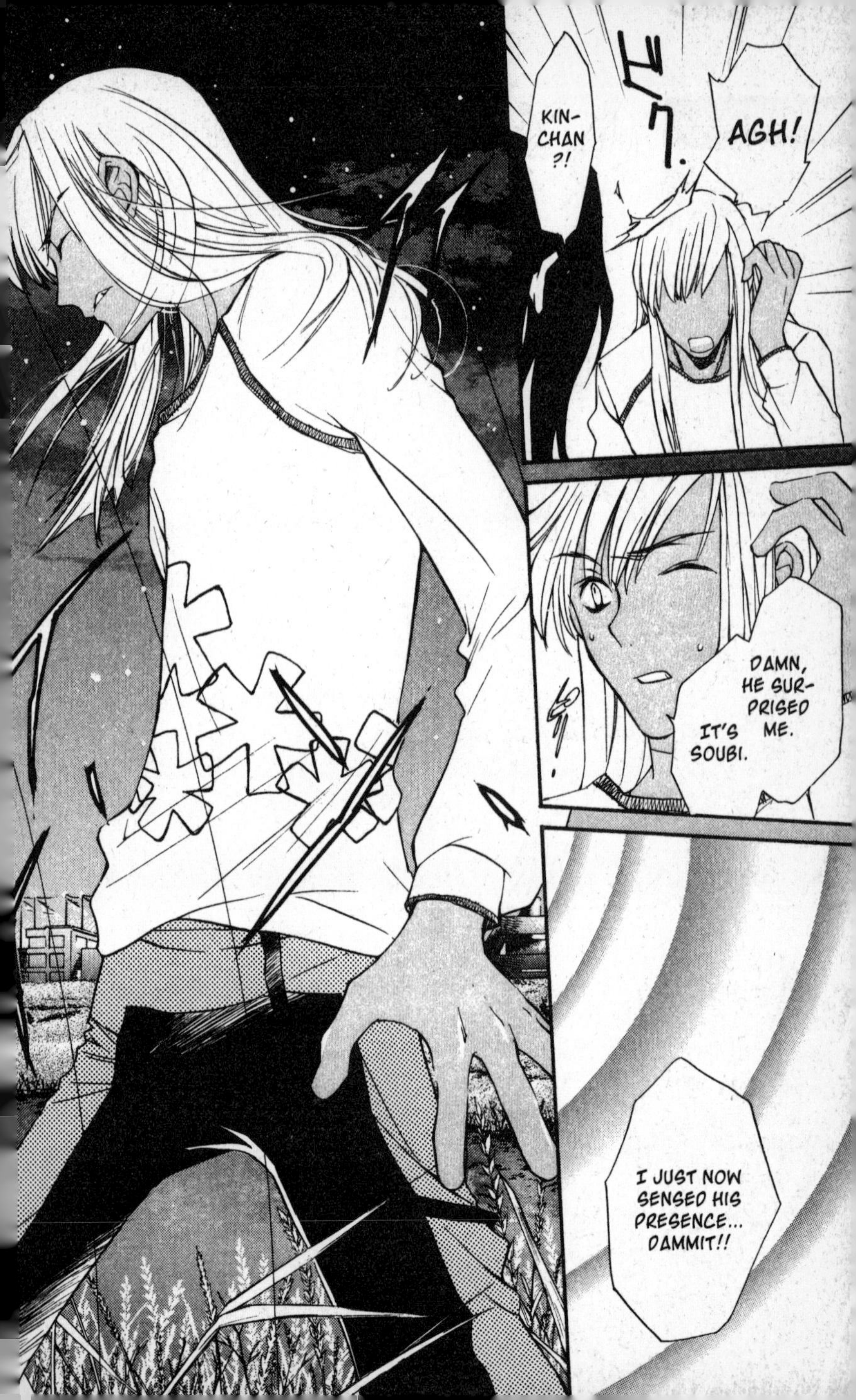
AGH!
ビク.
KIN-CHAN?!
DAMN, HE SURPRISED ME.
IT'S SOUBI.
I JUST NOW SENSED HIS PRESENCE... DAMMIT!!

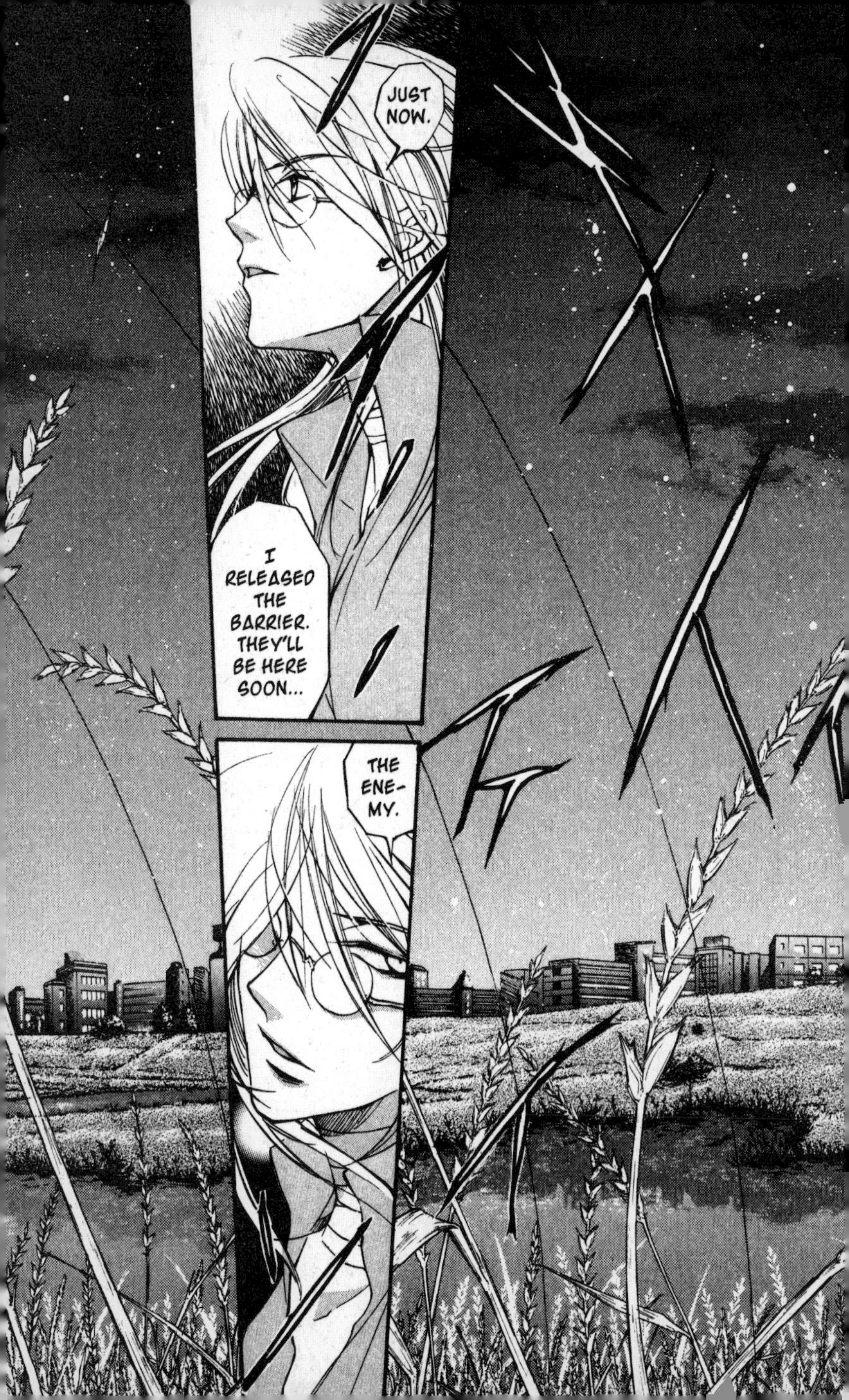
JUST NOW.
I RELEASED THE BARRIER. THEY'LL BE HERE SOON...
THE ENE-MY.

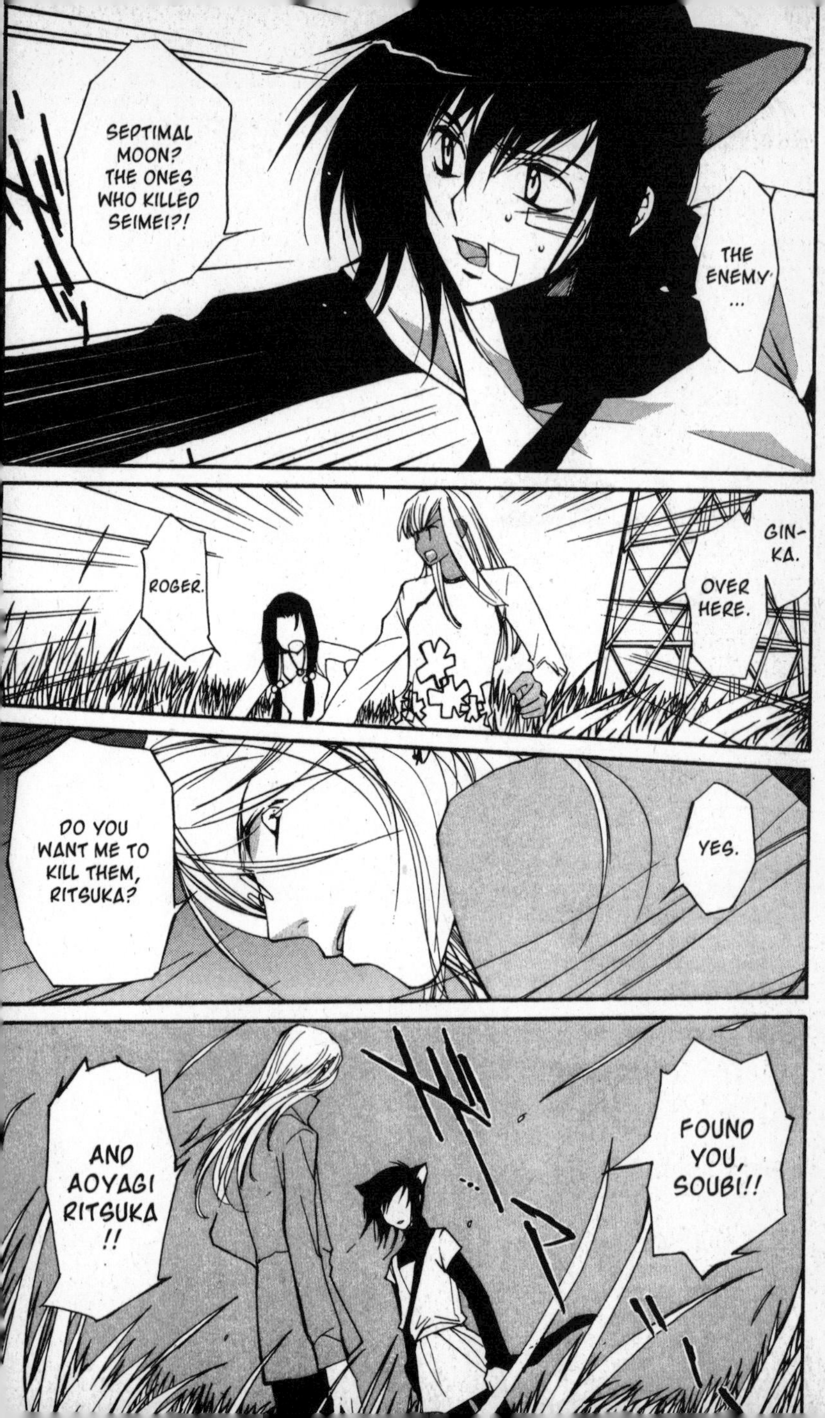

THE ENEMY ...
SEPTIMAL MOON? THE ONES WHO KILLED SEIMEI?!
GIN-KA. OVER HERE.
ROGER.
YES.
DO YOU WANT ME TO KILL THEM, RITSUKA?
FOUND YOU, SOUBI!!
AND AOYAGI RITSUKA !!

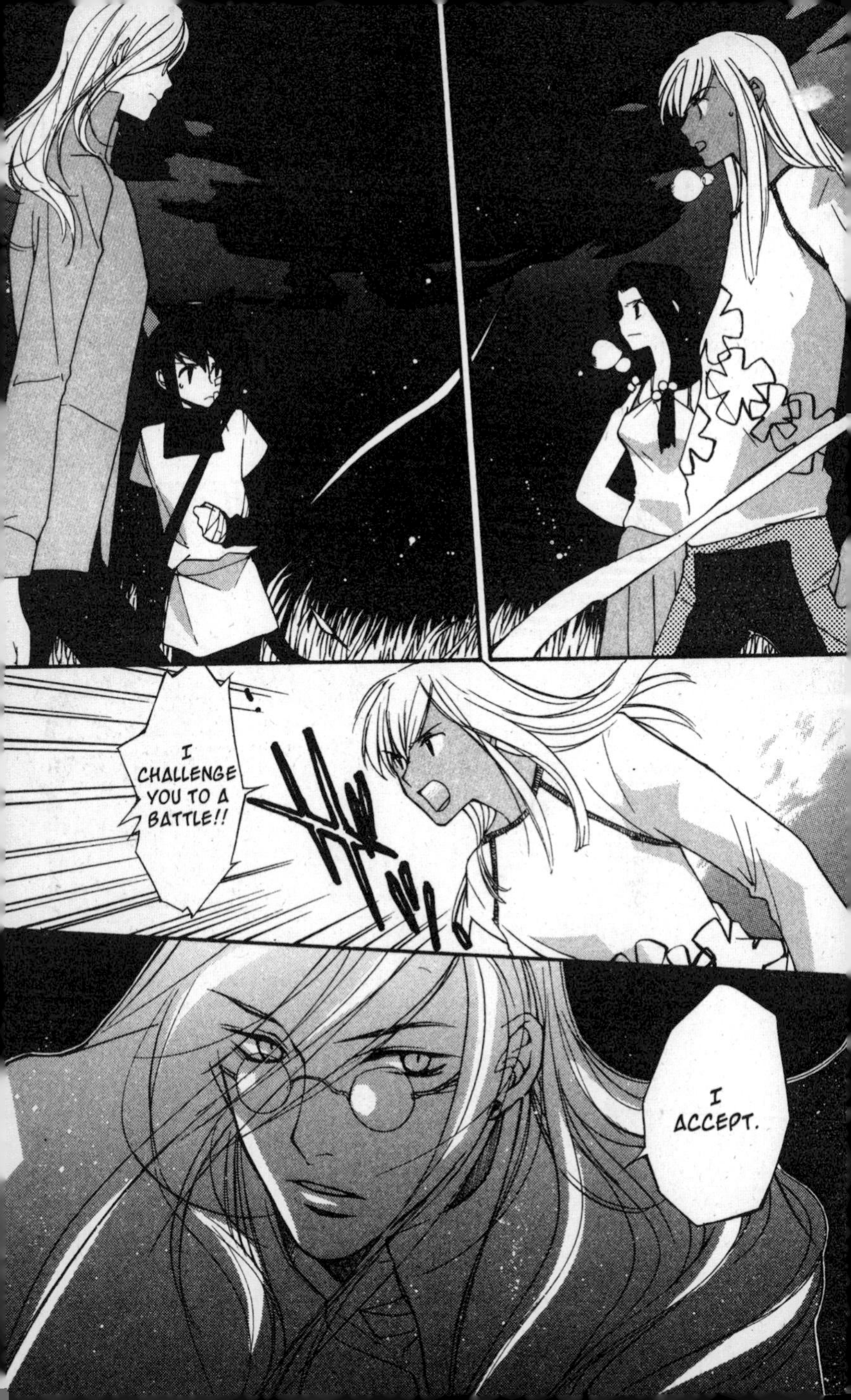
I CHALLENGE YOU TO A BATTLE!!
I ACCEPT.

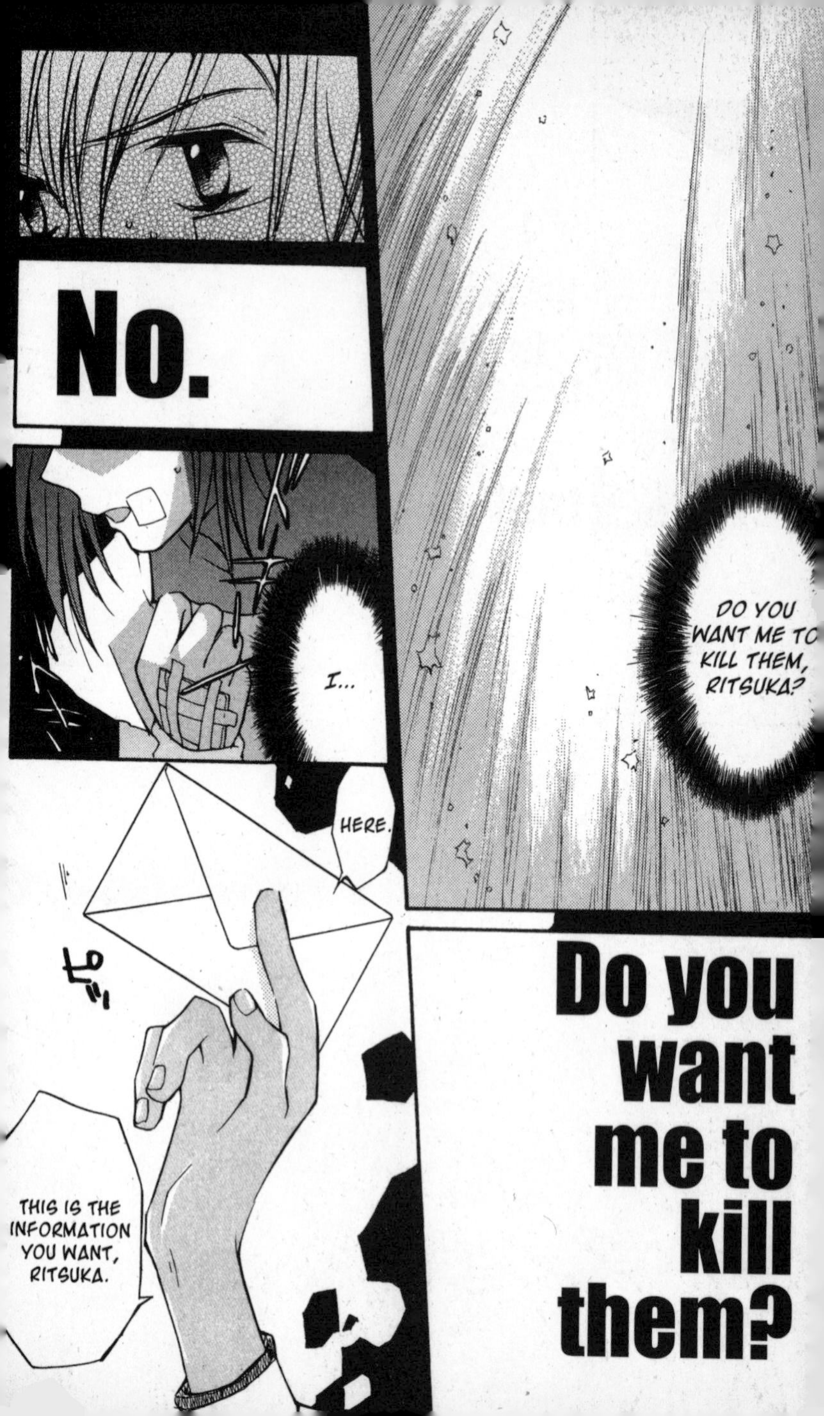
DO YOU WANT ME TO KILL THEM, RITSUKA?
No.
I...
Do you want me to kill them?
HERE.
THIS IS THE INFORMATION YOU WANT, RITSUKA.

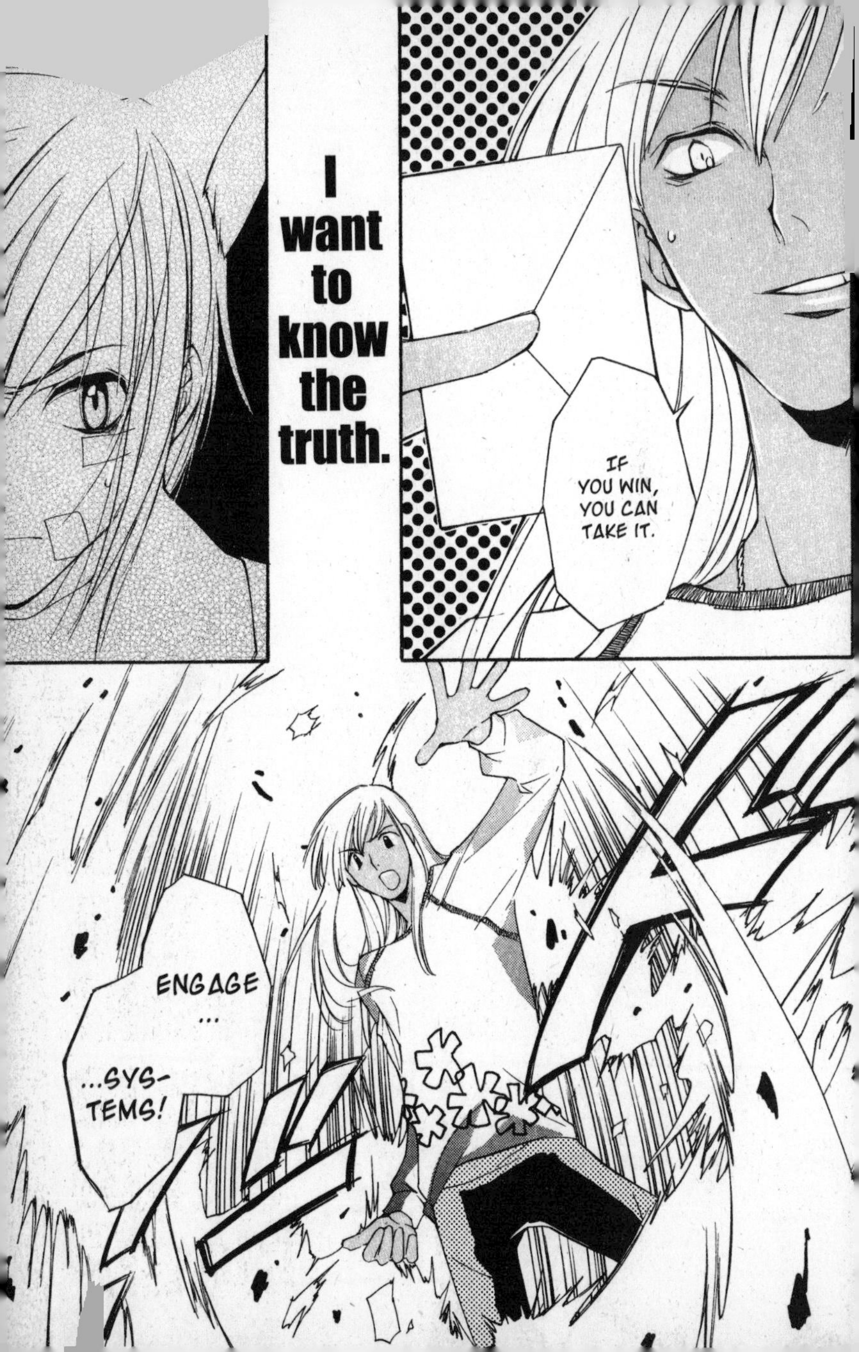
IF YOU WIN, YOU CAN TAKE IT.
I want to know the truth.
ENGAGE ...
...SYS-TEMS!

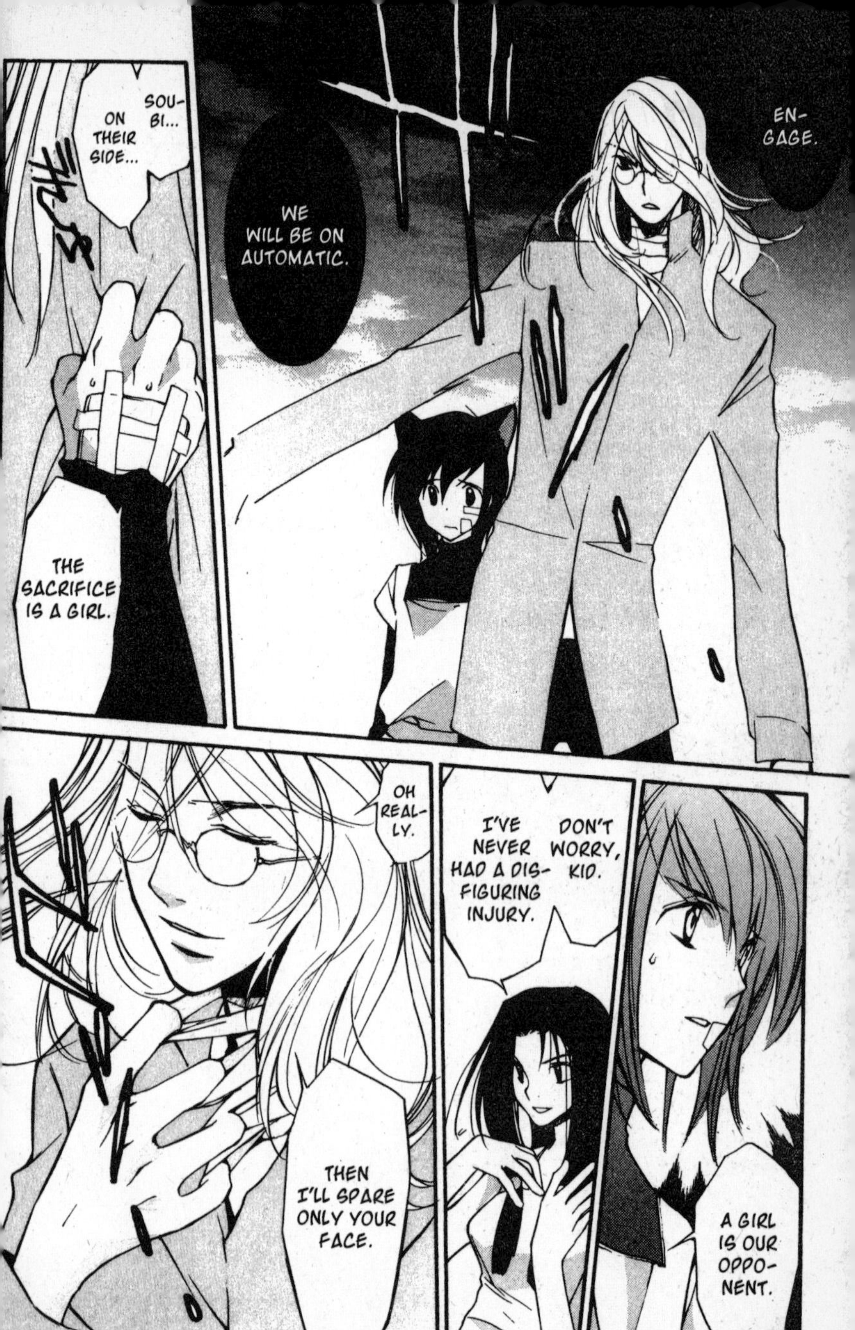

EN-GAGE.
WE WILL BE ON AUTOMATIC.
SOU-BI... ON THEIR SIDE...
THE SACRIFICE IS A GIRL.
A GIRL IS OUR OPPO-NENT.
DON'T WORRY, KID.
I'VE NEVER HAD A DIS-FIGURING INJURY.
OH REAL-LY.
THEN I'LL SPARE ONLY YOUR FACE.

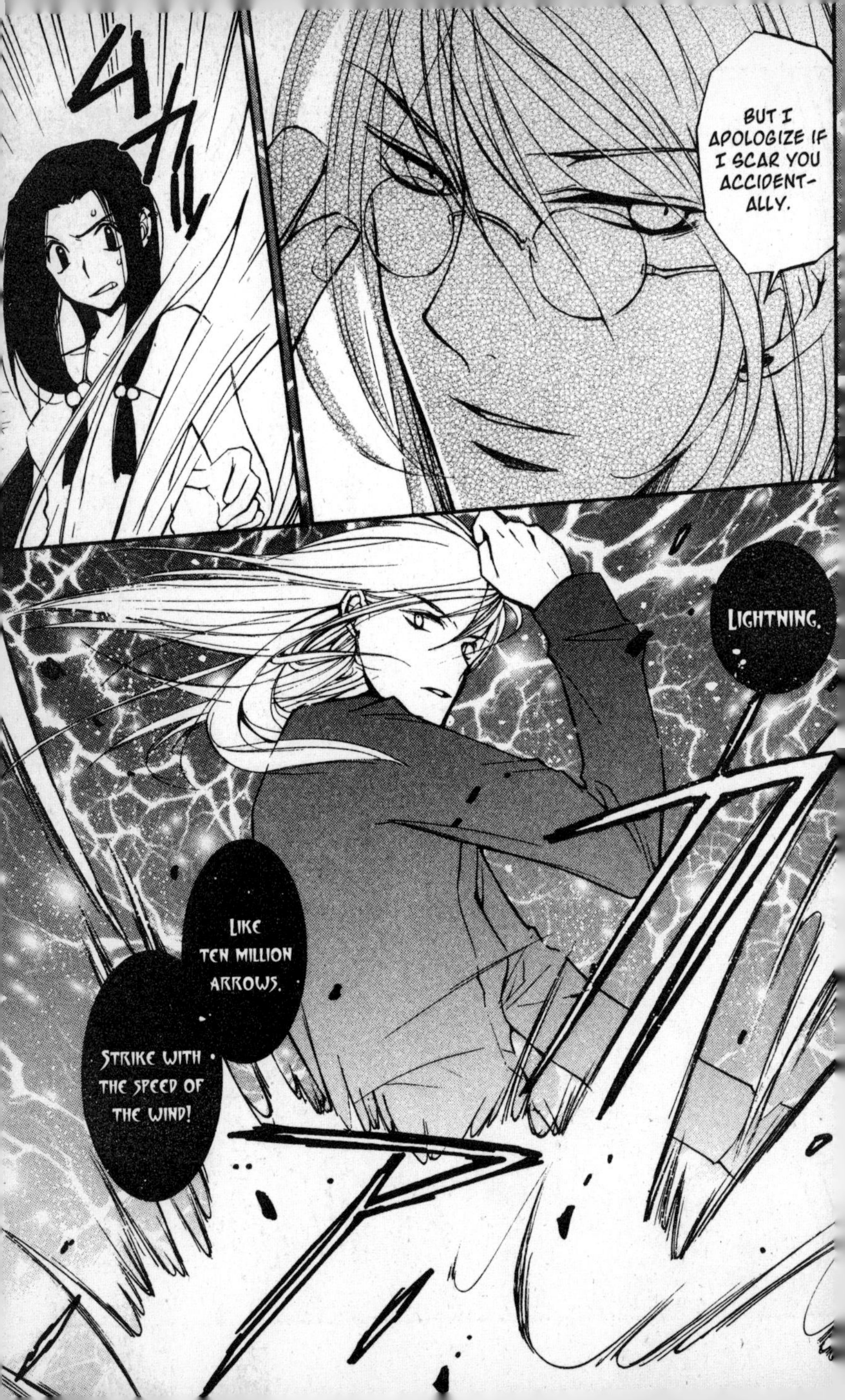
BUT I APOLOGIZE IF I SCAR YOU ACCIDENT-ALLY.
LIGHTNING.
LIKE TEN MILLION ARROWS.
STRIKE WITH THE SPEED OF THE WIND!

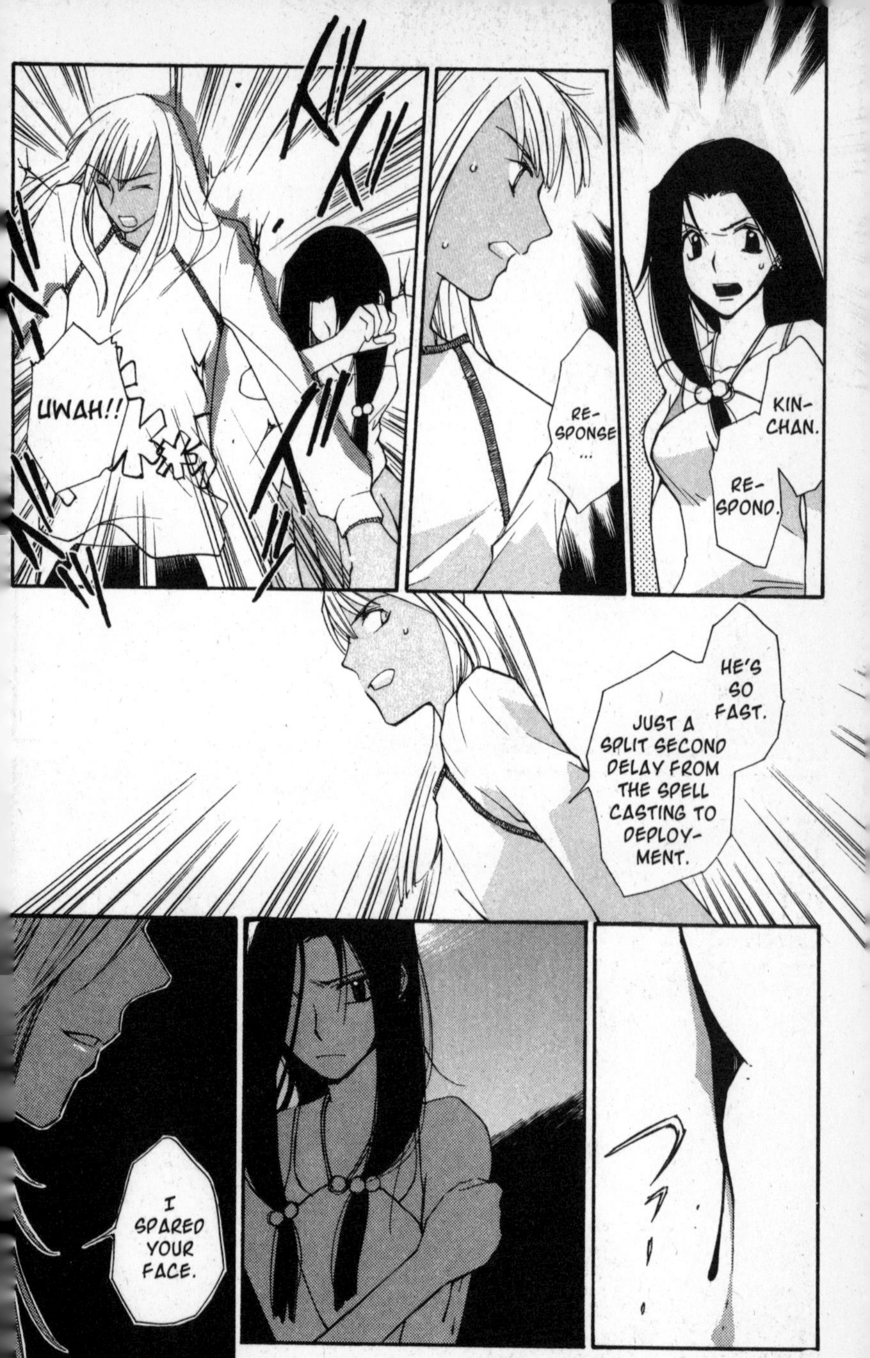
KIN-CHAN.
RE-SPOND.
RE-SPONSE...
UWAH!!
HE'S SO FAST.
JUST A SPLIT SECOND DELAY FROM THE SPELL CASTING TO DEPLOY-MENT.
I SPARED YOUR FACE.

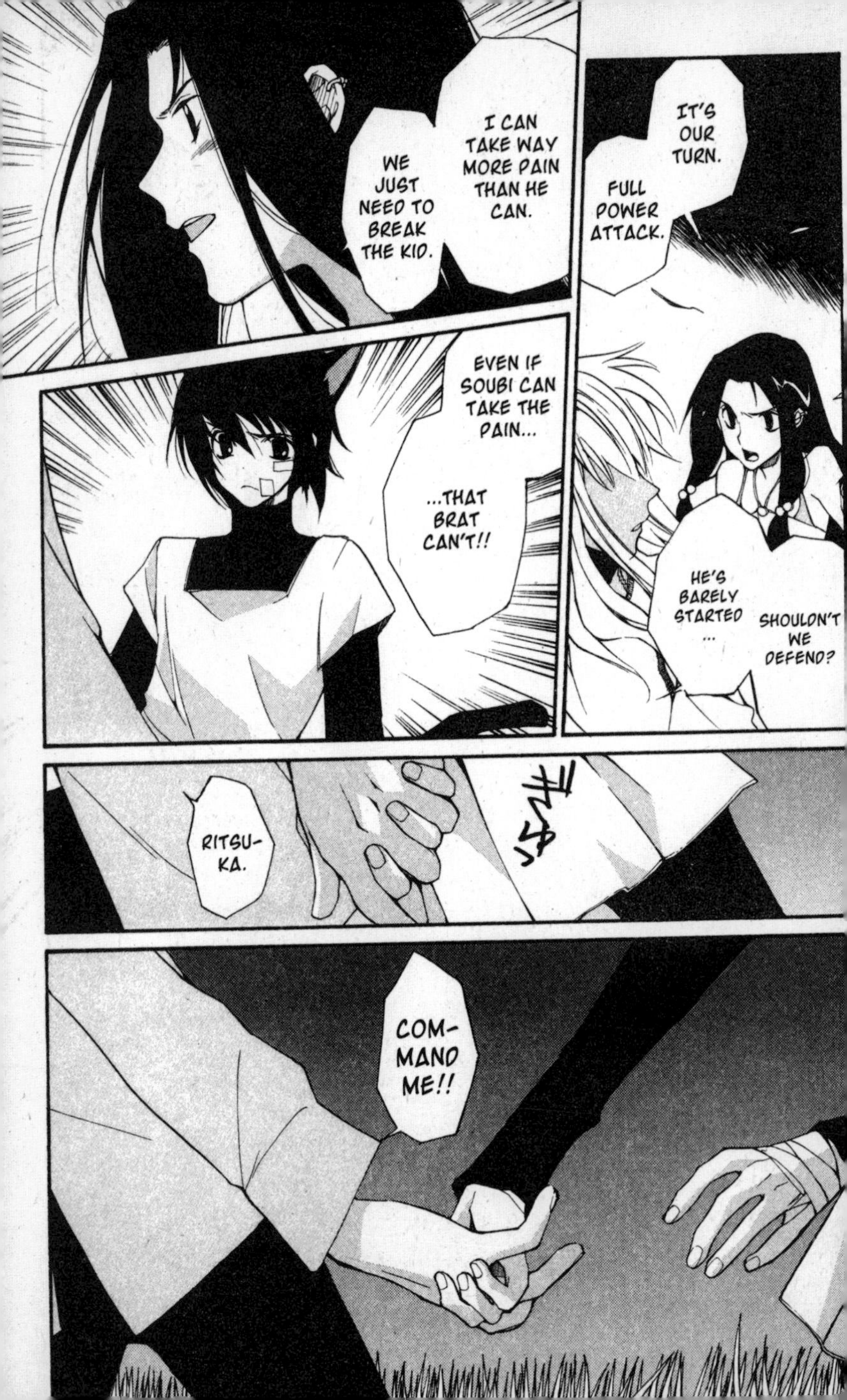
IT'S OUR TURN.
FULL POWER ATTACK.
I CAN TAKE WAY MORE PAIN THAN HE CAN.
WE JUST NEED TO BREAK THE KID.
HE'S BARELY STARTED...
SHOULDN'T WE DEFEND?
EVEN IF SOUBI CAN TAKE THE PAIN...
...THAT BRAT CAN'T!!
RITSU-KA.
COM-MAND ME!!

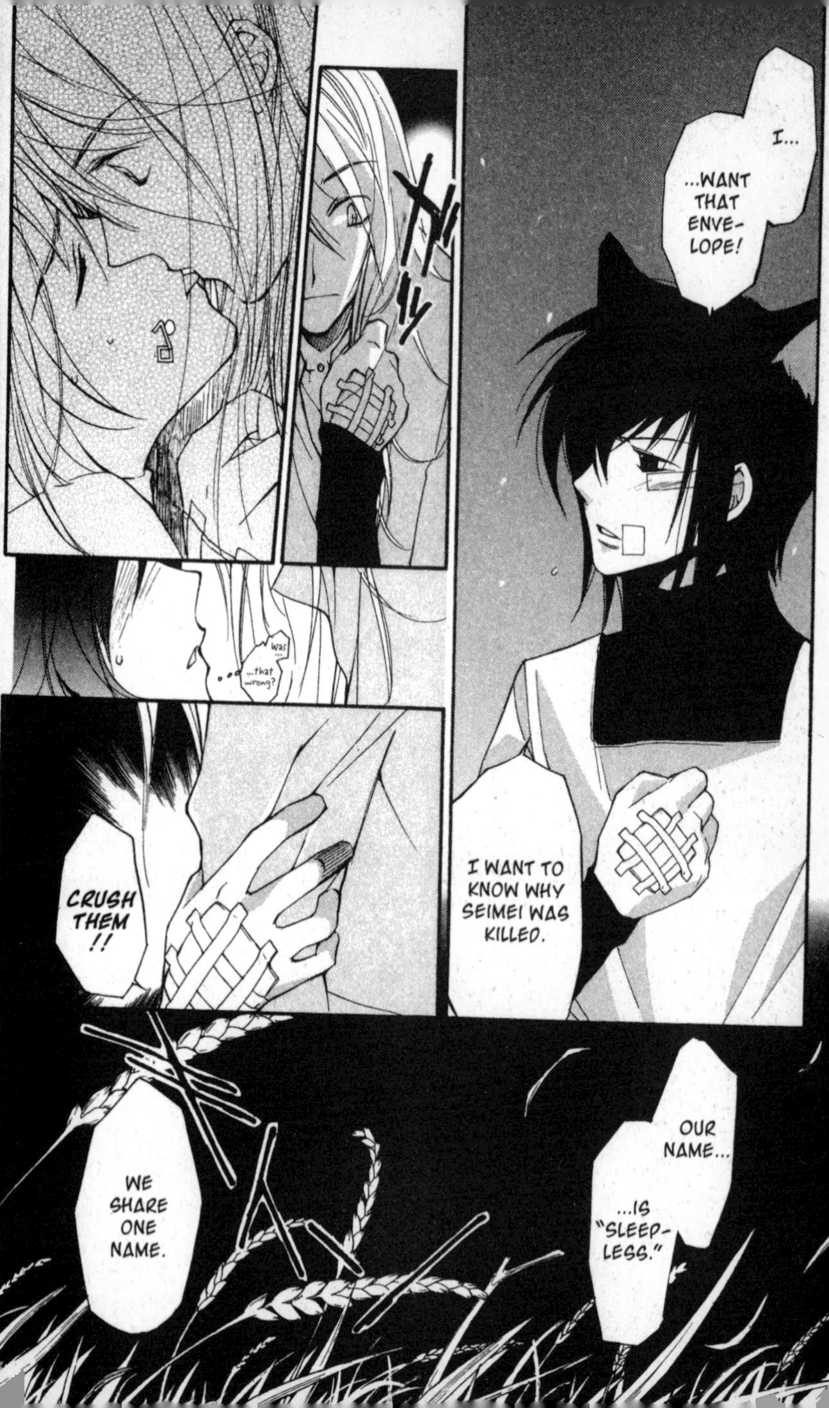
I...
...WANT THAT ENVELOPE!
I WANT TO KNOW WHY SEIMEI WAS KILLED.
...
Was...
...that wrong?
CRUSH THEM!!
OUR NAME...
...IS "SLEEPLESS."
WE SHARE ONE NAME.

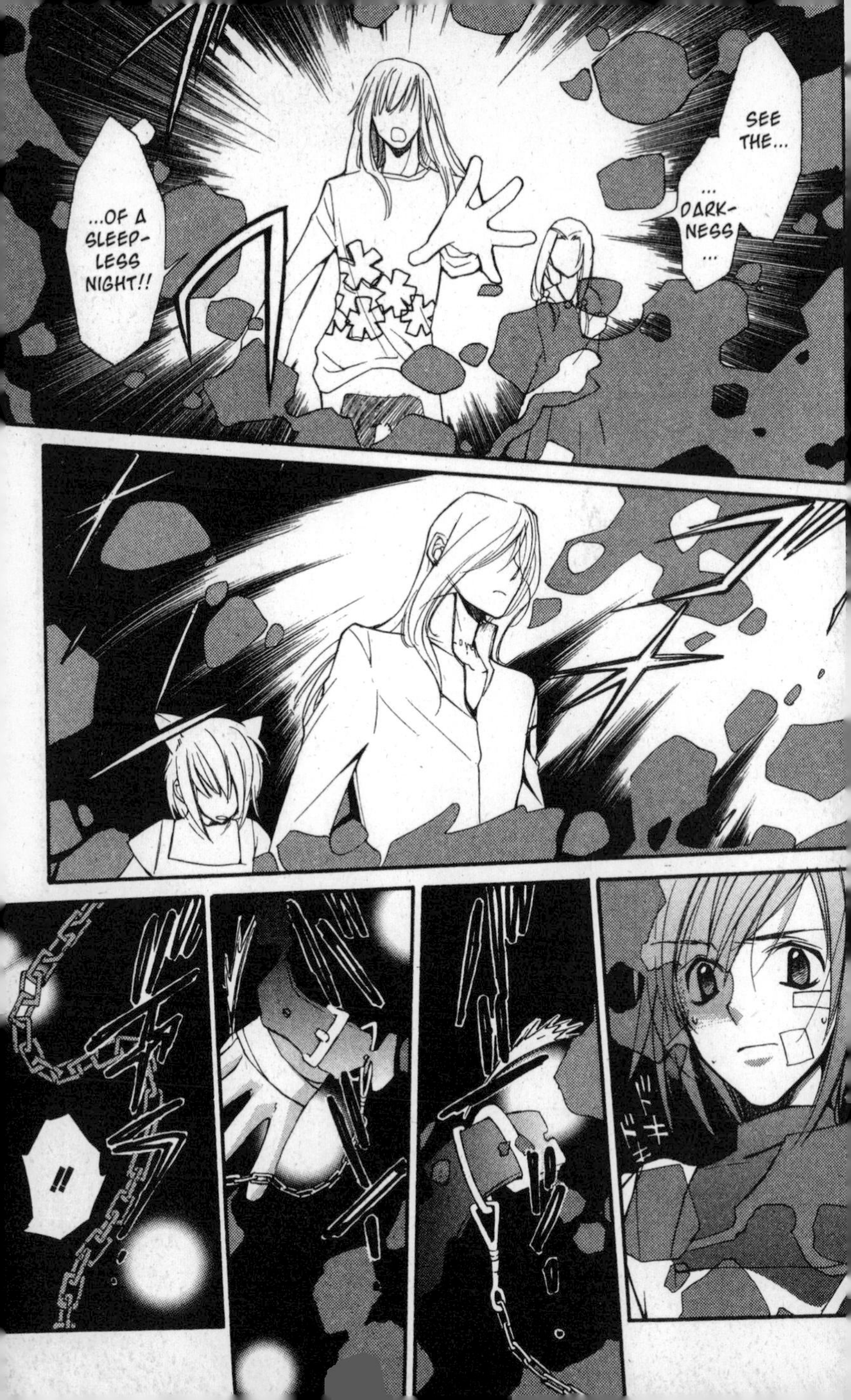
SEE THE...
...DARK-NESS...
...OF A SLEEP-LESS NIGHT!!
!!

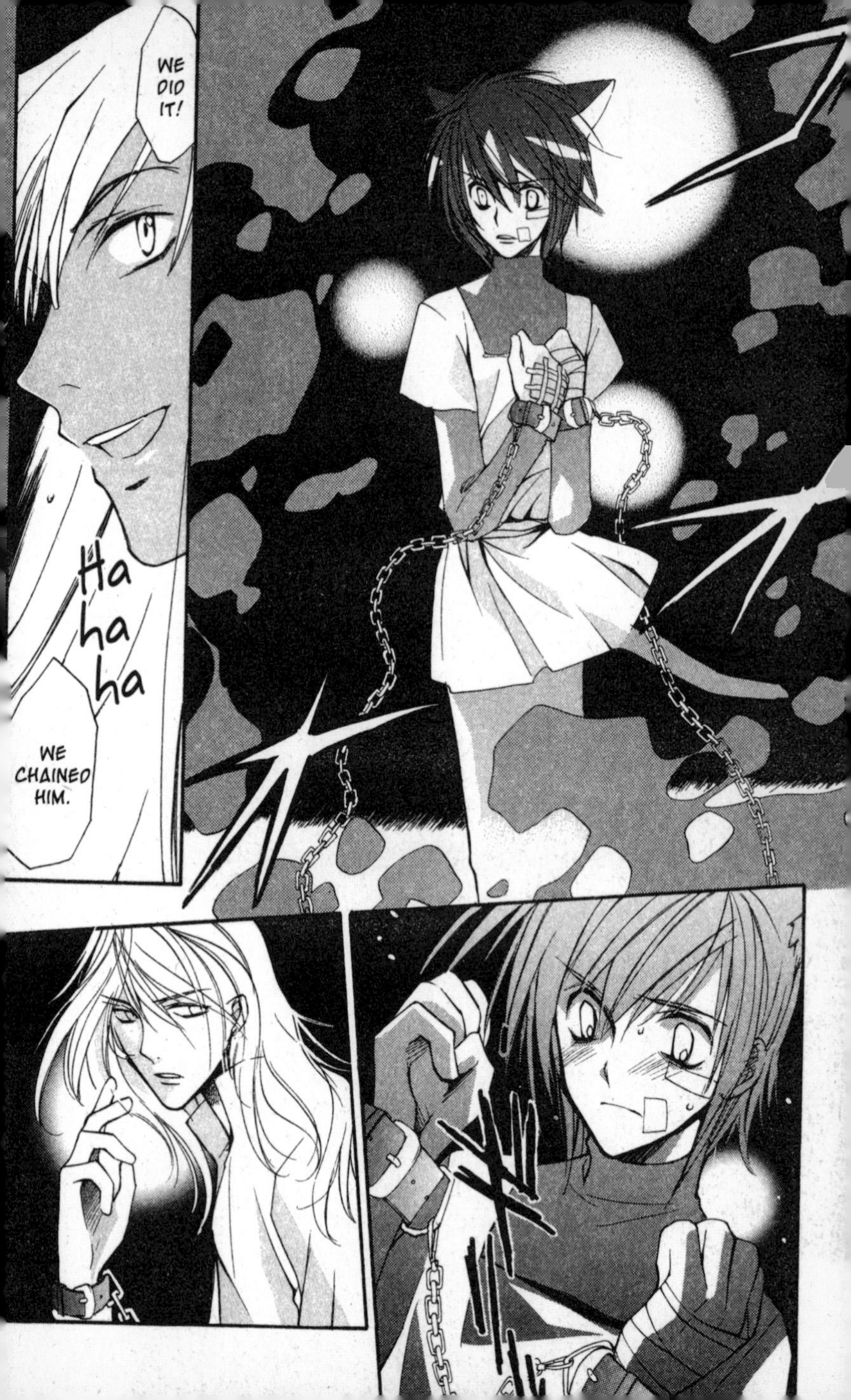
WE DID IT!
Ha ha ha
WE CHAINED HIM.

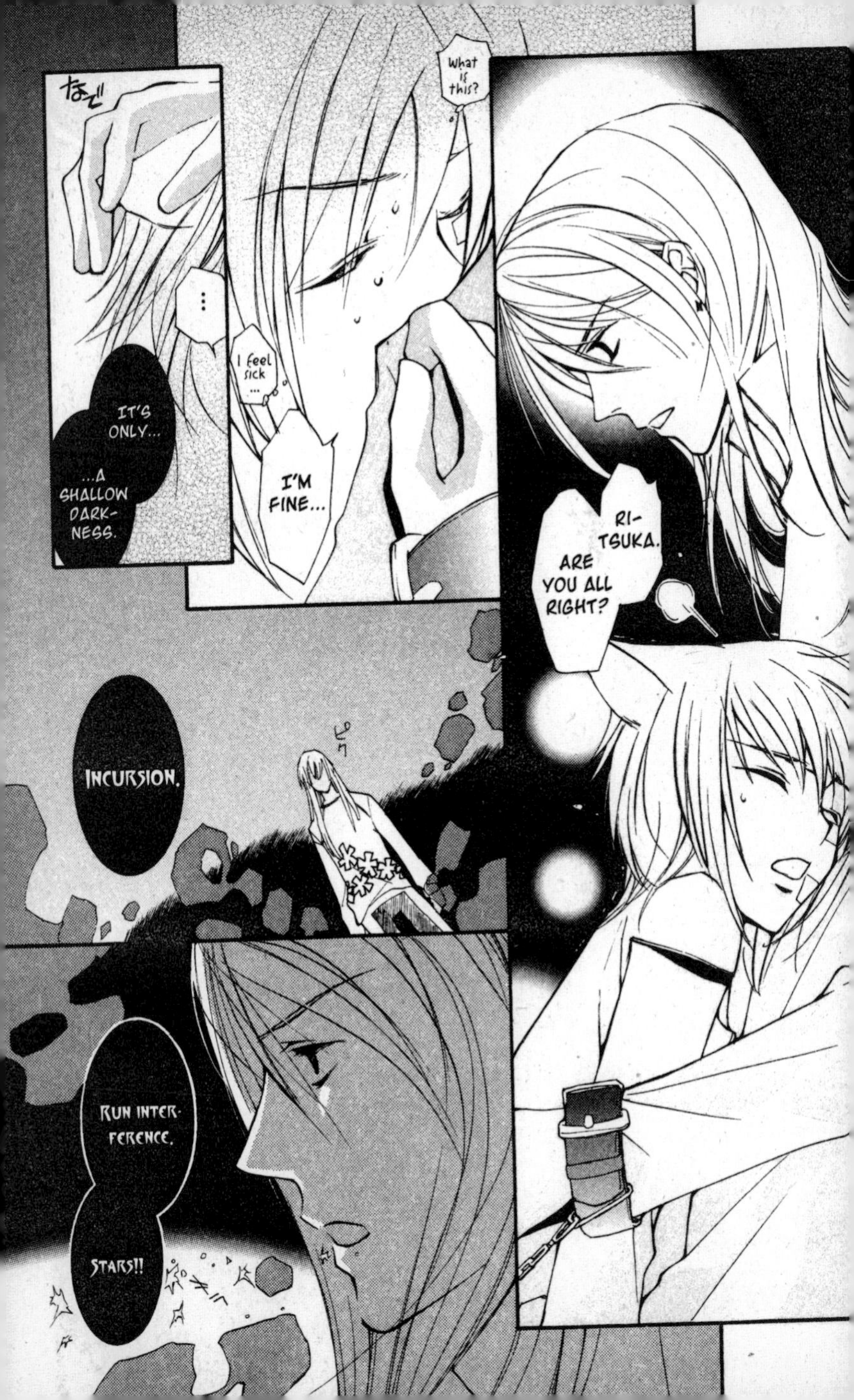
Ri-tsuka. Are you all right?
What is this?
I feel sick...
I'm fine...
なで
...
It's only...
...a shallow darkness.
ピク
Incursion.
Run interference.
Stars!!

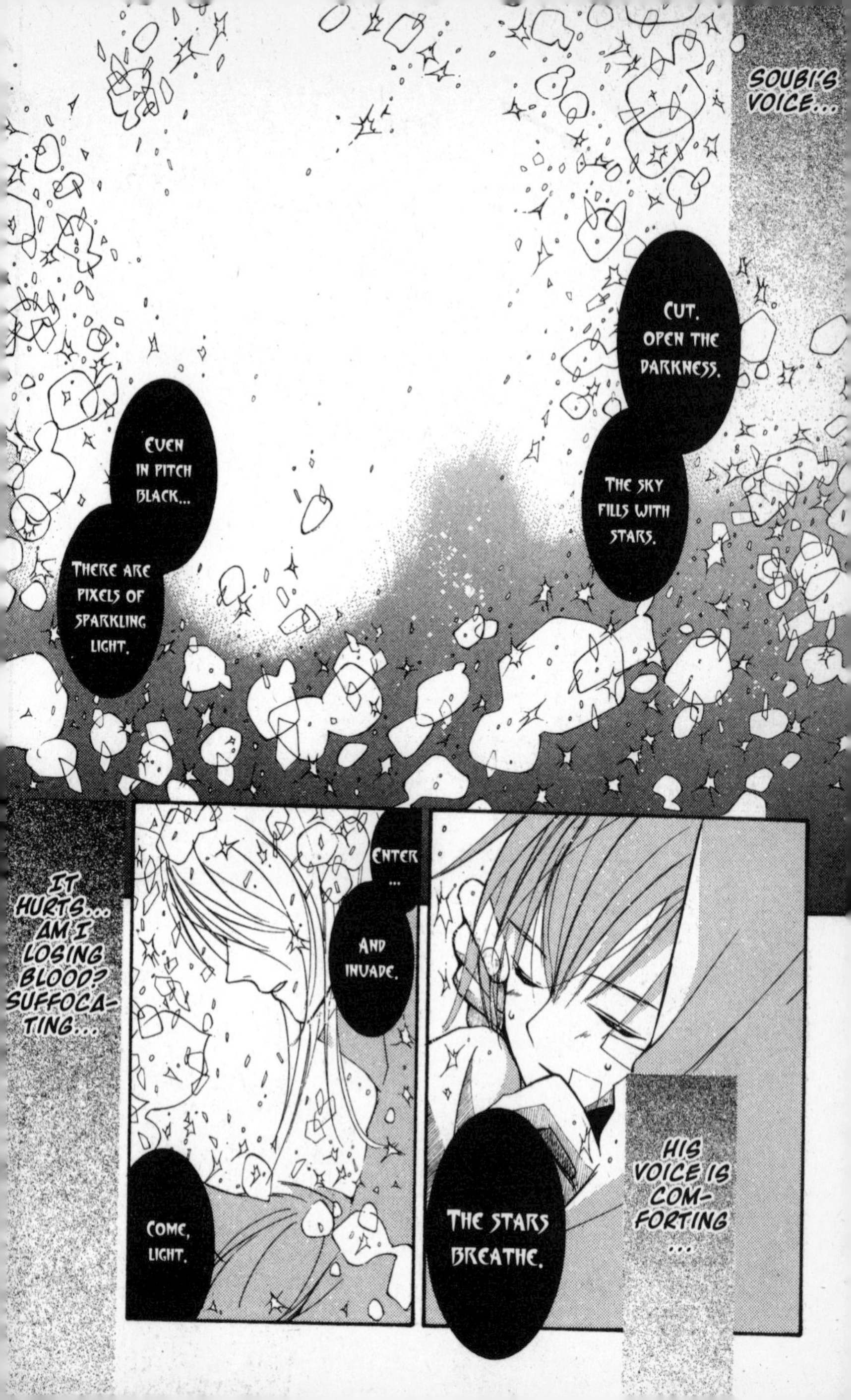
SOUBI'S VOICE...
CUT. OPEN THE DARKNESS.
THE SKY FILLS WITH STARS.
EVEN IN PITCH BLACK...
THERE ARE PIXELS OF SPARKLING LIGHT.
HIS VOICE IS COM-FORTING...
THE STARS BREATHE.
ENTER...
AND INVADE.
COME, LIGHT.
IT HURTS... AM I LOSING BLOOD? SUFFOCA-TING...

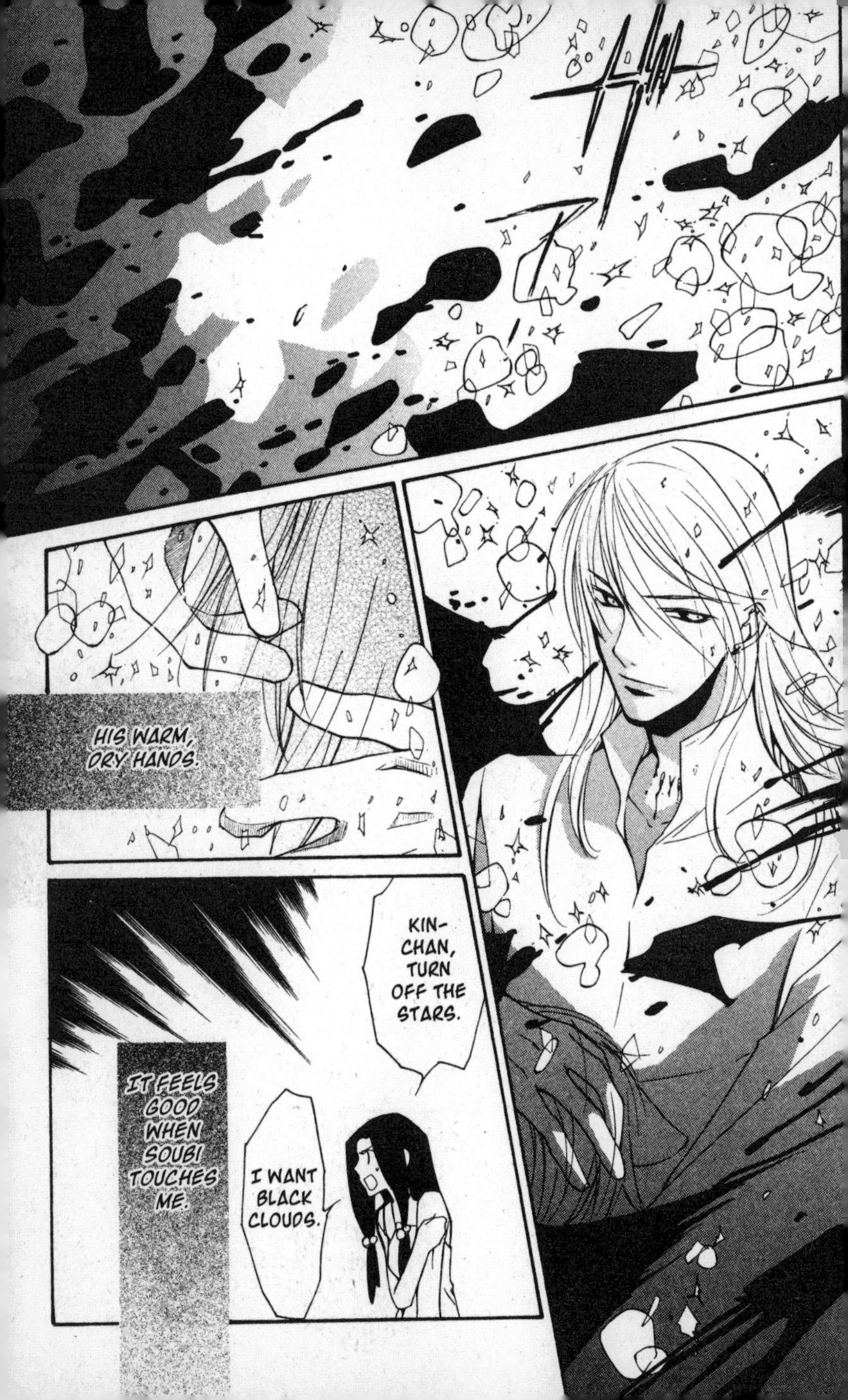
HIS WARM, DRY HANDS.
KIN-CHAN, TURN OFF THE STARS.
I WANT BLACK CLOUDS.
IT FEELS GOOD WHEN SOUBI TOUCHES ME.

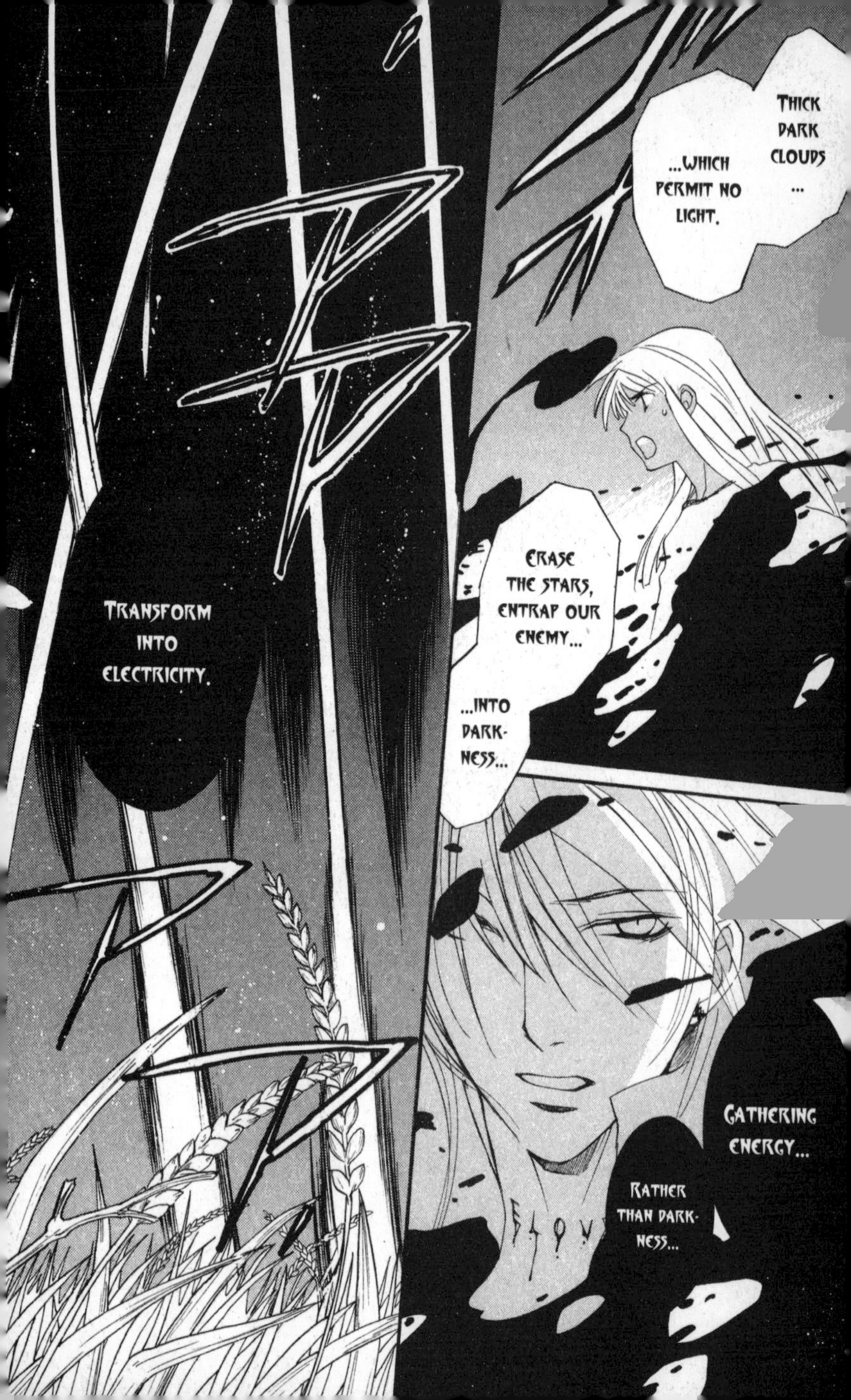
THICK DARK CLOUDS...
...WHICH PERMIT NO LIGHT.
ERASE THE STARS, ENTRAP OUR ENEMY...
...INTO DARK-NESS...
GATHERING ENERGY...
RATHER THAN DARK-NESS...
TRANSFORM INTO ELECTRICITY.

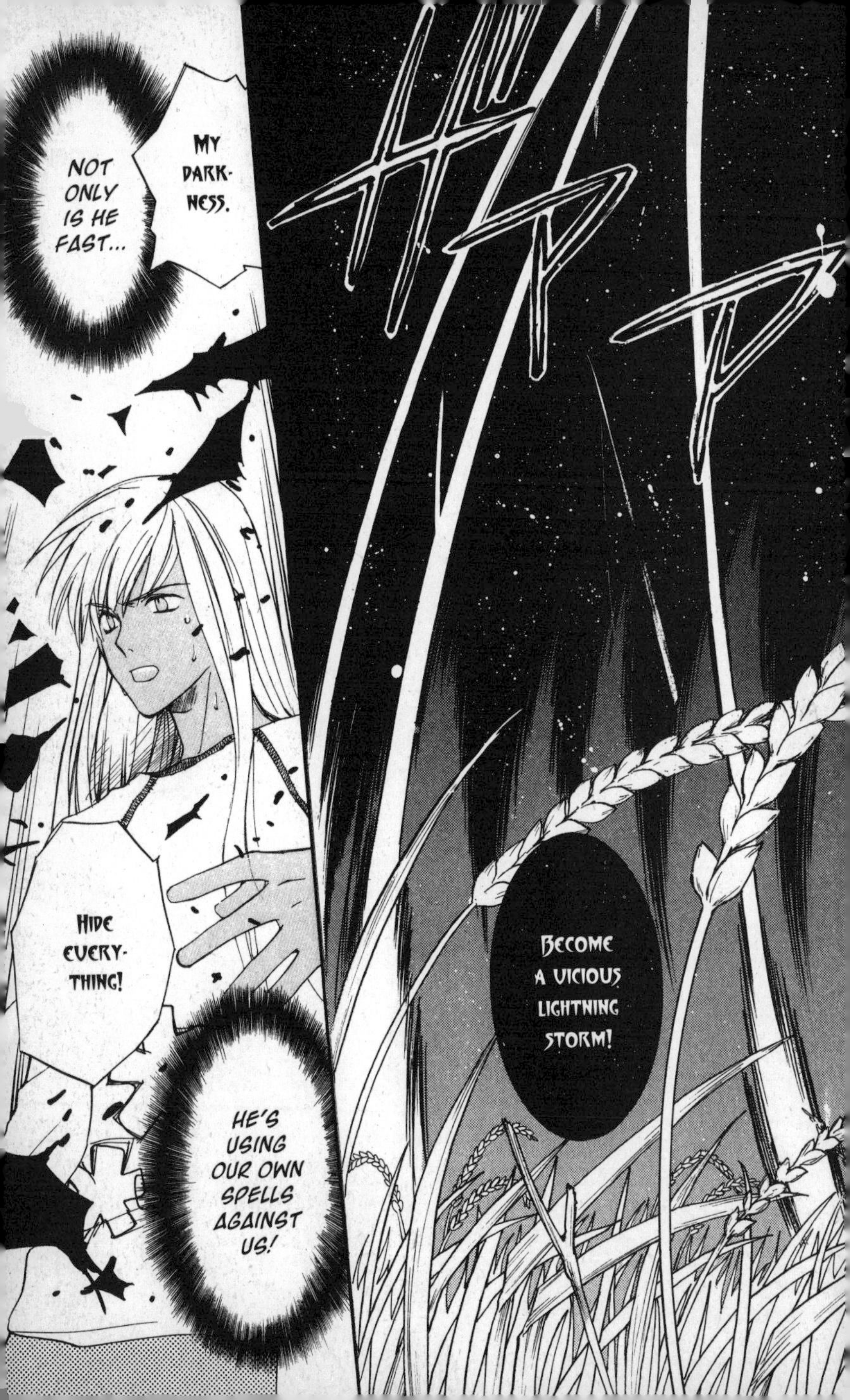
Become a vicious lightning storm!
My darkness.
Not only is he fast...
Hide everything!
He's using our own spells against us!

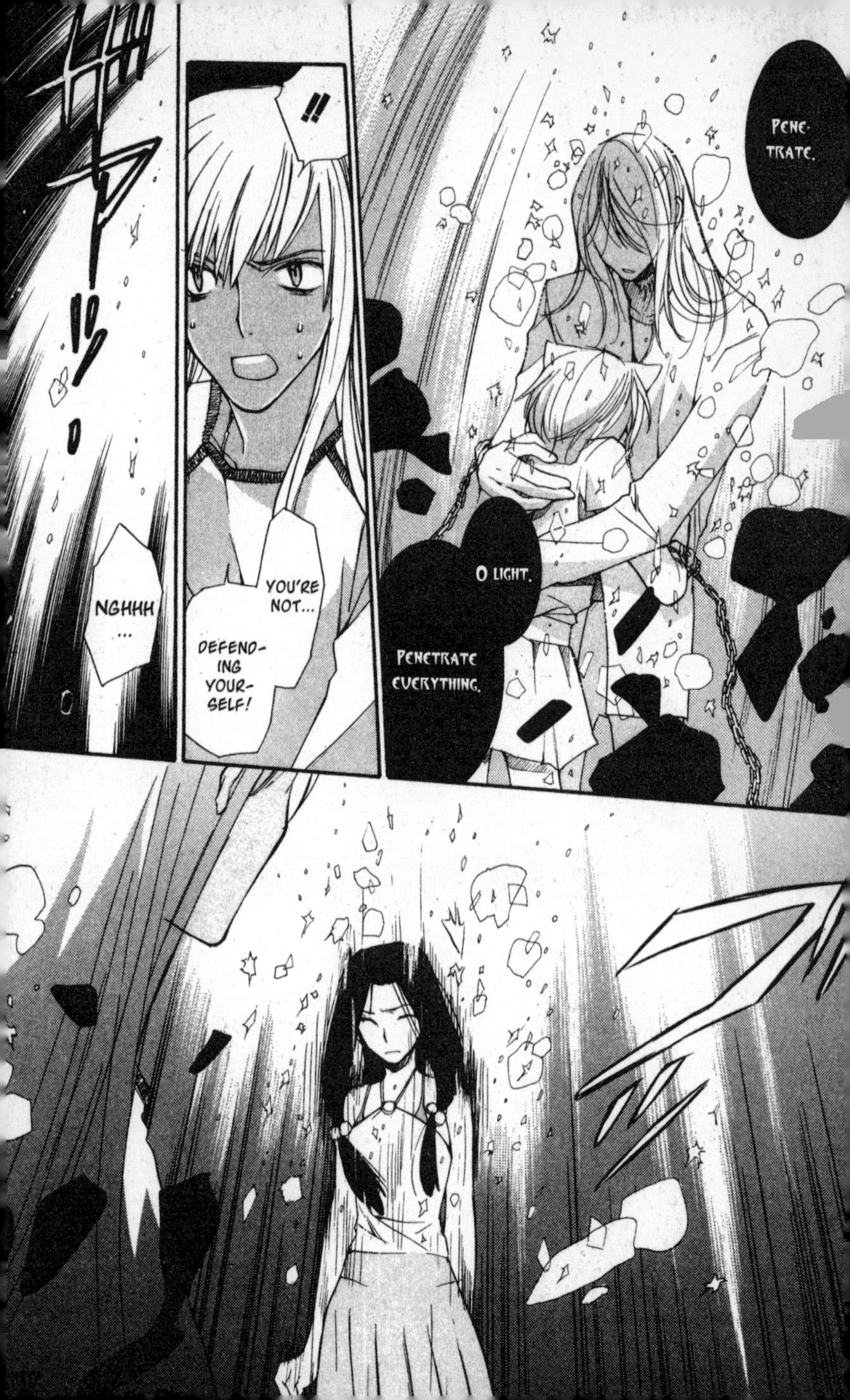
PENE-TRATE.
O LIGHT.
PENETRATE EVERYTHING.
!!
YOU'RE NOT...
DEFEND-ING YOUR-SELF!
NGHHH...

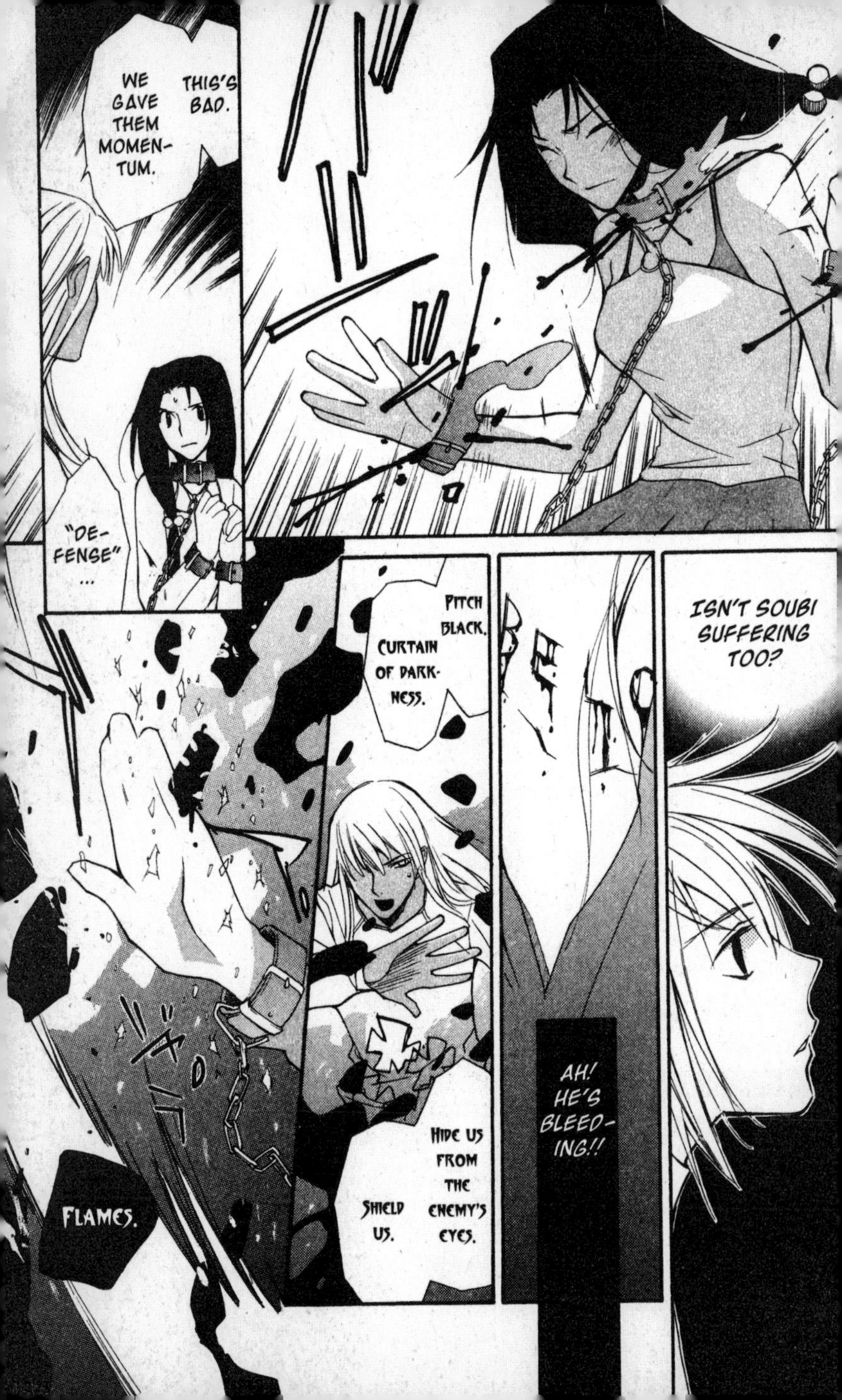
THIS'S BAD.
WE GAVE THEM MOMEN-TUM.
"DE-FENSE" ...
ISN'T SOUBI SUFFERING TOO?
AH! HE'S BLEED-ING!!
PITCH BLACK.
CURTAIN OF DARK-NESS.
HIDE US FROM THE ENEMY'S EYES.
SHIELD US.
FLAMES.

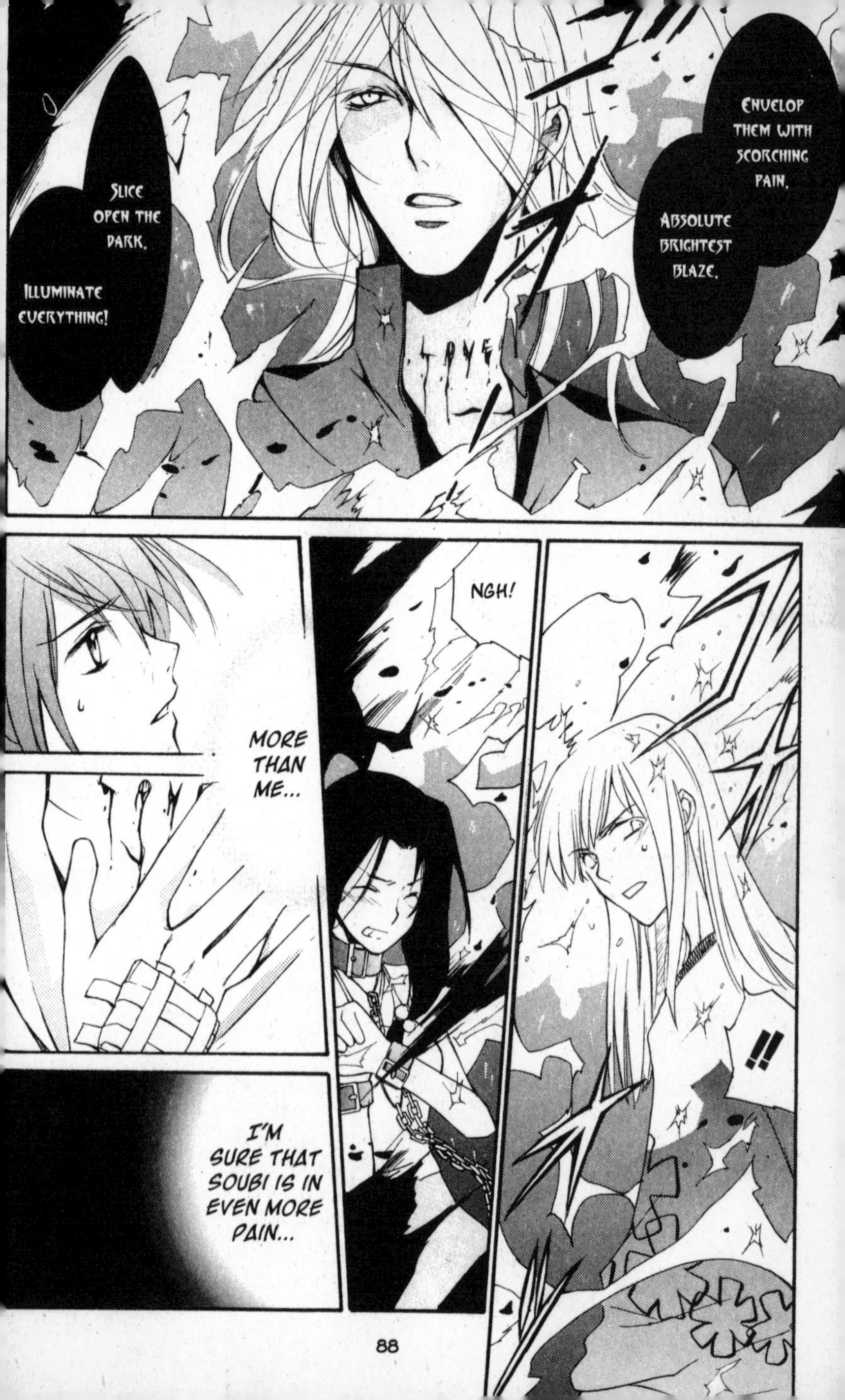
Envelop them with scorching pain.
Absolute brightest blaze.
Slice open the dark.
Illuminate everything!
!!
NGH!
MORE THAN ME...
I'M SURE THAT SOUBI IS IN EVEN MORE PAIN...

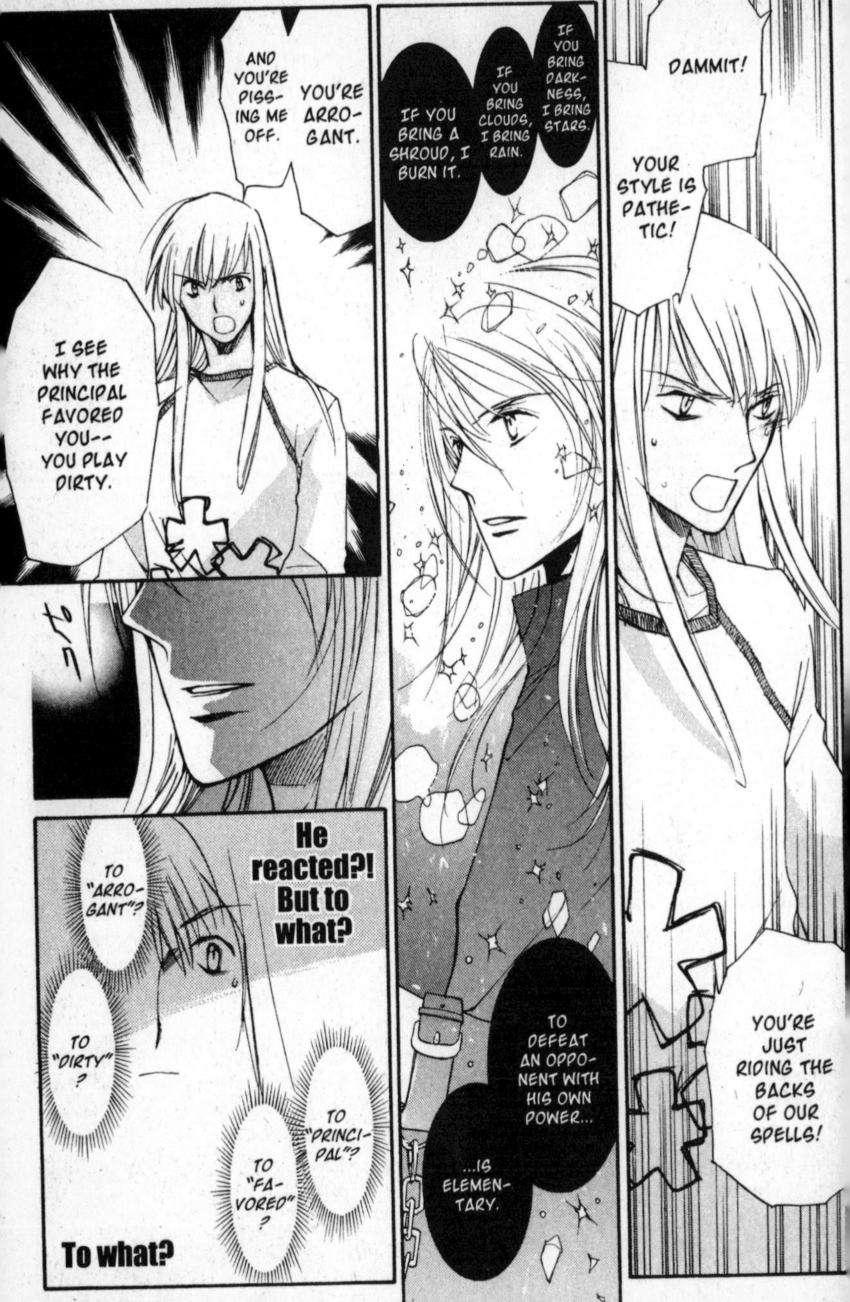
DAMMIT!
YOUR STYLE IS PATHETIC!
YOU'RE JUST RIDING THE BACKS OF OUR SPELLS!
IF YOU BRING DARKNESS, I BRING STARS.
IF YOU BRING CLOUDS, I BRING RAIN.
IF YOU BRING A SHROUD, I BURN IT.
TO DEFEAT AN OPPONENT WITH HIS OWN POWER...
...IS ELEMENTARY.
YOU'RE ARROGANT.
AND YOU'RE PISSING ME OFF.
I SEE WHY THE PRINCIPAL FAVORED YOU-- YOU PLAY DIRTY.
He reacted?! But to what?
TO "ARROGANT"?
TO "PRINCIPAL"?
TO "DIRTY"?
TO "FAVORED"?
To what?

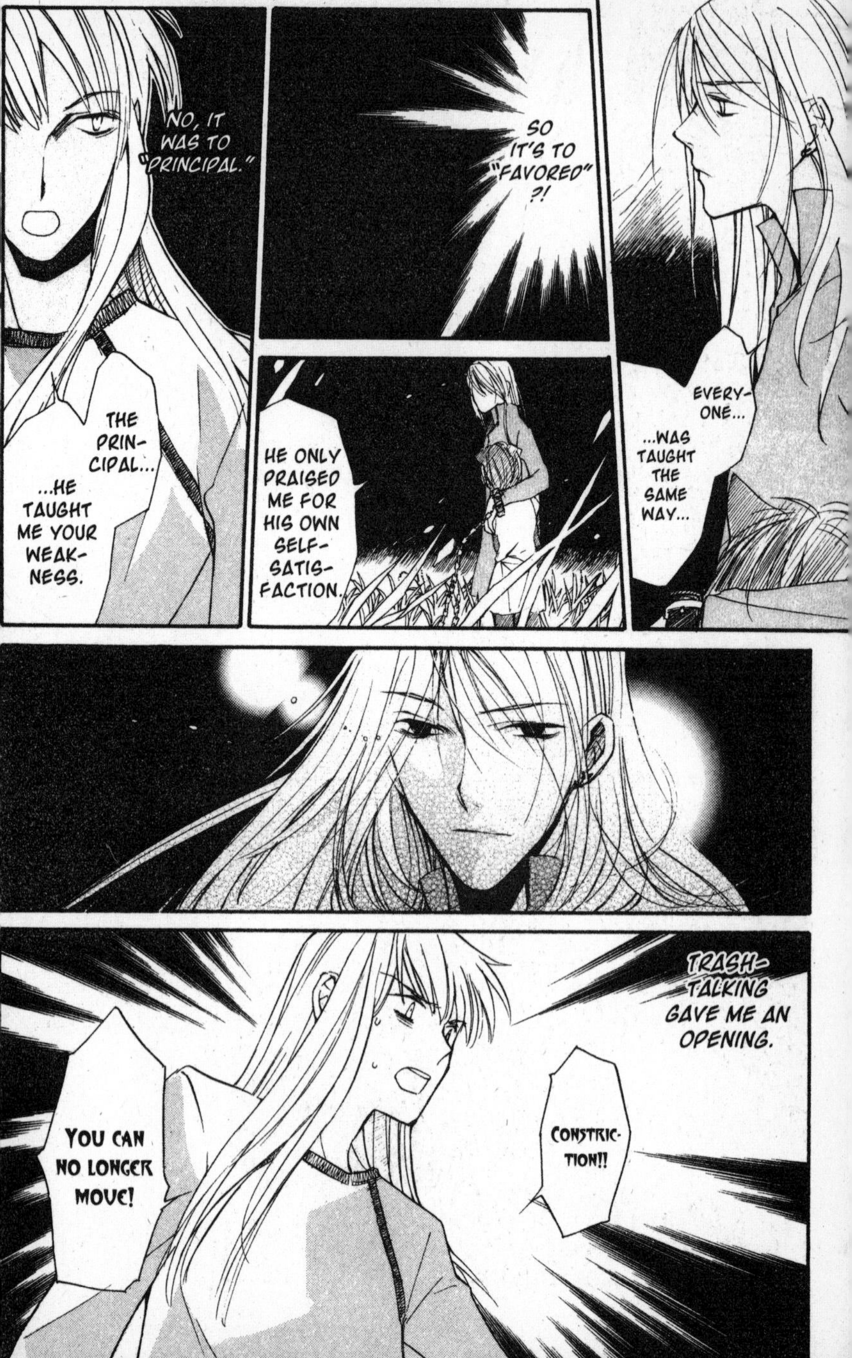
EVERY-ONE...
...WAS TAUGHT THE SAME WAY...
SO IT'S TO "FAVORED"?!
HE ONLY PRAISED ME FOR HIS OWN SELF-SATIS-FACTION.
NO, IT WAS TO "PRINCIPAL."
THE PRIN-CIPAL...
...HE TAUGHT ME YOUR WEAK-NESS.
TRASH-TALKING GAVE ME AN OPENING.
CONSTRIC-TION!!
YOU CAN NO LONGER MOVE!

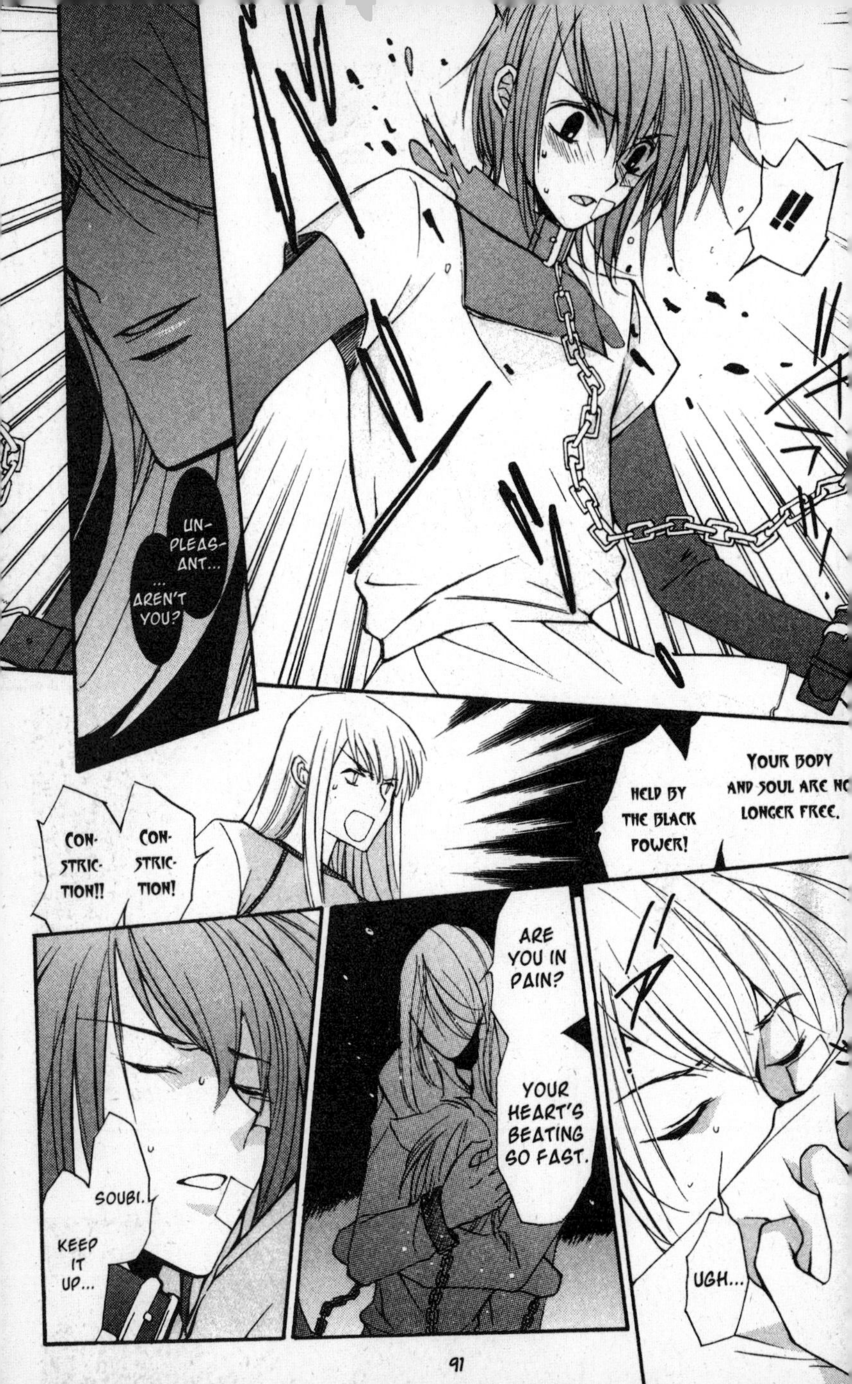
!!
UN-PLEAS-ANT... ...AREN'T YOU?
YOUR BODY AND SOUL ARE NO LONGER FREE.
HELD BY THE BLACK POWER!
CON-STRIC-TION!
CON-STRIC-TION!!
UGH...
ARE YOU IN PAIN?
YOUR HEART'S BEATING SO FAST.
SOUBI.
KEEP IT UP...

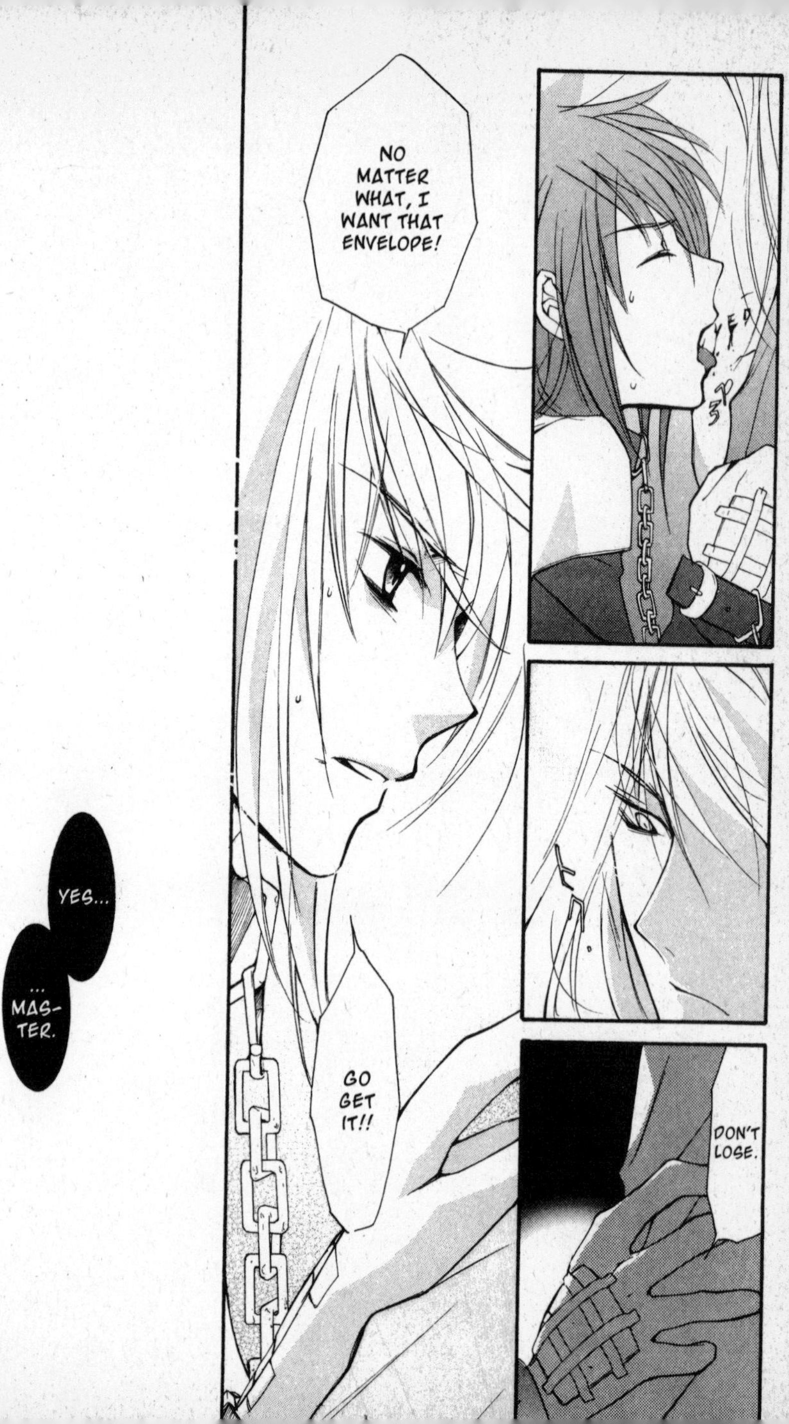
DON'T LOSE.
NO MATTER WHAT, I WANT THAT ENVELOPE!
GO GET IT!!
YES...
...MASTER.

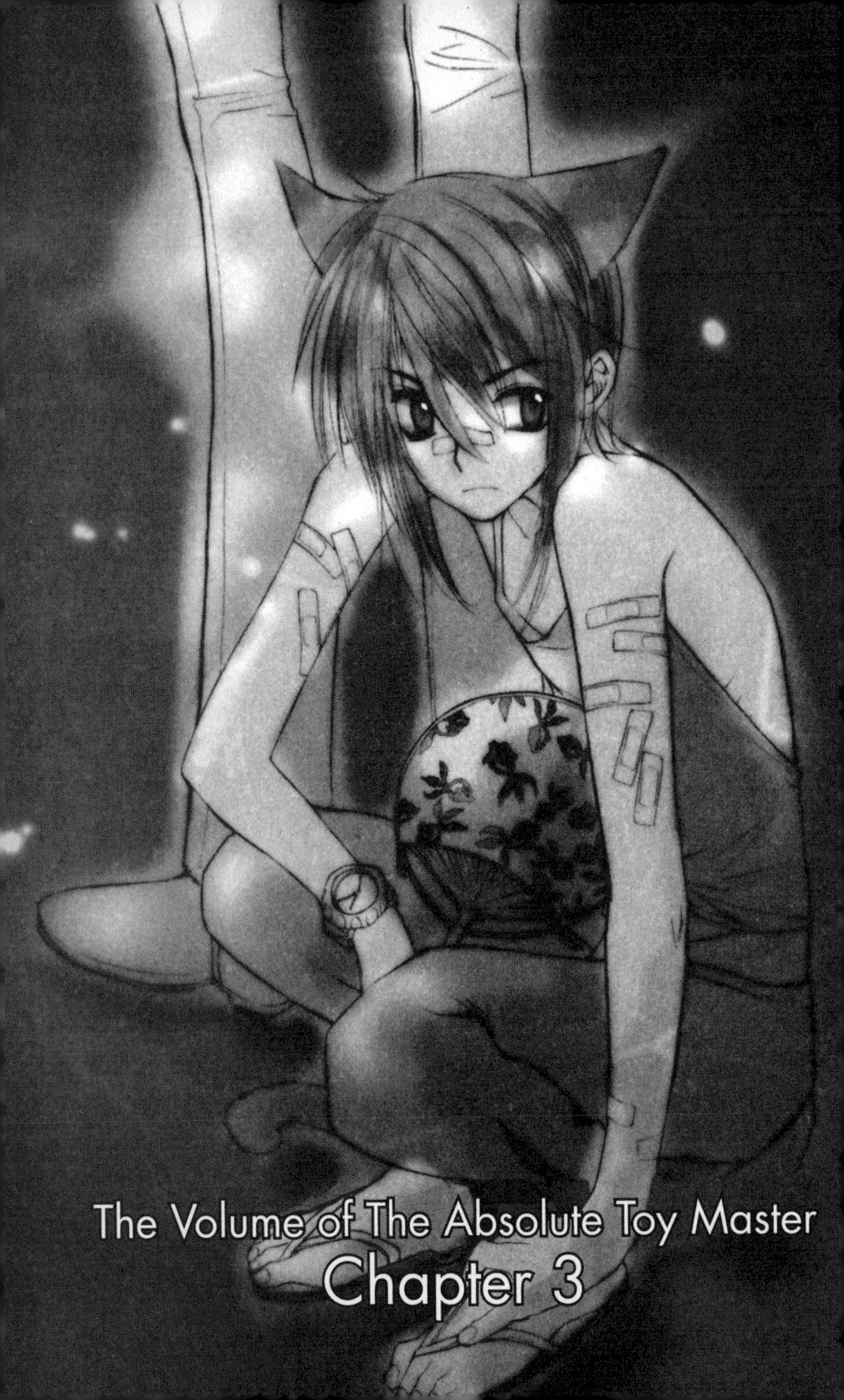
The Volume of The Absolute Toy Master
Chapter 3

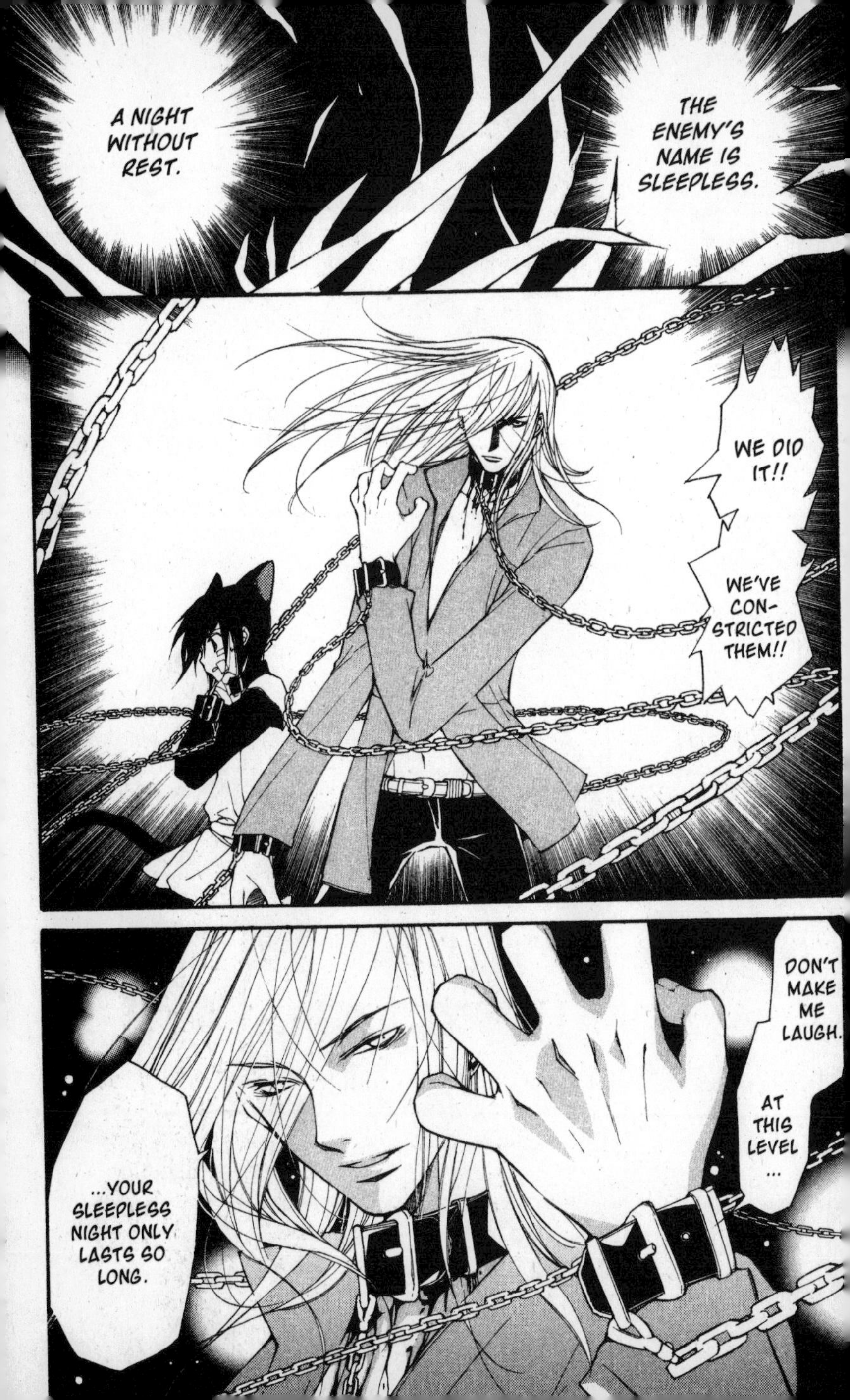
THE ENEMY'S NAME IS SLEEPLESS.
A NIGHT WITHOUT REST.
WE DID IT!!
WE'VE CON-STRICTED THEM!!
DON'T MAKE ME LAUGH.
AT THIS LEVEL ...
...YOUR SLEEPLESS NIGHT ONLY LASTS SO LONG.

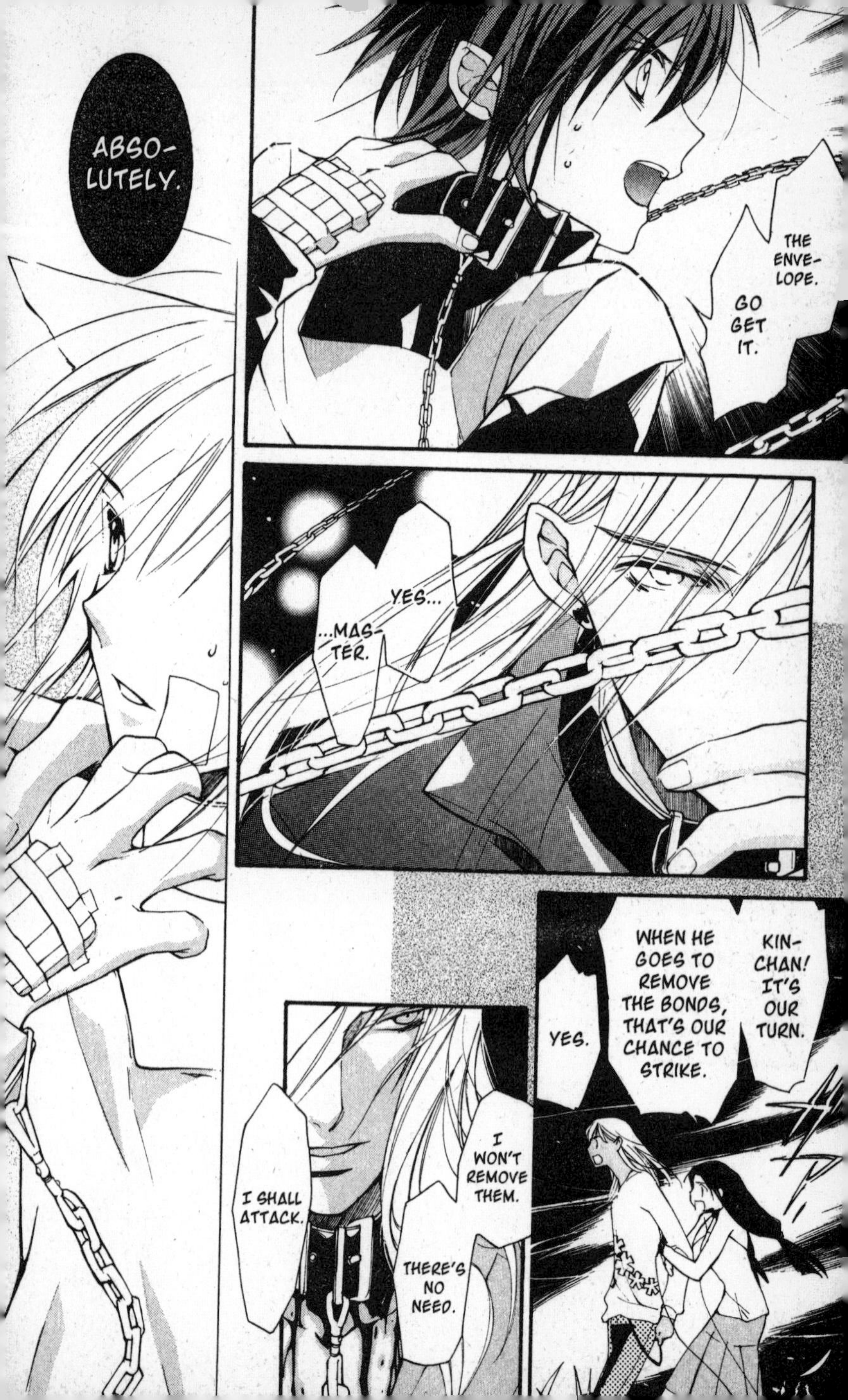
THE ENVELOPE.
GO GET IT.
YES...
...MASTER.
KIN-CHAN! IT'S OUR TURN.
WHEN HE GOES TO REMOVE THE BONDS, THAT'S OUR CHANCE TO STRIKE.
YES.
I WON'T REMOVE THEM.
THERE'S NO NEED.
I SHALL ATTACK.
ABSOLUTELY.

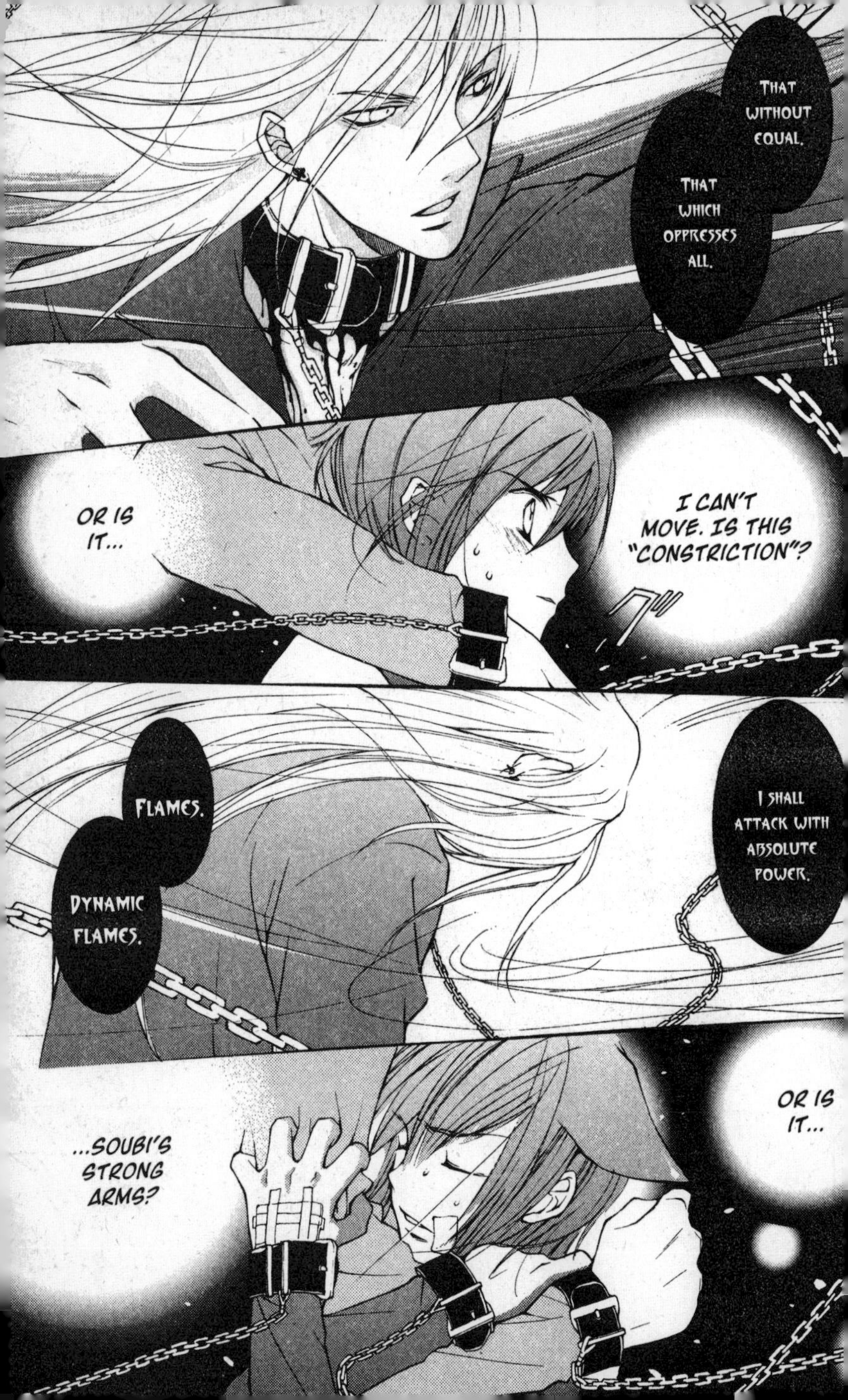
THAT WITHOUT EQUAL.
THAT WHICH OPPRESSES ALL.
I CAN'T MOVE. IS THIS "CONSTRICTION"?
グ
OR IS IT...
I SHALL ATTACK WITH ABSOLUTE POWER.
FLAMES.
DYNAMIC FLAMES.
OR IS IT...
...SOUBI'S STRONG ARMS?

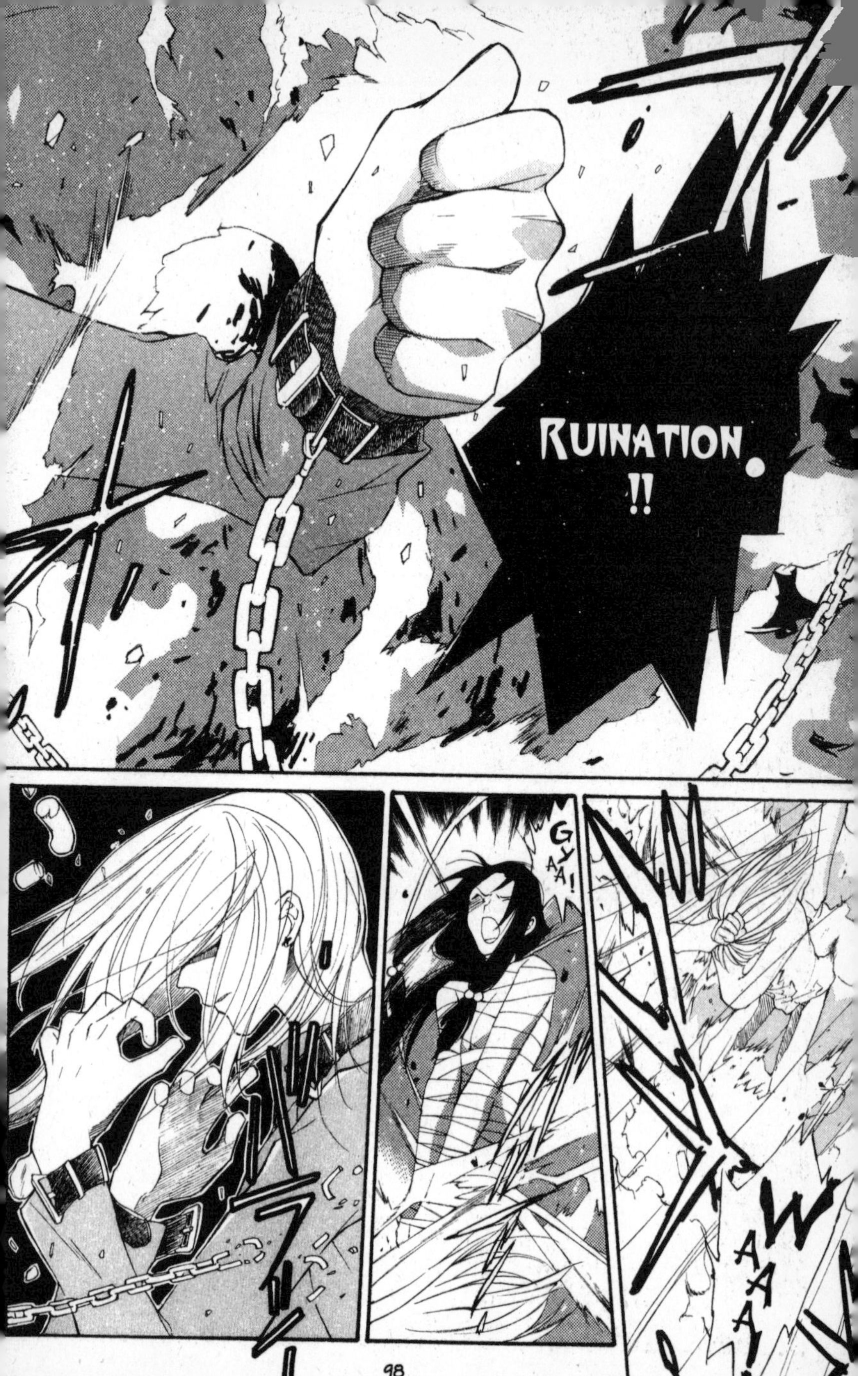
RUINATION !!
WAAAA!
GYAA!

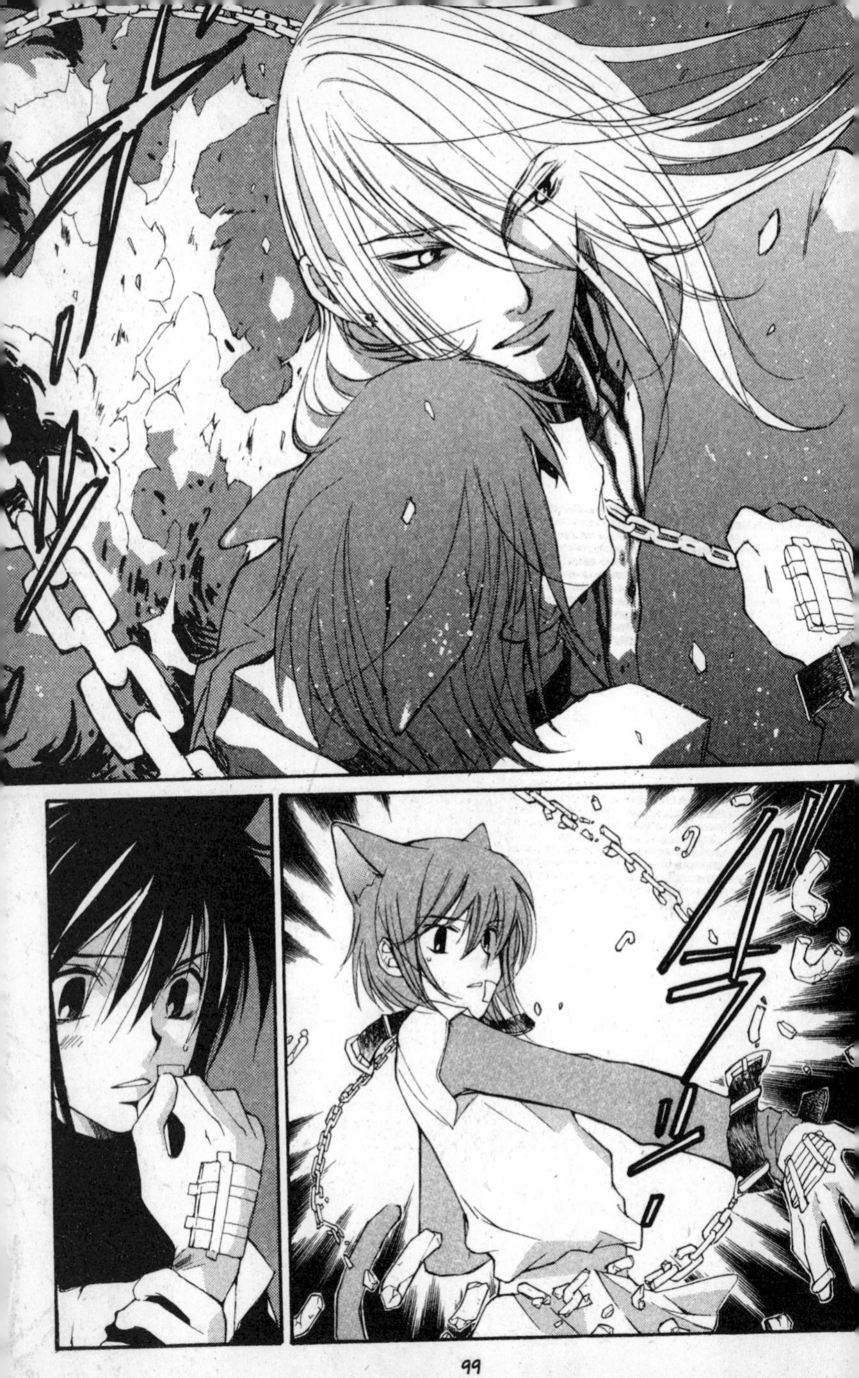

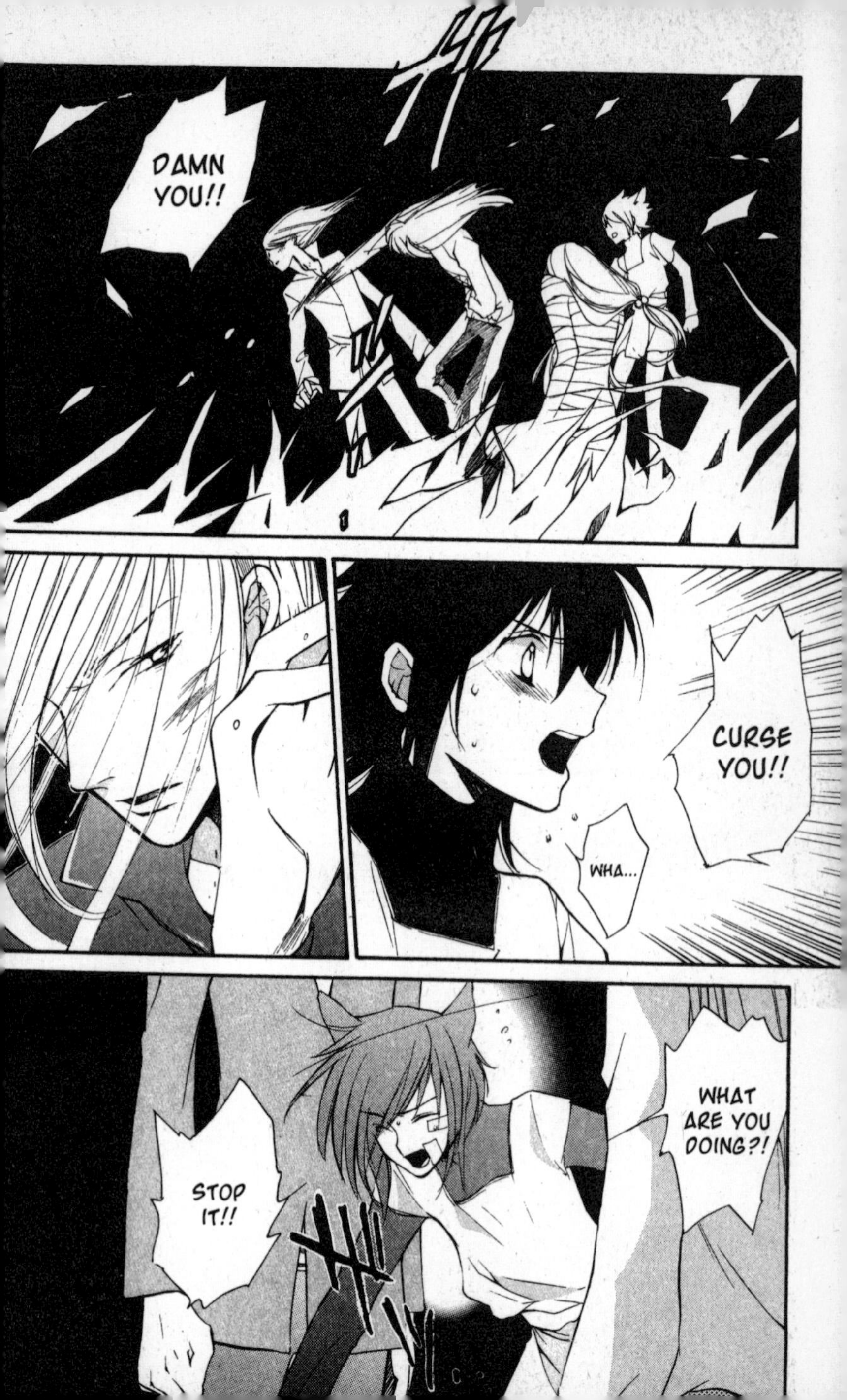
DAMN YOU!!
CURSE YOU!!
WHA...
WHAT ARE YOU DOING?!
STOP IT!!

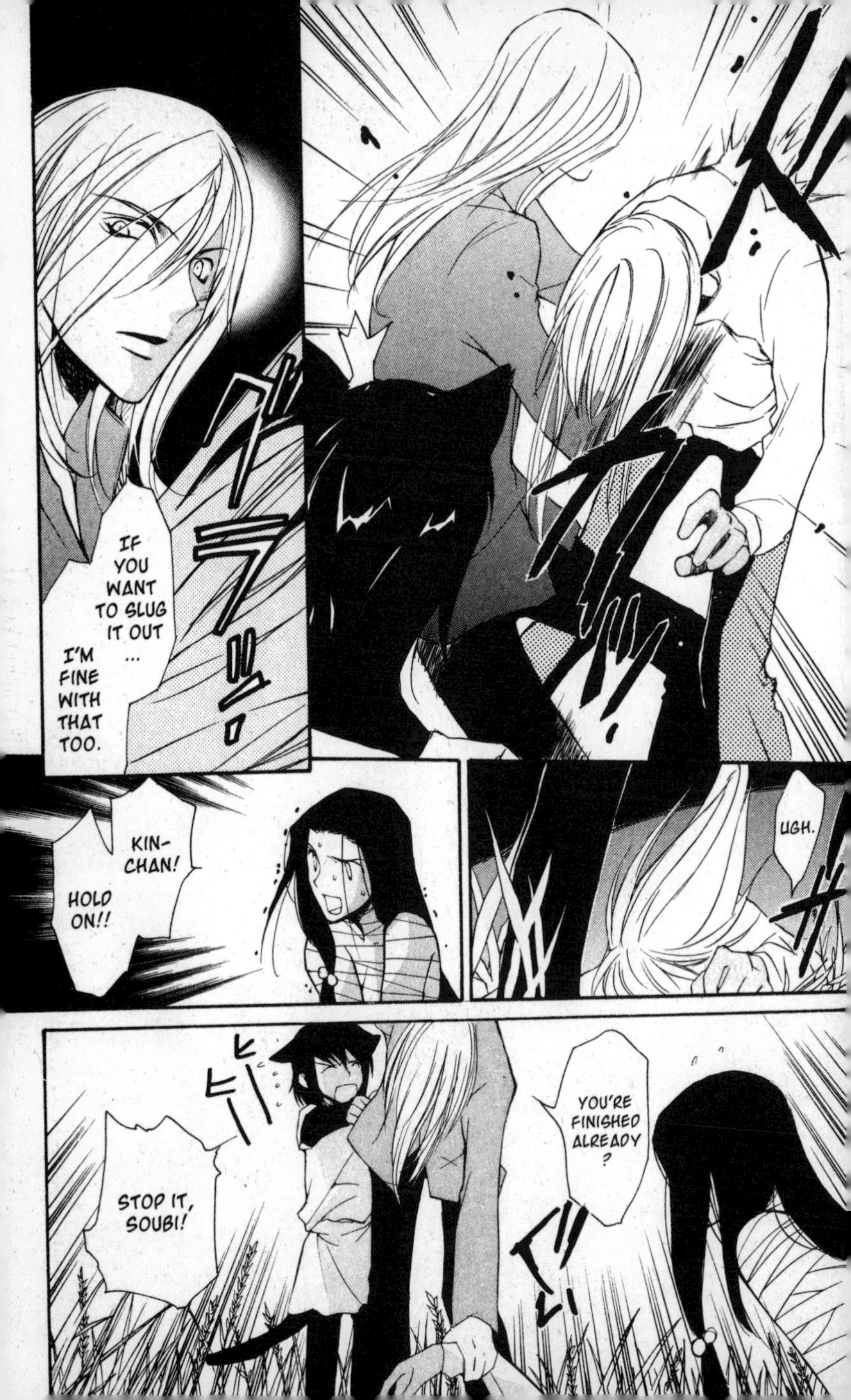
IF YOU WANT TO SLUG IT OUT... I'M FINE WITH THAT TOO.
UGH.
KIN-CHAN! HOLD ON!!
YOU'RE FINISHED ALREADY?
STOP IT, SOUBI!

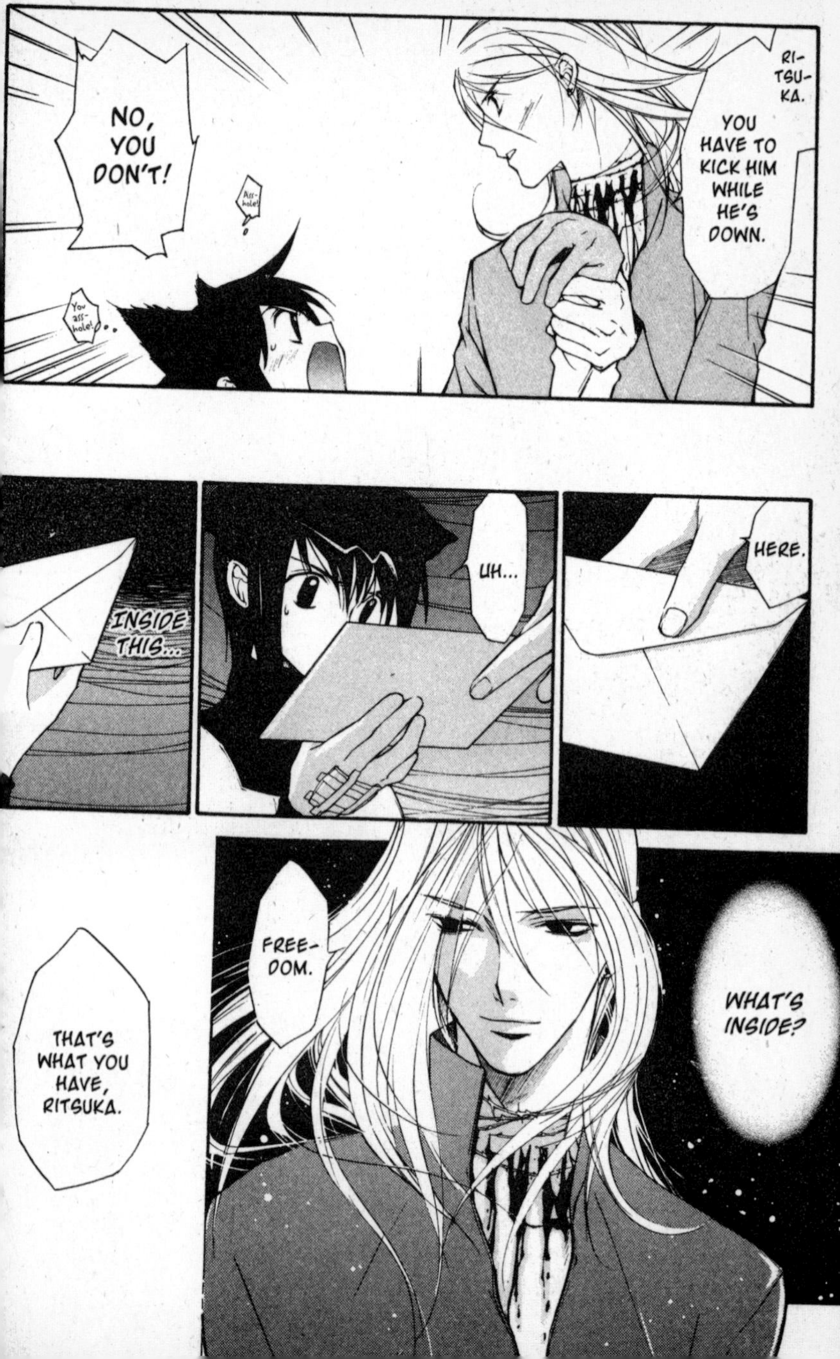
RI-TSU-KA.
YOU HAVE TO KICK HIM WHILE HE'S DOWN.
NO, YOU DON'T!
Ass-hole!
You ass-hole!
HERE.
UH...
INSIDE THIS...
WHAT'S INSIDE?
FREE-DOM.
THAT'S WHAT YOU HAVE, RITSUKA.

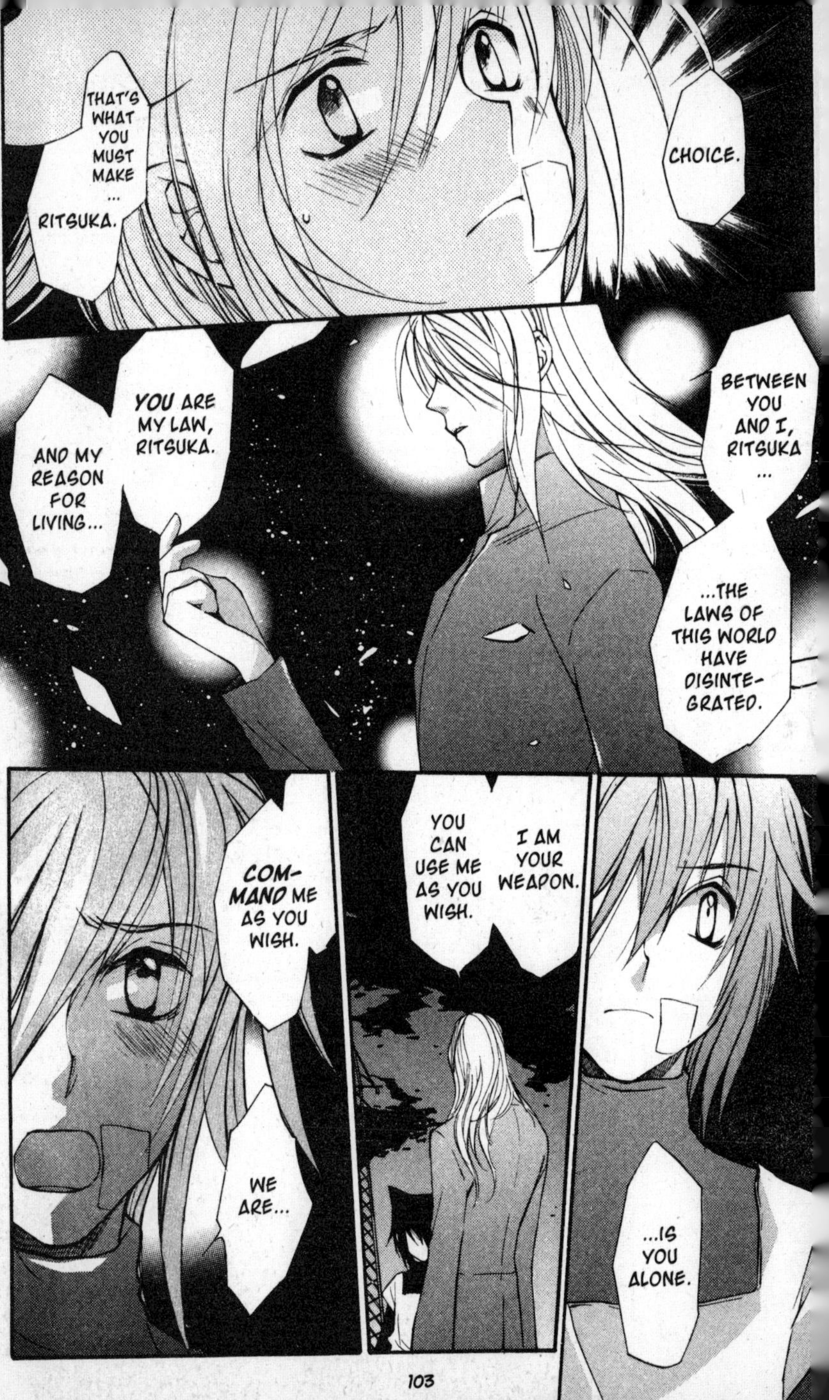
CHOICE.
THAT'S WHAT YOU MUST MAKE ... RITSUKA.
BETWEEN YOU AND I, RITSUKA ...
...THE LAWS OF THIS WORLD HAVE DISINTEGRATED.
YOU ARE MY LAW, RITSUKA.
AND MY REASON FOR LIVING...
...IS YOU ALONE.
I AM YOUR WEAPON.
YOU CAN USE ME AS YOU WISH.
COMMAND ME AS YOU WISH.
WE ARE...

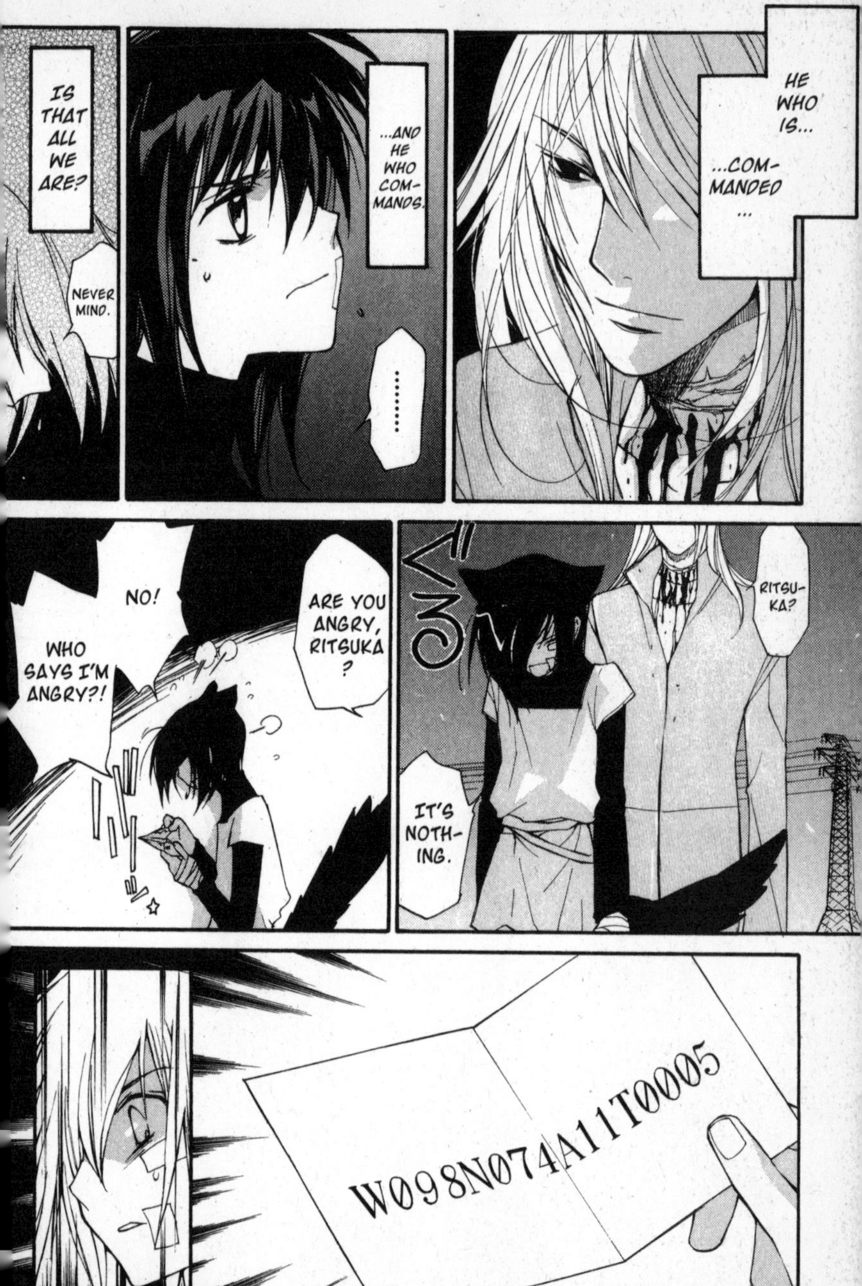
HE WHO IS...
...COM-MANDED ...
...AND HE WHO COM-MANDS.
....
IS THAT ALL WE ARE?
NEVER MIND.
RITSU-KA?
IT'S NOTH-ING.
ARE YOU ANGRY, RITSUKA ?
NO!
WHO SAYS I'M ANGRY?!
W098N074A11T0005

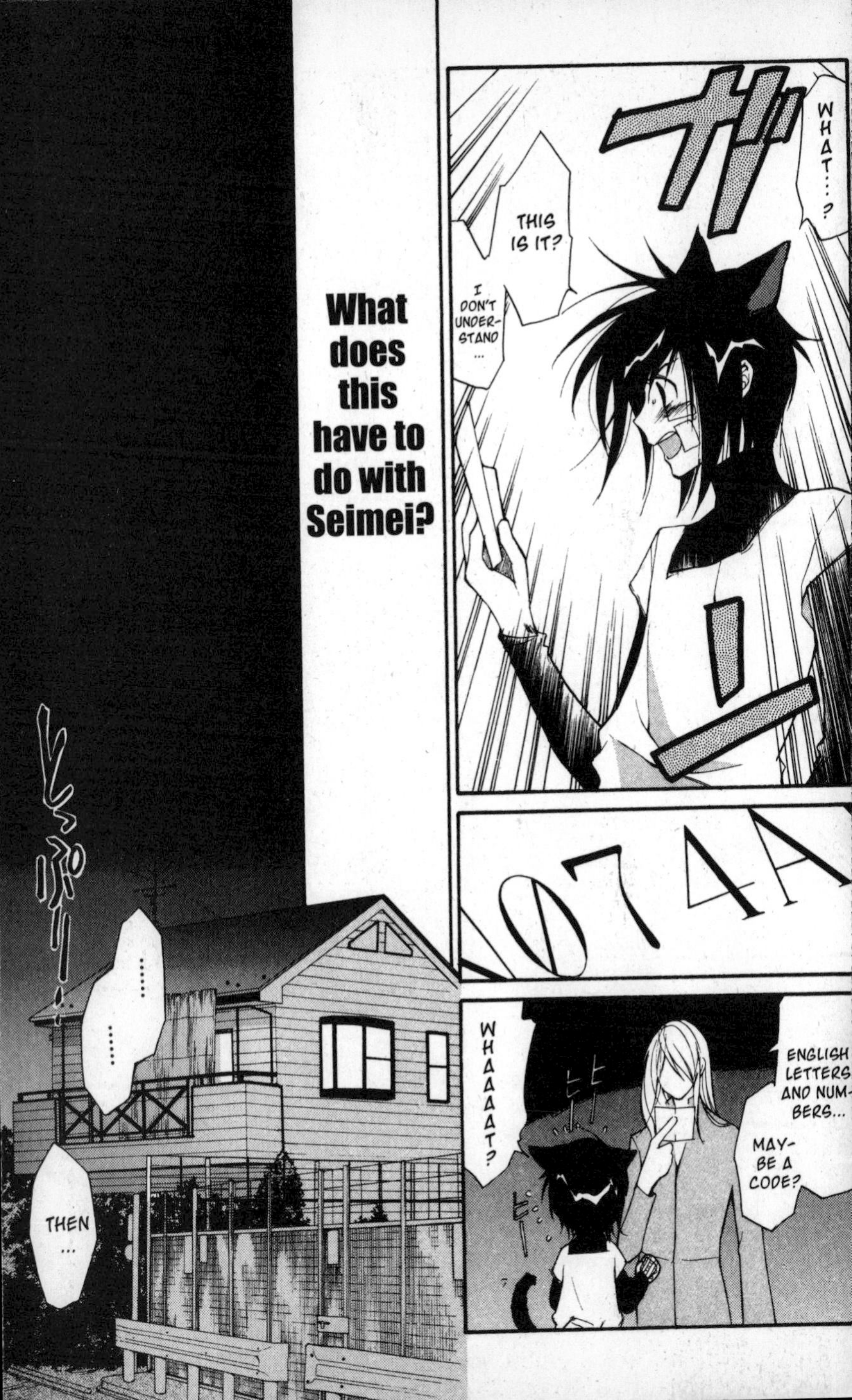
WHAT...?
THIS IS IT?
I DON'T UNDERSTAND...
074A
ENGLISH LETTERS AND NUMBERS...
MAYBE A CODE?
WHAAAAT?
What does this have to do with Seimei?
......
......
THEN...

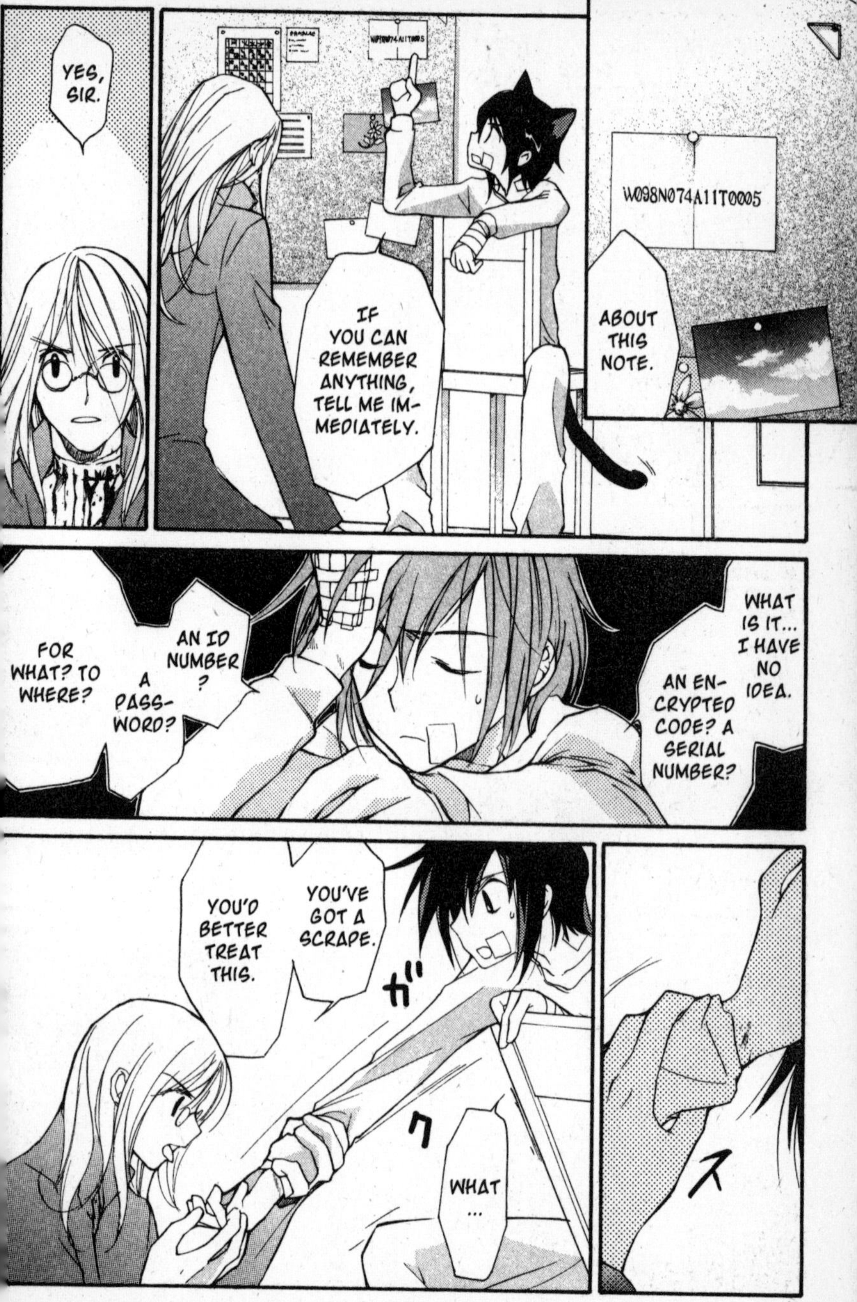
W098N074A11T0005
ABOUT THIS NOTE.
IF YOU CAN REMEMBER ANYTHING, TELL ME IM-MEDIATELY.
YES, SIR.
WHAT IS IT... I HAVE NO IDEA.
AN EN-CRYPTED CODE? A SERIAL NUMBER?
AN ID NUMBER?
A PASS-WORD?
FOR WHAT? TO WHERE?
ス
YOU'VE GOT A SCRAPE.
YOU'D BETTER TREAT THIS.
ガ
ク
WHAT ...

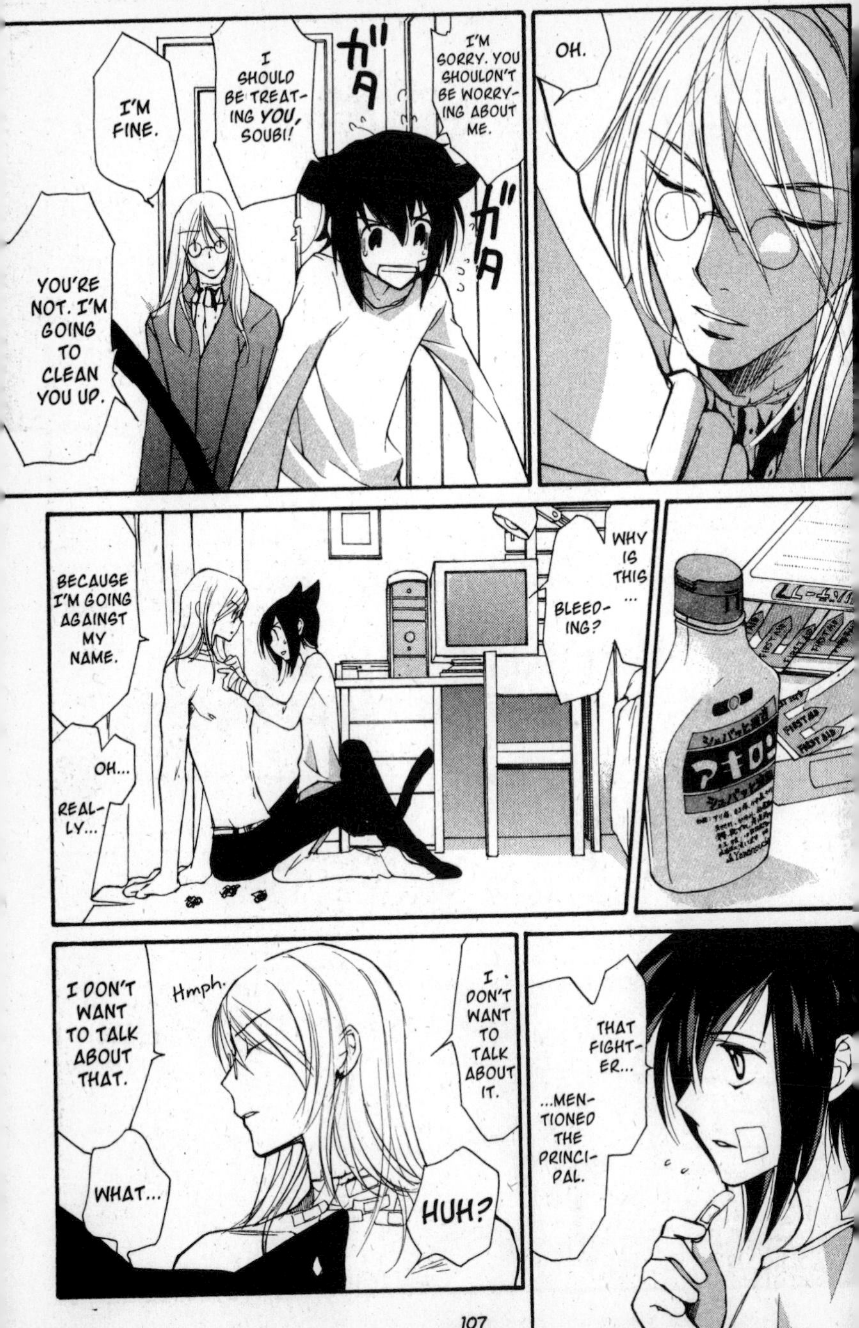
OH.
I'M SORRY. YOU SHOULDN'T BE WORRYING ABOUT ME.
ガタ
ガタ
I SHOULD BE TREATING YOU, SOUBI!
I'M FINE.
YOU'RE NOT. I'M GOING TO CLEAN YOU UP.
FIRST AID
WHY IS THIS...
BLEEDING?
BECAUSE I'M GOING AGAINST MY NAME.
OH...
REALLY...
THAT FIGHTER...
...MENTIONED THE PRINCIPAL.
I DON'T WANT TO TALK ABOUT IT.
HUH?
Hmph.
I DON'T WANT TO TALK ABOUT THAT.
WHAT...

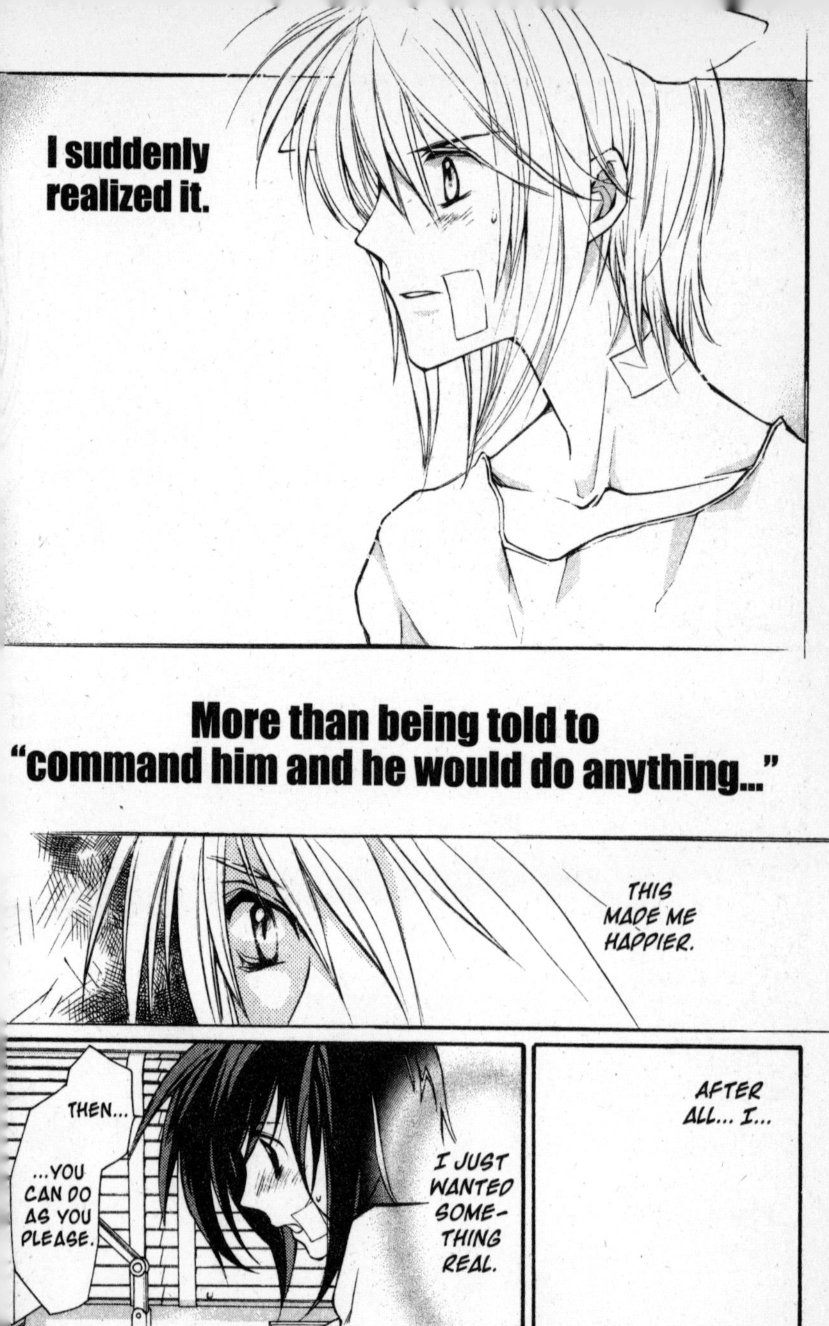
I suddenly realized it.
More than being told to "command him and he would do anything..."
THIS MADE ME HAPPIER.
AFTER ALL... I...
I JUST WANTED SOME-THING REAL.
THEN...
...YOU CAN DO AS YOU PLEASE.

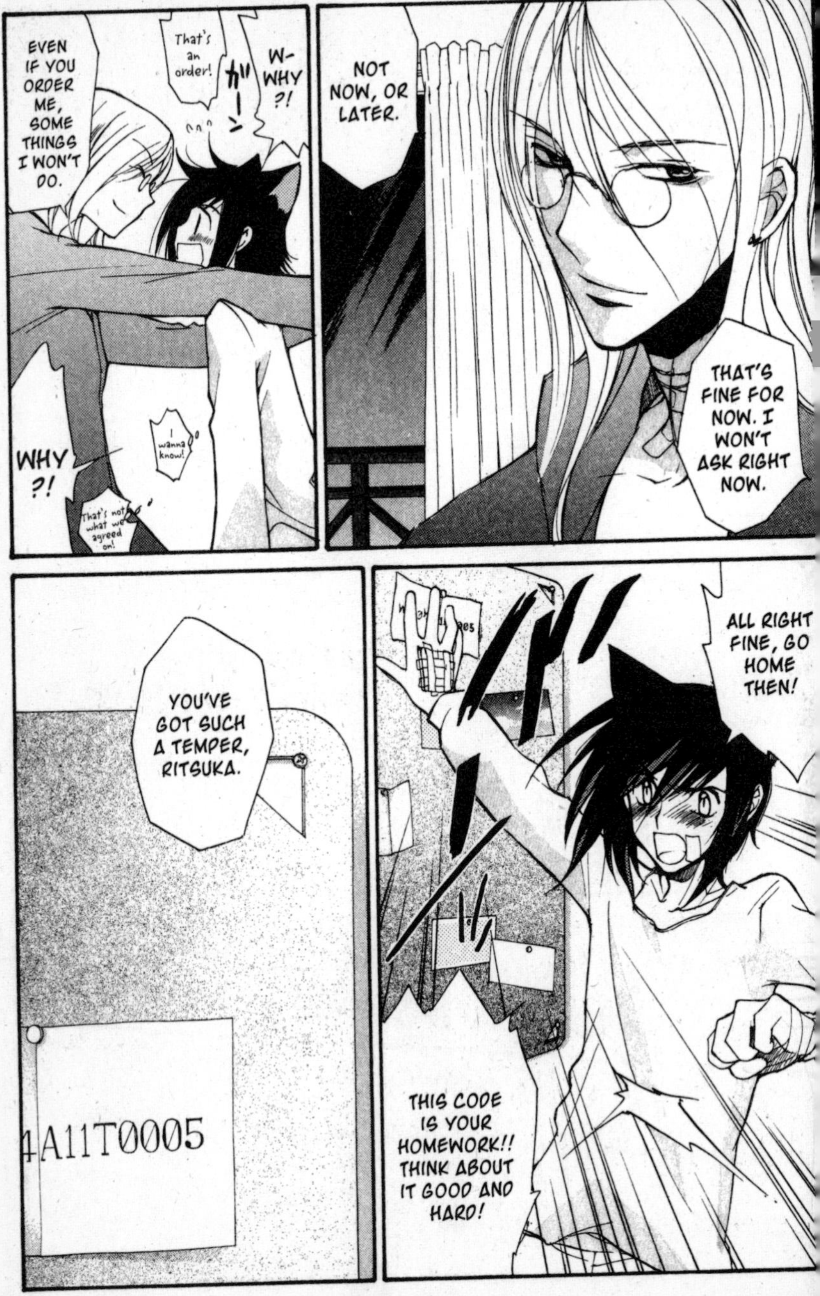
NOT NOW, OR LATER.
THAT'S FINE FOR NOW. I WON'T ASK RIGHT NOW.
W-WHY?!
That's an order!
EVEN IF YOU ORDER ME, SOME THINGS I WON'T DO.
I wanna know!
WHY?!
That's not what we agreed on!
ALL RIGHT FINE, GO HOME THEN!
THIS CODE IS YOUR HOMEWORK!! THINK ABOUT IT GOOD AND HARD!
YOU'VE GOT SUCH A TEMPER, RITSUKA.
4A11T0005

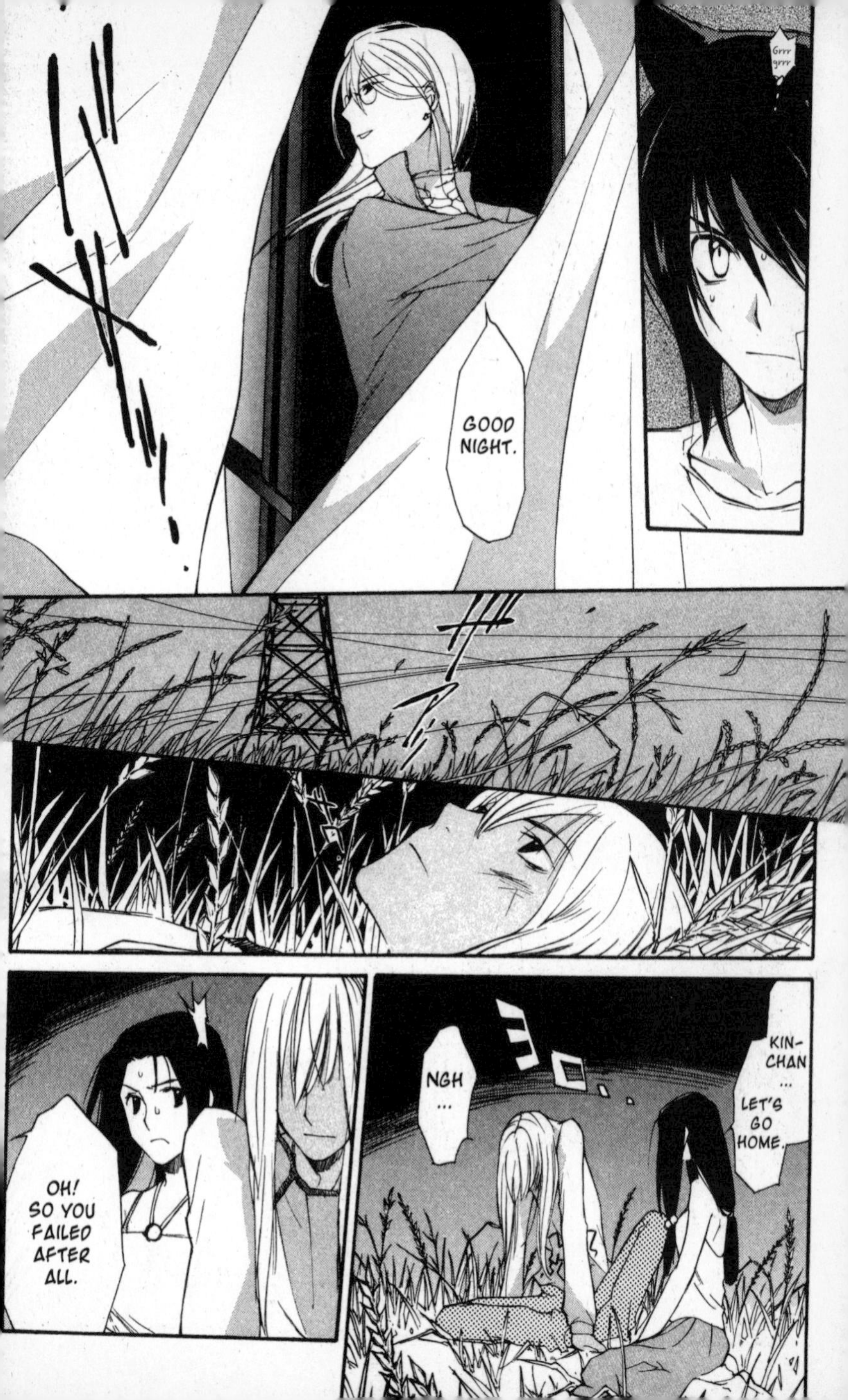
Grrr grrr
GOOD NIGHT.
KIN-CHAN ... LET'S GO HOME.
NGH ...
OH! SO YOU FAILED AFTER ALL.

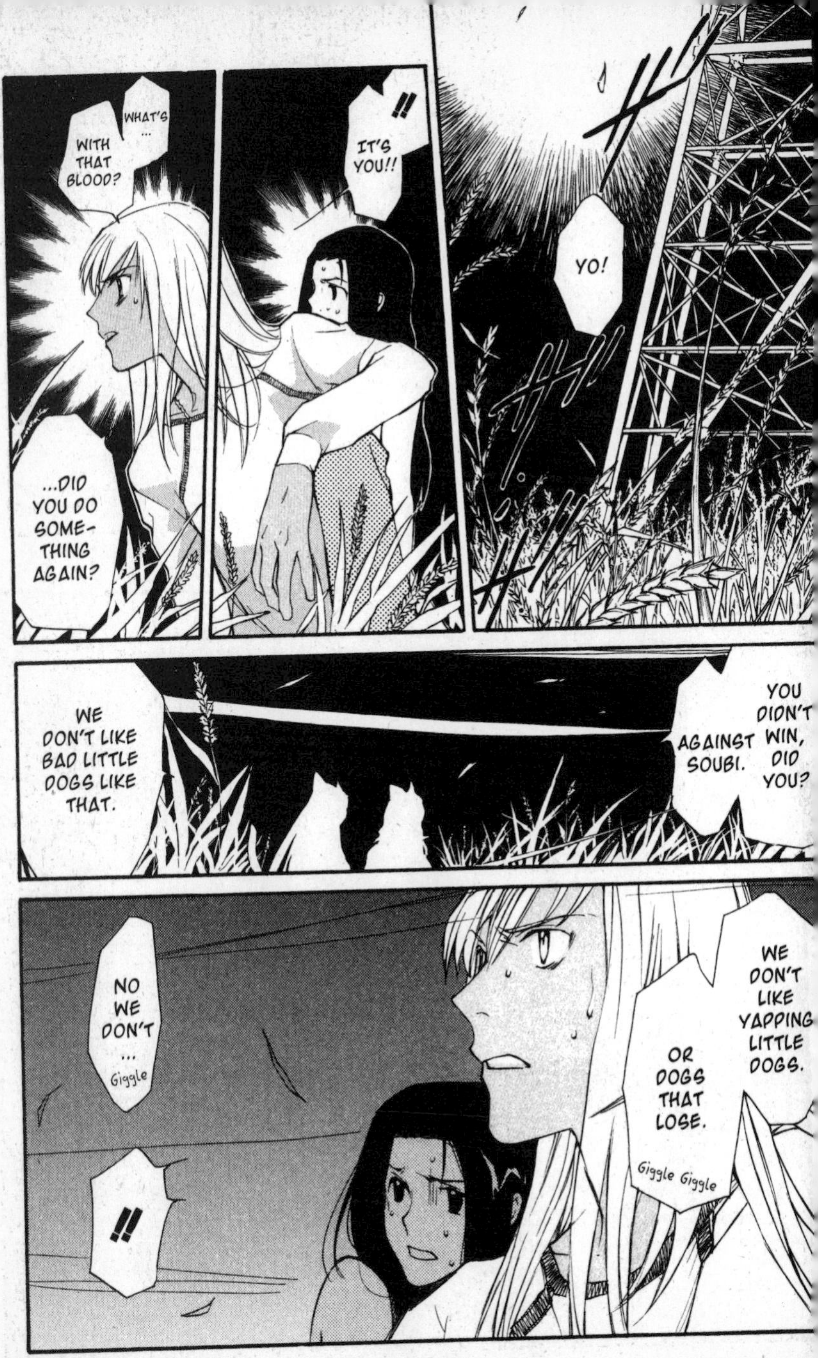
YO!
!!
IT'S YOU!!
WHAT'S ...
WITH THAT BLOOD?
...DID YOU DO SOME-THING AGAIN?
YOU DIDN'T WIN, DID YOU?
AGAINST SOUBI.
WE DON'T LIKE BAD LITTLE DOGS LIKE THAT.
WE DON'T LIKE YAPPING LITTLE DOGS.
OR DOGS THAT LOSE.
Giggle Giggle
NO WE DON'T ...
Giggle
!!

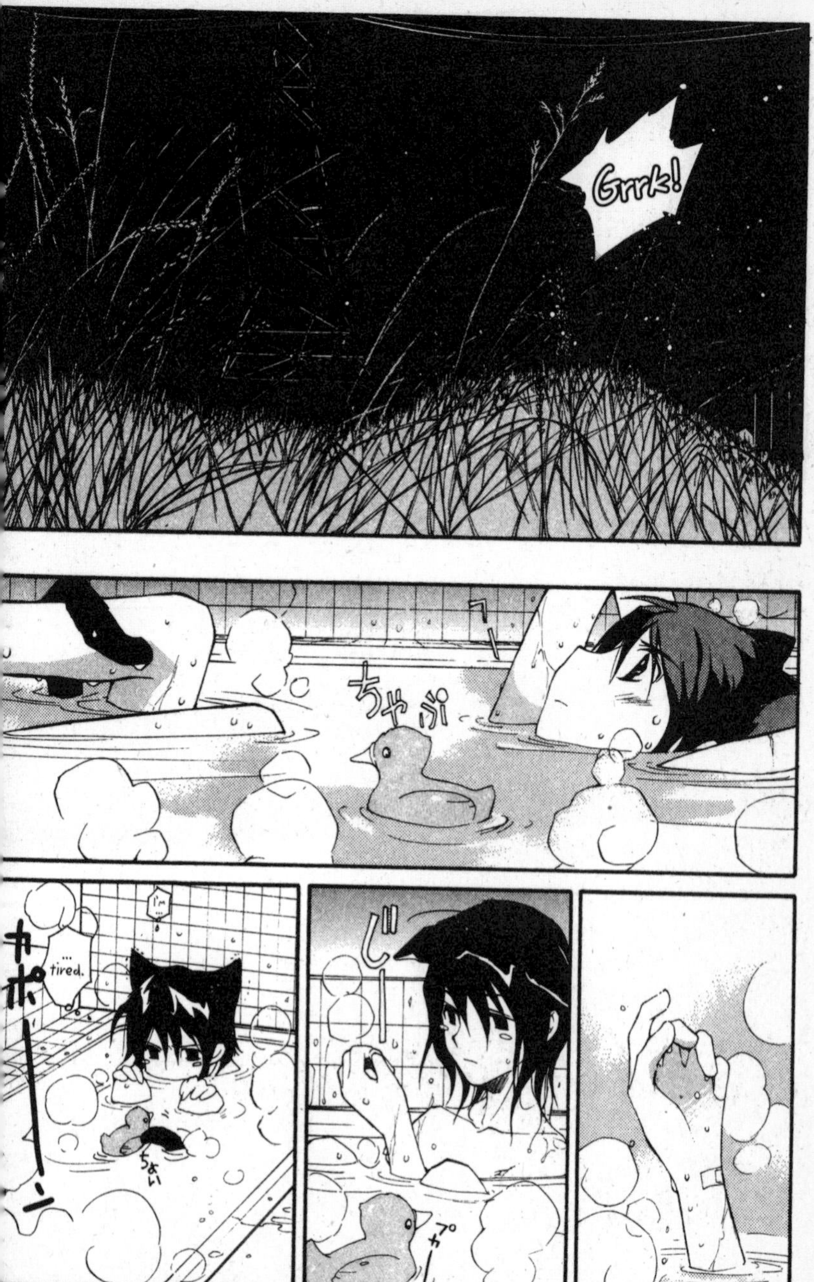

Grrk!
ちゃぷ
じー
プカー
I'm ...
... tired.
カポーン
ちょい

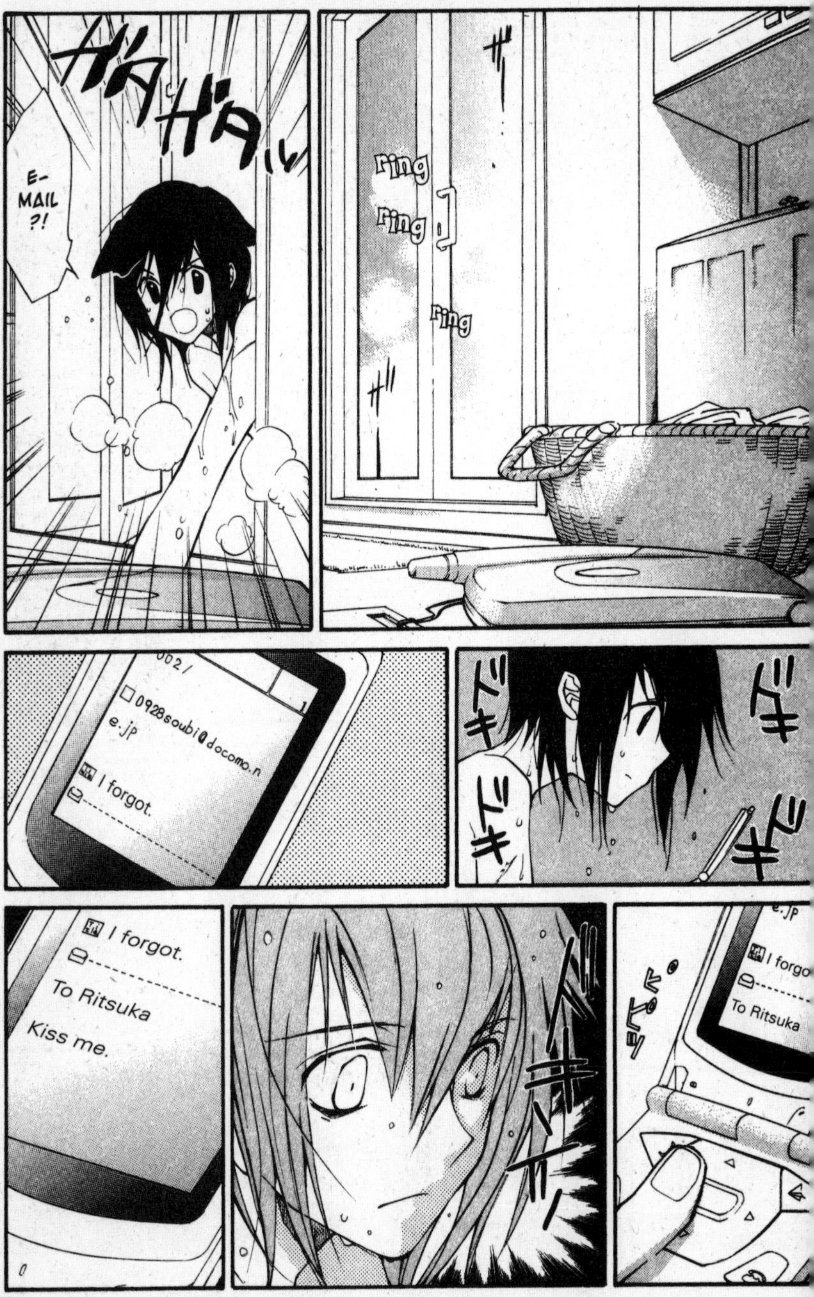

ring
ring
ring
E-MAIL ?!
ドキドキ
ドキドキ
0928soubi@docomo.n
e.jp
I forgot.
e.jp
I forgo
To Ritsuka
I forgot.
To Ritsuka
Kiss me.

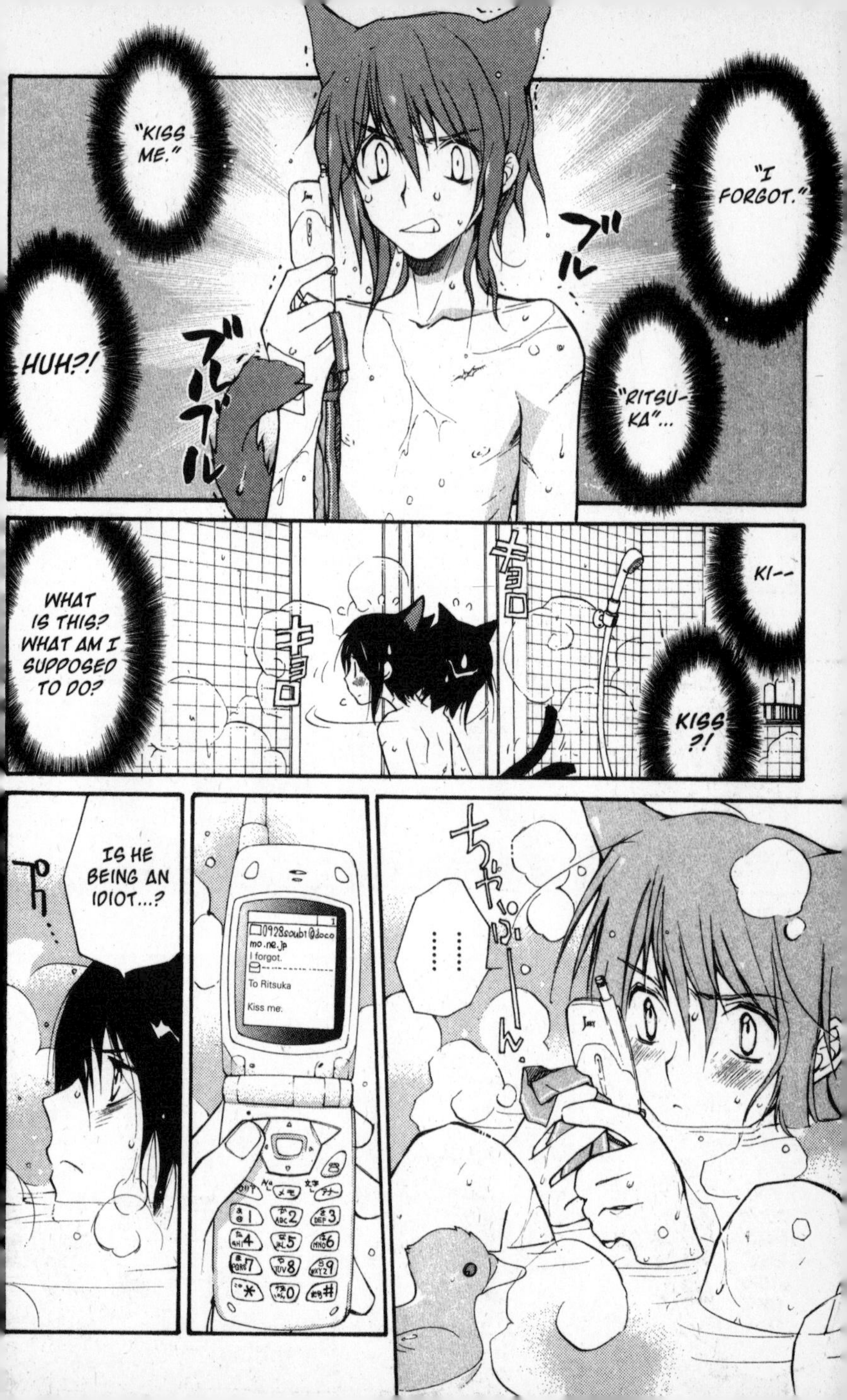
"I FORGOT."
"RITSU-KA"...
ブル
"KISS ME."
ブルブル
HUH?!
KI--
KISS ?!
キョロ
キョロ
WHAT IS THIS? WHAT AM I SUPPOSED TO DO?
ちゃぷーん
......
0928soub1@docomo.ne.jp
I forgot.
To Ritsuka
Kiss me.
IS HE BEING AN IDIOT...?
ぴ...

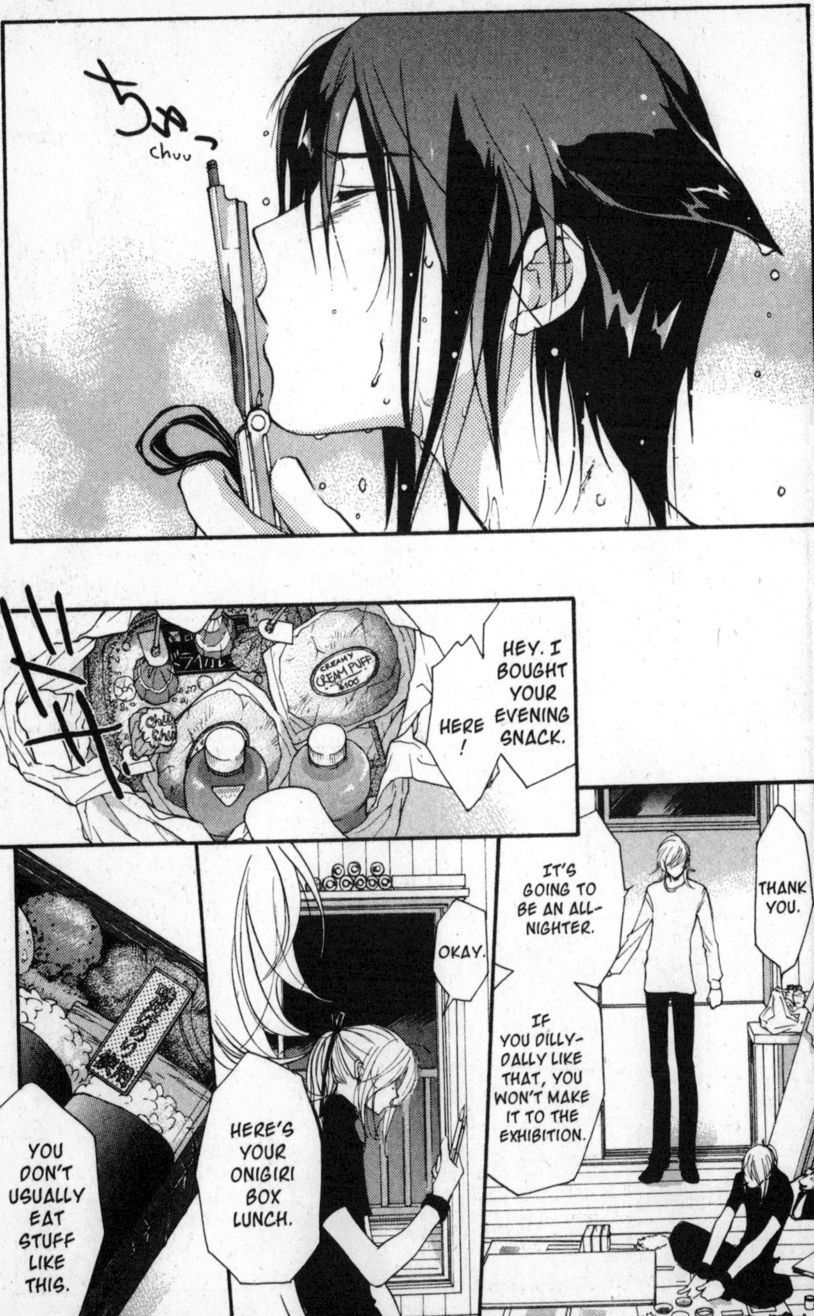
chuu
HEY. I BOUGHT YOUR EVENING SNACK.
HERE!
CREAMY CREAM PUFF ¥100
THANK YOU.
IT'S GOING TO BE AN ALL-NIGHTER.
OKAY.
IF YOU DILLY-DALLY LIKE THAT, YOU WON'T MAKE IT TO THE EXHIBITION.
HERE'S YOUR ONIGIRI BOX LUNCH.
YOU DON'T USUALLY EAT STUFF LIKE THIS.

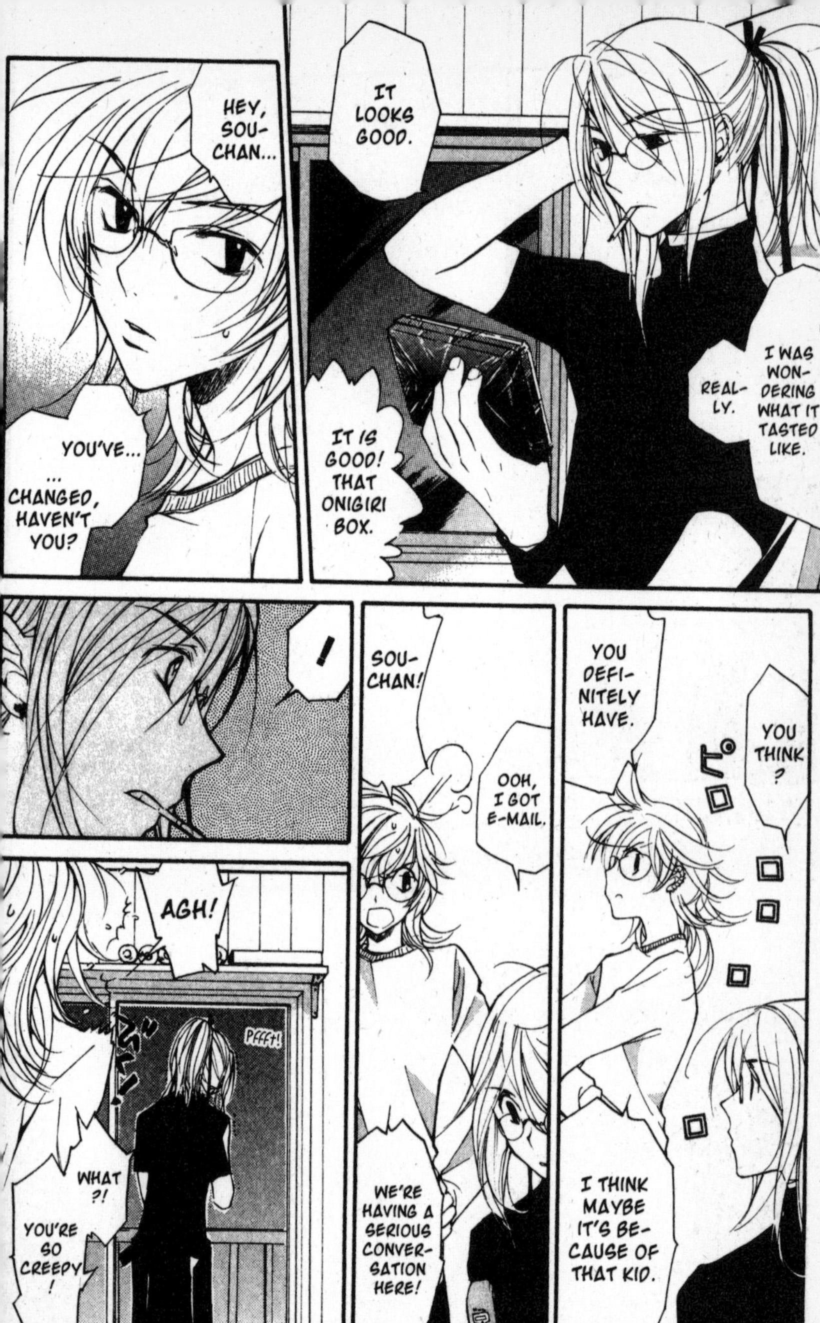

IT LOOKS GOOD.
I WAS WONDERING WHAT IT TASTED LIKE.
REALLY.
IT IS GOOD! THAT ONIGIRI BOX.
HEY, SOU-CHAN...
YOU'VE...
... CHANGED, HAVEN'T YOU?
YOU DEFINITELY HAVE.
YOU THINK?
I THINK MAYBE IT'S BECAUSE OF THAT KID.
SOU-CHAN!
OOH, I GOT E-MAIL.
WE'RE HAVING A SERIOUS CONVERSATION HERE!
!
AGH!
PFFFT!
WHAT?!
YOU'RE SO CREEPY!

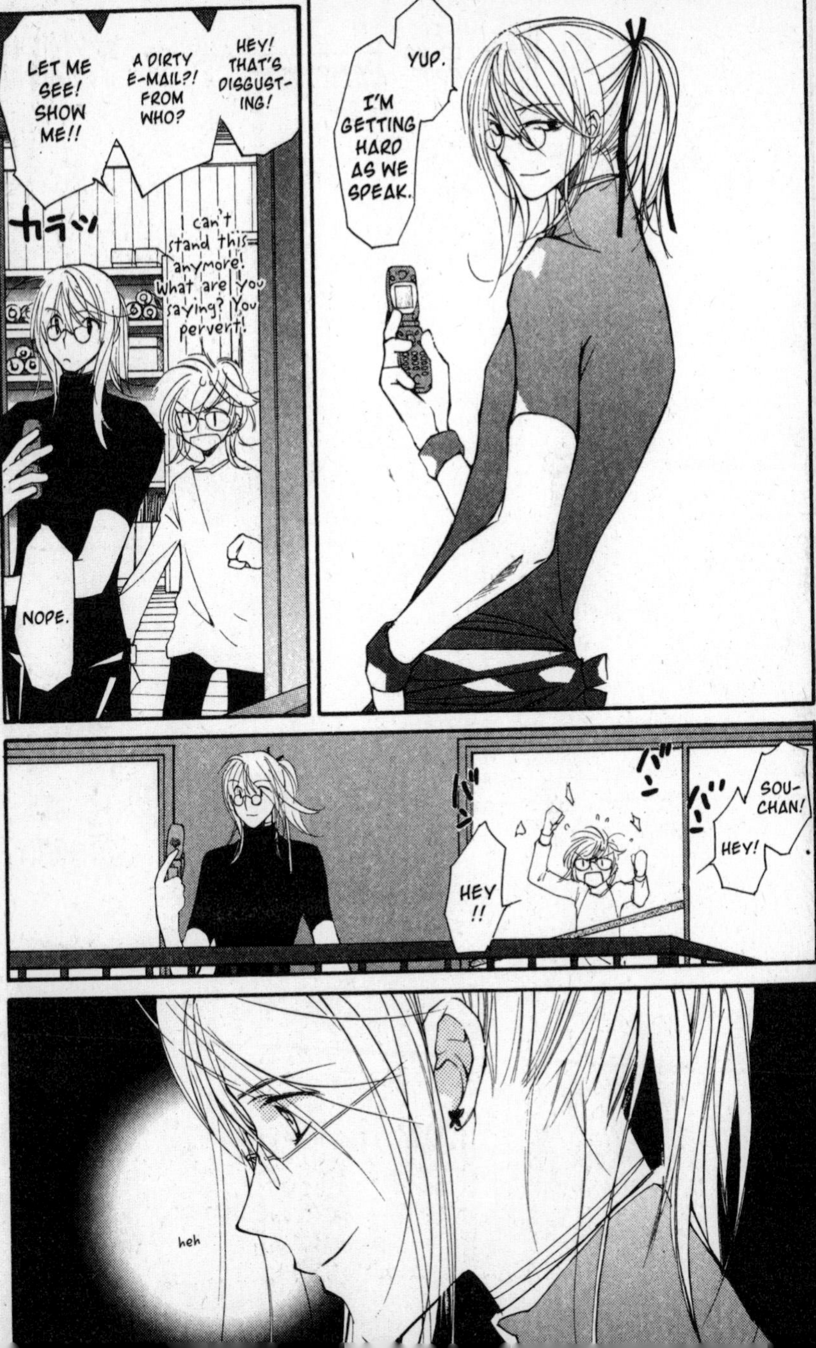
YUP.
I'M GETTING HARD AS WE SPEAK.
HEY! THAT'S DISGUSTING!
A DIRTY E-MAIL?! FROM WHO?
LET ME SEE! SHOW ME!!
カラッ
I can't stand this anymore! What are you saying? You pervert!
NOPE.
SOU-CHAN!
HEY!
HEY !!
heh

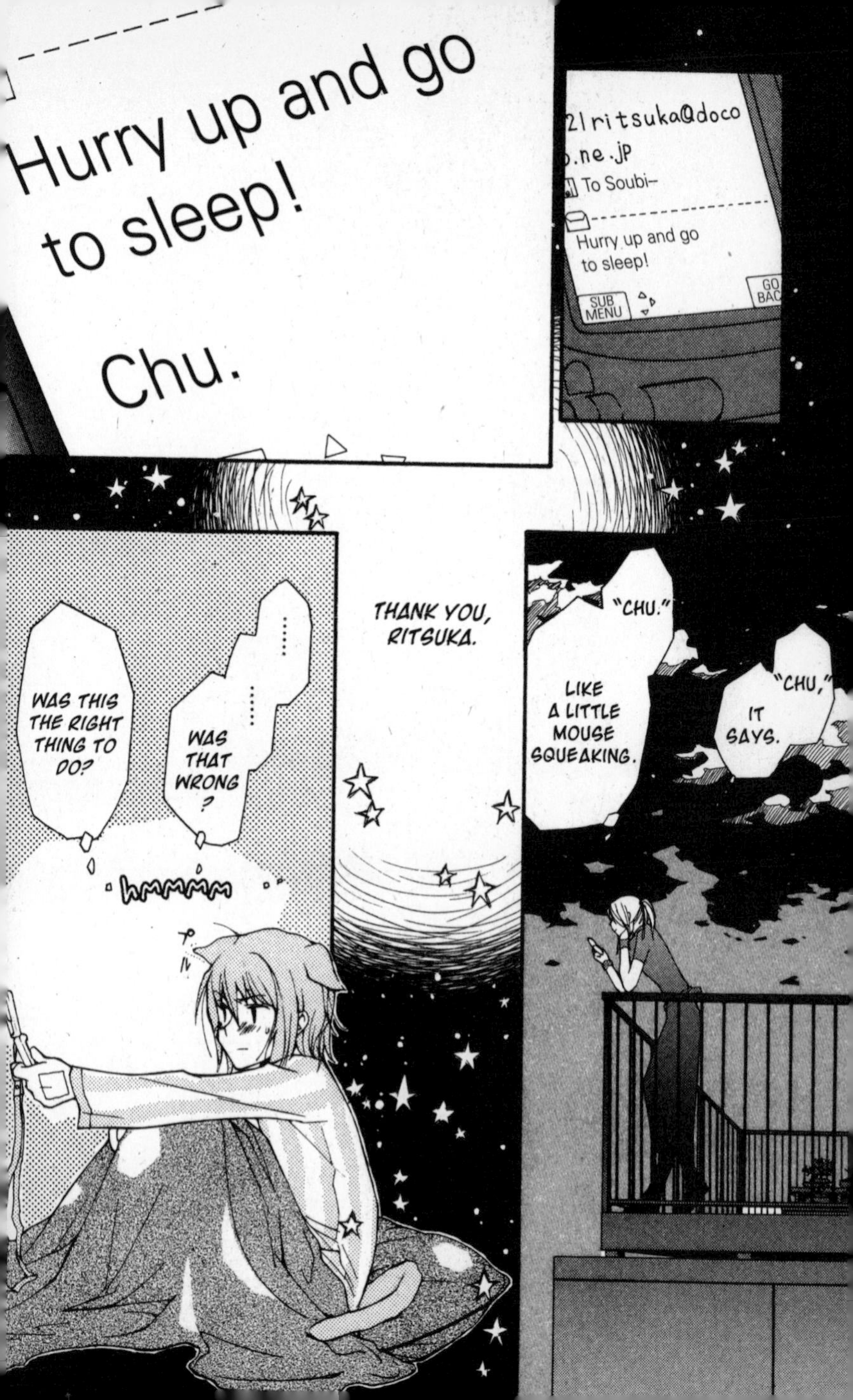
21ritsuka@doco
.ne.jp
To Soubi–
Hurry up and go to sleep!
SUB MENU
GO BAC
Hurry up and go to sleep!
Chu.
"CHU," IT SAYS.
"CHU." LIKE A LITTLE MOUSE SQUEAKING.
THANK YOU, RITSUKA.
......
WAS THAT WRONG?
WAS THIS THE RIGHT THING TO DO?
hmmmm

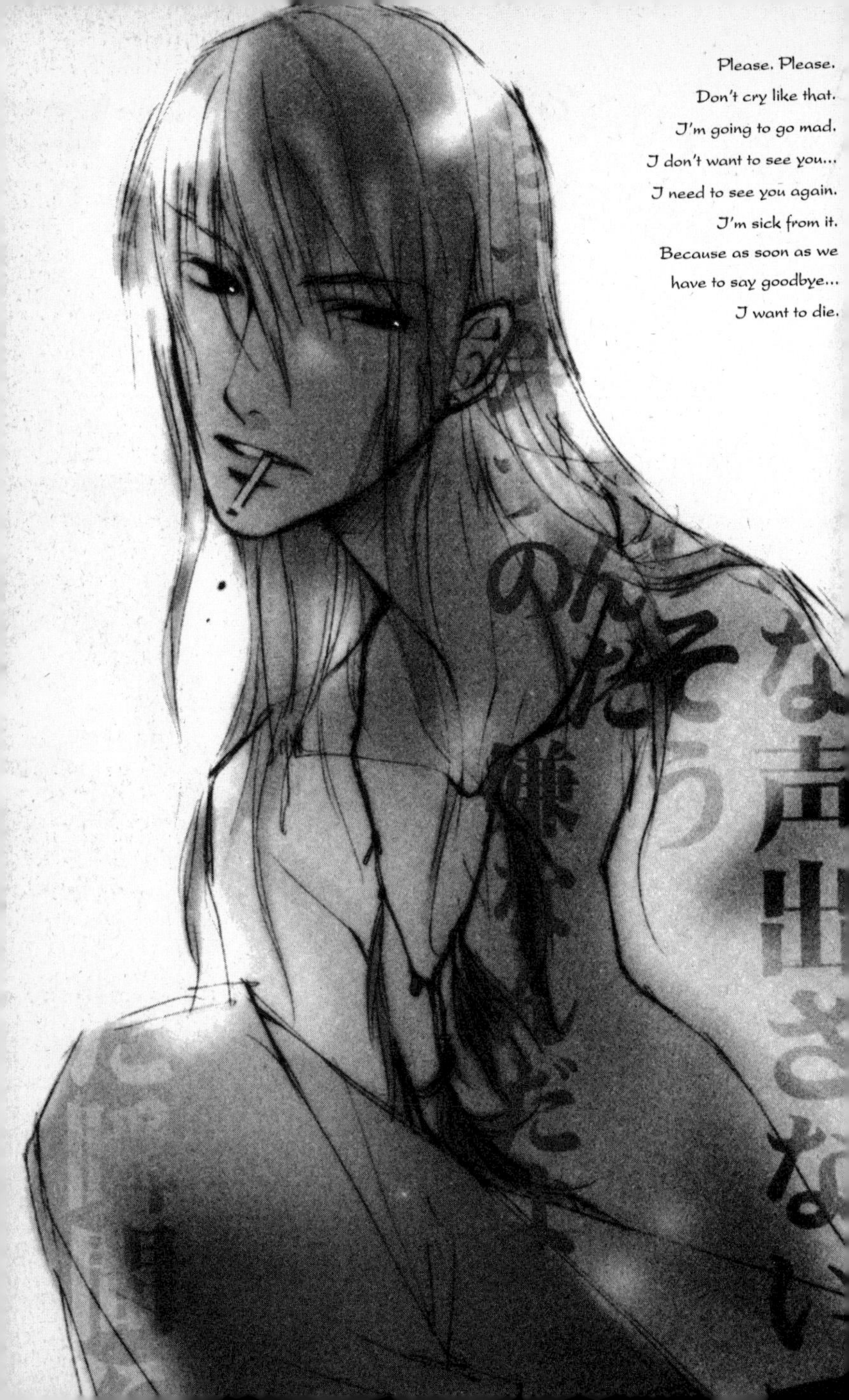
Please. Please.
Don't cry like that.
I'm going to go mad.
I don't want to see you...
I need to see you again.
I'm sick from it.
Because as soon as we
have to say goodbye...
I want to die.

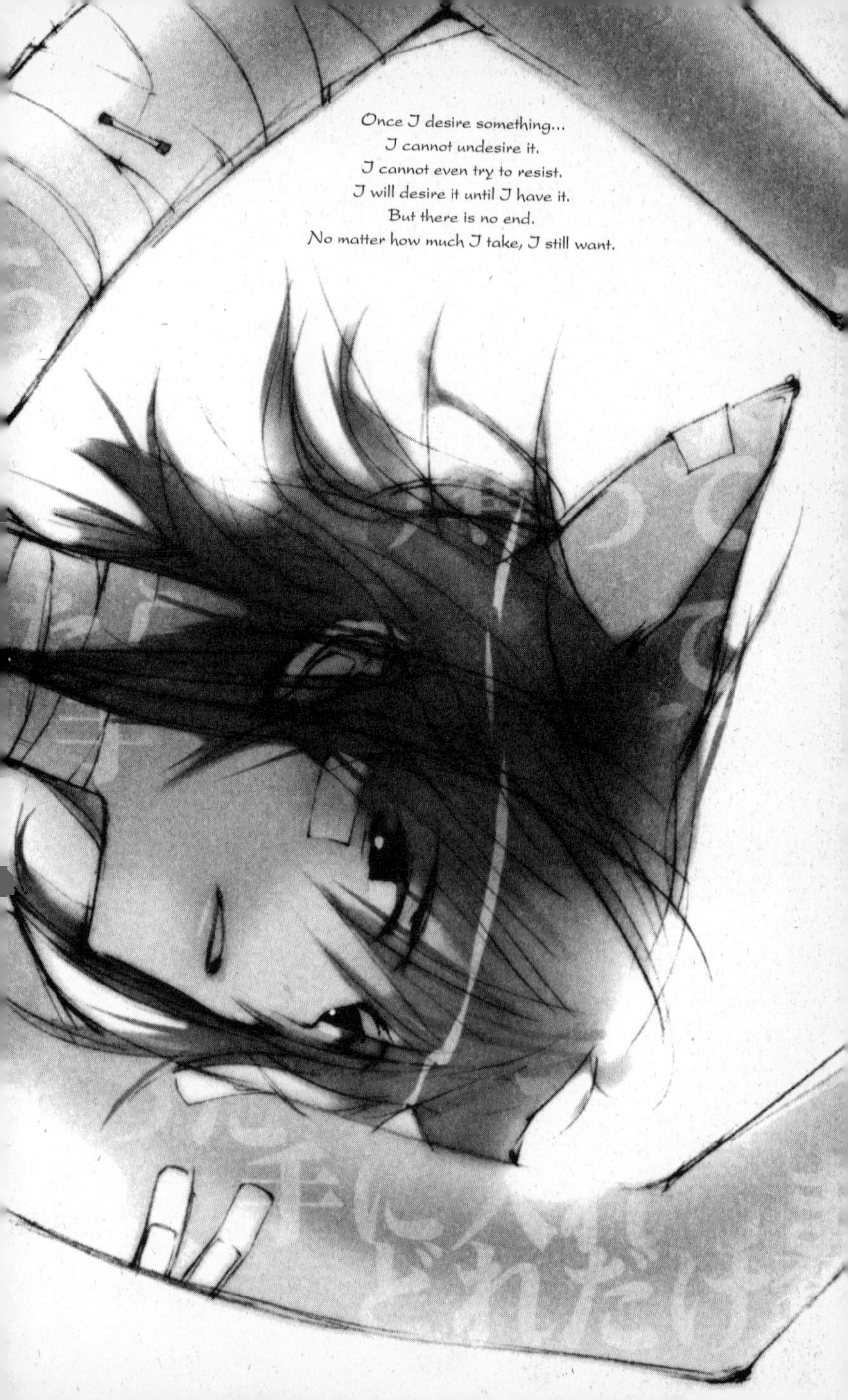
Once I desire something...
I cannot undesire it.
I cannot even try to resist.
I will desire it until I have it.
But there is no end.
No matter how much I take, I still want.

LOVELESS
YUN KOUGA
NO:04

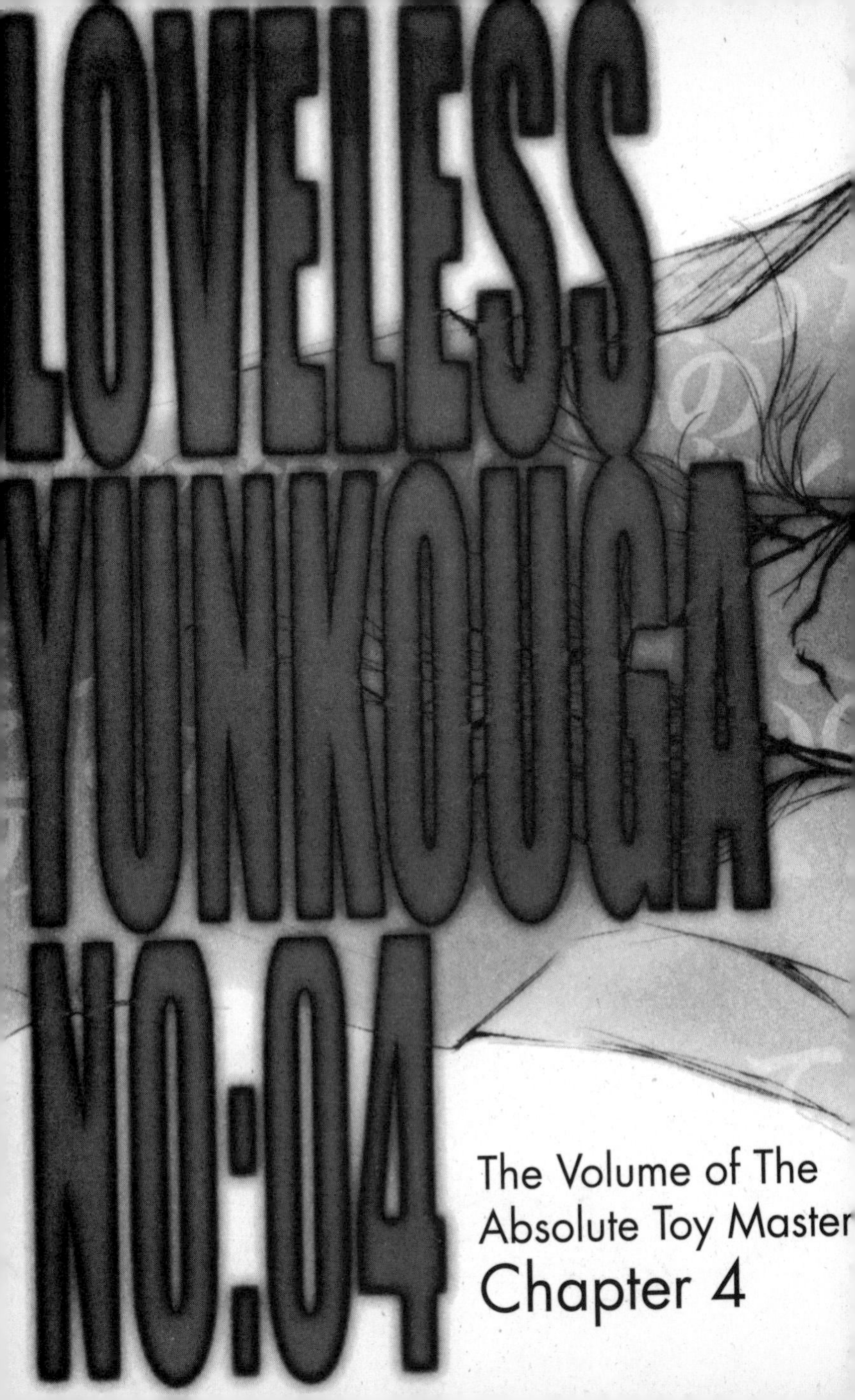

The Volume of The Absolute Toy Master
Chapter 4

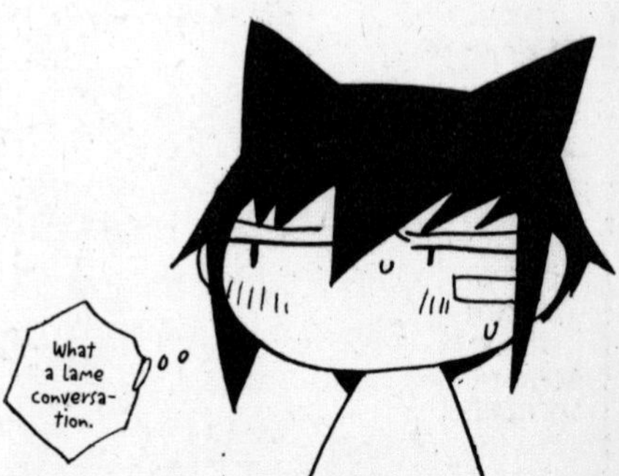
What a lame conversa-tion.

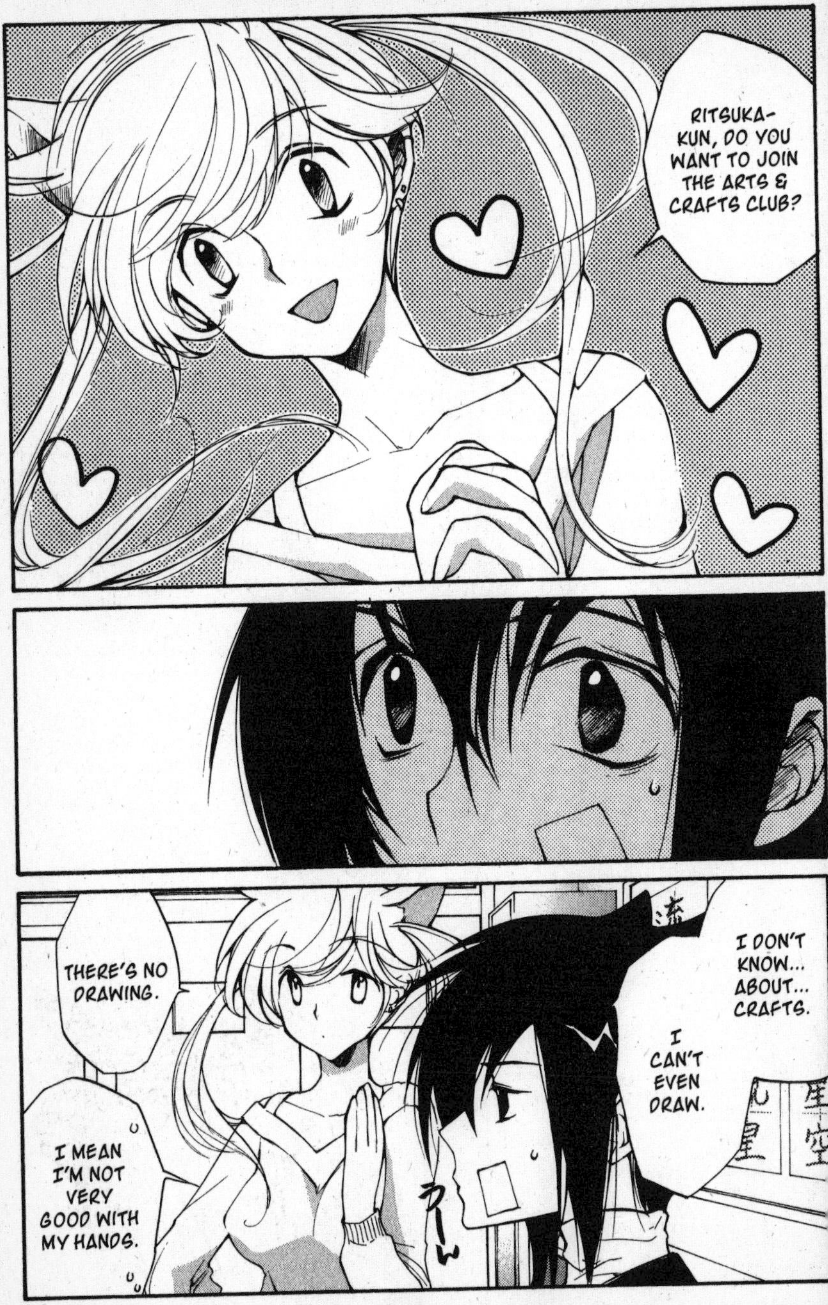
RITSUKA-KUN, DO YOU WANT TO JOIN THE ARTS & CRAFTS CLUB?
I DON'T KNOW... ABOUT... CRAFTS.
I CAN'T EVEN DRAW.
THERE'S NO DRAWING.
I MEAN I'M NOT VERY GOOD WITH MY HANDS.

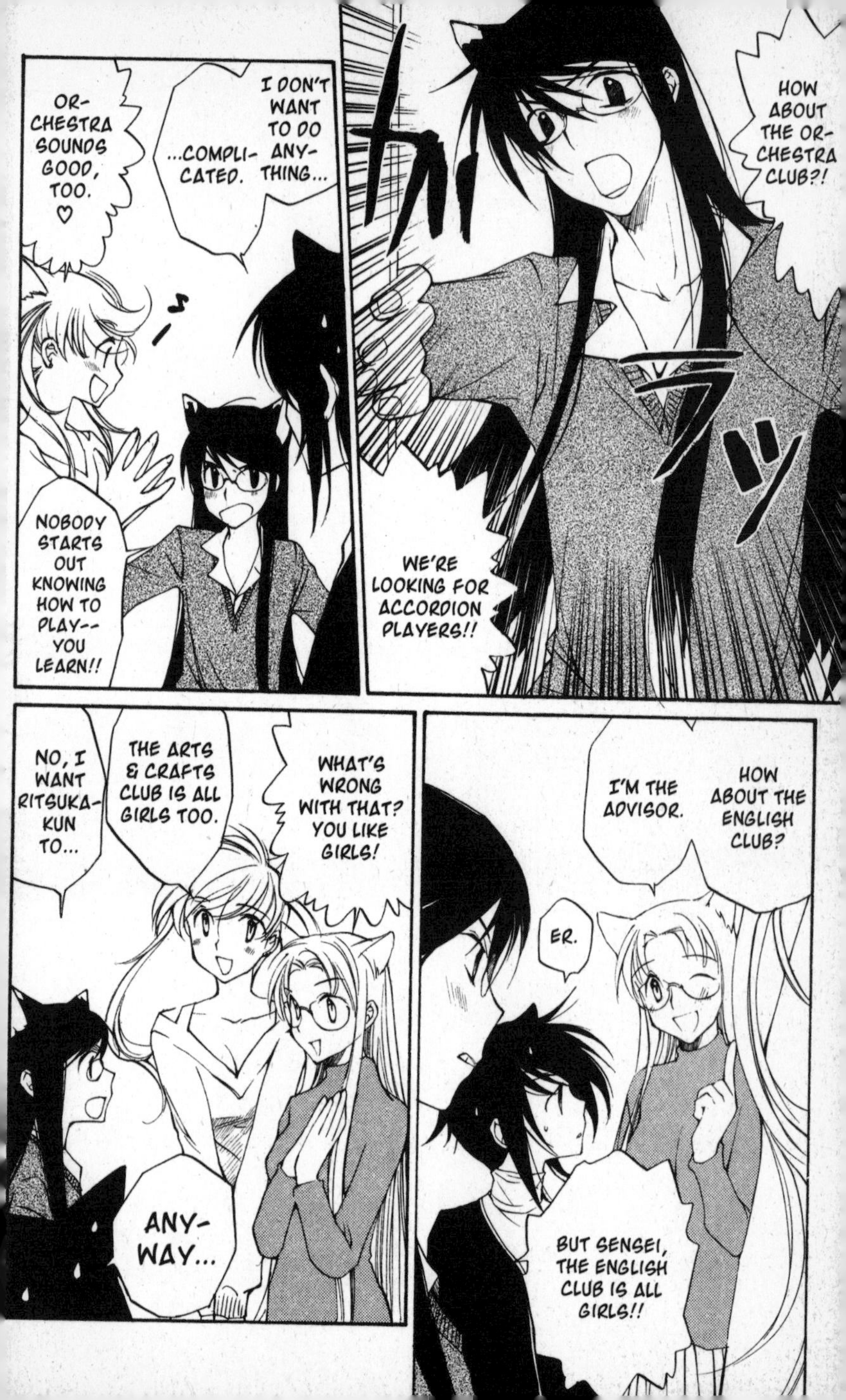
HOW ABOUT THE ORCHESTRA CLUB?!
WE'RE LOOKING FOR ACCORDION PLAYERS!!
I DON'T WANT TO DO ANYTHING...
...COMPLICATED.
ORCHESTRA SOUNDS GOOD, TOO. ♡
NOBODY STARTS OUT KNOWING HOW TO PLAY--YOU LEARN!!
HOW ABOUT THE ENGLISH CLUB?
I'M THE ADVISOR.
ER.
BUT SENSEI, THE ENGLISH CLUB IS ALL GIRLS!!
WHAT'S WRONG WITH THAT? YOU LIKE GIRLS!
THE ARTS & CRAFTS CLUB IS ALL GIRLS TOO.
NO, I WANT RITSUKA-KUN TO...
ANYWAY...

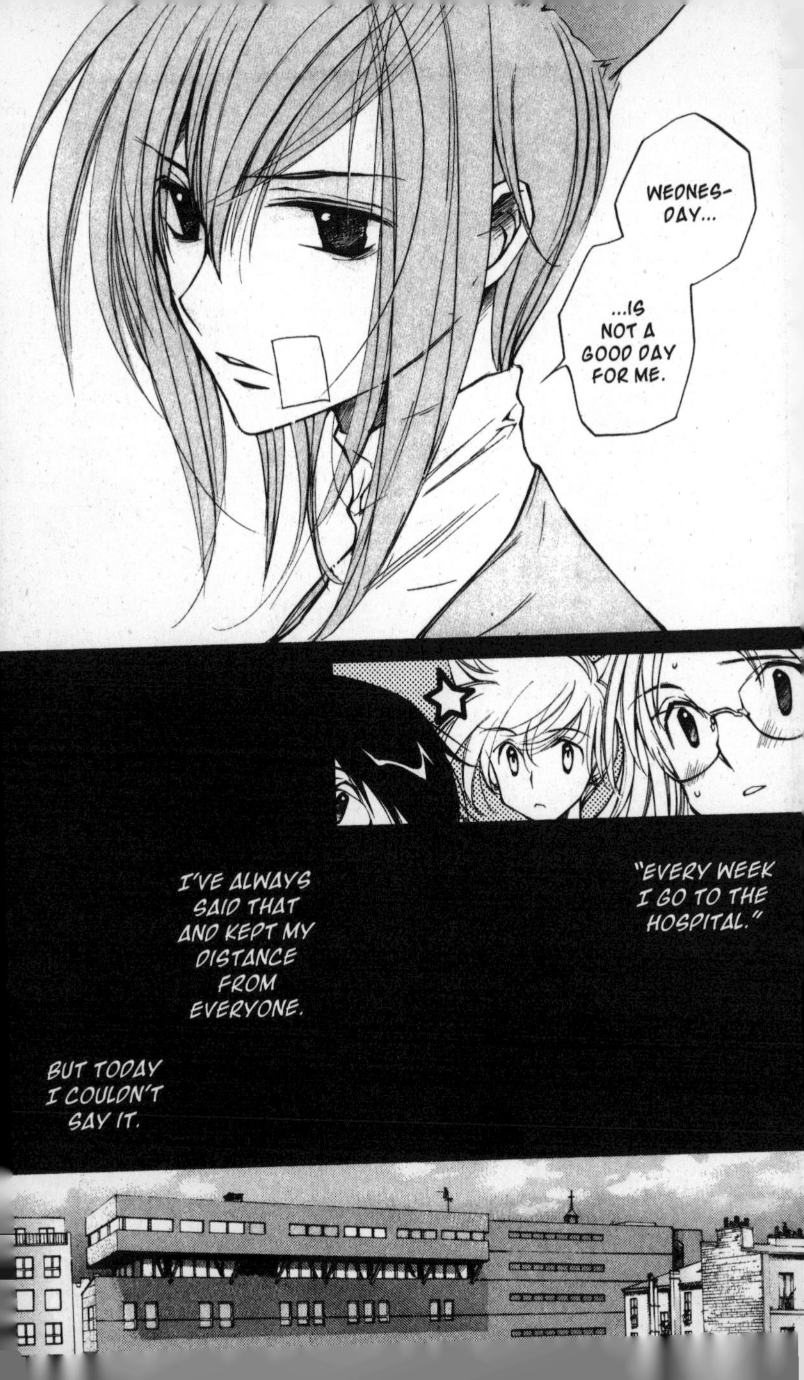
WEDNES-DAY...
...IS NOT A GOOD DAY FOR ME.
"EVERY WEEK I GO TO THE HOSPITAL."
I'VE ALWAYS SAID THAT AND KEPT MY DISTANCE FROM EVERYONE.
BUT TODAY I COULDN'T SAY IT.

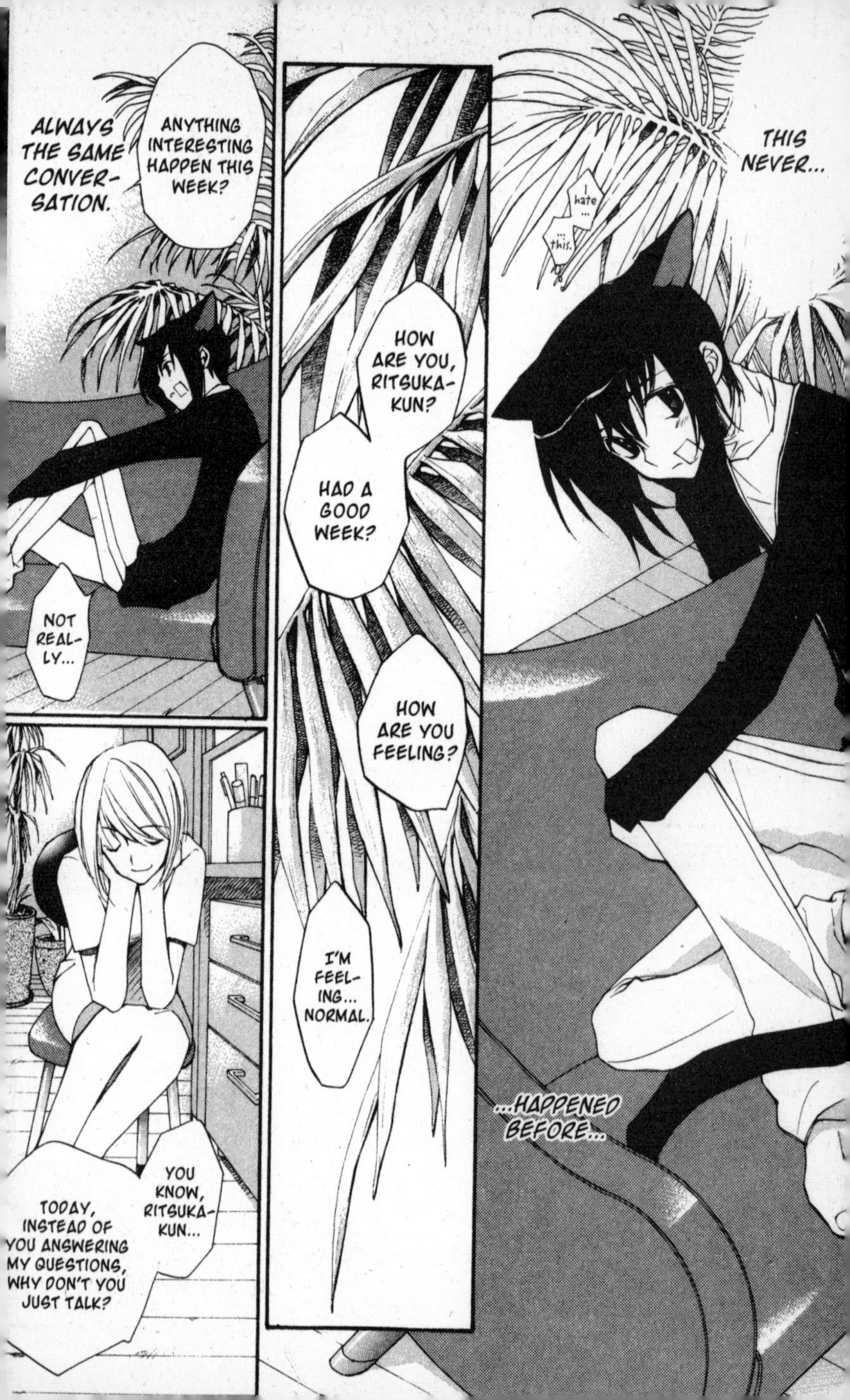
THIS NEVER...
I hate... ...this.
...HAPPENED BEFORE...
HOW ARE YOU, RITSUKA-KUN?
HAD A GOOD WEEK?
HOW ARE YOU FEELING?
I'M FEELING... NORMAL.
ANYTHING INTERESTING HAPPEN THIS WEEK?
ALWAYS THE SAME CONVERSATION.
NOT REALLY...
YOU KNOW, RITSUKA-KUN...
TODAY, INSTEAD OF YOU ANSWERING MY QUESTIONS, WHY DON'T YOU JUST TALK?

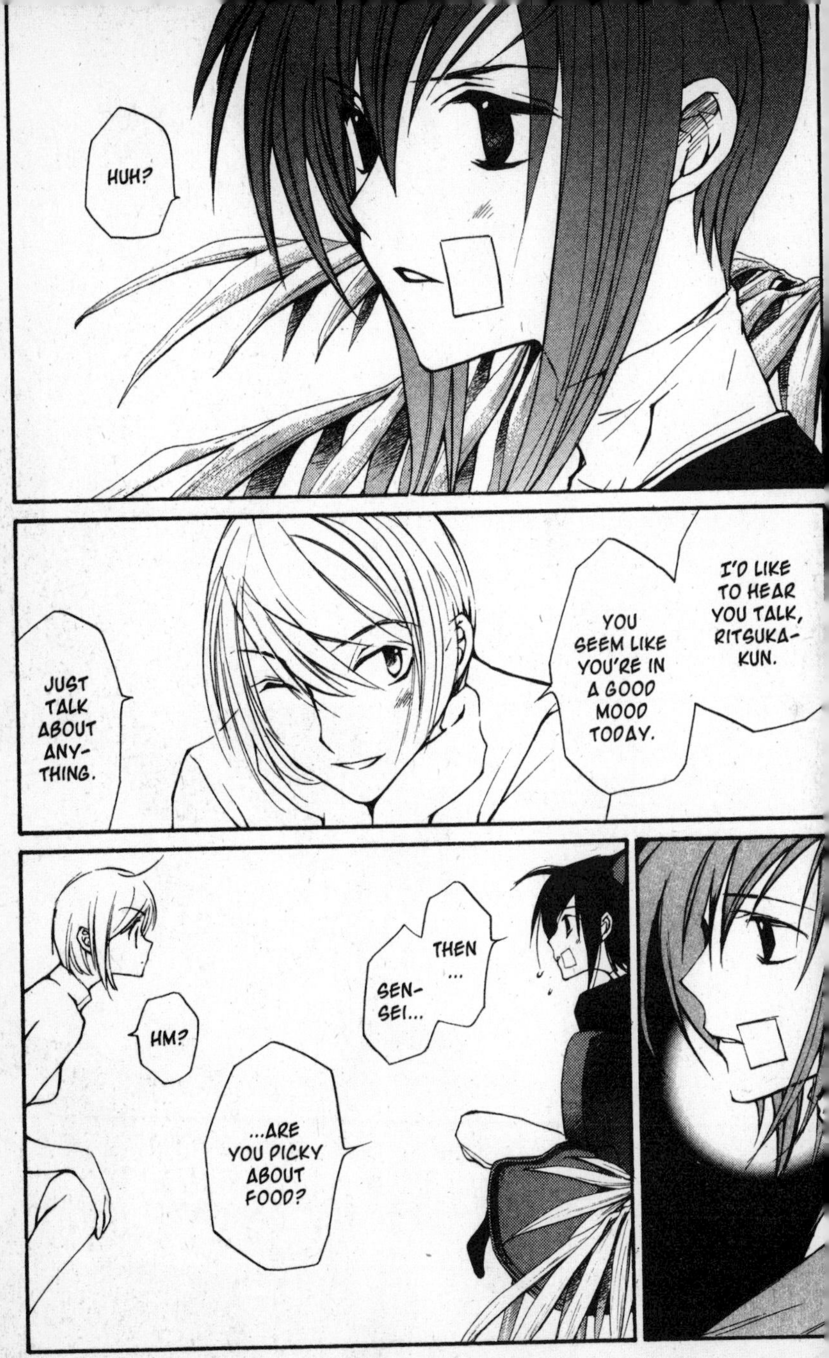
HUH?
I'D LIKE TO HEAR YOU TALK, RITSUKA-KUN.
YOU SEEM LIKE YOU'RE IN A GOOD MOOD TODAY.
JUST TALK ABOUT ANY-THING.
THEN...
SEN-SEI...
HM?
...ARE YOU PICKY ABOUT FOOD?

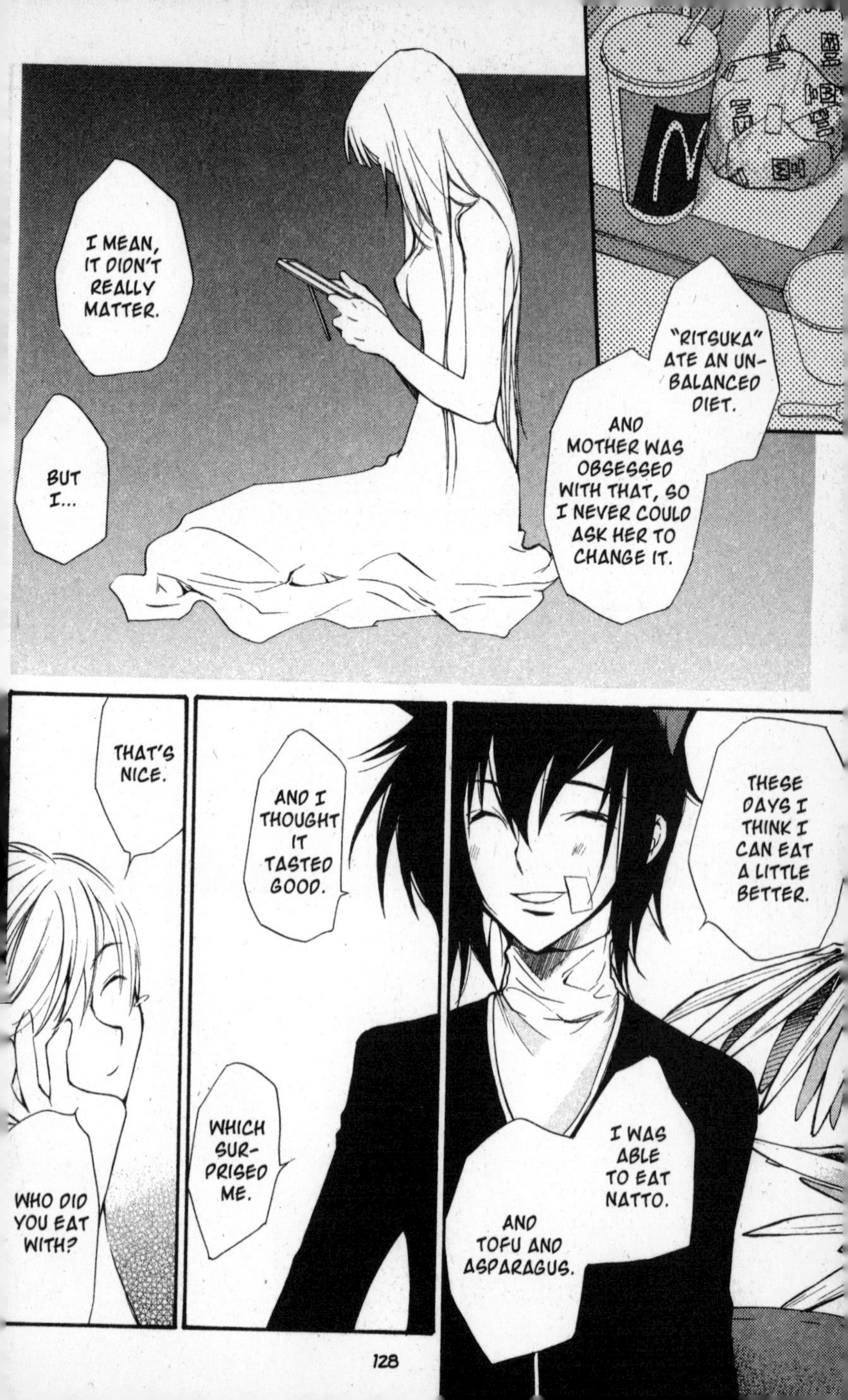
"RITSUKA" ATE AN UN-BALANCED DIET.
AND MOTHER WAS OBSESSED WITH THAT, SO I NEVER COULD ASK HER TO CHANGE IT.
I MEAN, IT DIDN'T REALLY MATTER.
BUT I...
THESE DAYS I THINK I CAN EAT A LITTLE BETTER.
I WAS ABLE TO EAT NATTO.
AND TOFU AND ASPARAGUS.
AND I THOUGHT IT TASTED GOOD.
WHICH SUR-PRISED ME.
THAT'S NICE.
WHO DID YOU EAT WITH?

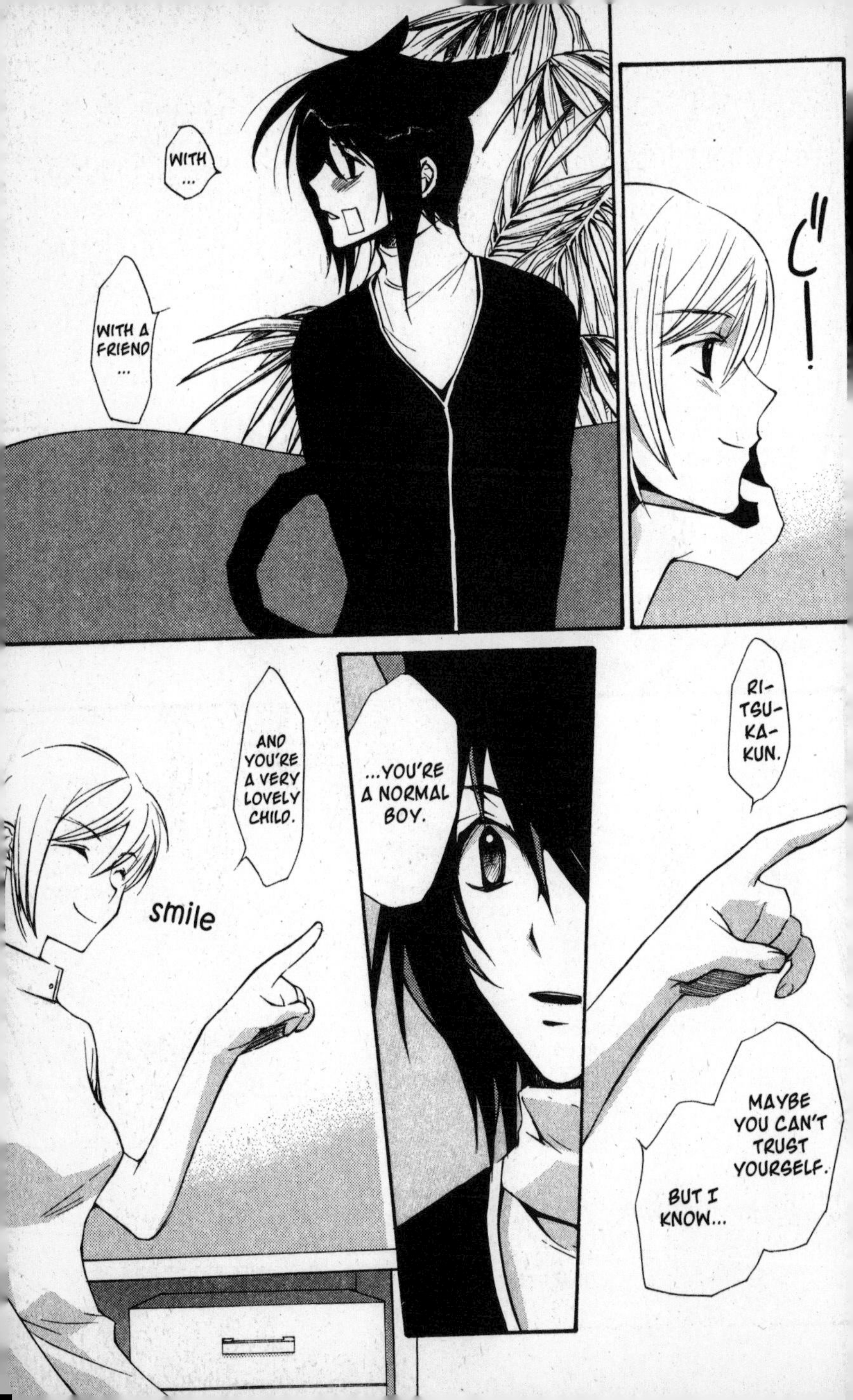

じー!
WITH ...
WITH A FRIEND ...
RI-TSU-KA-KUN.
MAYBE YOU CAN'T TRUST YOURSELF.
BUT I KNOW...
...YOU'RE A NORMAL BOY.
AND YOU'RE A VERY LOVELY CHILD.
smile

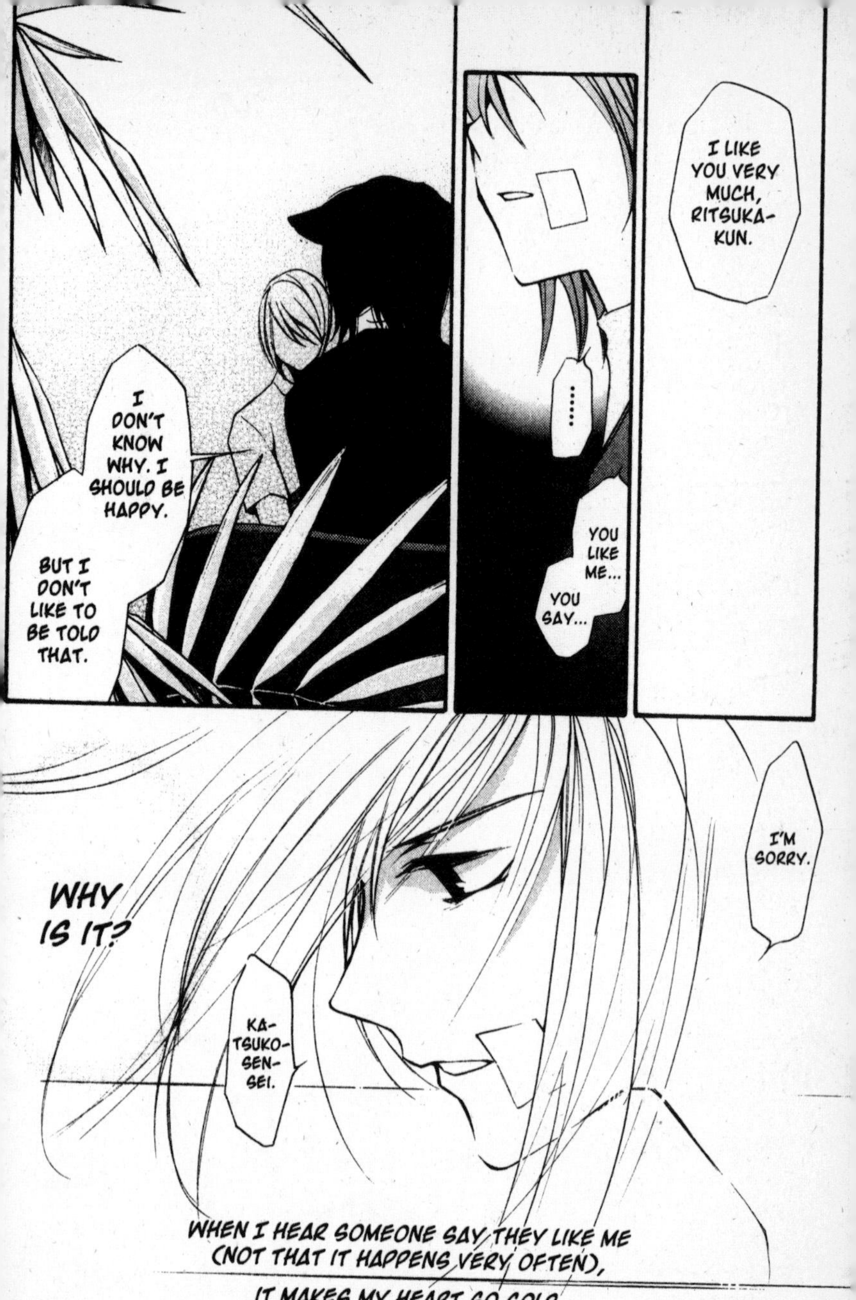
I LIKE YOU VERY MUCH, RITSUKA-KUN.
......
YOU LIKE ME... YOU SAY...
I DON'T KNOW WHY. I SHOULD BE HAPPY.
BUT I DON'T LIKE TO BE TOLD THAT.
I'M SORRY.
KA-TSUKO-SEN-SEI.
WHY IS IT?
WHEN I HEAR SOMEONE SAY THEY LIKE ME (NOT THAT IT HAPPENS VERY OFTEN),
IT MAKES MY HEART GO COLD.

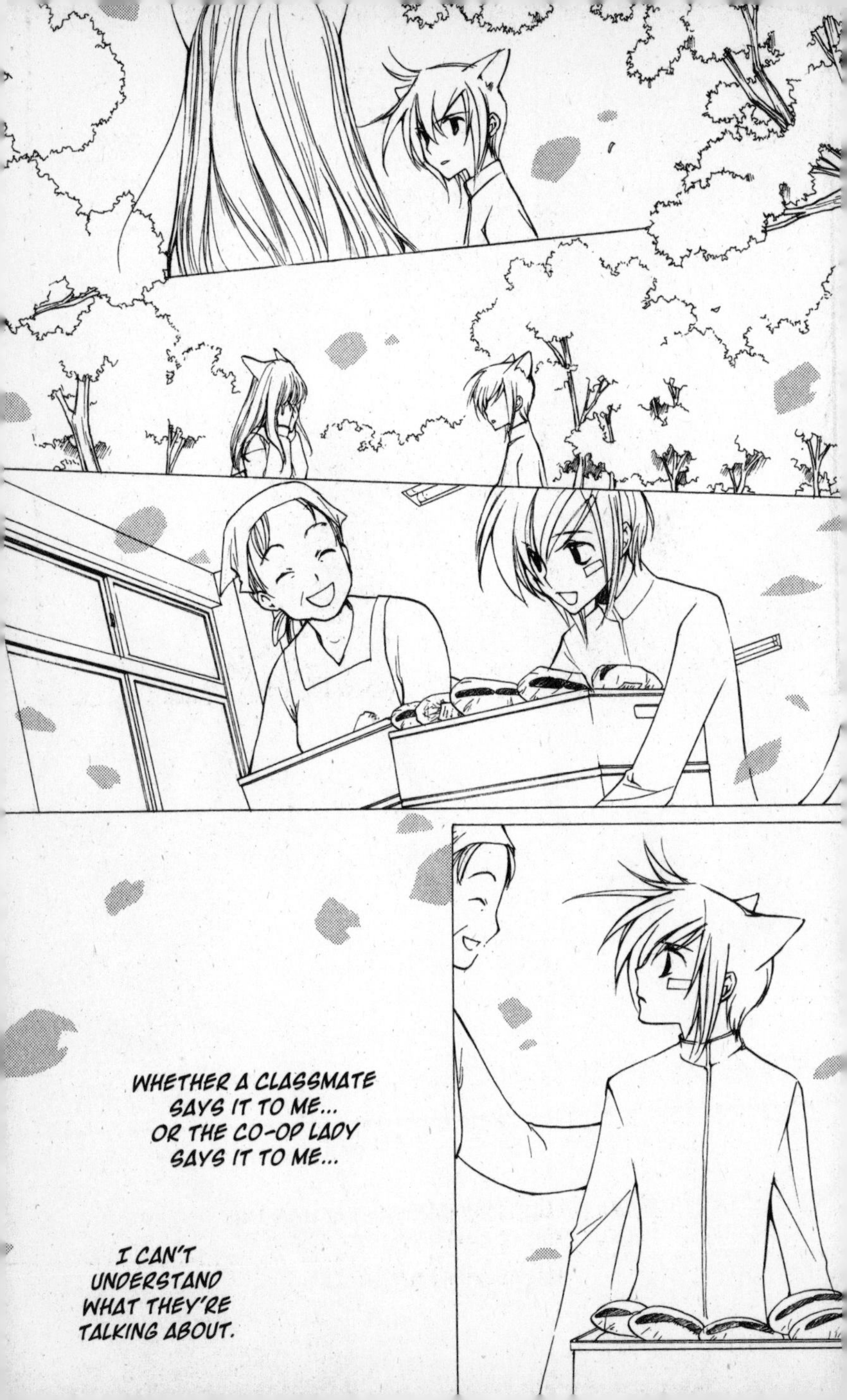
WHETHER A CLASSMATE SAYS IT TO ME... OR THE CO-OP LADY SAYS IT TO ME...
I CAN'T UNDERSTAND WHAT THEY'RE TALKING ABOUT.

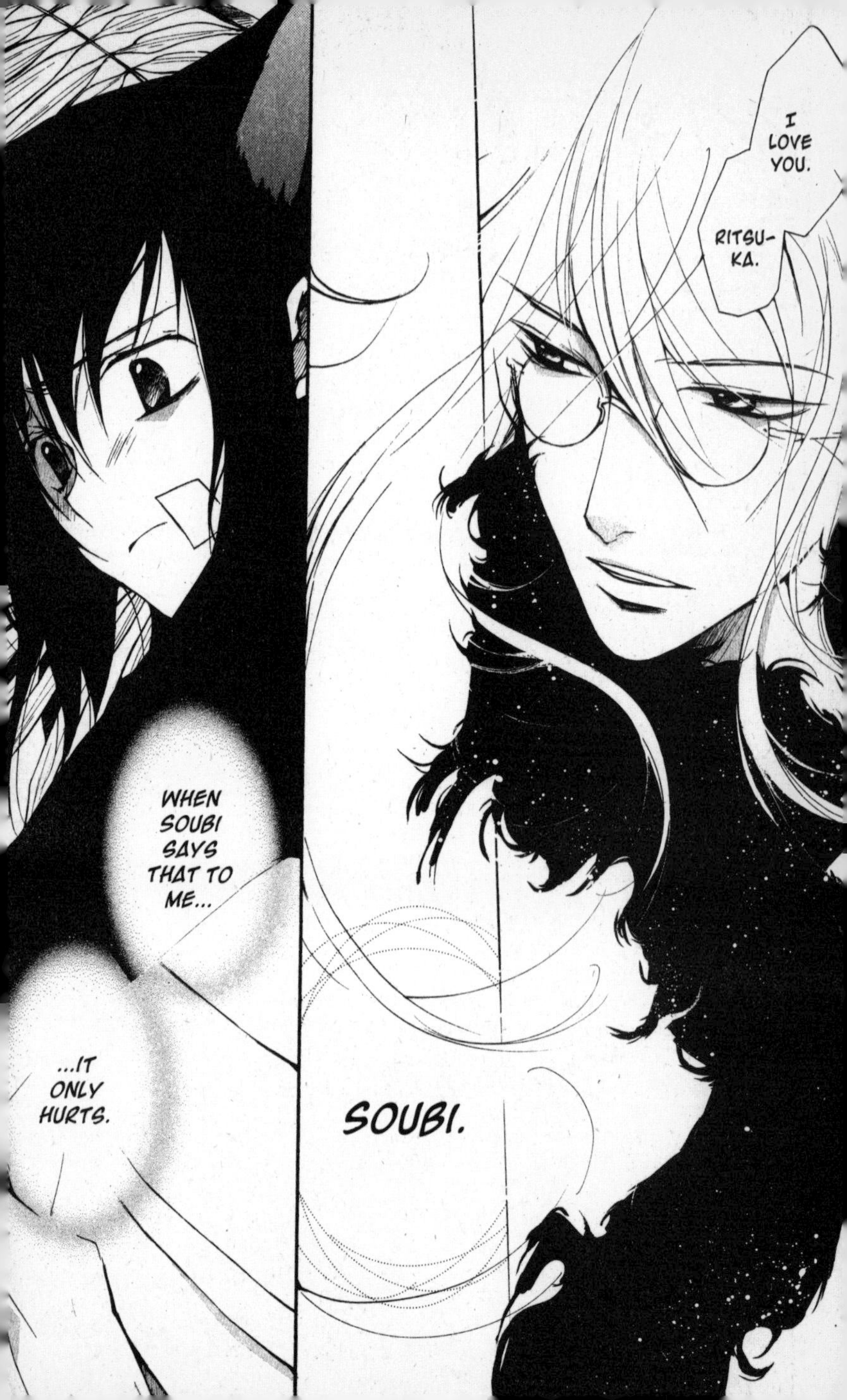
I LOVE YOU.
RITSU-KA.
SOUBI.
WHEN SOUBI SAYS THAT TO ME...
...IT ONLY HURTS.

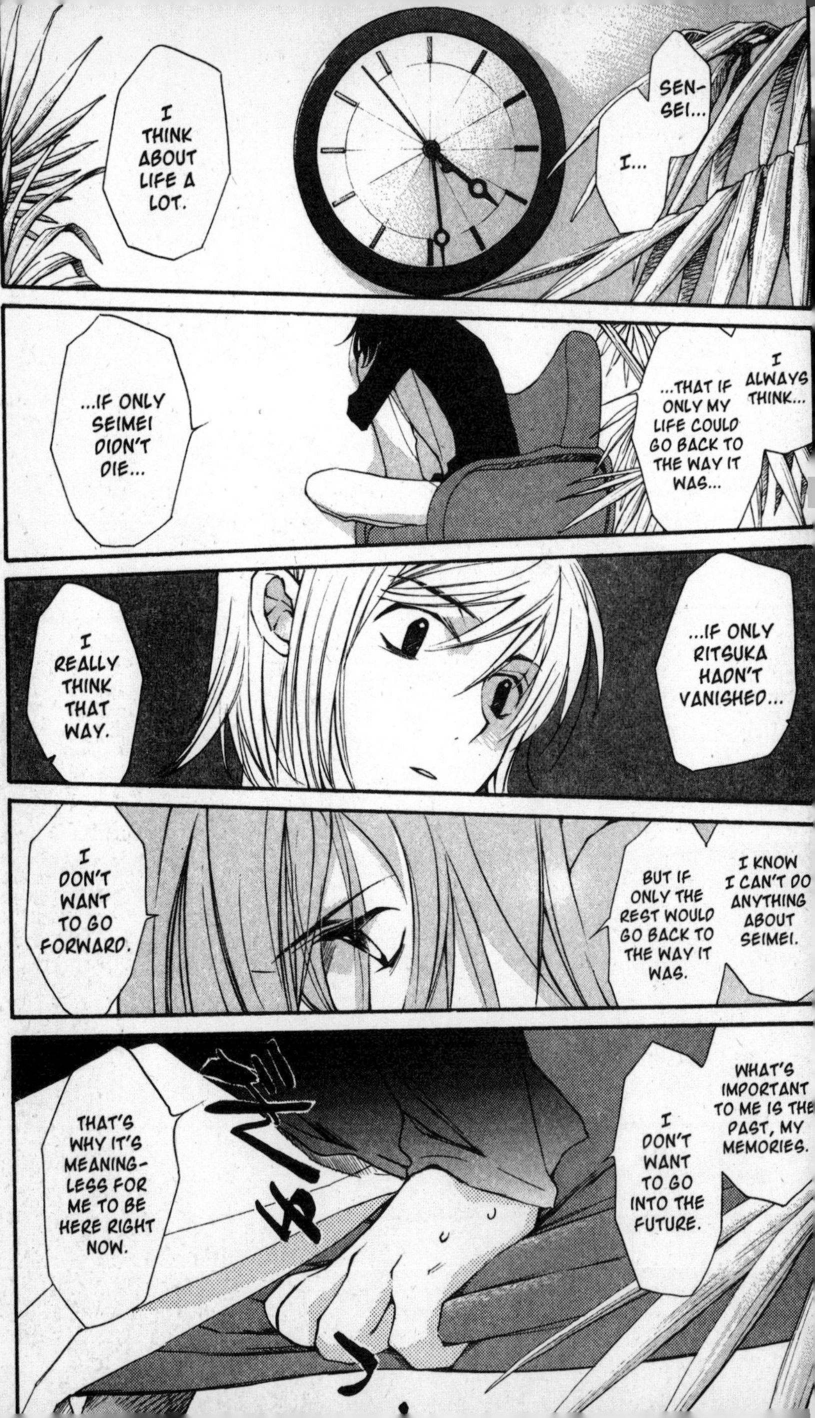
SEN-SEI...
I...
I THINK ABOUT LIFE A LOT.
I ALWAYS THINK...
...THAT IF ONLY MY LIFE COULD GO BACK TO THE WAY IT WAS...
...IF ONLY SEIMEI DIDN'T DIE...
...IF ONLY RITSUKA HADN'T VANISHED...
I REALLY THINK THAT WAY.
I KNOW I CAN'T DO ANYTHING ABOUT SEIMEI.
BUT IF ONLY THE REST WOULD GO BACK TO THE WAY IT WAS.
I DON'T WANT TO GO FORWARD.
WHAT'S IMPORTANT TO ME IS THE PAST, MY MEMORIES.
I DON'T WANT TO GO INTO THE FUTURE.
THAT'S WHY IT'S MEANING-LESS FOR ME TO BE HERE RIGHT NOW.

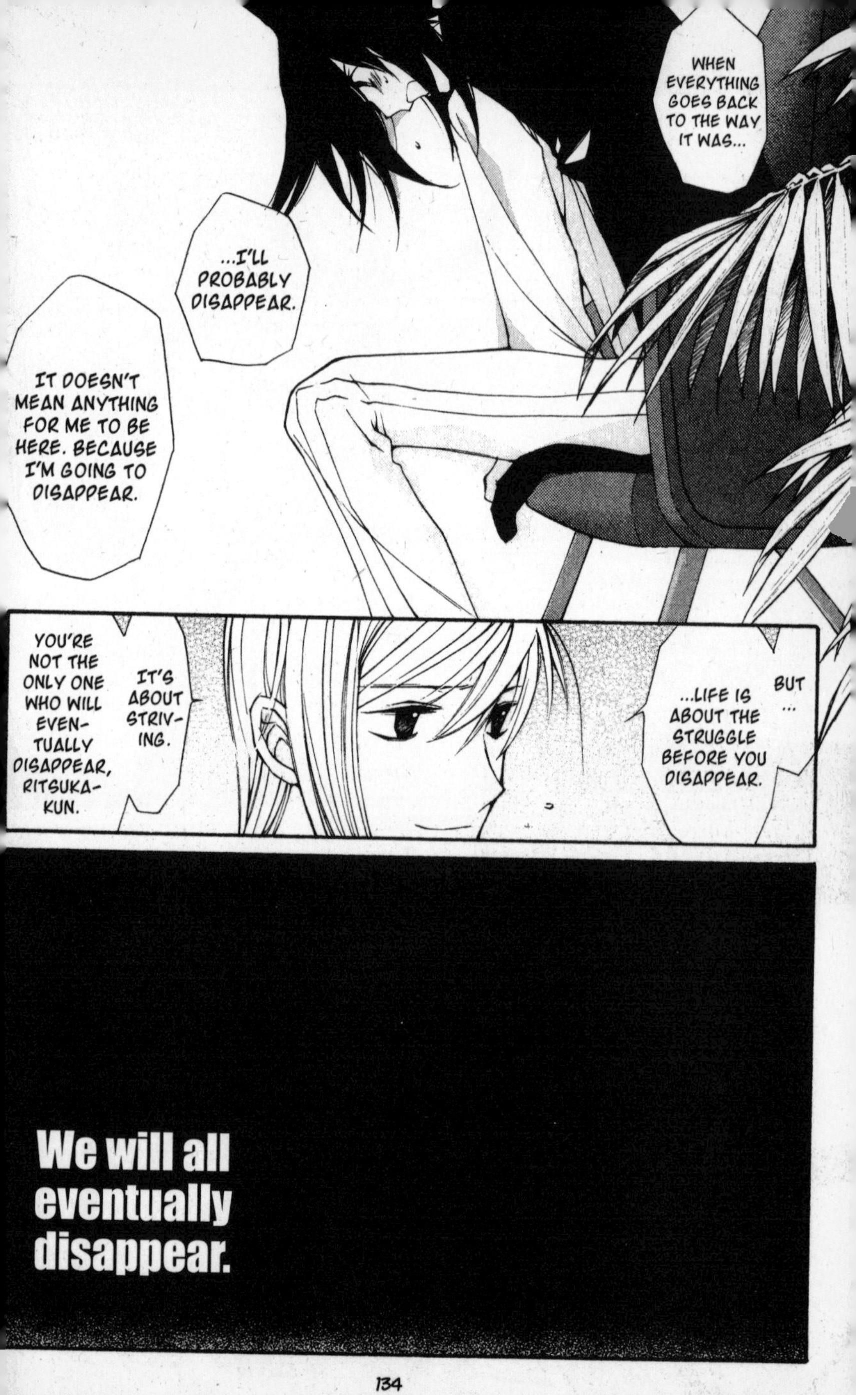
WHEN EVERYTHING GOES BACK TO THE WAY IT WAS...
...I'LL PROBABLY DISAPPEAR.
IT DOESN'T MEAN ANYTHING FOR ME TO BE HERE. BECAUSE I'M GOING TO DISAPPEAR.
BUT ...
...LIFE IS ABOUT THE STRUGGLE BEFORE YOU DISAPPEAR.
IT'S ABOUT STRIV-ING.
YOU'RE NOT THE ONLY ONE WHO WILL EVEN-TUALLY DISAPPEAR, RITSUKA-KUN.
We will all eventually disappear.

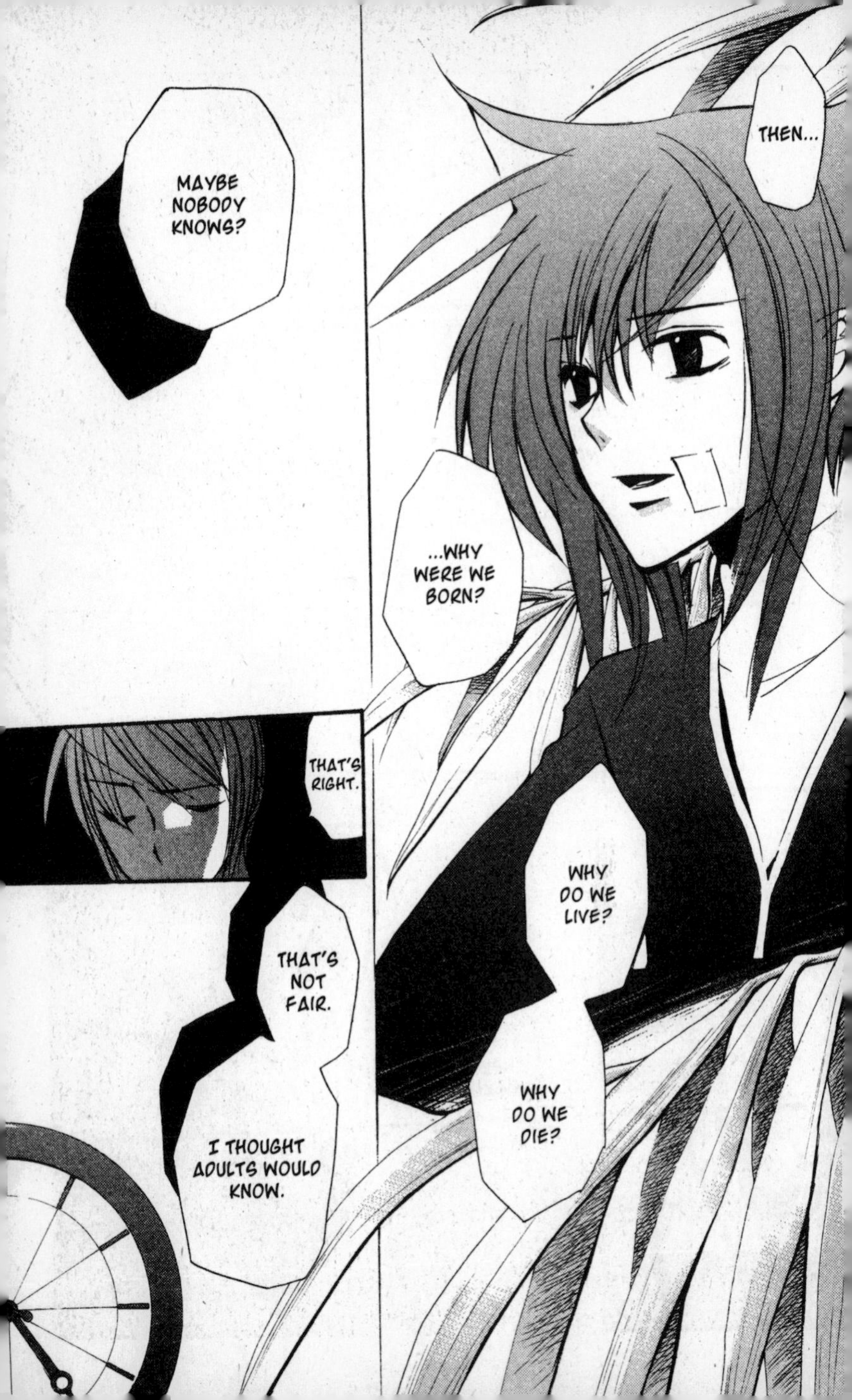
THEN...
...WHY WERE WE BORN?
WHY DO WE LIVE?
WHY DO WE DIE?
MAYBE NOBODY KNOWS?
THAT'S RIGHT.
THAT'S NOT FAIR.
I THOUGHT ADULTS WOULD KNOW.

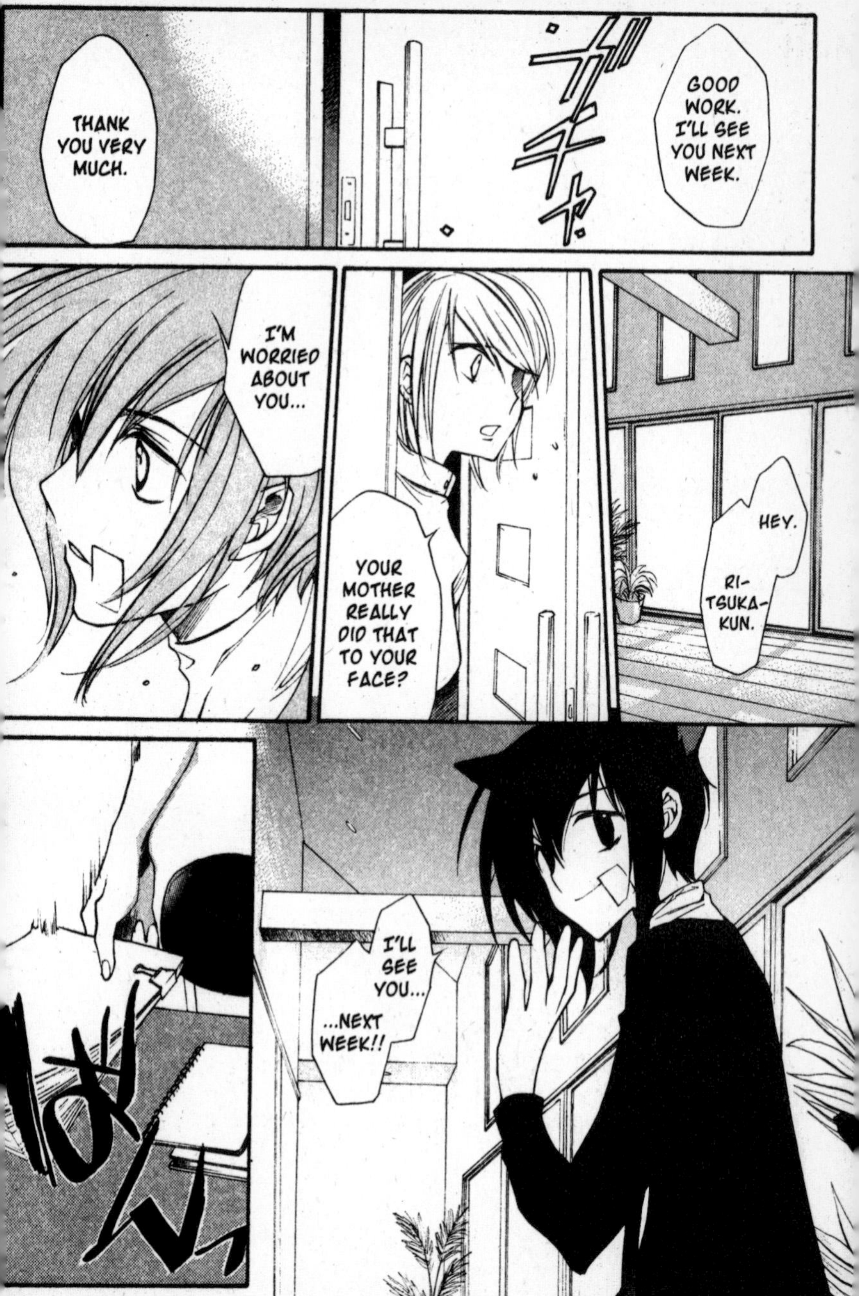
ガチャ
GOOD WORK. I'LL SEE YOU NEXT WEEK.
THANK YOU VERY MUCH.
HEY.
RI-TSUKA-KUN.
YOUR MOTHER REALLY DID THAT TO YOUR FACE?
I'M WORRIED ABOUT YOU...
I'LL SEE YOU...
...NEXT WEEK!!

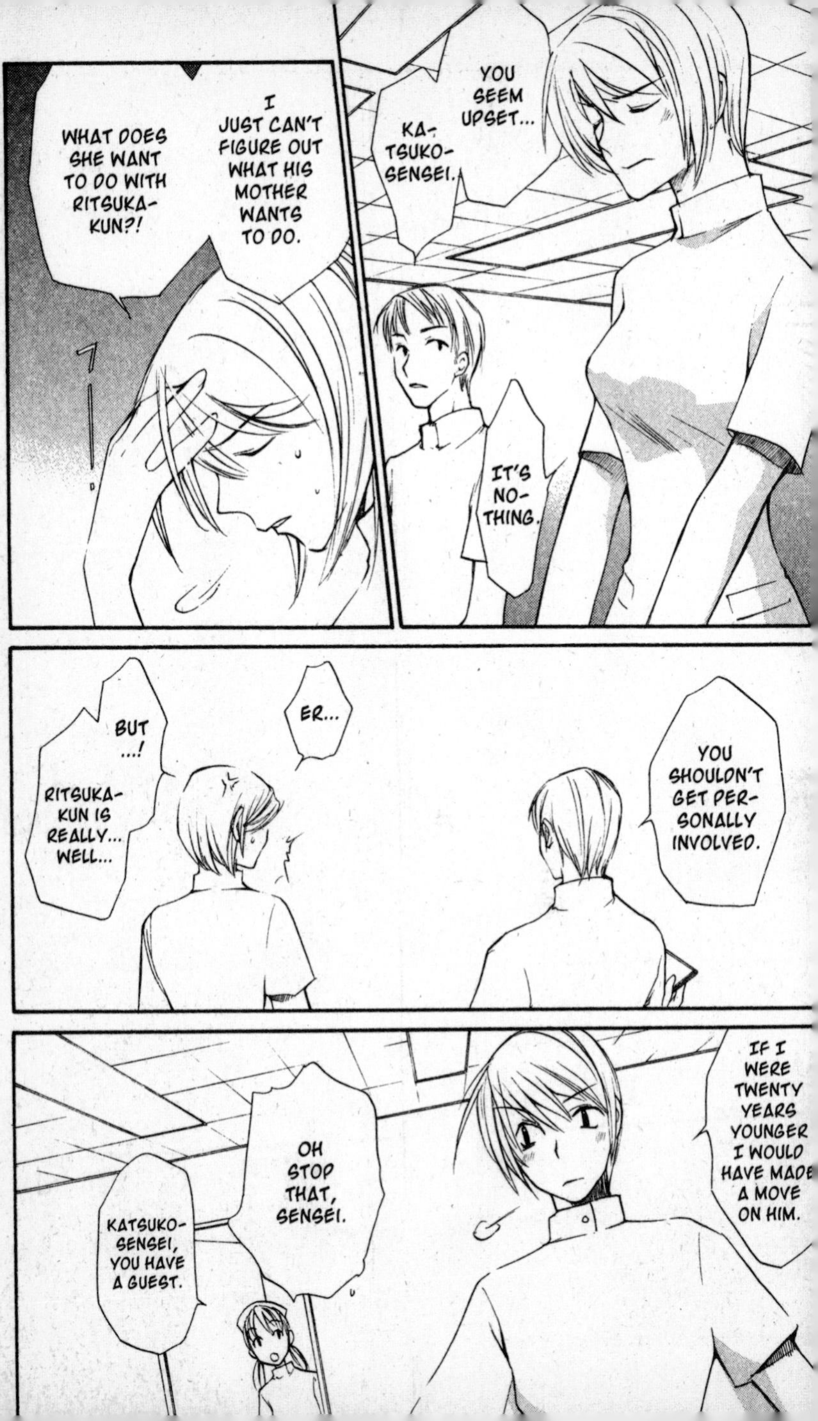
YOU SEEM UPSET...
KA-TSUKO-SENSEI.
IT'S NO-THING.
I JUST CAN'T FIGURE OUT WHAT HIS MOTHER WANTS TO DO.
WHAT DOES SHE WANT TO DO WITH RITSUKA-KUN?!
YOU SHOULDN'T GET PER-SONALLY INVOLVED.
ER...
BUT ...!
RITSUKA-KUN IS REALLY... WELL...
IF I WERE TWENTY YEARS YOUNGER I WOULD HAVE MADE A MOVE ON HIM.
OH STOP THAT, SENSEI.
KATSUKO-SENSEI, YOU HAVE A GUEST.

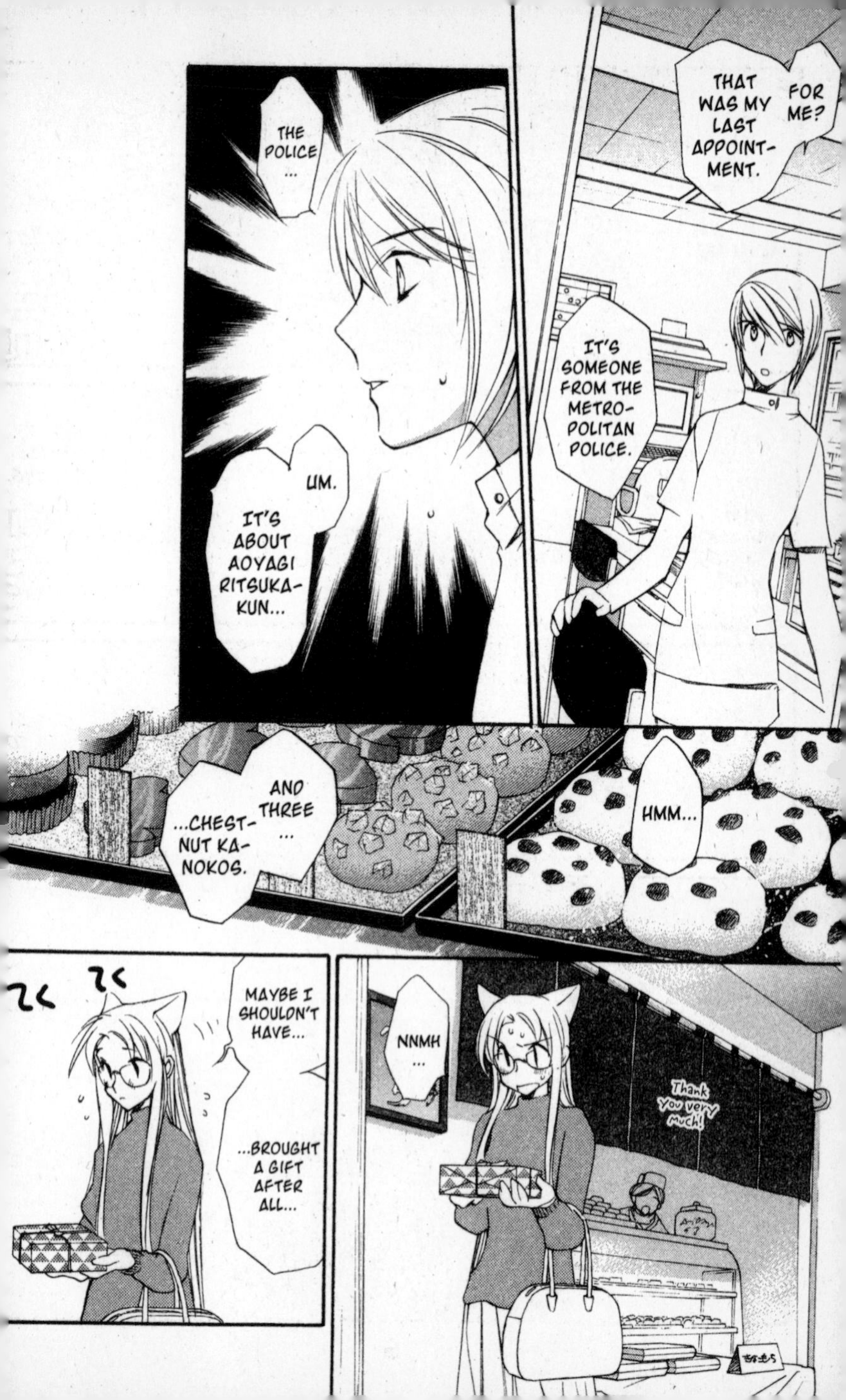
FOR ME?
THAT WAS MY LAST APPOINT-MENT.
IT'S SOMEONE FROM THE METRO-POLITAN POLICE.
THE POLICE ...
UM.
IT'S ABOUT AOYAGI RITSUKA-KUN...
HMM...
AND THREE ...
...CHEST-NUT KA-NOKOS.
NNMH ...
Thank you very much!
MAYBE I SHOULDN'T HAVE...
...BROUGHT A GIFT AFTER ALL...

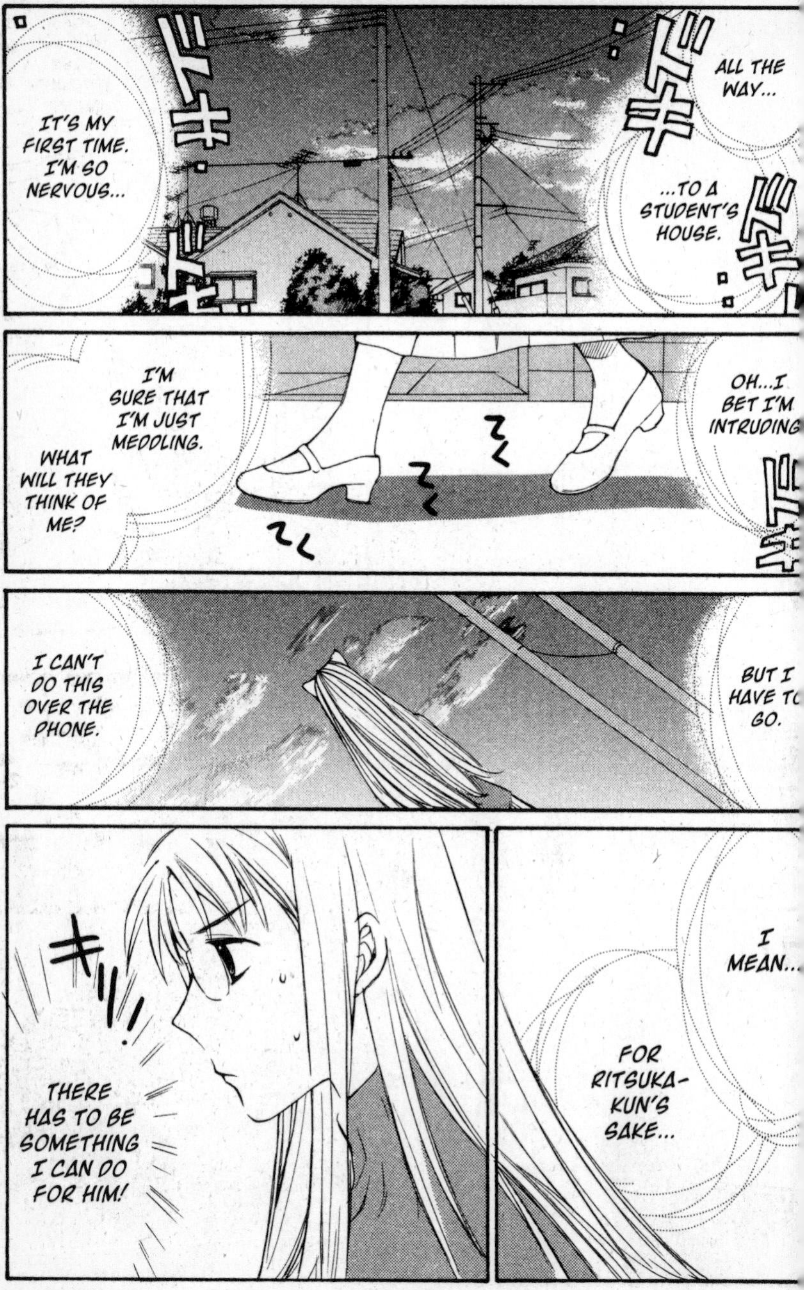
ALL THE WAY...
...TO A STUDENT'S HOUSE.
IT'S MY FIRST TIME. I'M SO NERVOUS...
OH...I BET I'M INTRUDING
I'M SURE THAT I'M JUST MEDDLING.
WHAT WILL THEY THINK OF ME?
BUT I HAVE TO GO.
I CAN'T DO THIS OVER THE PHONE.
I MEAN...
FOR RITSUKA-KUN'S SAKE...
THERE HAS TO BE SOMETHING I CAN DO FOR HIM!

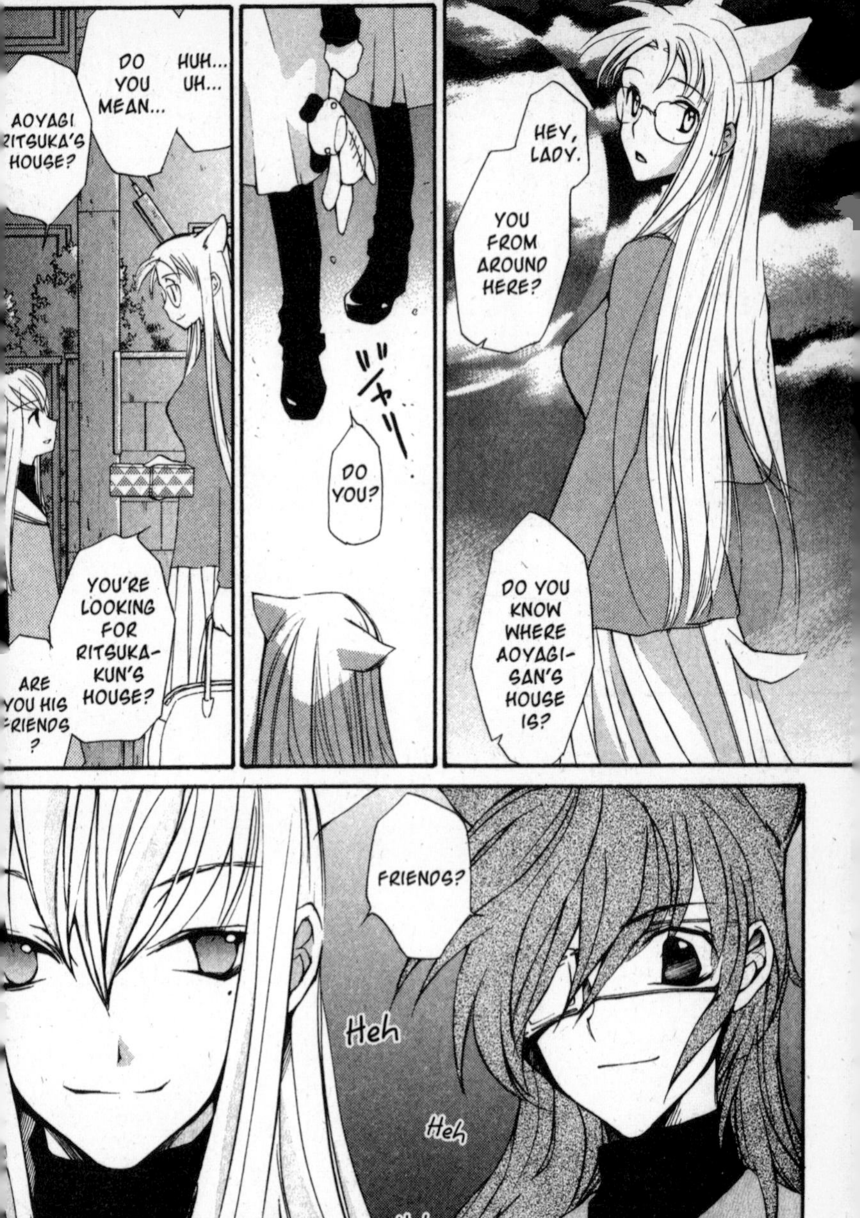
HEY, LADY.
YOU FROM AROUND HERE?
DO YOU KNOW WHERE AOYAGI-SAN'S HOUSE IS?
ジャリ
DO YOU?
HUH... UH...
DO YOU MEAN...
AOYAGI RITSUKA'S HOUSE?
YOU'RE LOOKING FOR RITSUKA-KUN'S HOUSE?
ARE YOU HIS FRIENDS?
FRIENDS?
Heh
Heh
Heh

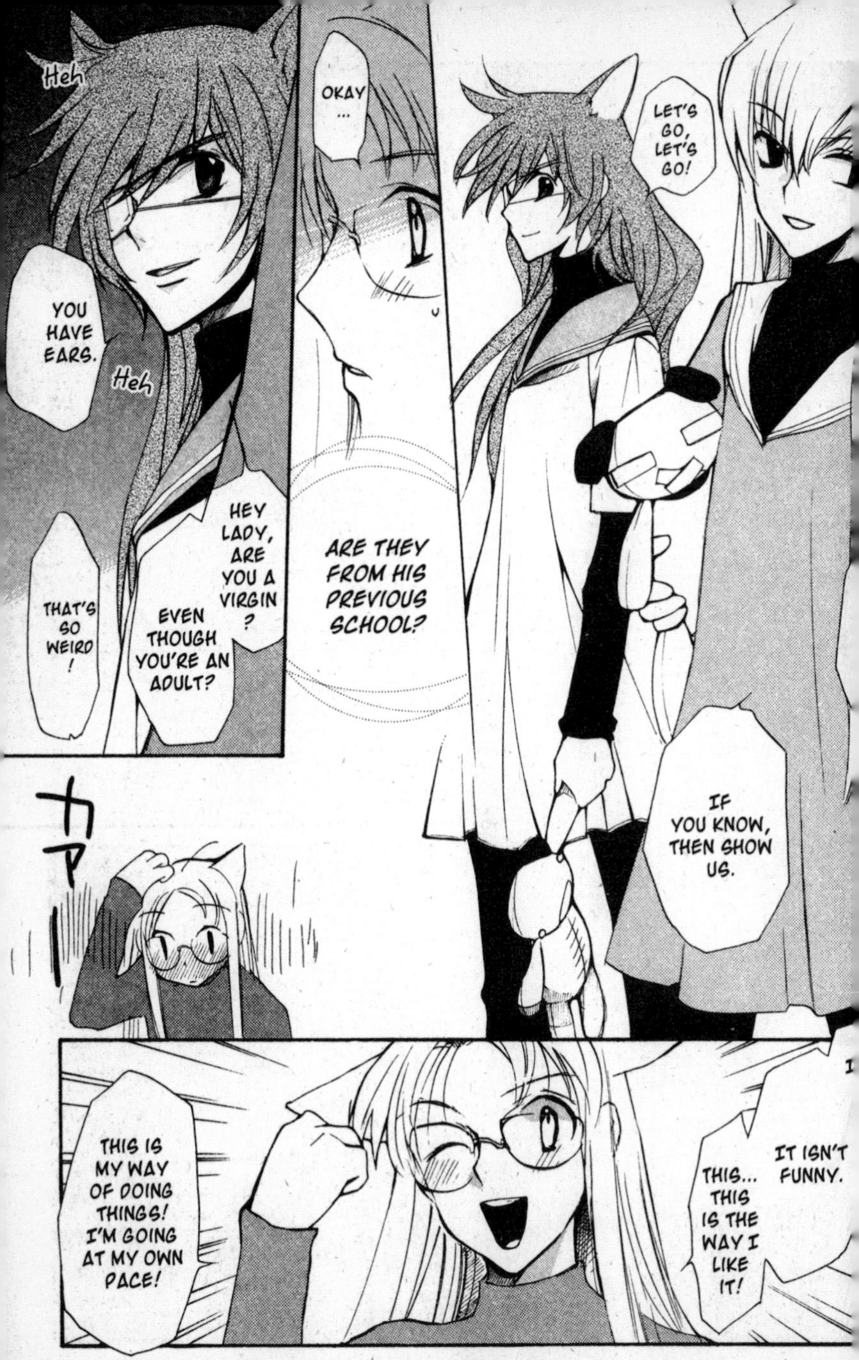
LET'S GO, LET'S GO!
IF YOU KNOW, THEN SHOW US.
OKAY ...
ARE THEY FROM HIS PREVIOUS SCHOOL?
Heh
YOU HAVE EARS.
Heh
HEY LADY, ARE YOU A VIRGIN?
EVEN THOUGH YOU'RE AN ADULT?
THAT'S SO WEIRD!
カァー
IT ISN'T FUNNY.
THIS... THIS IS THE WAY I LIKE IT!
THIS IS MY WAY OF DOING THINGS! I'M GOING AT MY OWN PACE!

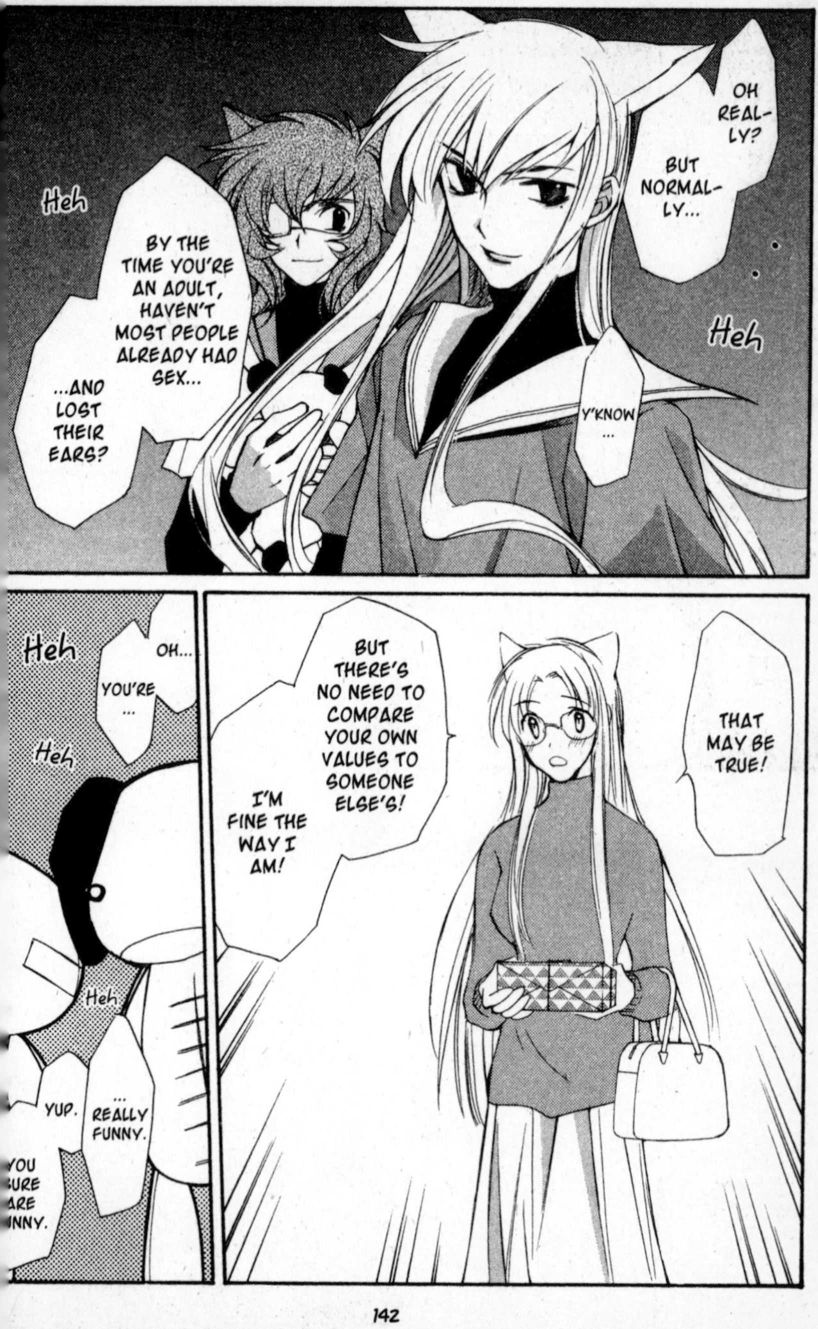
OH REALLY?
BUT NORMALLY...
Heh
Y'KNOW ...
Heh
BY THE TIME YOU'RE AN ADULT, HAVEN'T MOST PEOPLE ALREADY HAD SEX...
...AND LOST THEIR EARS?
THAT MAY BE TRUE!
BUT THERE'S NO NEED TO COMPARE YOUR OWN VALUES TO SOMEONE ELSE'S!
I'M FINE THE WAY I AM!
Heh
OH...
YOU'RE ...
Heh
Heh
... REALLY FUNNY.
YUP.
YOU URE ARE NNY.

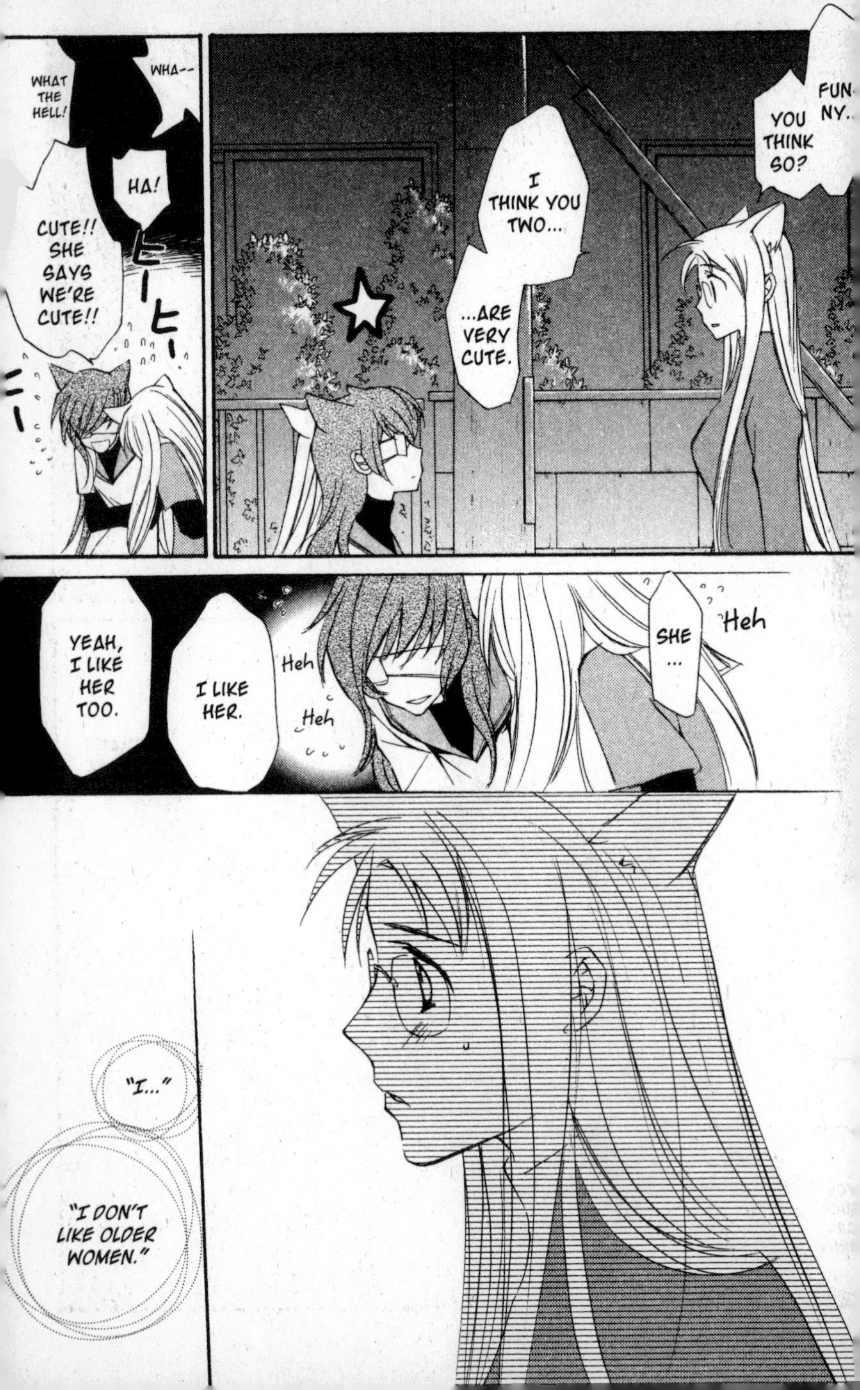
FUN-NY..
YOU THINK SO?
I THINK YOU TWO...
...ARE VERY CUTE.
WHA--
WHAT THE HELL!
HA!
CUTE!! SHE SAYS WE'RE CUTE!!
Heh
SHE ...
Heh
Heh
I LIKE HER.
YEAH, I LIKE HER TOO.
"I..."
"I DON'T LIKE OLDER WOMEN."

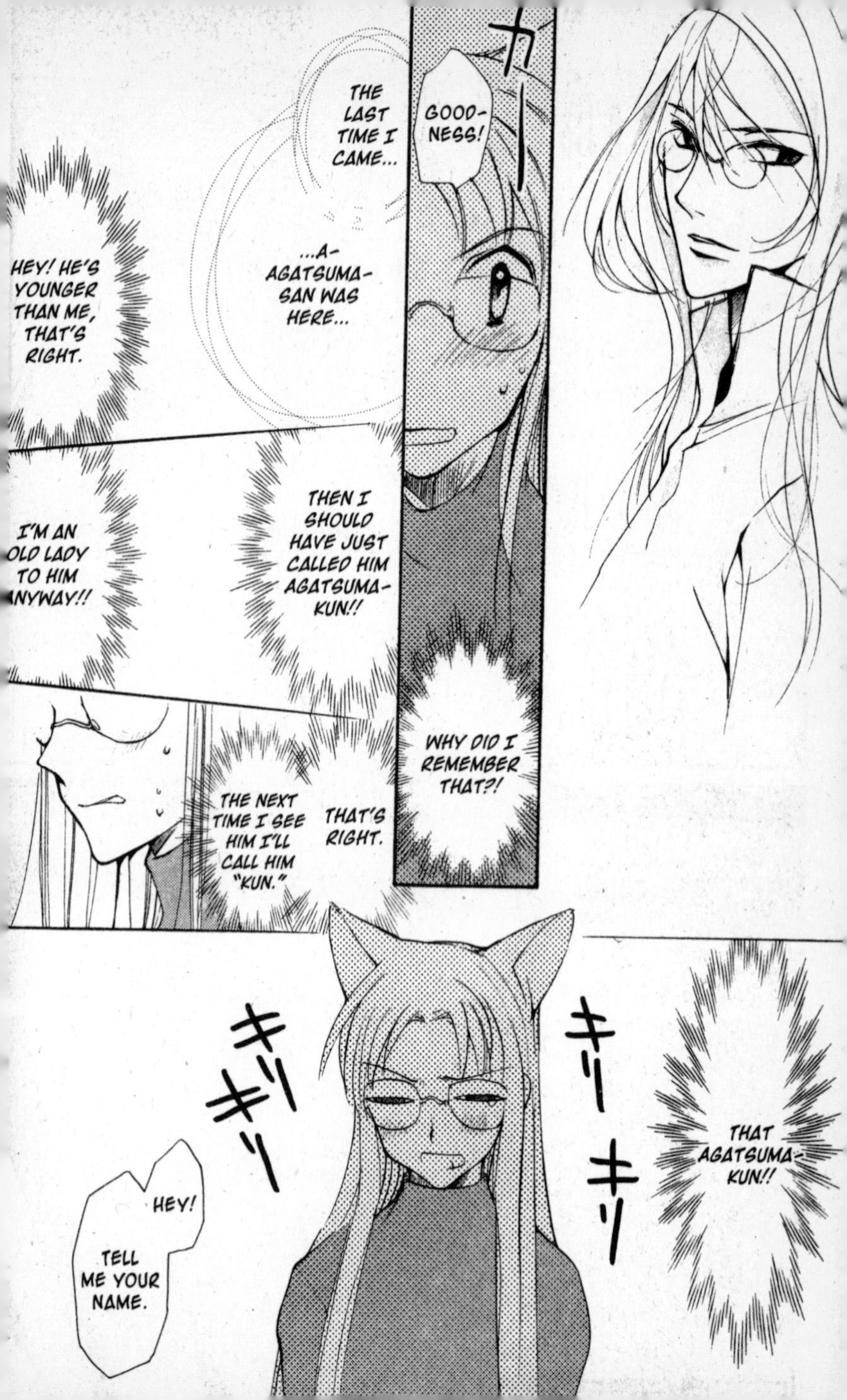
カー
GOODNESS!
WHY DID I REMEMBER THAT?!
THE LAST TIME I CAME...
...A-AGATSUMA-SAN WAS HERE...
HEY! HE'S YOUNGER THAN ME, THAT'S RIGHT.
THEN I SHOULD HAVE JUST CALLED HIM AGATSUMA-KUN!!
I'M AN OLD LADY TO HIM ANYWAY!!
THAT'S RIGHT.
THE NEXT TIME I SEE HIM I'LL CALL HIM "KUN."
THAT AGATSUMA-KUN!!
キリキリ
キリキリ
HEY!
TELL ME YOUR NAME.

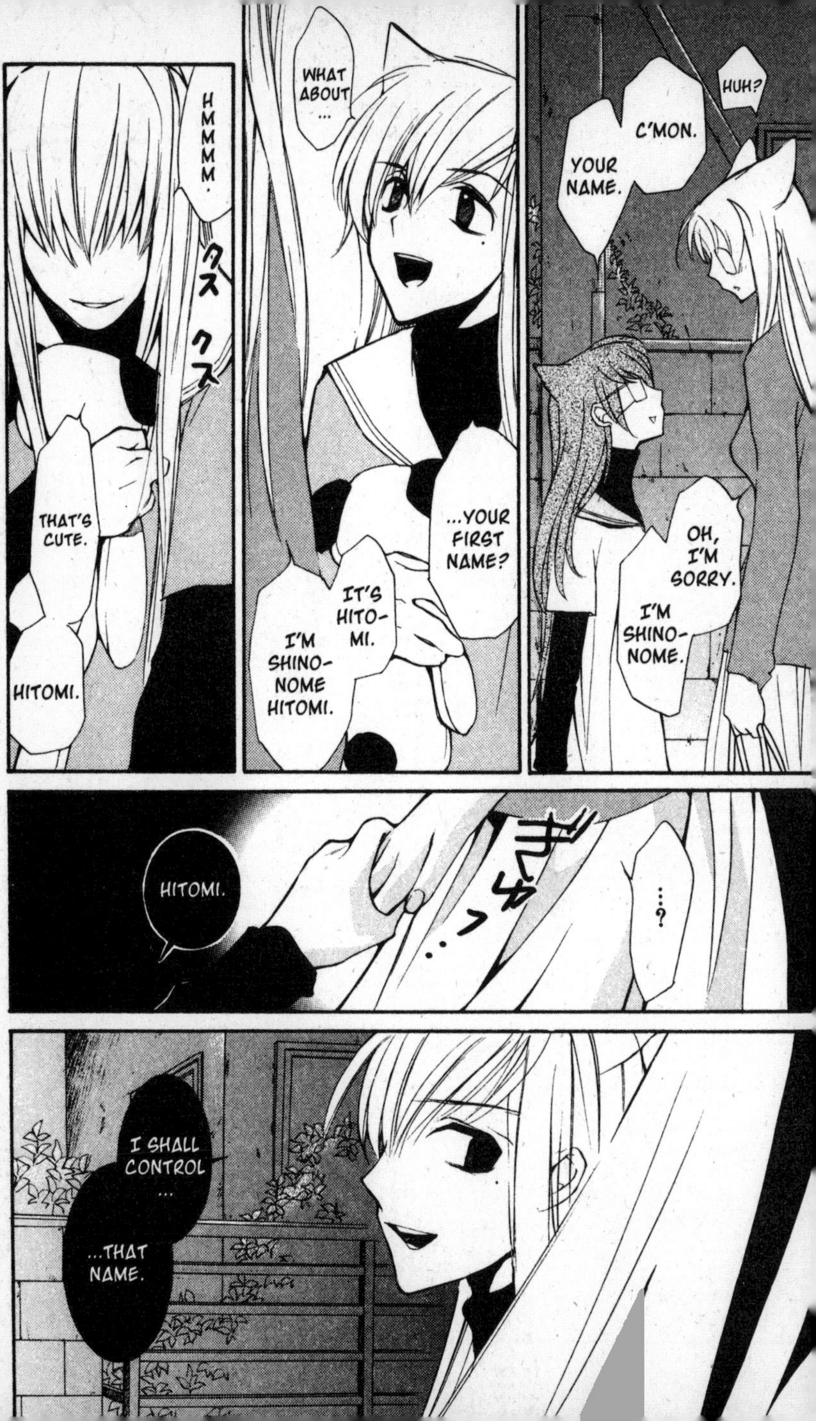
HUH?
C'MON.
YOUR NAME.
OH, I'M SORRY.
I'M SHINONOME.
WHAT ABOUT...
...YOUR FIRST NAME?
IT'S HITOMI.
I'M SHINONOME HITOMI.
HMMMM.
クス クス
THAT'S CUTE.
HITOMI.
...?
ぎゅっ...
HITOMI.
I SHALL CONTROL...
...THAT NAME.

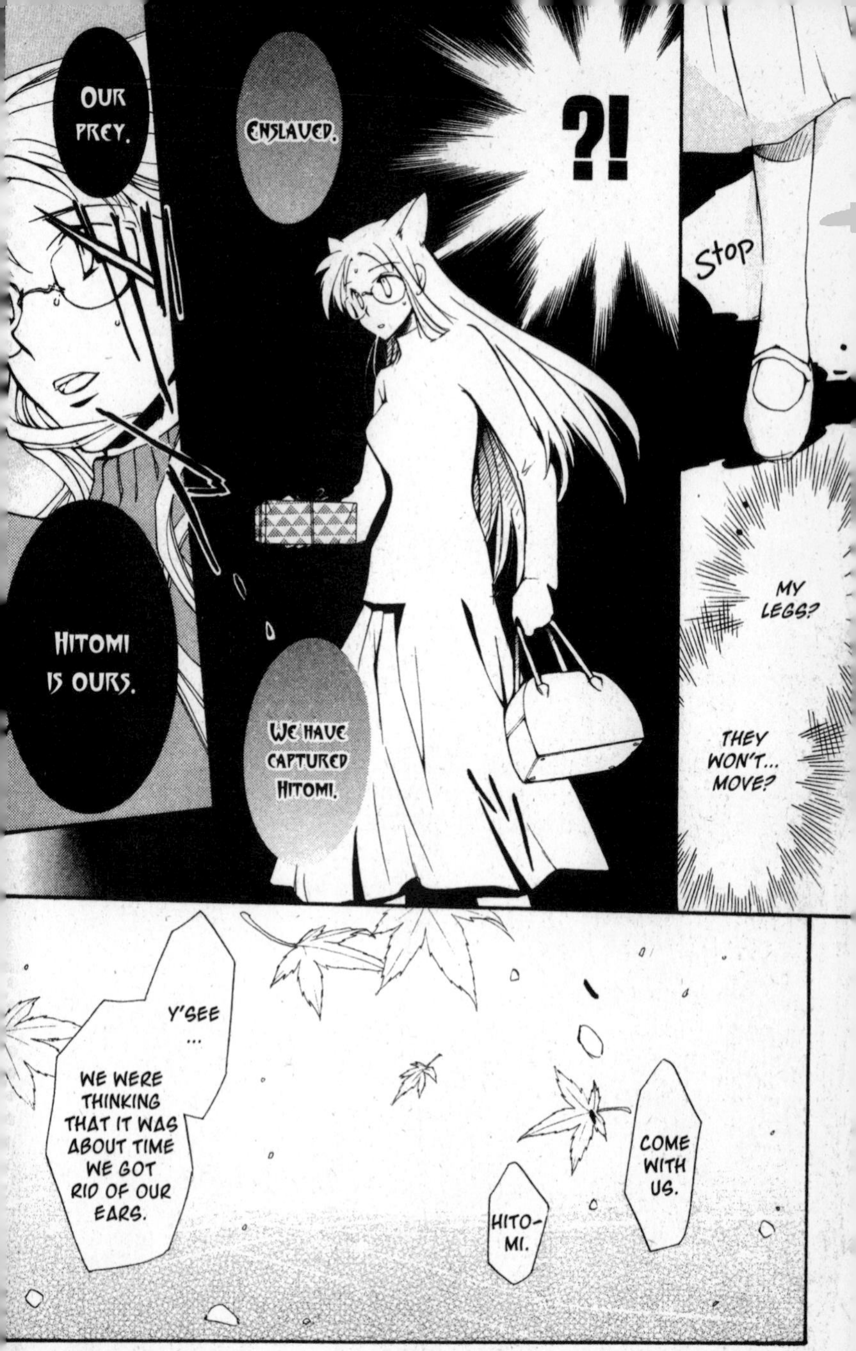
Stop
MY LEGS?
THEY WON'T... MOVE?
?!
ENSLAVED.
WE HAVE CAPTURED HITOMI.
OUR PREY.
HITOMI IS OURS.
COME WITH US.
HITO-MI.
Y'SEE ...
WE WERE THINKING THAT IT WAS ABOUT TIME WE GOT RID OF OUR EARS.

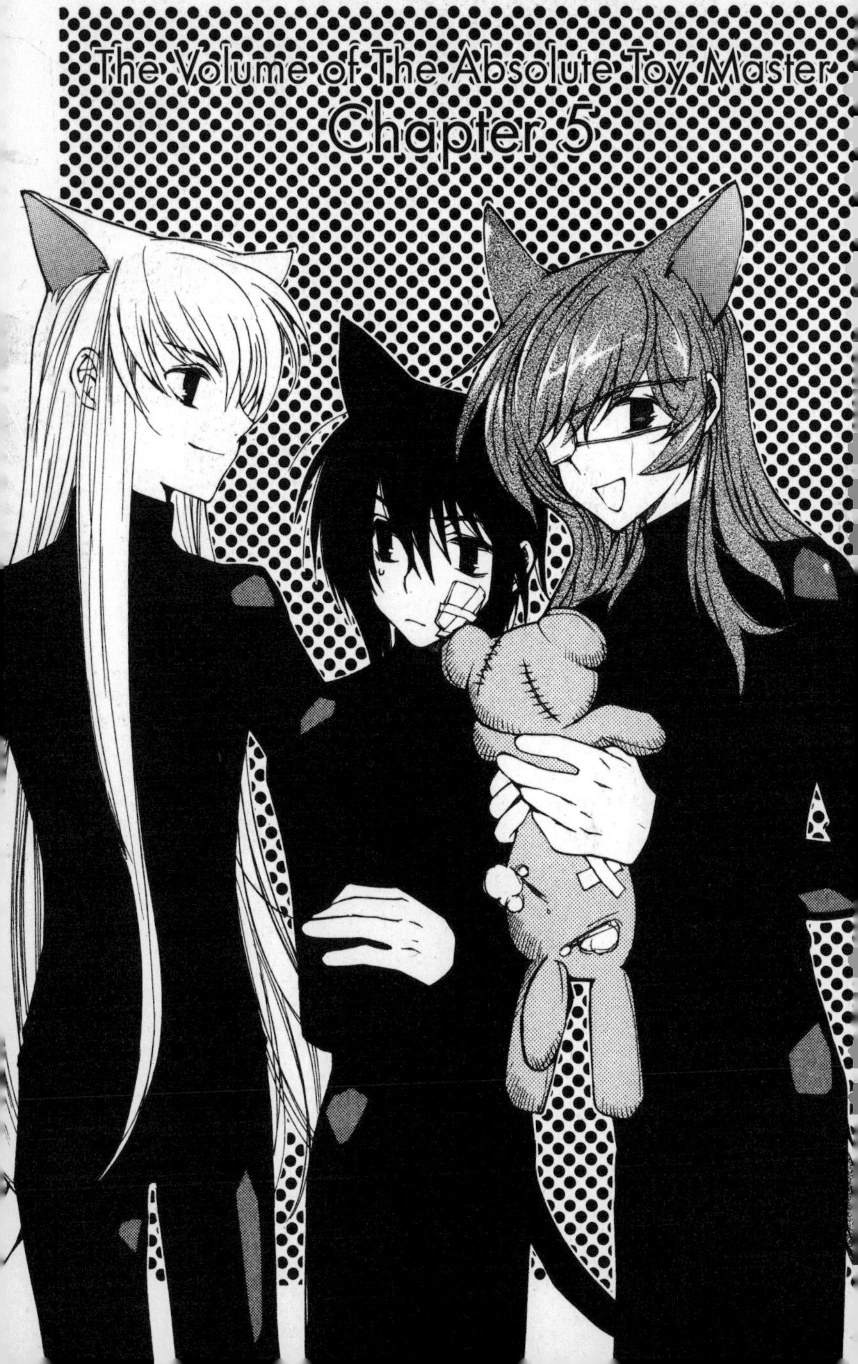
The Volume of The Absolute Toy Master
Chapter 5

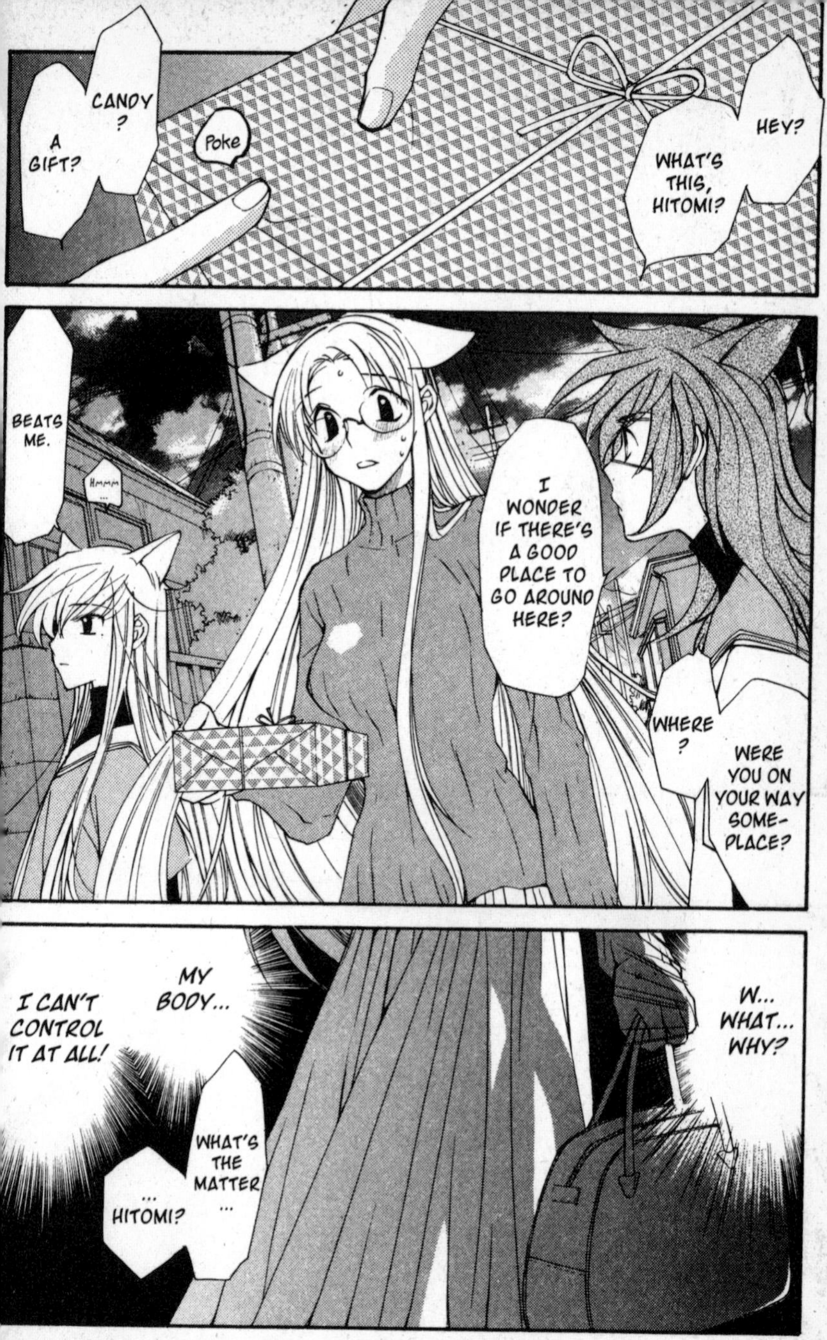
HEY?
WHAT'S THIS, HITOMI?
Poke
CANDY?
A GIFT?
WHERE?
WERE YOU ON YOUR WAY SOME-PLACE?
I WONDER IF THERE'S A GOOD PLACE TO GO AROUND HERE?
Hmmm...
BEATS ME.
W... WHAT... WHY?
MY BODY...
I CAN'T CONTROL IT AT ALL!
WHAT'S THE MATTER...
... HITOMI?

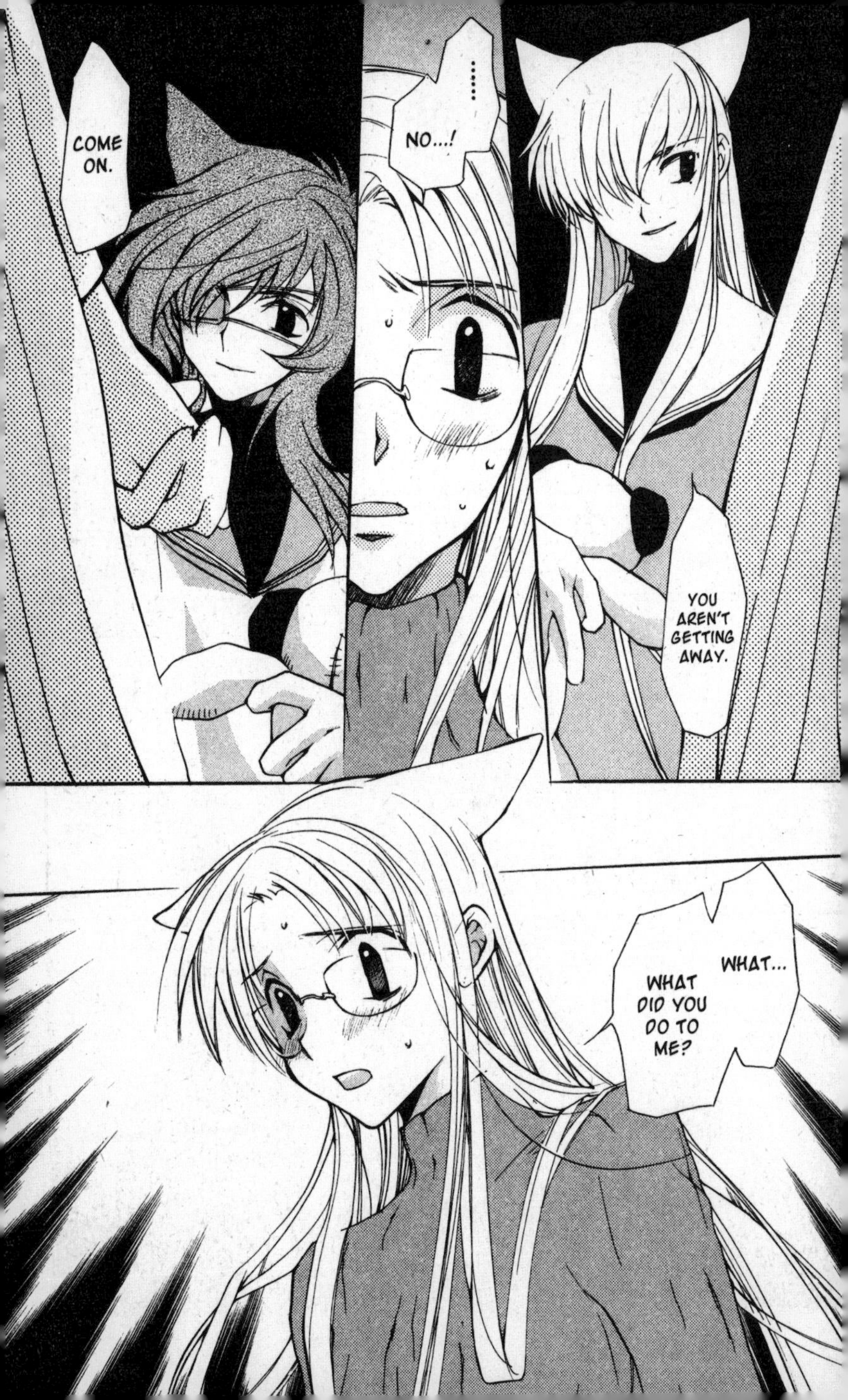
YOU AREN'T GETTING AWAY.
......
NO...!
COME ON.
WHAT...
WHAT DID YOU DO TO ME?

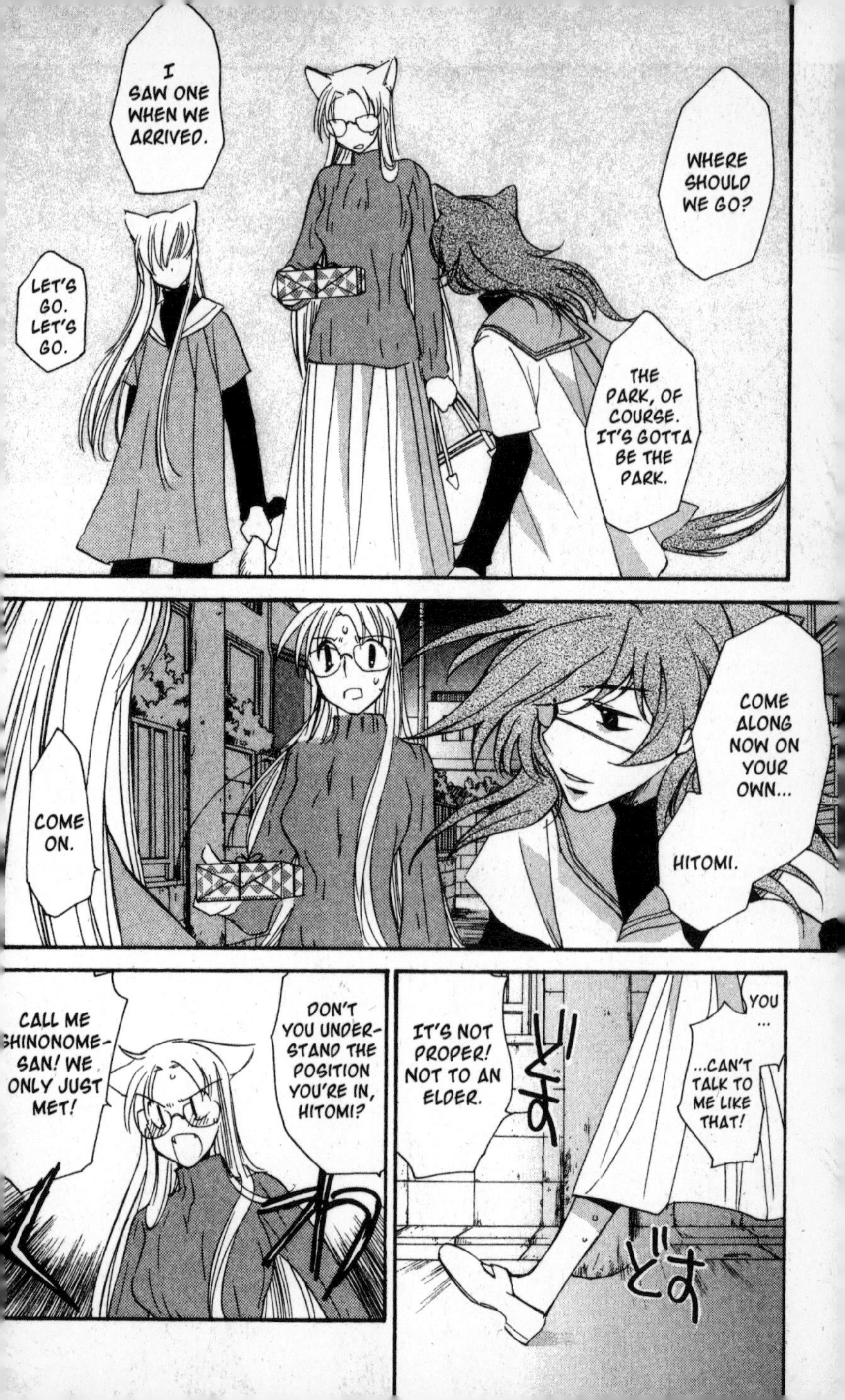
WHERE SHOULD WE GO?
THE PARK, OF COURSE. IT'S GOTTA BE THE PARK.
I SAW ONE WHEN WE ARRIVED.
LET'S GO. LET'S GO.
COME ALONG NOW ON YOUR OWN...
HITOMI.
COME ON.
YOU ...
...CAN'T TALK TO ME LIKE THAT!
どす
どす
IT'S NOT PROPER! NOT TO AN ELDER.
DON'T YOU UNDER-STAND THE POSITION YOU'RE IN, HITOMI?
CALL ME SHINONOME-SAN! WE ONLY JUST MET!

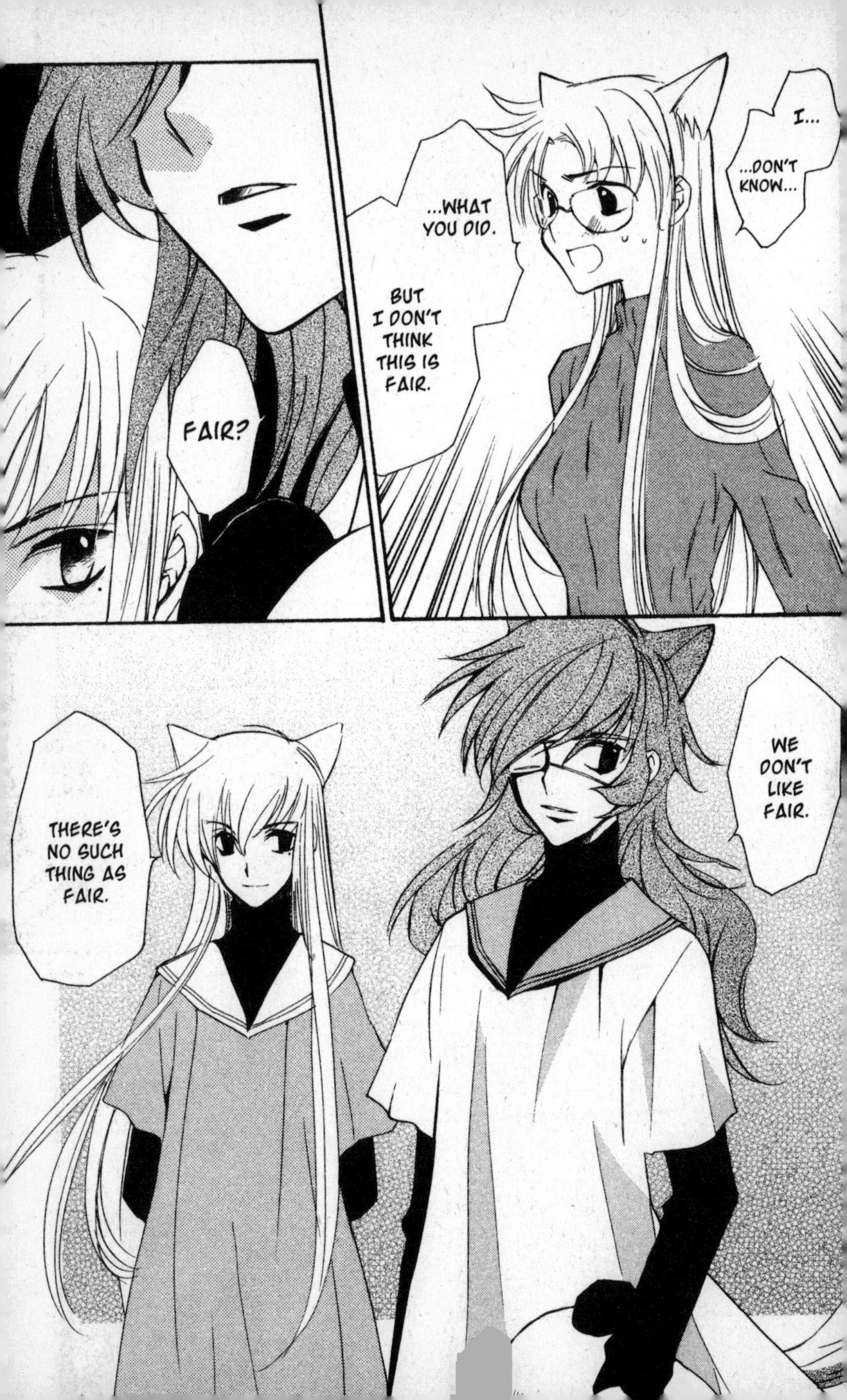
I...
...DON'T KNOW...
...WHAT YOU DID.
BUT I DON'T THINK THIS IS FAIR.
FAIR?
WE DON'T LIKE FAIR.
THERE'S NO SUCH THING AS FAIR.

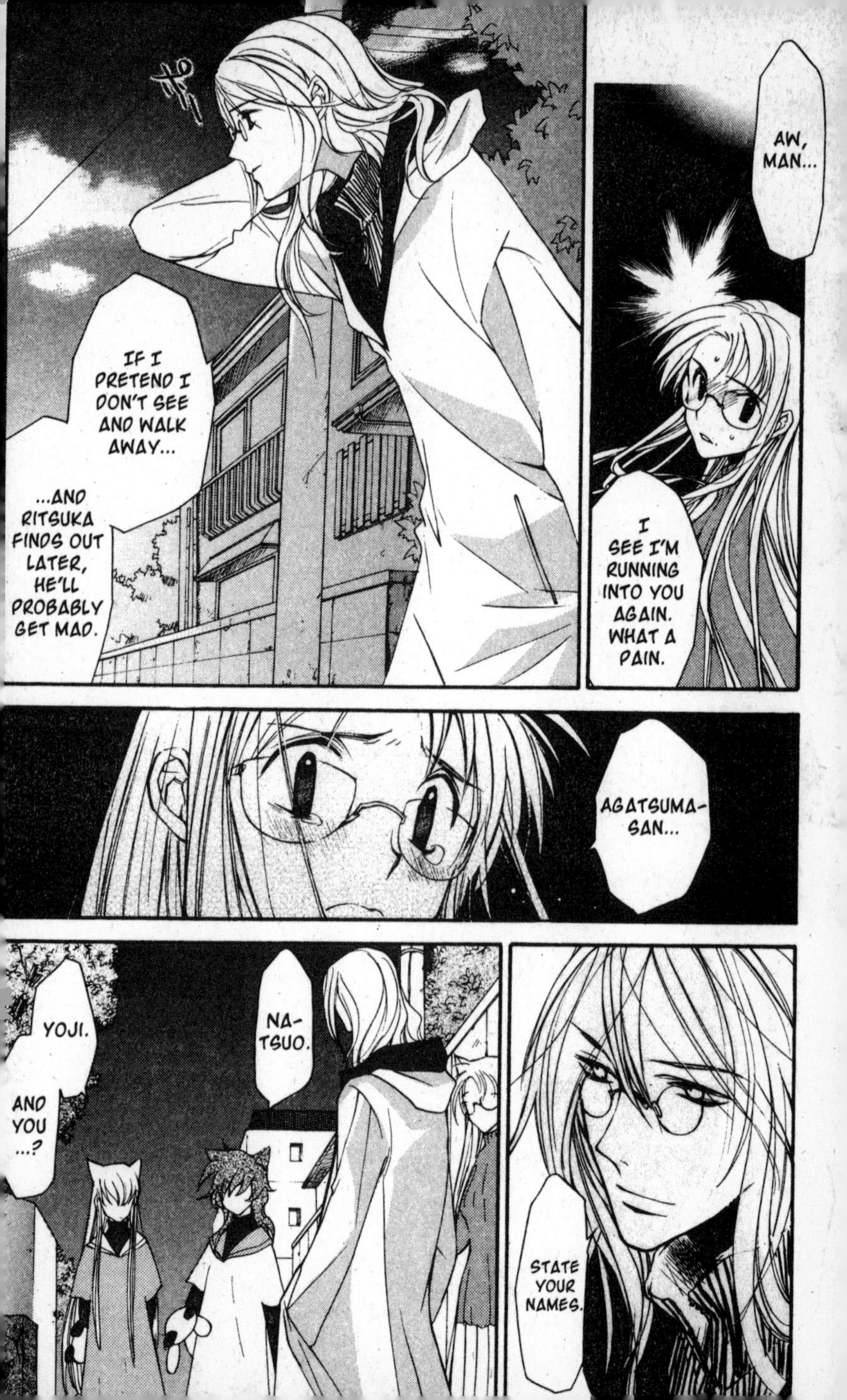
AW, MAN...
I SEE I'M RUNNING INTO YOU AGAIN. WHAT A PAIN.
IF I PRETEND I DON'T SEE AND WALK AWAY...
...AND RITSUKA FINDS OUT LATER, HE'LL PROBABLY GET MAD.
AGATSUMA-SAN...
STATE YOUR NAMES.
NA-TSUO.
YOJI.
AND YOU ...?

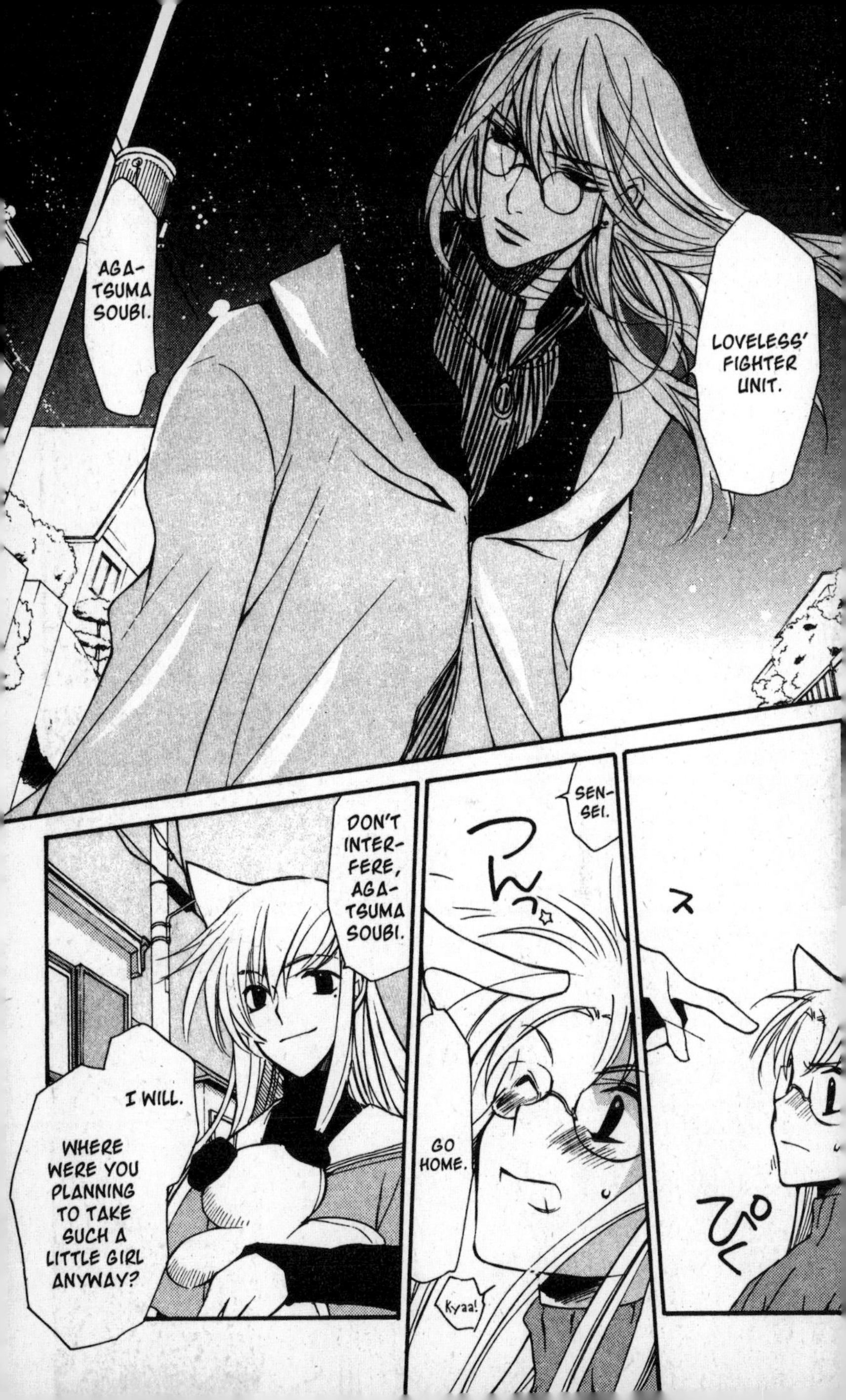
AGATSUMA SOUBI.
LOVELESS' FIGHTER UNIT.
SENSEI.
GO HOME.
Kyaa!
DON'T INTERFERE, AGATSUMA SOUBI.
I WILL.
WHERE WERE YOU PLANNING TO TAKE SUCH A LITTLE GIRL ANYWAY?

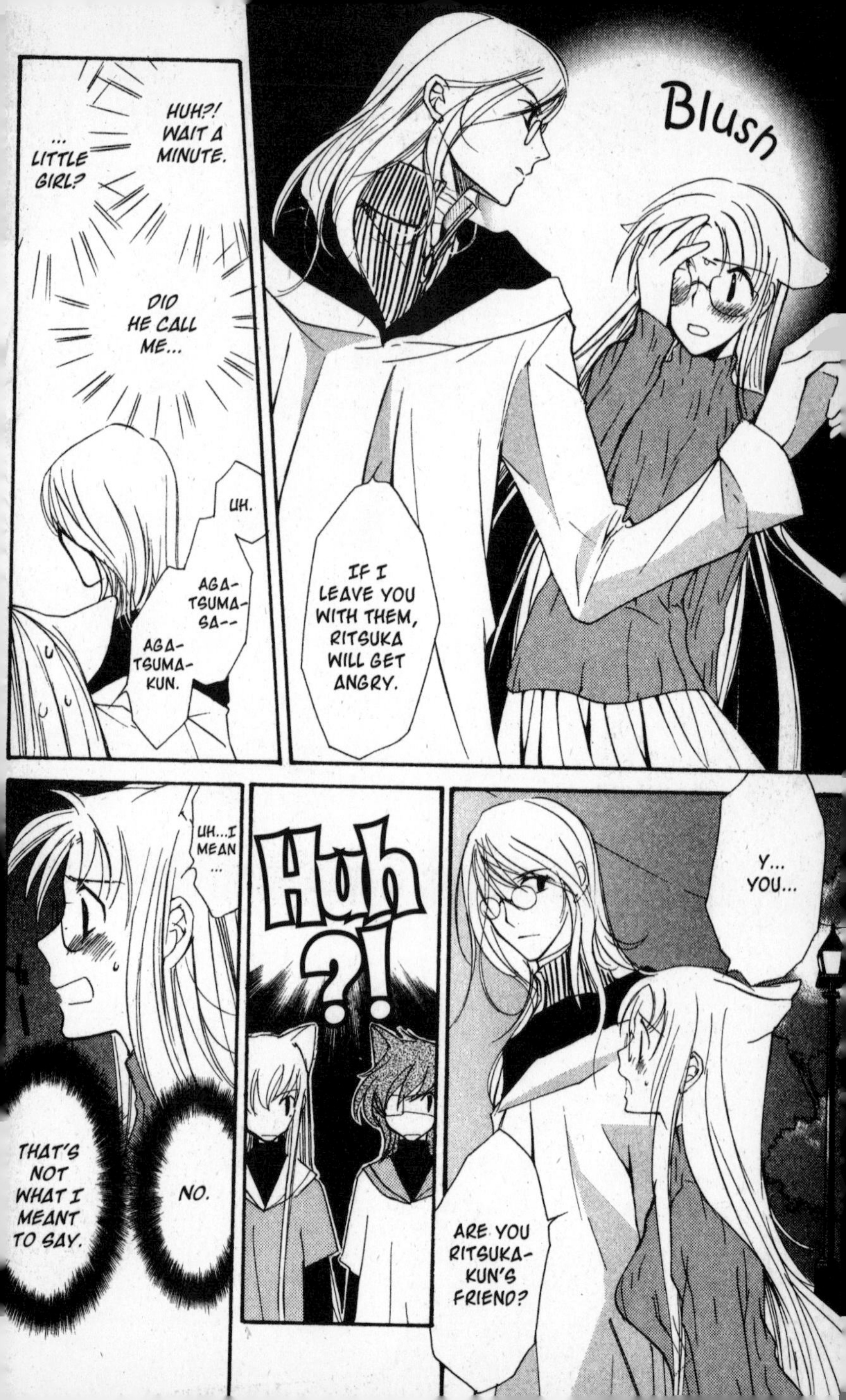
Blush
IF I LEAVE YOU WITH THEM, RITSUKA WILL GET ANGRY.
HUH?! WAIT A MINUTE.
... LITTLE GIRL?
DID HE CALL ME...
UH.
AGA-TSUMA-SA--
AGA-TSUMA-KUN.
Y... YOU...
ARE YOU RITSUKA-KUN'S FRIEND?
Huh?!
UH...I MEAN ...
NO.
THAT'S NOT WHAT I MEANT TO SAY.

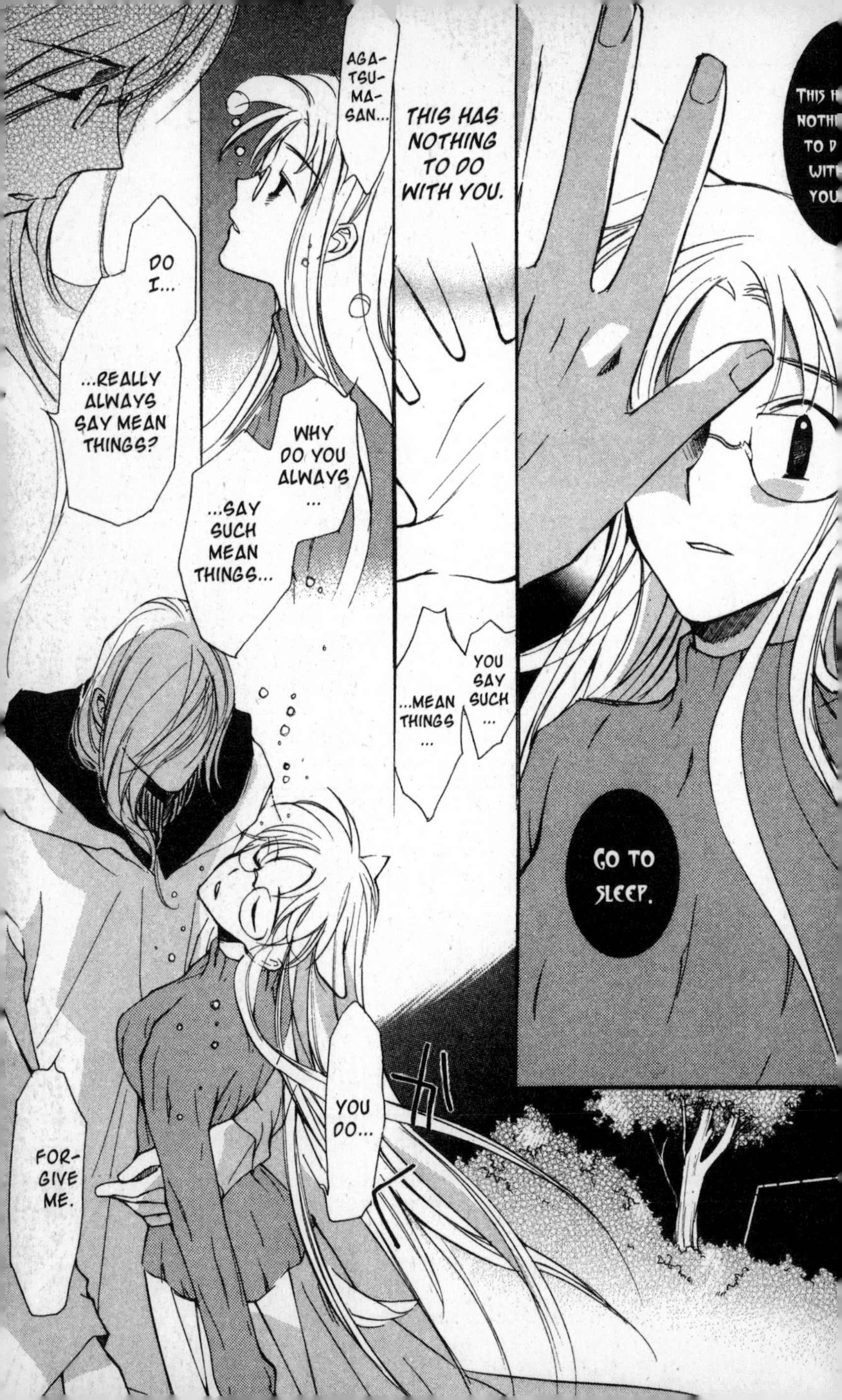
THIS H NOTHI TO D WIT YOU
GO TO SLEEP.
THIS HAS NOTHING TO DO WITH YOU.
YOU SAY SUCH...
...MEAN THINGS...
AGA-TSU-MA-SAN...
WHY DO YOU ALWAYS...
...SAY SUCH MEAN THINGS...
DO I...
...REALLY ALWAYS SAY MEAN THINGS?
YOU DO...
FOR-GIVE ME.

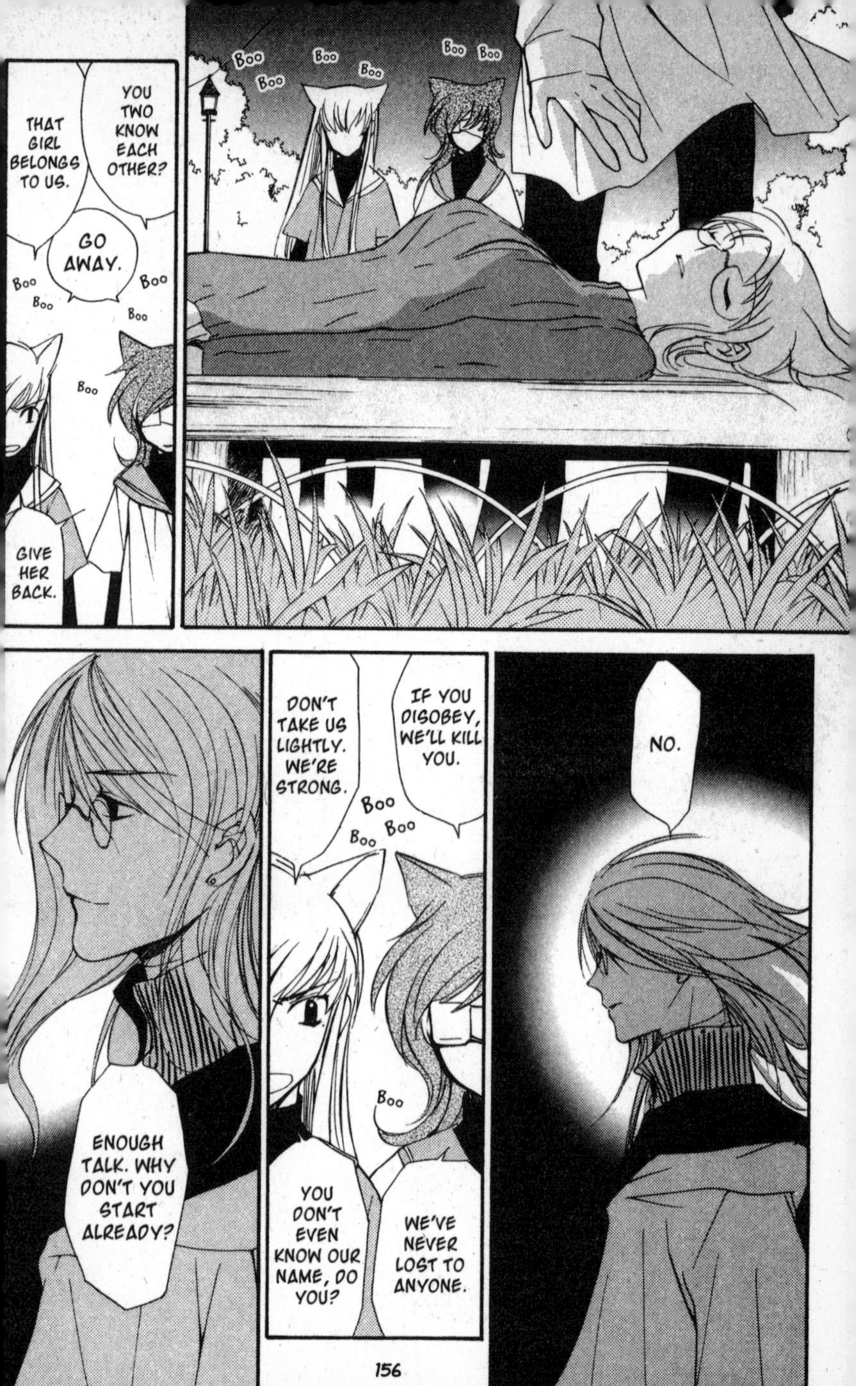

Boo Boo Boo Boo Boo Boo
YOU TWO KNOW EACH OTHER?
THAT GIRL BELONGS TO US.
GO AWAY.
Boo Boo Boo Boo Boo
GIVE HER BACK.
NO.
IF YOU DISOBEY, WE'LL KILL YOU.
DON'T TAKE US LIGHTLY. WE'RE STRONG.
Boo Boo Boo
Boo
WE'VE NEVER LOST TO ANYONE.
YOU DON'T EVEN KNOW OUR NAME, DO YOU?
ENOUGH TALK. WHY DON'T YOU START ALREADY?

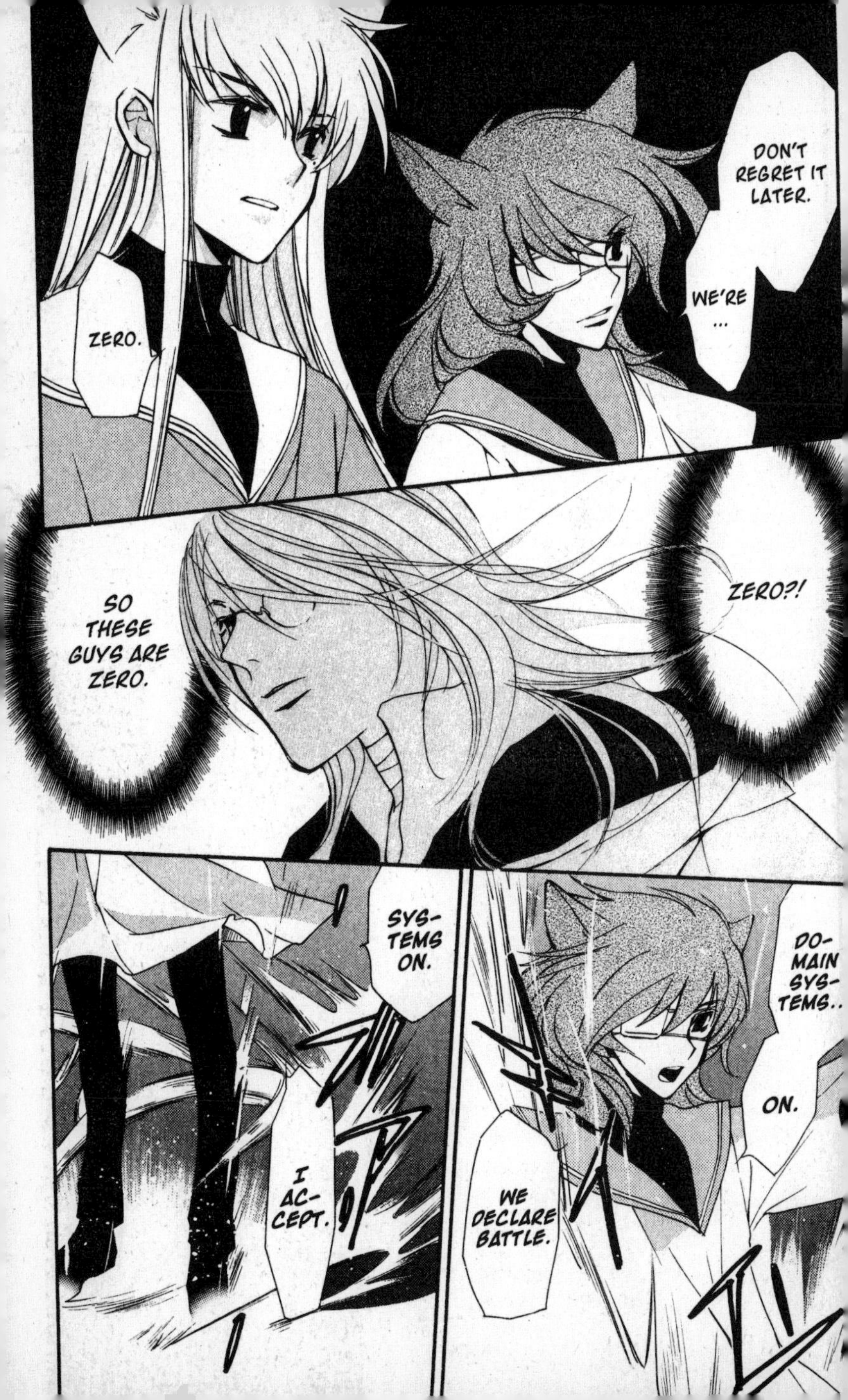
DON'T REGRET IT LATER.
WE'RE ...
ZERO.
ZERO?!
SO THESE GUYS ARE ZERO.
DOMAIN SYSTEMS..
ON.
WE DECLARE BATTLE.
SYSTEMS ON.
I ACCEPT.

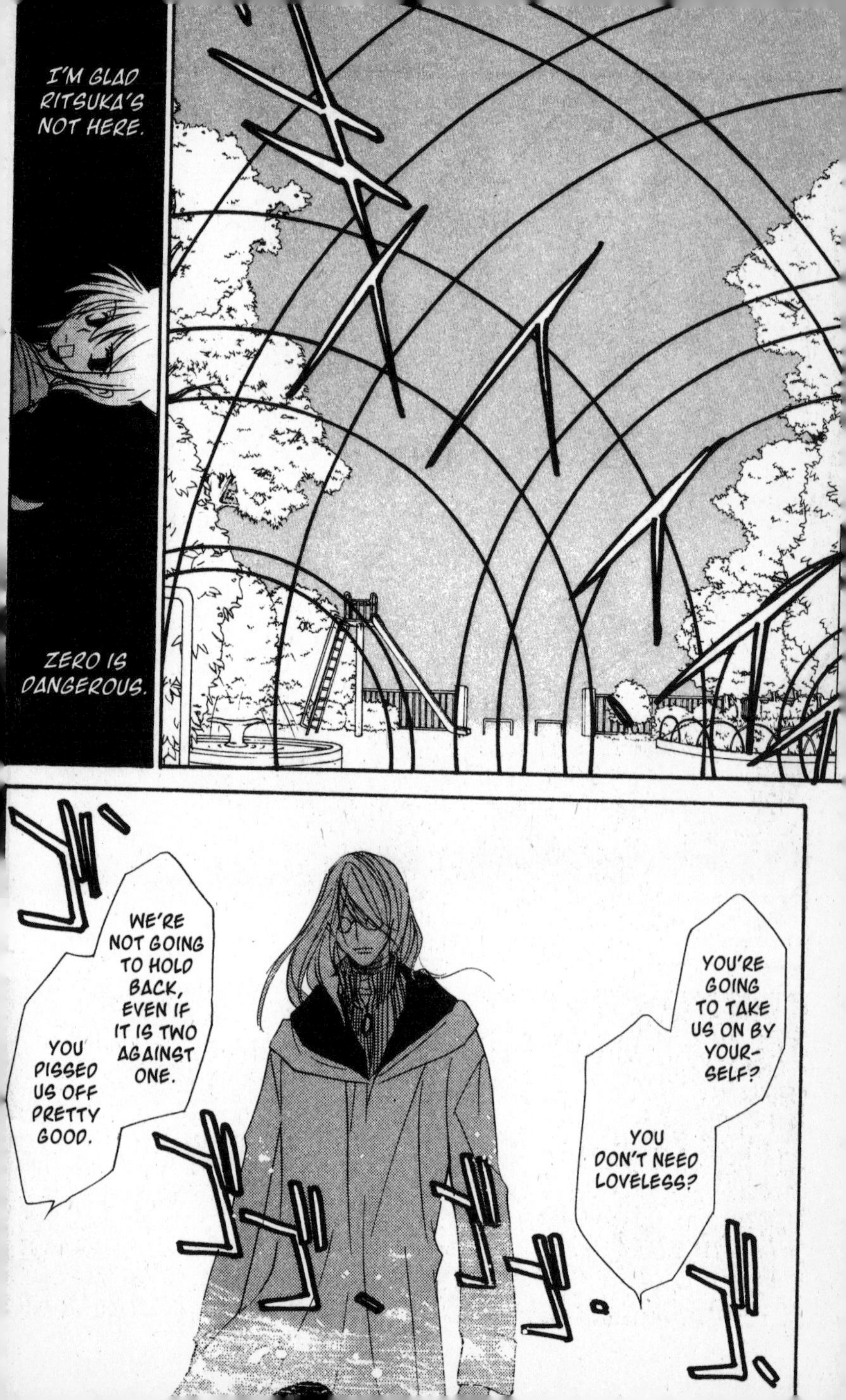
I'M GLAD RITSUKA'S NOT HERE.
ZERO IS DANGEROUS.
YOU'RE GOING TO TAKE US ON BY YOUR-SELF?
YOU DON'T NEED LOVELESS?
WE'RE NOT GOING TO HOLD BACK, EVEN IF IT IS TWO AGAINST ONE.
YOU PISSED US OFF PRETTY GOOD.

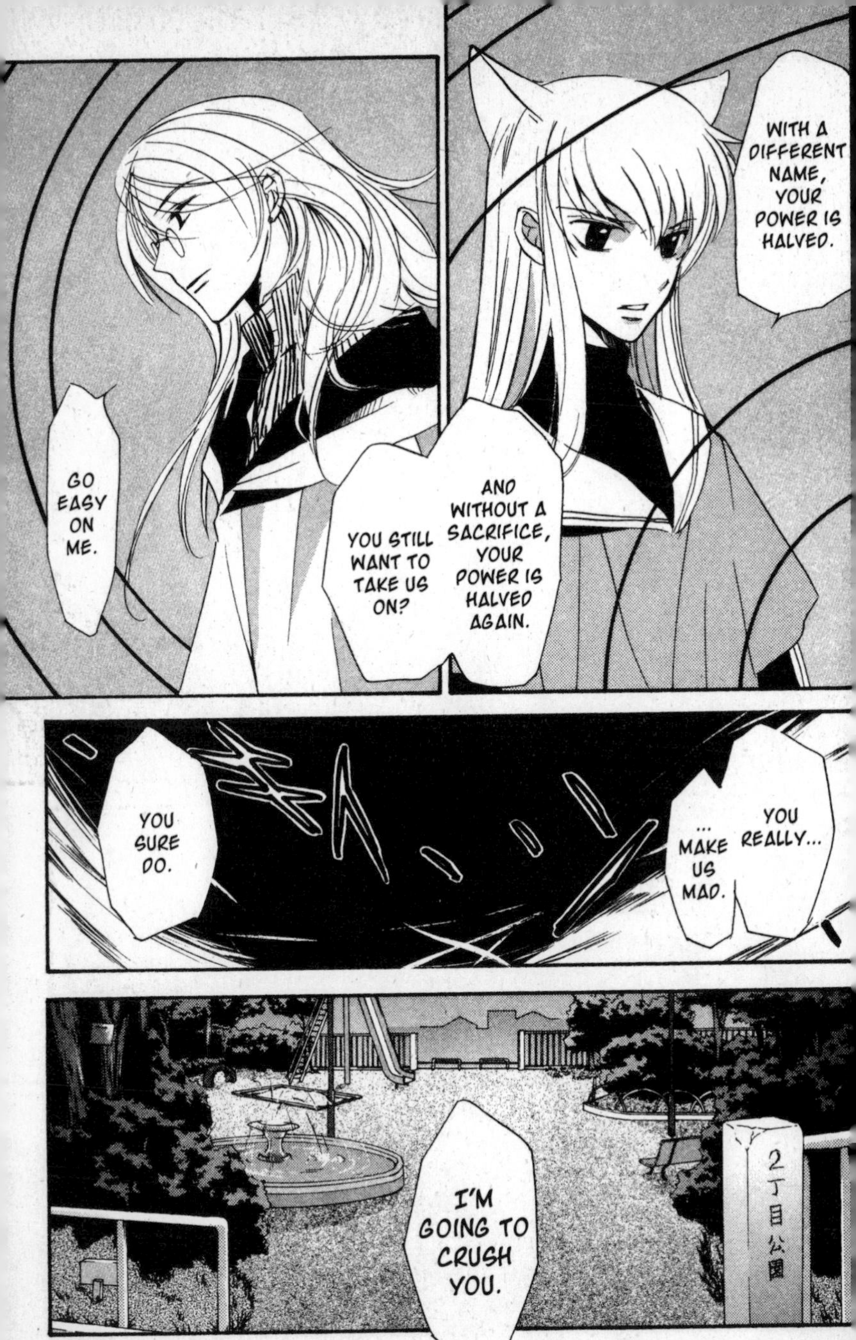
WITH A DIFFERENT NAME, YOUR POWER IS HALVED.
AND WITHOUT A SACRIFICE, YOUR POWER IS HALVED AGAIN.
YOU STILL WANT TO TAKE US ON?
GO EASY ON ME.
YOU REALLY...
... MAKE US MAD.
YOU SURE DO.
2丁目公園
I'M GOING TO CRUSH YOU.

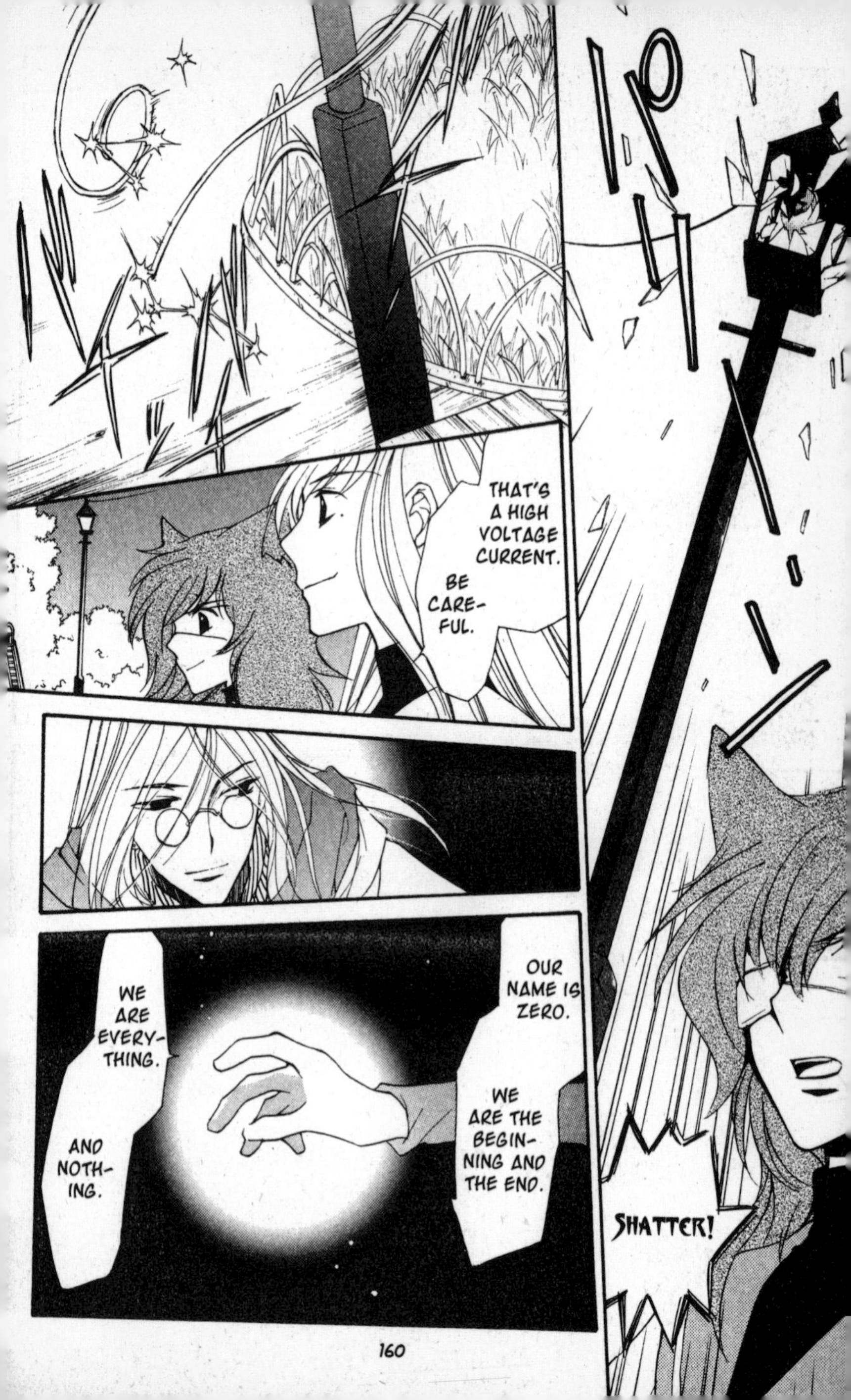
SHATTER!
THAT'S A HIGH VOLTAGE CURRENT.
BE CAREFUL.
OUR NAME IS ZERO.
WE ARE THE BEGINNING AND THE END.
WE ARE EVERYTHING.
AND NOTHING.

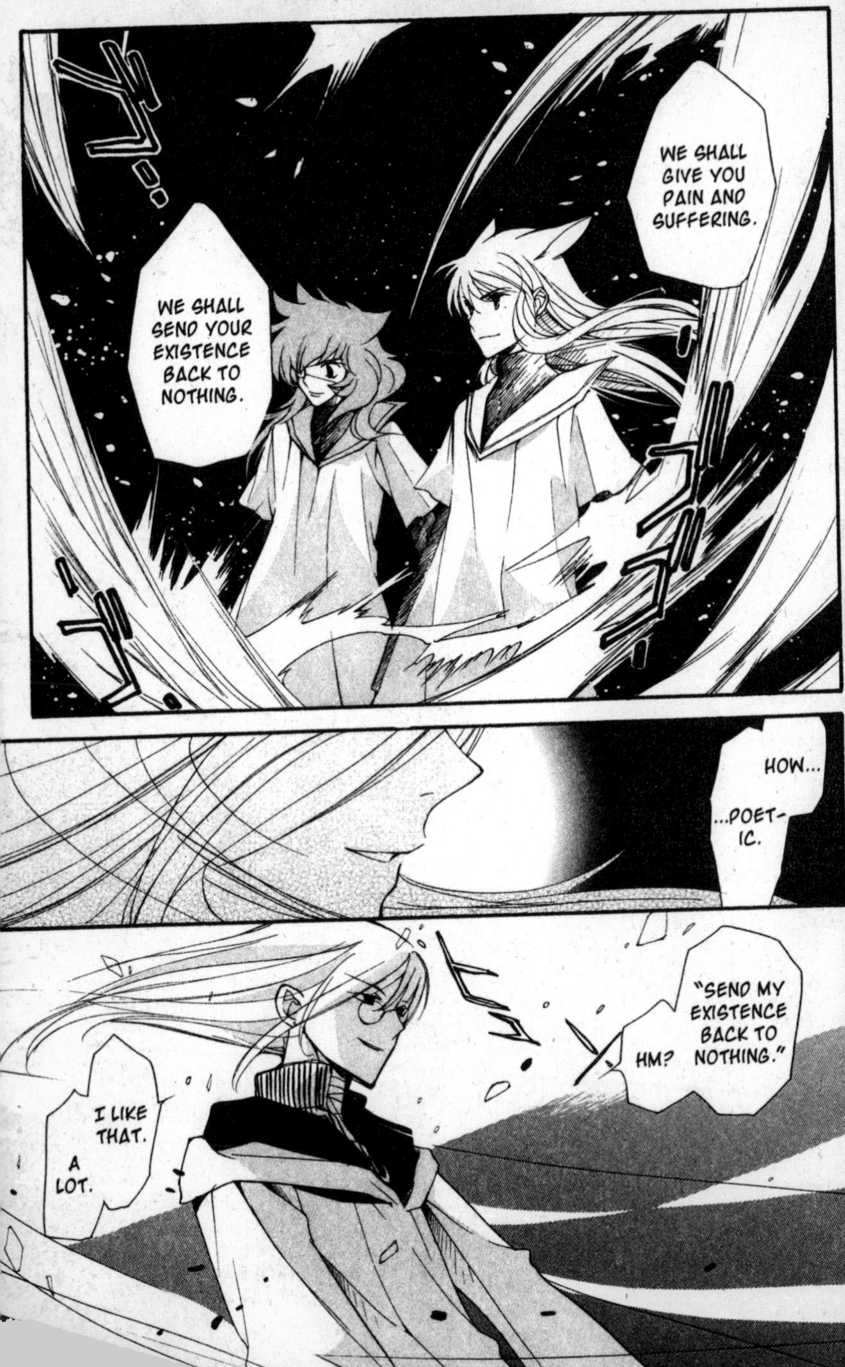
WE SHALL GIVE YOU PAIN AND SUFFERING.
WE SHALL SEND YOUR EXISTENCE BACK TO NOTHING.
HOW...
...POET-IC.
"SEND MY EXISTENCE BACK TO NOTHING."
HM?
I LIKE THAT.
A LOT.

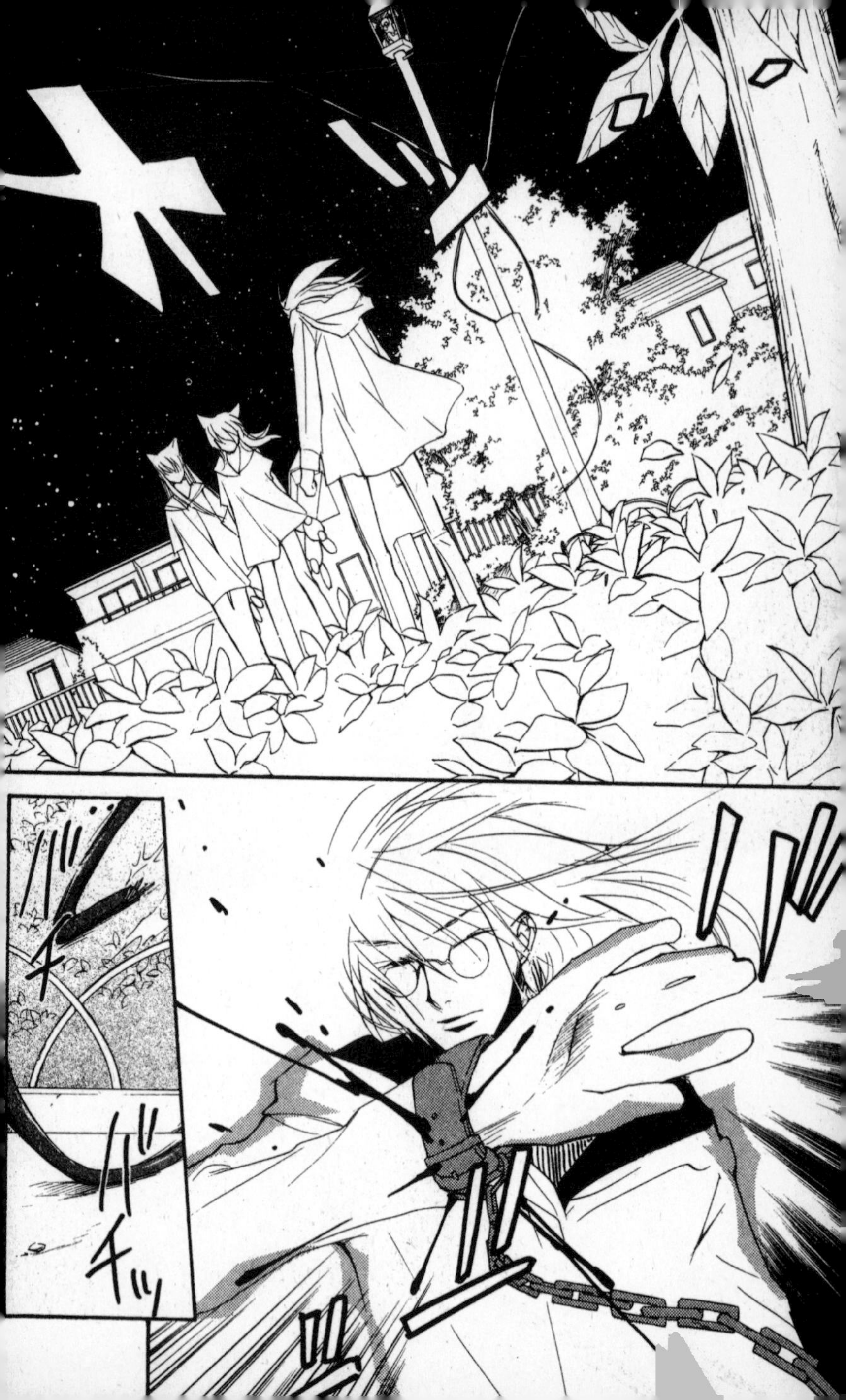
バチ
バチッ

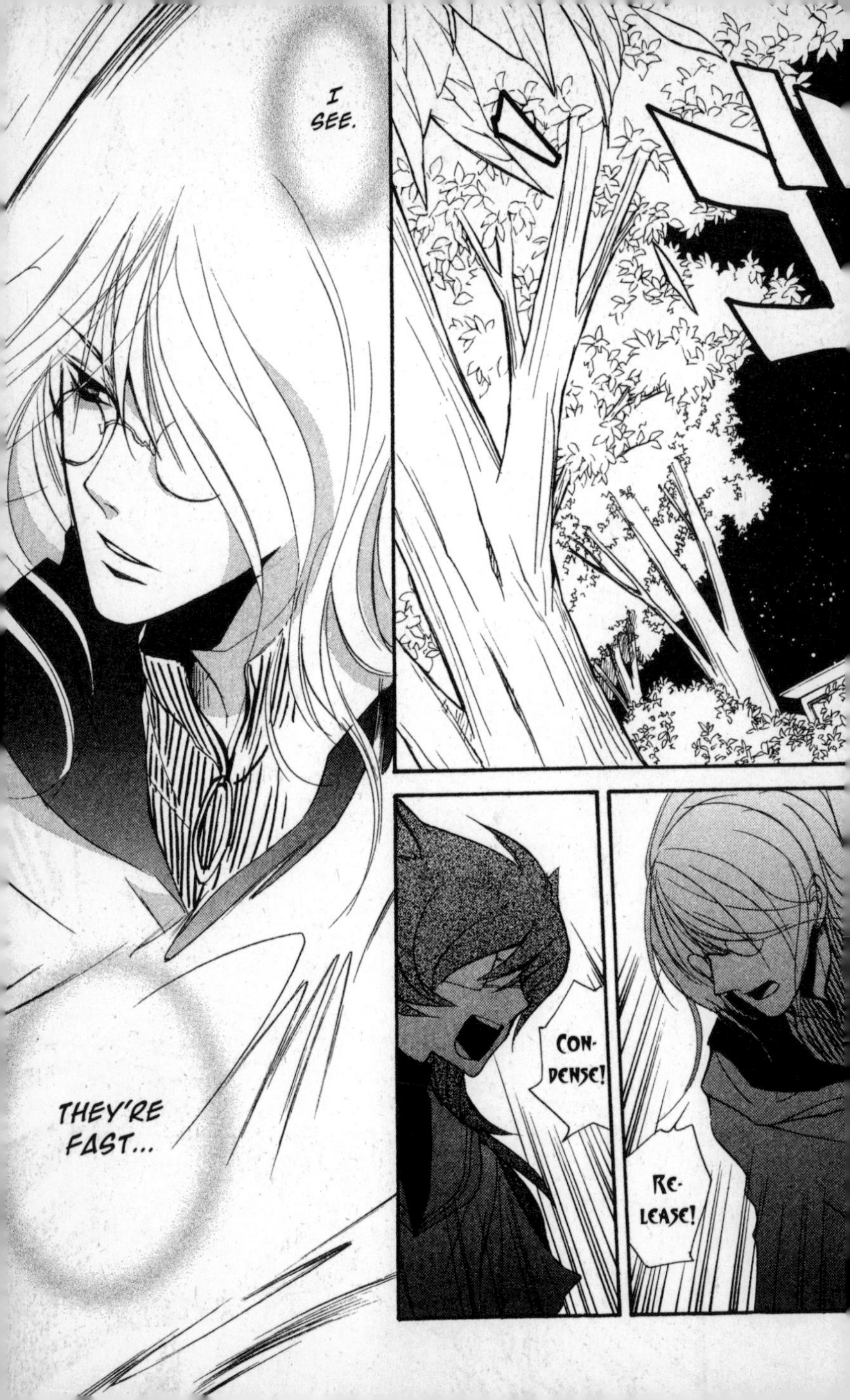
RE-LEASE!
CON-DENSE!
I SEE.
THEY'RE FAST...

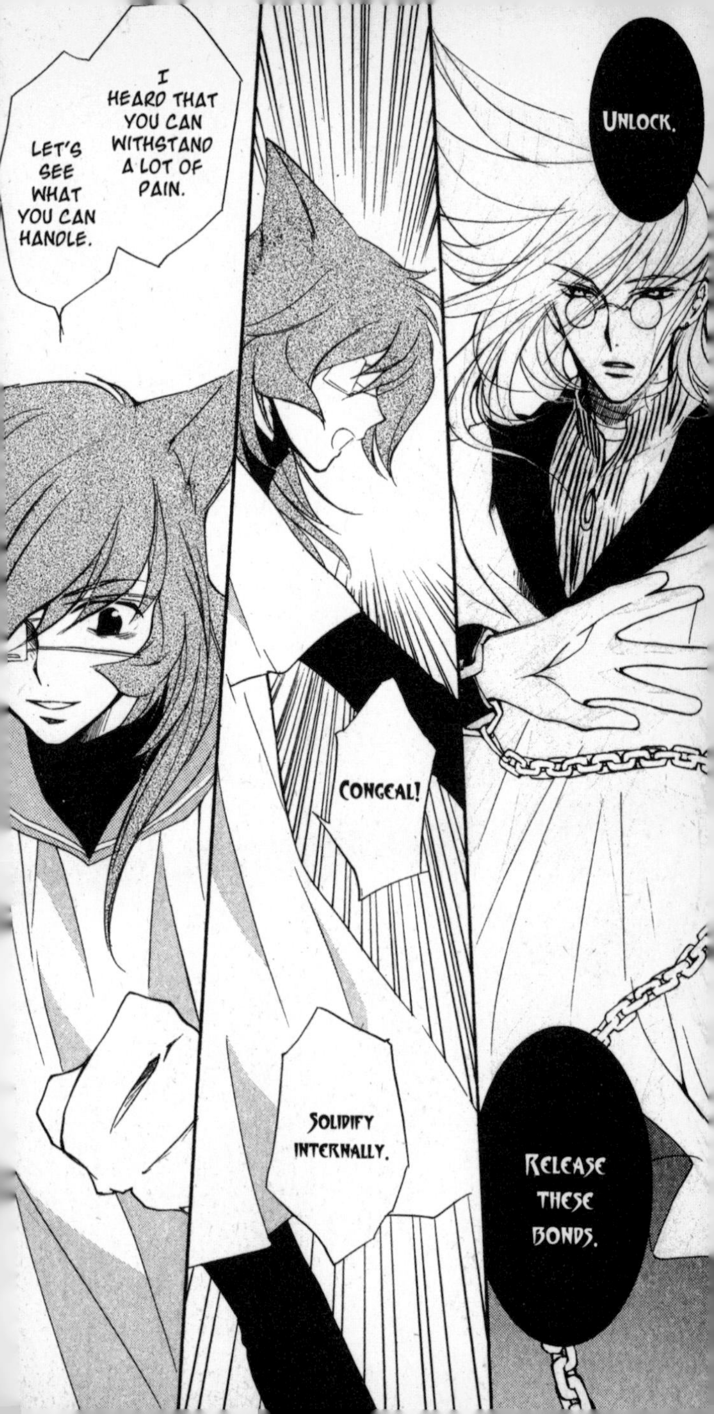
UNLOCK.
RELEASE THESE BONDS.
CONGEAL!
SOLIDIFY INTERNALLY.
I HEARD THAT YOU CAN WITHSTAND A LOT OF PAIN.
LET'S SEE WHAT YOU CAN HANDLE.

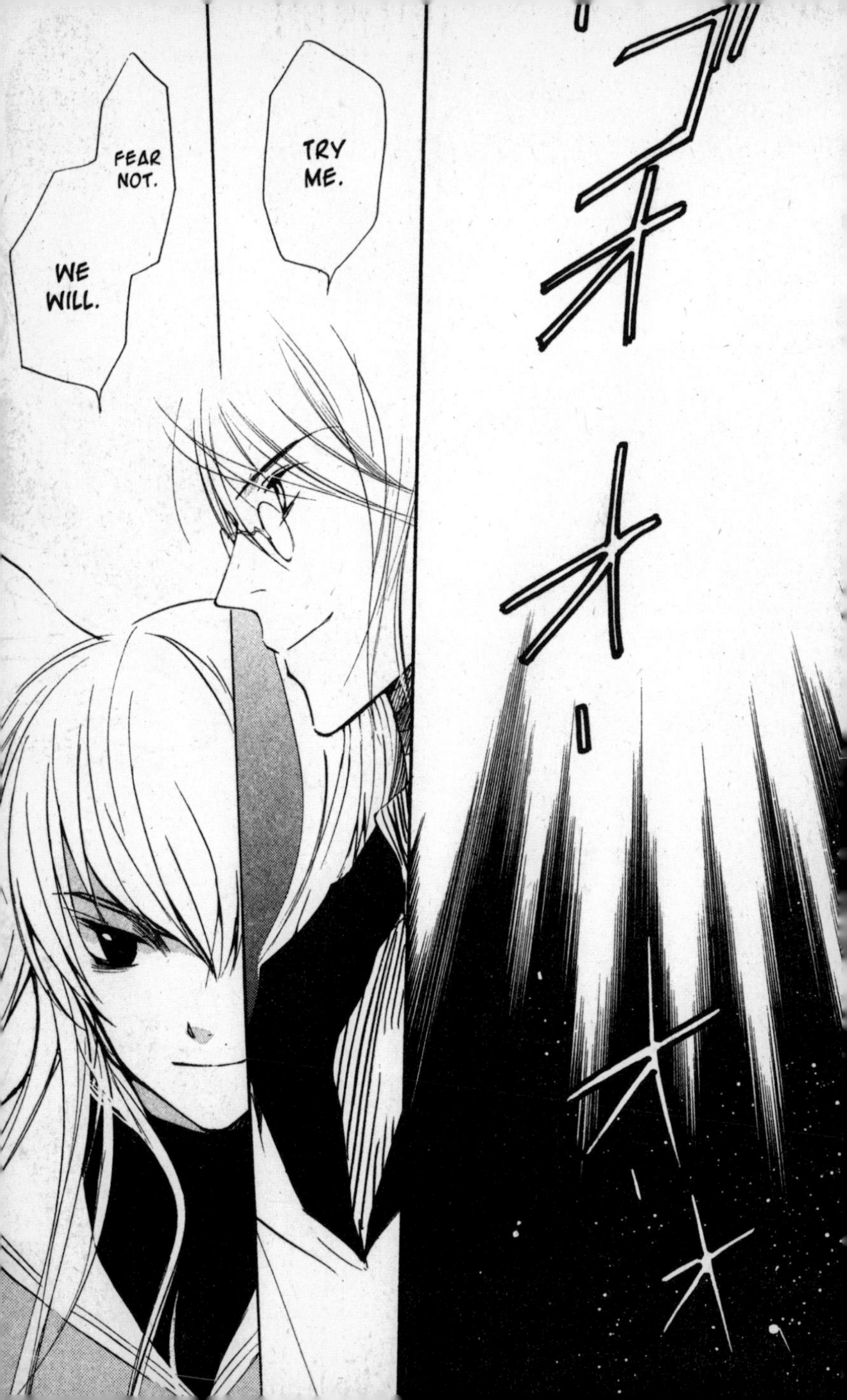
TRY ME.
FEAR NOT.
WE WILL.

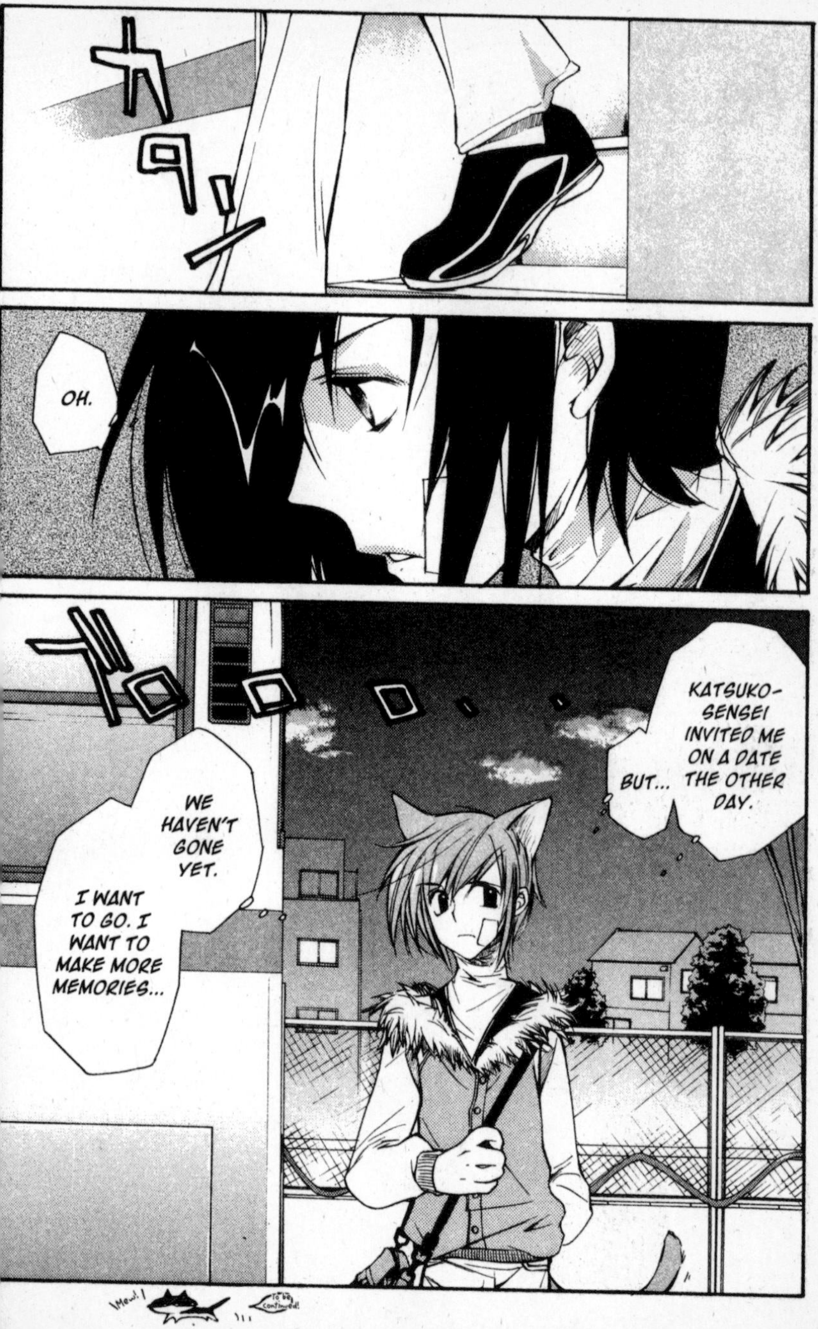
カタッ
OH.
KATSUKO-SENSEI INVITED ME ON A DATE THE OTHER DAY.
BUT...
WE HAVEN'T GONE YET.
I WANT TO GO. I WANT TO MAKE MORE MEMORIES...
Mew!
To be continued!

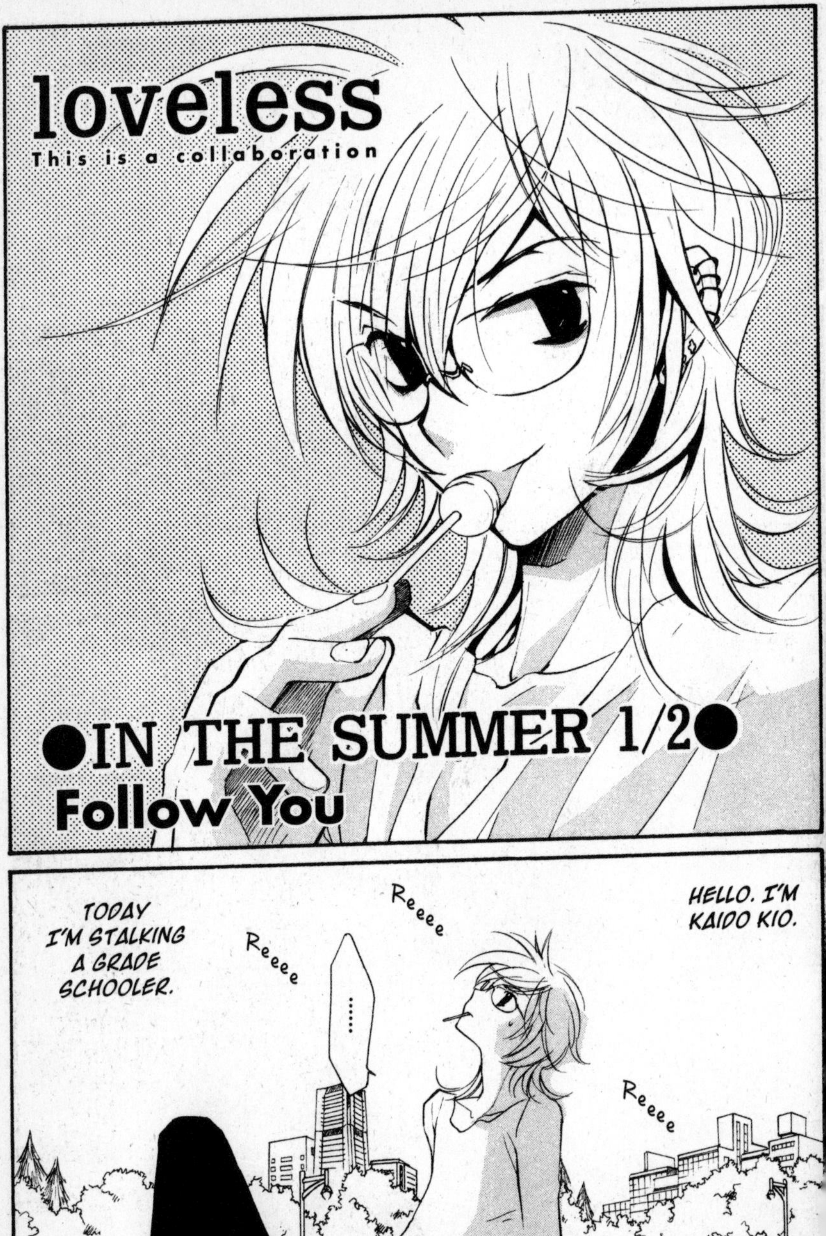
loveless
This is a collaboration
●IN THE SUMMER 1/2●
Follow You
HELLO. I'M KAIDO KIO.
Reeeee
Reeeee
......
TODAY I'M STALKING A GRADE SCHOOLER.
Reeeee

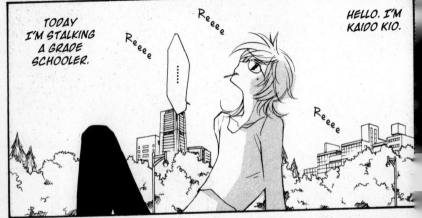

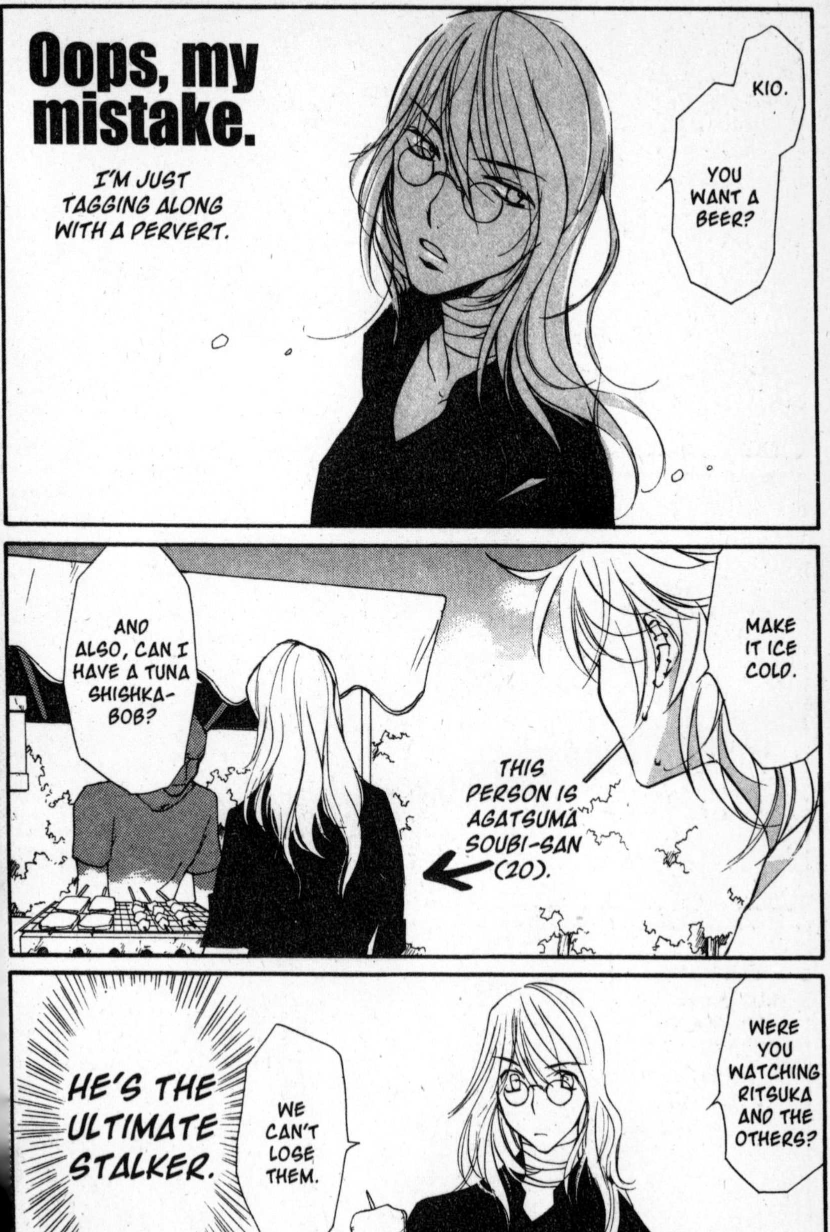
KIO.
YOU WANT A BEER?
Oops, my mistake.
I'M JUST TAGGING ALONG WITH A PERVERT.
MAKE IT ICE COLD.
THIS PERSON IS AGATSUMA SOUBI-SAN (20).
AND ALSO, CAN I HAVE A TUNA SHISHKA-BOB?
WERE YOU WATCHING RITSUKA AND THE OTHERS?
WE CAN'T LOSE THEM.
HE'S THE ULTIMATE STALKER.

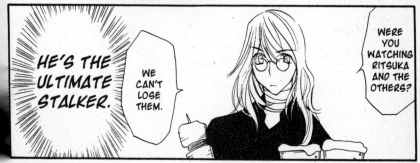

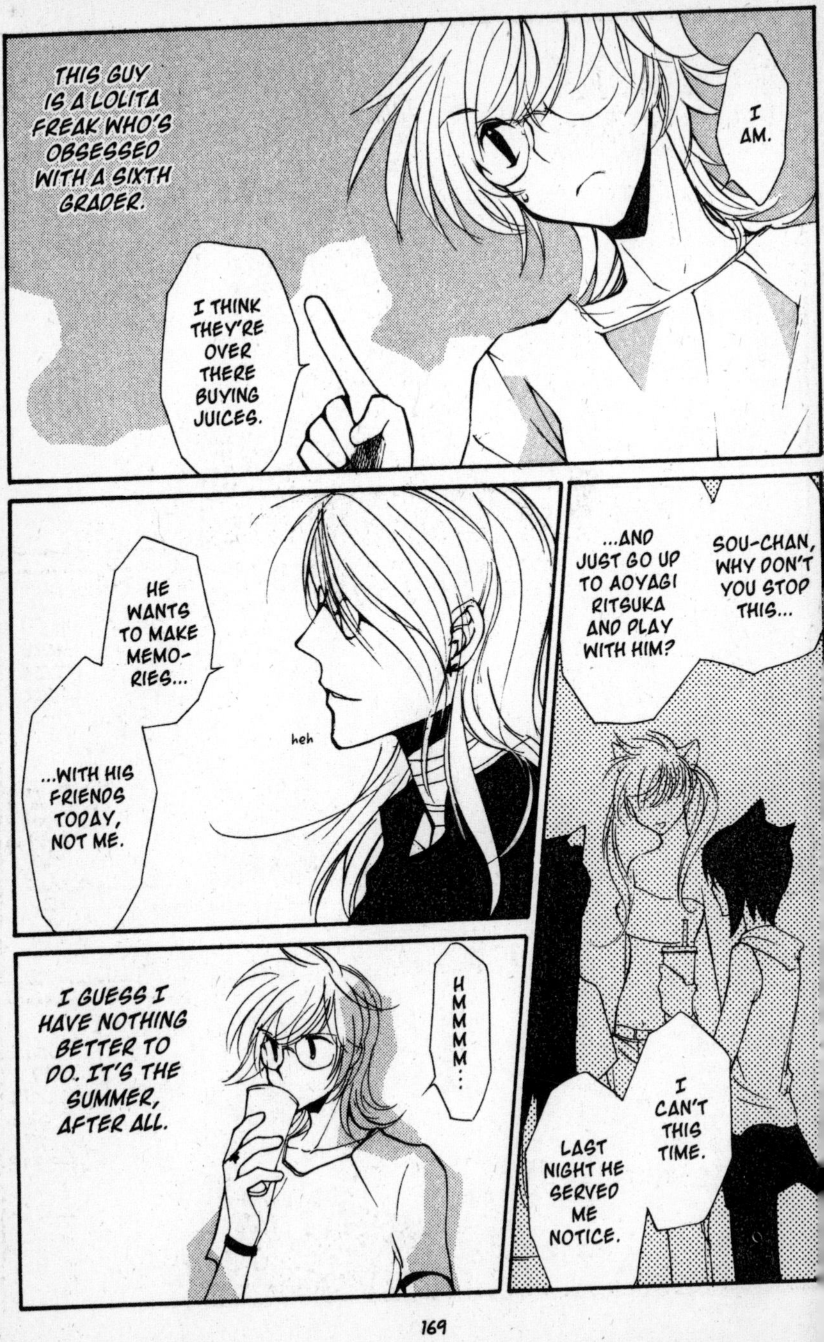
I AM.
THIS GUY IS A LOLITA FREAK WHO'S OBSESSED WITH A SIXTH GRADER.
I THINK THEY'RE OVER THERE BUYING JUICES.
SOU-CHAN, WHY DON'T YOU STOP THIS...
...AND JUST GO UP TO AOYAGI RITSUKA AND PLAY WITH HIM?
I CAN'T THIS TIME.
LAST NIGHT HE SERVED ME NOTICE.
HE WANTS TO MAKE MEMO-RIES...
heh
...WITH HIS FRIENDS TODAY, NOT ME.
HMMMM...
I GUESS I HAVE NOTHING BETTER TO DO. IT'S THE SUMMER, AFTER ALL.

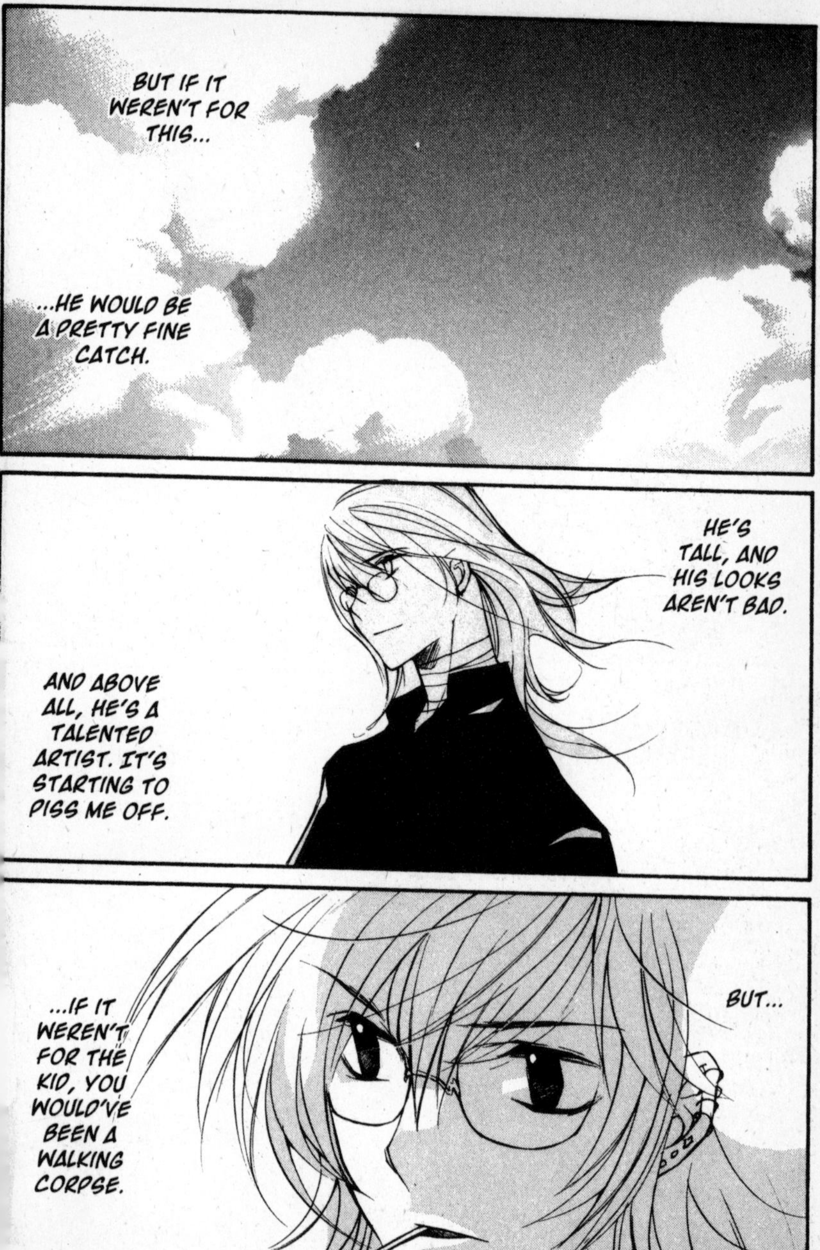
BUT IF IT WEREN'T FOR THIS...
...HE WOULD BE A PRETTY FINE CATCH.
HE'S TALL, AND HIS LOOKS AREN'T BAD.
AND ABOVE ALL, HE'S A TALENTED ARTIST. IT'S STARTING TO PISS ME OFF.
BUT...
...IF IT WEREN'T FOR THE KID, YOU WOULD'VE BEEN A WALKING CORPSE.

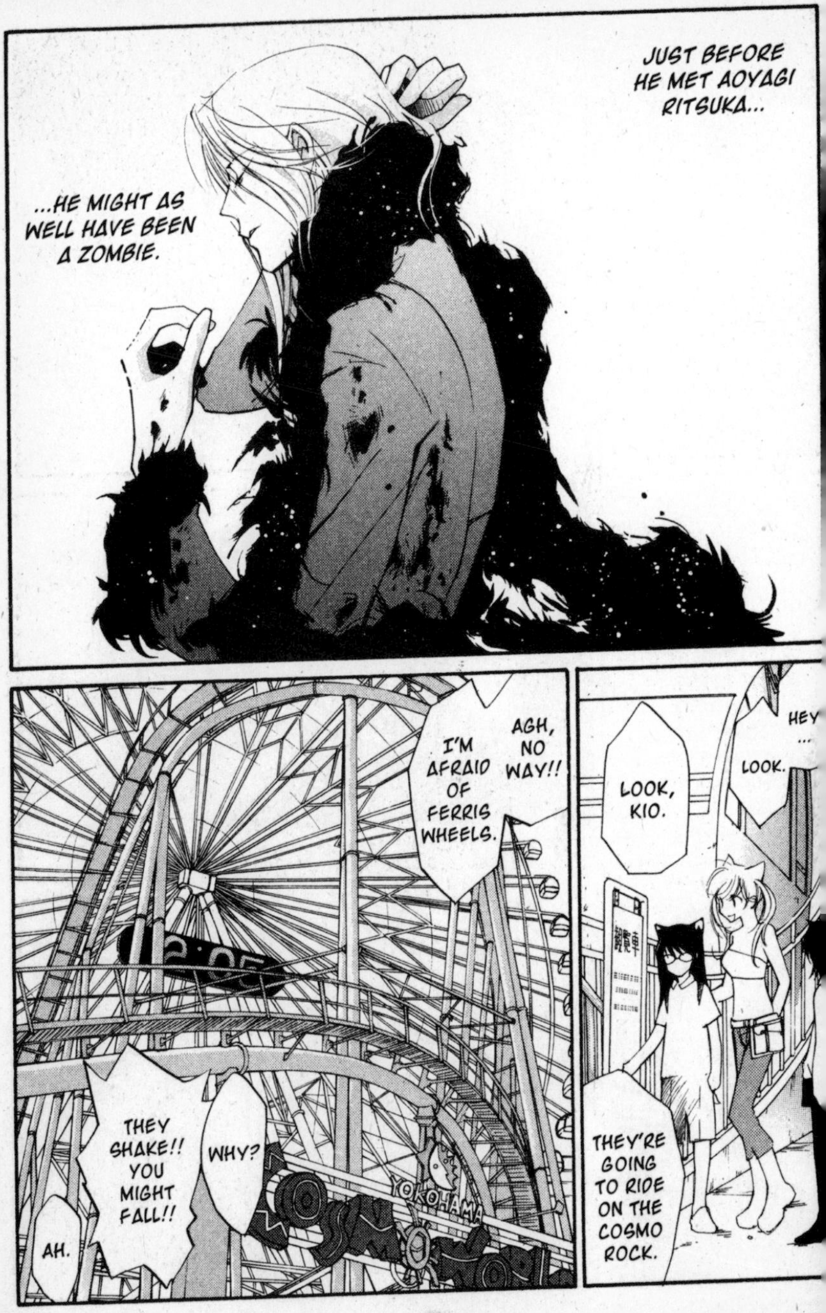
JUST BEFORE HE MET AOYAGI RITSUKA...
...HE MIGHT AS WELL HAVE BEEN A ZOMBIE.
HEY ...
LOOK.
LOOK, KIO.
THEY'RE GOING TO RIDE ON THE COSMO ROCK.
AGH, NO WAY!!
I'M AFRAID OF FERRIS WHEELS.
WHY?
THEY SHAKE!! YOU MIGHT FALL!!
YOKOHAMA
AH.

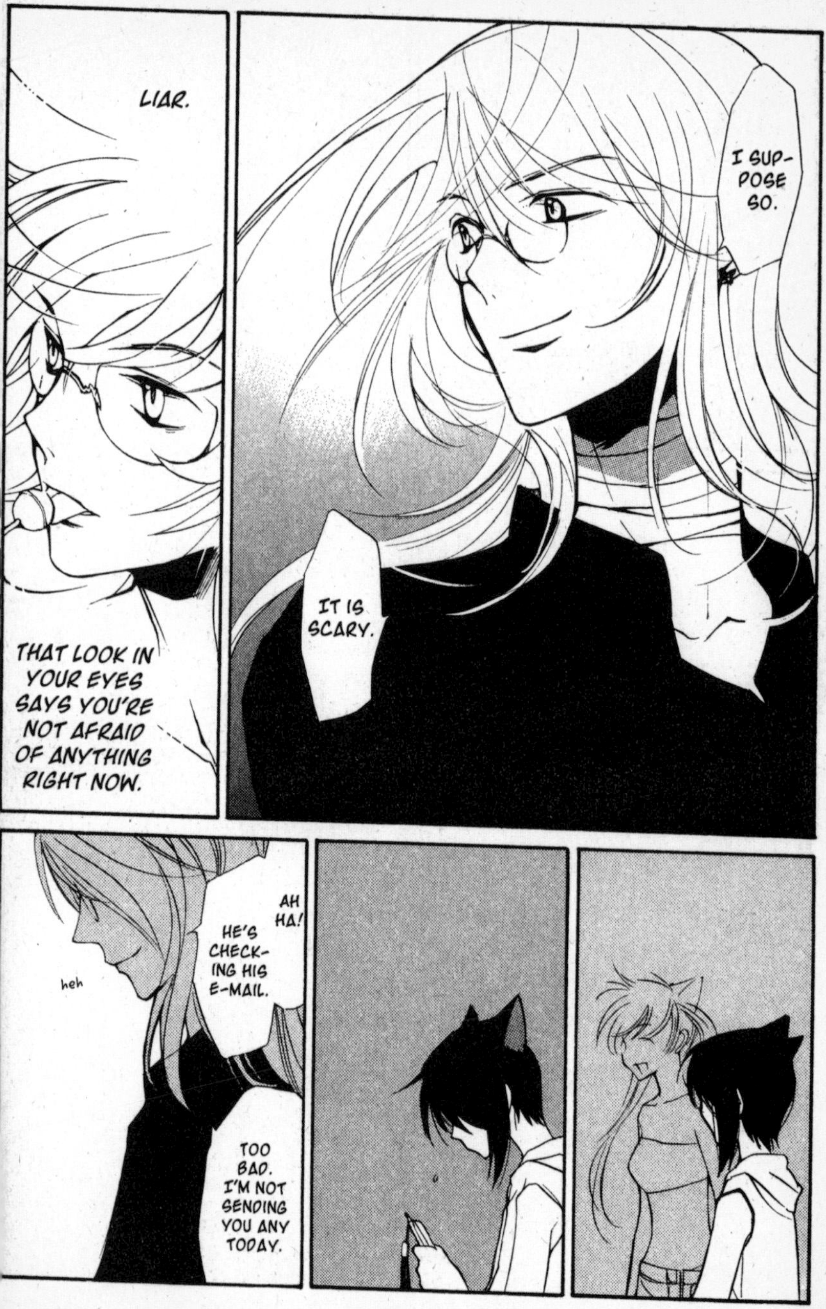
I SUP-
POSE
SO.
IT IS
SCARY.
LIAR.
THAT LOOK IN
YOUR EYES
SAYS YOU'RE
NOT AFRAID
OF ANYTHING
RIGHT NOW.
AH
HA!
HE'S
CHECK-
ING HIS
E-MAIL.
heh
TOO
BAD.
I'M NOT
SENDING
YOU ANY
TODAY.

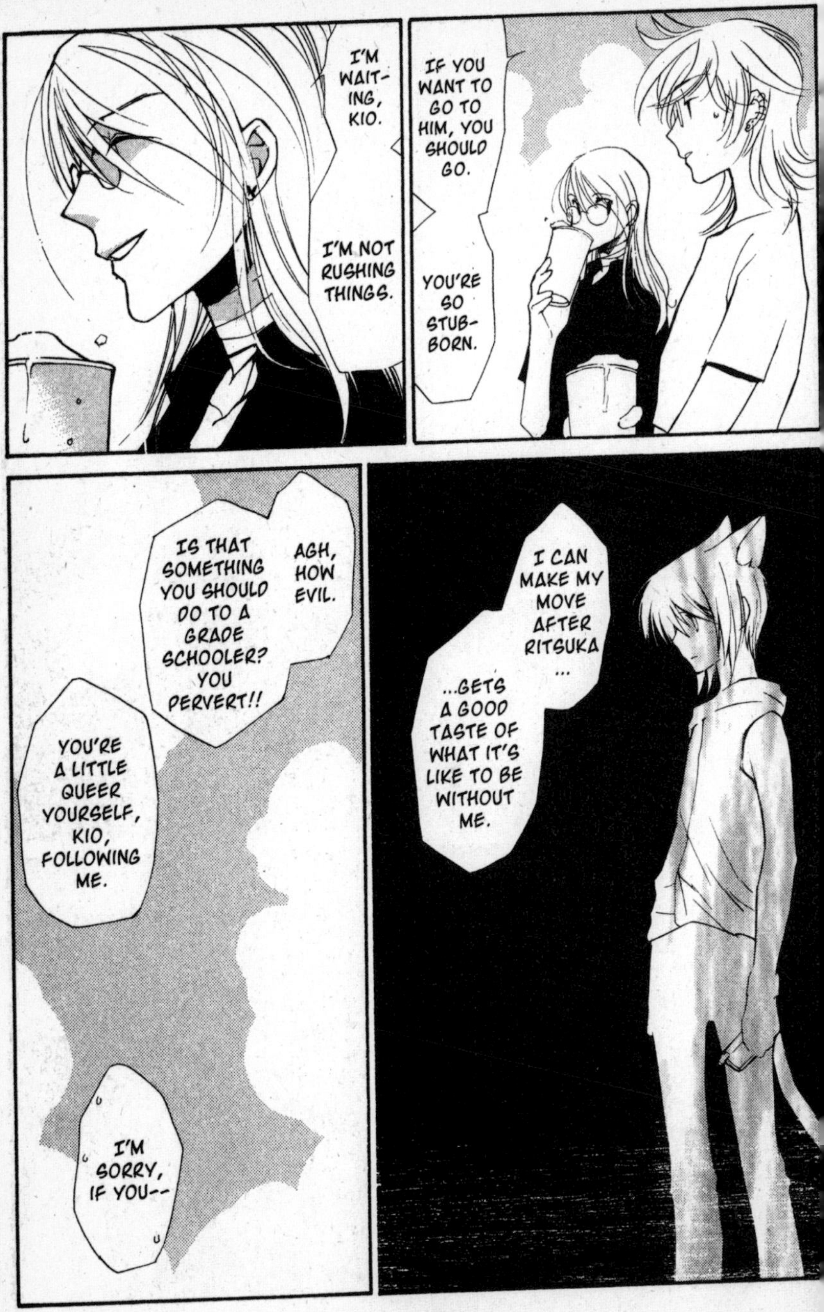
IF YOU WANT TO GO TO HIM, YOU SHOULD GO.
YOU'RE SO STUB-BORN.
I'M WAIT-ING, KIO.
I'M NOT RUSHING THINGS.
I CAN MAKE MY MOVE AFTER RITSUKA...
...GETS A GOOD TASTE OF WHAT IT'S LIKE TO BE WITHOUT ME.
AGH, HOW EVIL.
IS THAT SOMETHING YOU SHOULD DO TO A GRADE SCHOOLER? YOU PERVERT!!
YOU'RE A LITTLE QUEER YOURSELF, KIO, FOLLOWING ME.
I'M SORRY, IF YOU--

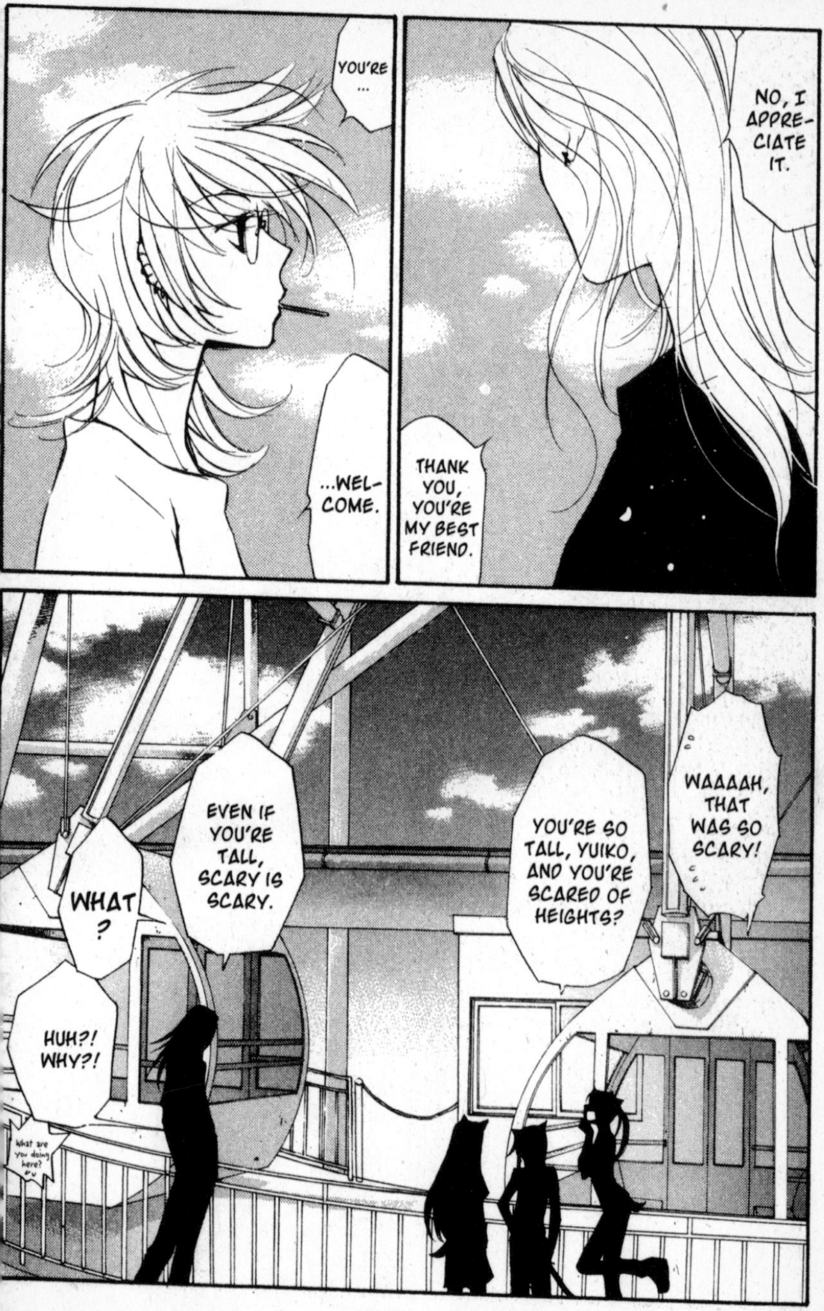
NO, I APPRECIATE IT.
THANK YOU, YOU'RE MY BEST FRIEND.
YOU'RE ...
...WELCOME.
WAAAAH, THAT WAS SO SCARY!
YOU'RE SO TALL, YUIKO, AND YOU'RE SCARED OF HEIGHTS?
EVEN IF YOU'RE TALL, SCARY IS SCARY.
WHAT?
HUH?! WHY?!
What are you doing here?

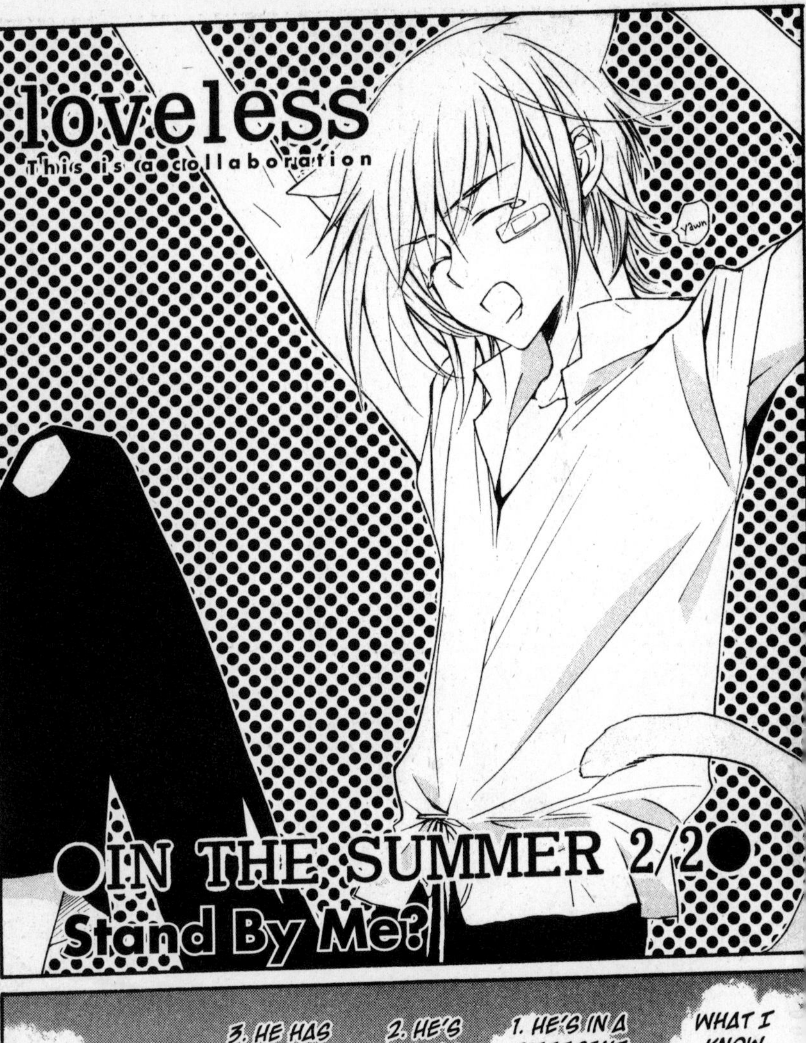
loveless
This is a collaboration
Yawn
IN THE SUMMER 2/2
Stand By Me?

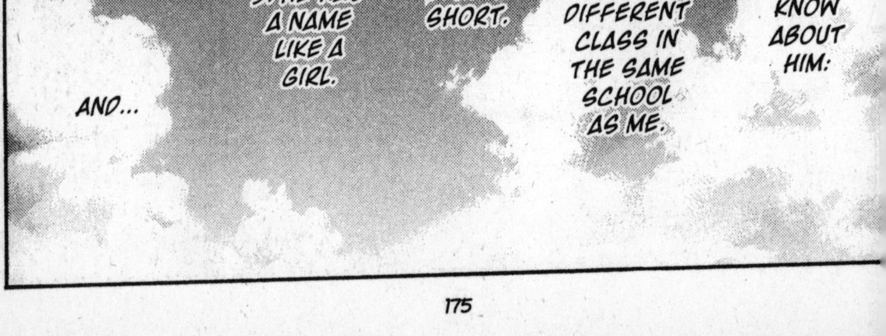
WHAT I KNOW ABOUT HIM:
1. HE'S IN A DIFFERENT CLASS IN THE SAME SCHOOL AS ME.
2. HE'S SHORT.
3. HE HAS A NAME LIKE A GIRL.
AND...

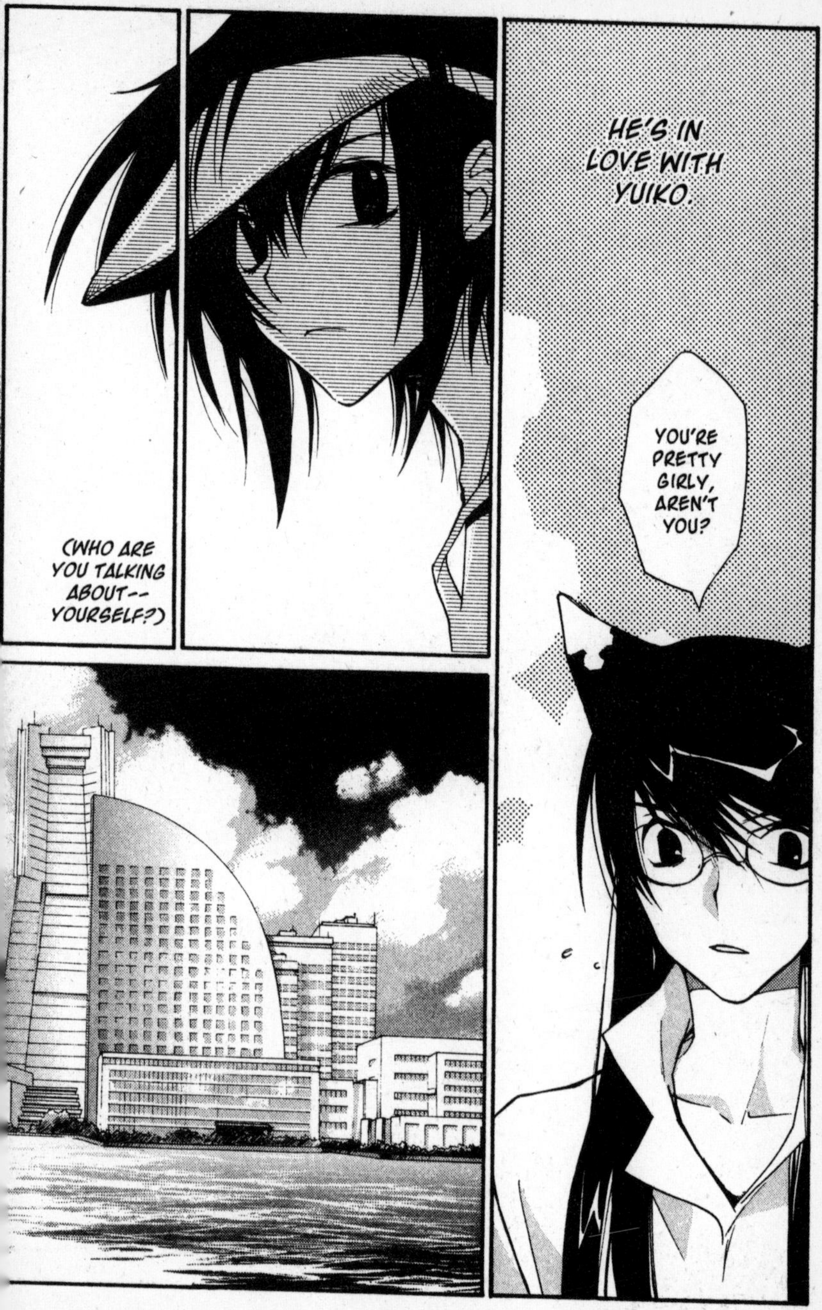
HE'S IN LOVE WITH YUIKO.
YOU'RE PRETTY GIRLY, AREN'T YOU?
(WHO ARE YOU TALKING ABOUT--YOURSELF?)

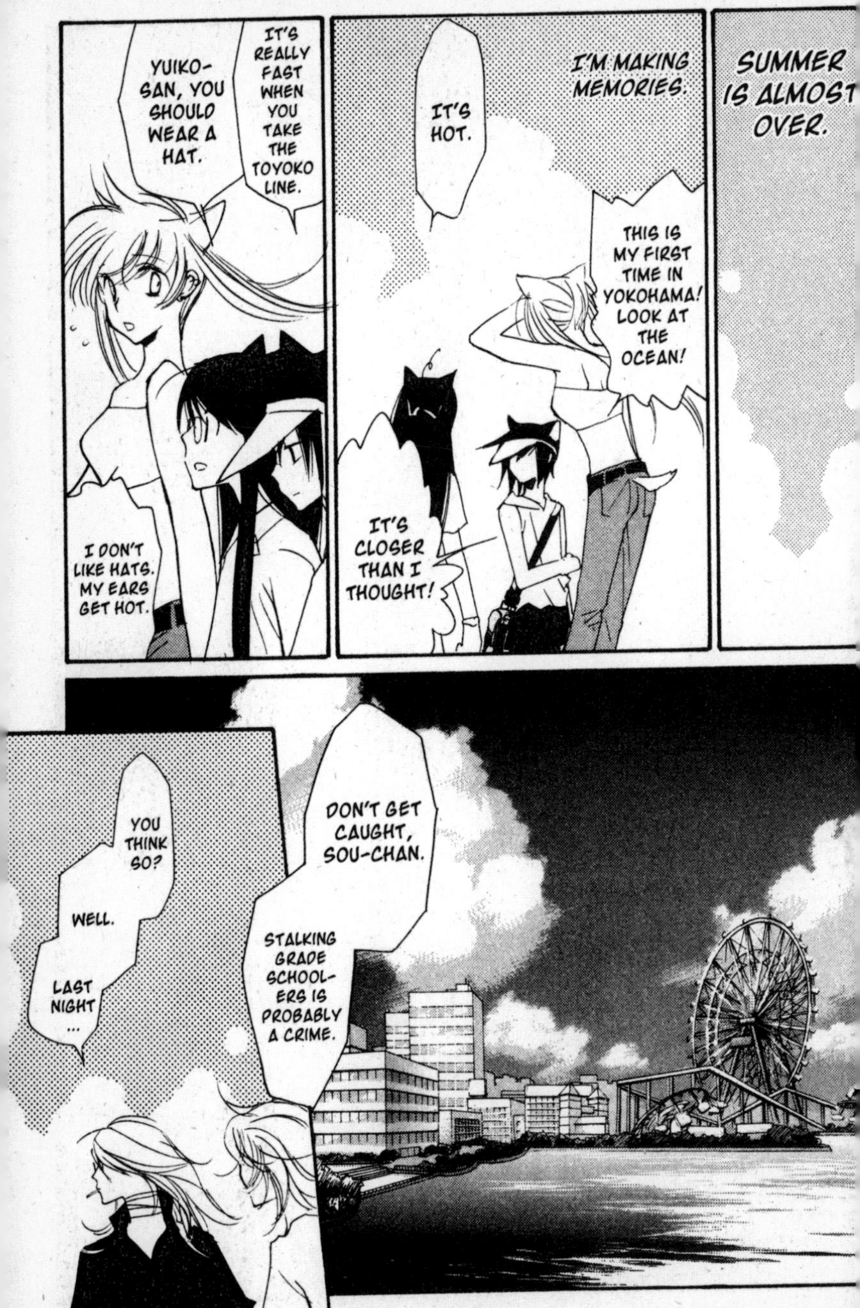
SUMMER IS ALMOST OVER.
I'M MAKING MEMORIES.
IT'S HOT.
THIS IS MY FIRST TIME IN YOKOHAMA! LOOK AT THE OCEAN!
IT'S CLOSER THAN I THOUGHT!
IT'S REALLY FAST WHEN YOU TAKE THE TOYOKO LINE.
YUIKO-SAN, YOU SHOULD WEAR A HAT.
I DON'T LIKE HATS. MY EARS GET HOT.
DON'T GET CAUGHT, SOU-CHAN.
STALKING GRADE SCHOOL-ERS IS PROBABLY A CRIME.
YOU THINK SO?
WELL.
LAST NIGHT ...

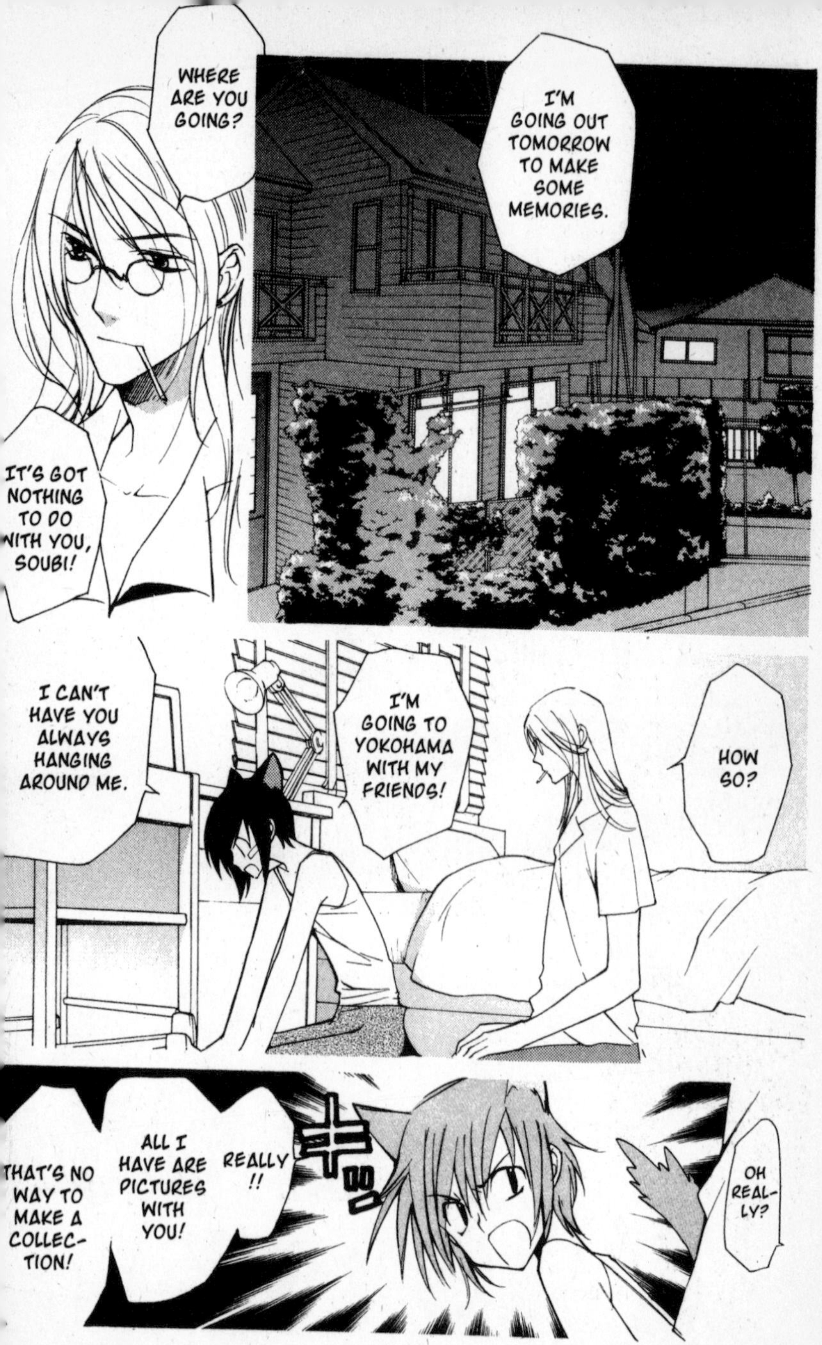
I'M GOING OUT TOMORROW TO MAKE SOME MEMORIES.
WHERE ARE YOU GOING?
IT'S GOT NOTHING TO DO WITH YOU, SOUBI!
HOW SO?
I'M GOING TO YOKOHAMA WITH MY FRIENDS!
I CAN'T HAVE YOU ALWAYS HANGING AROUND ME.
OH REAL-LY?
REALLY !!
ALL I HAVE ARE PICTURES WITH YOU!
THAT'S NO WAY TO MAKE A COLLEC-TION!

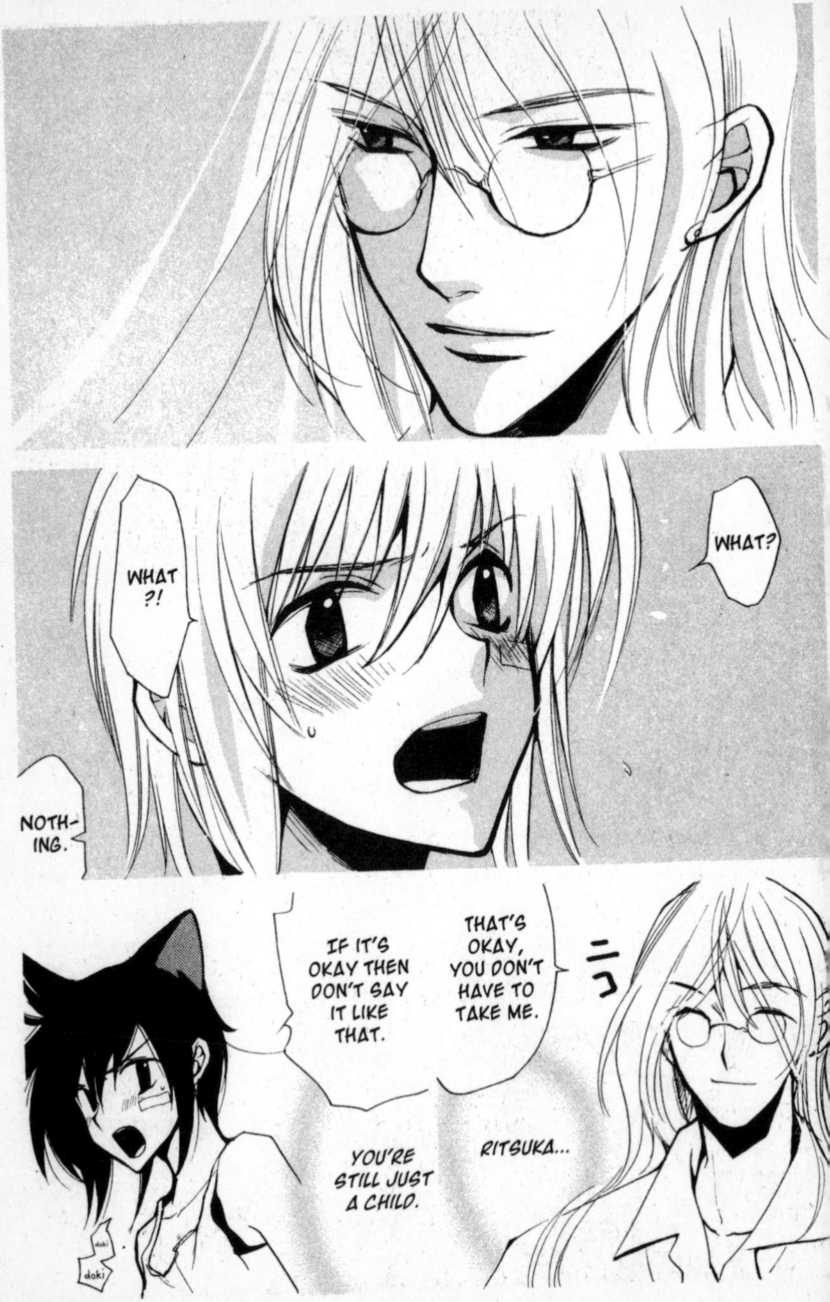
WHAT?
WHAT ?!
NOTH-ING.
ニコ
THAT'S OKAY, YOU DON'T HAVE TO TAKE ME.
IF IT'S OKAY THEN DON'T SAY IT LIKE THAT.
RITSUKA...
YOU'RE STILL JUST A CHILD.
doki doki

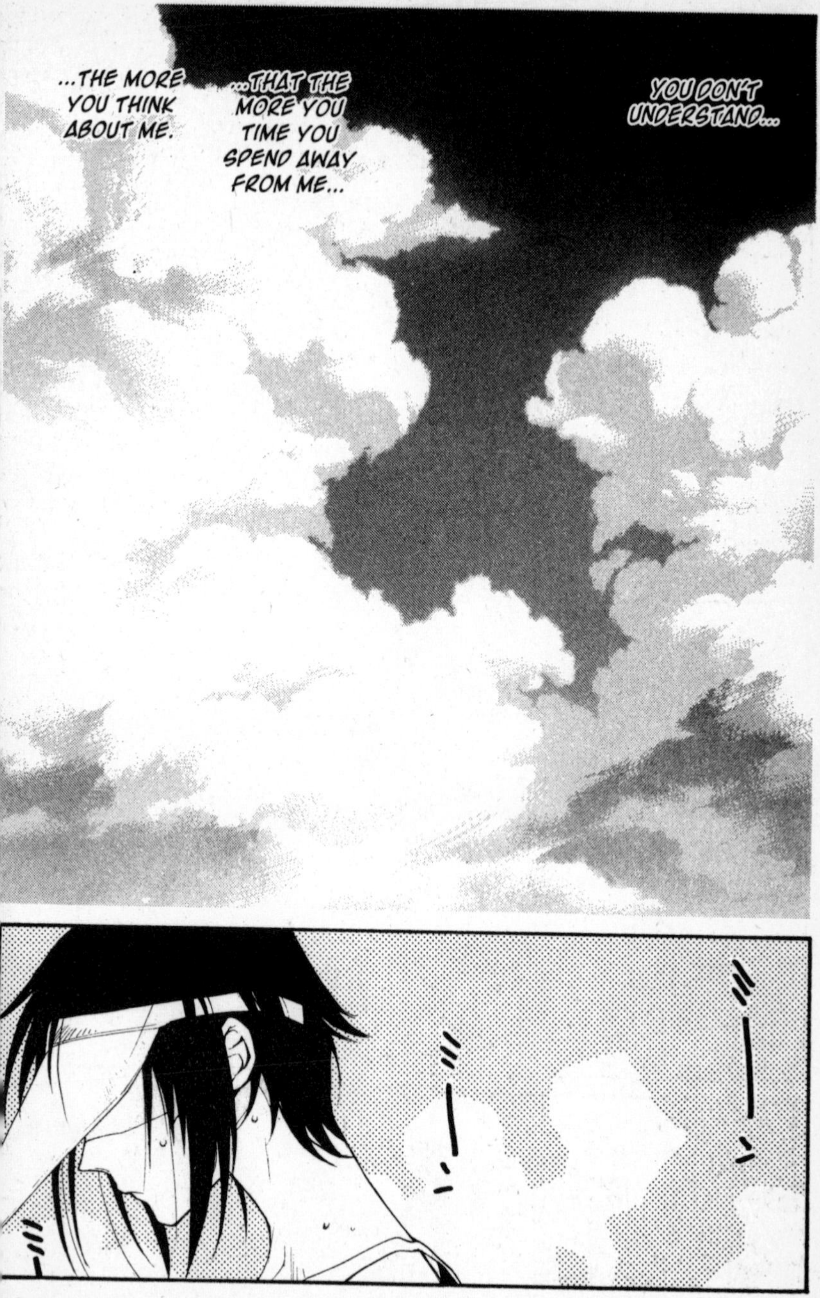
YOU DON'T UNDERSTAND...
...THAT THE MORE YOU TIME YOU SPEND AWAY FROM ME...
...THE MORE YOU THINK ABOUT ME.

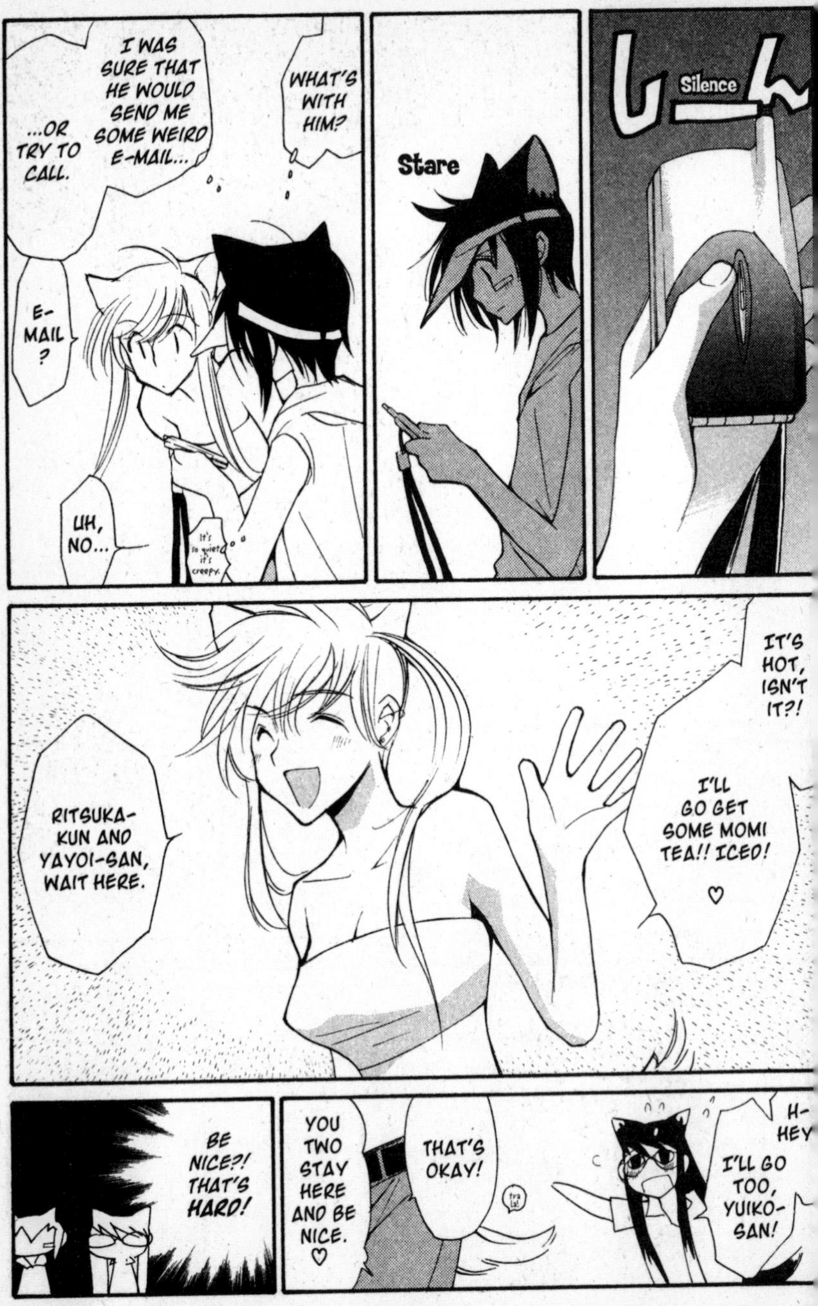
Silence
Stare
WHAT'S WITH HIM?
I WAS SURE THAT HE WOULD SEND ME SOME WEIRD E-MAIL...
...OR TRY TO CALL.
E-MAIL?
It's so quiet it's creepy.
UH, NO...
IT'S HOT, ISN'T IT?!
I'LL GO GET SOME MOMI TEA!! ICED! ♡
RITSUKA-KUN AND YAYOI-SAN, WAIT HERE.
H-HEY
I'LL GO TOO, YUIKO-SAN!
tra la!
THAT'S OKAY!
YOU TWO STAY HERE AND BE NICE. ♡
BE NICE?! THAT'S HARD!

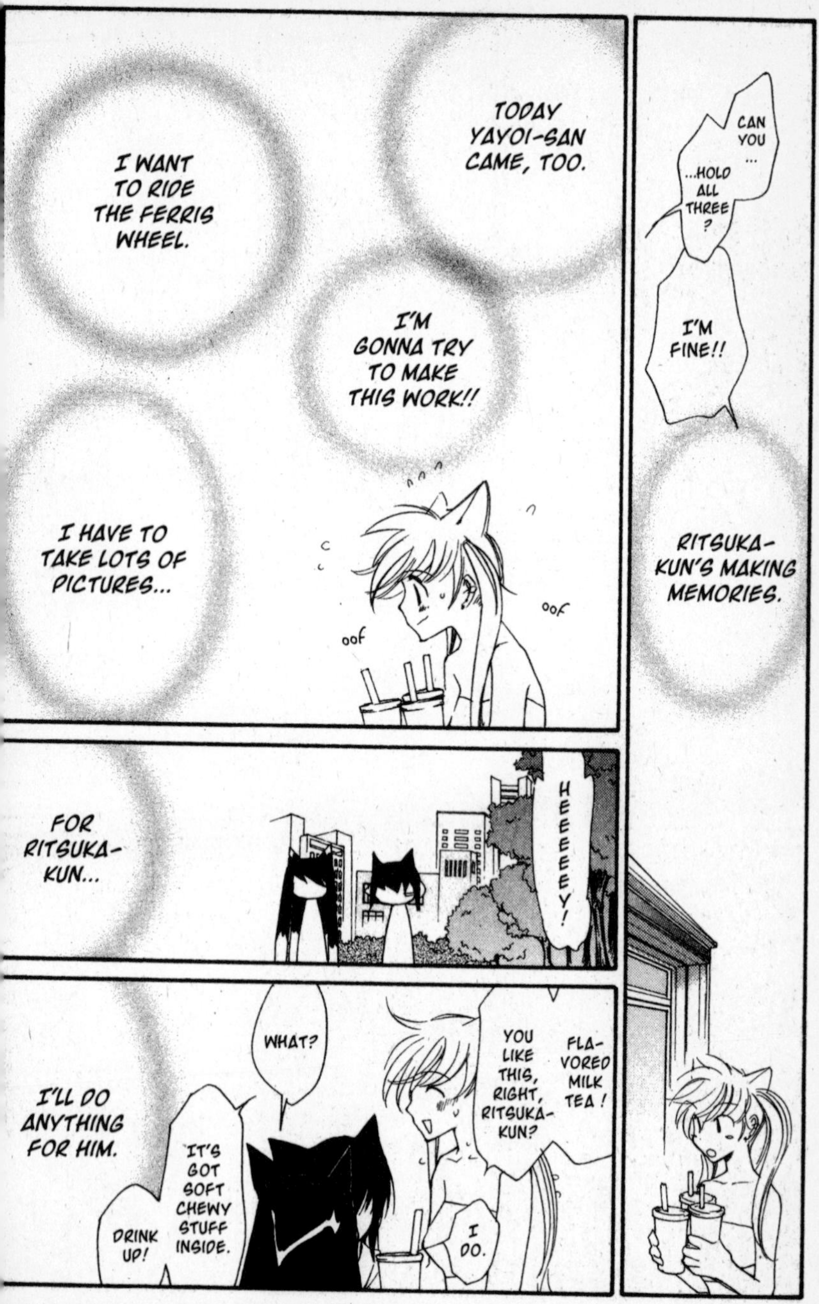
CAN YOU ...
...HOLD ALL THREE ?
I'M FINE!!
RITSUKA-KUN'S MAKING MEMORIES.
TODAY YAYOI-SAN CAME, TOO.
I WANT TO RIDE THE FERRIS WHEEL.
I'M GONNA TRY TO MAKE THIS WORK!!
oof
oof
I HAVE TO TAKE LOTS OF PICTURES...
HEEEEEY!
FOR RITSUKA-KUN...
FLAVORED MILK TEA !
YOU LIKE THIS, RIGHT, RITSUKA-KUN?
I DO.
WHAT?
IT'S GOT SOFT CHEWY STUFF INSIDE.
DRINK UP!
I'LL DO ANYTHING FOR HIM.

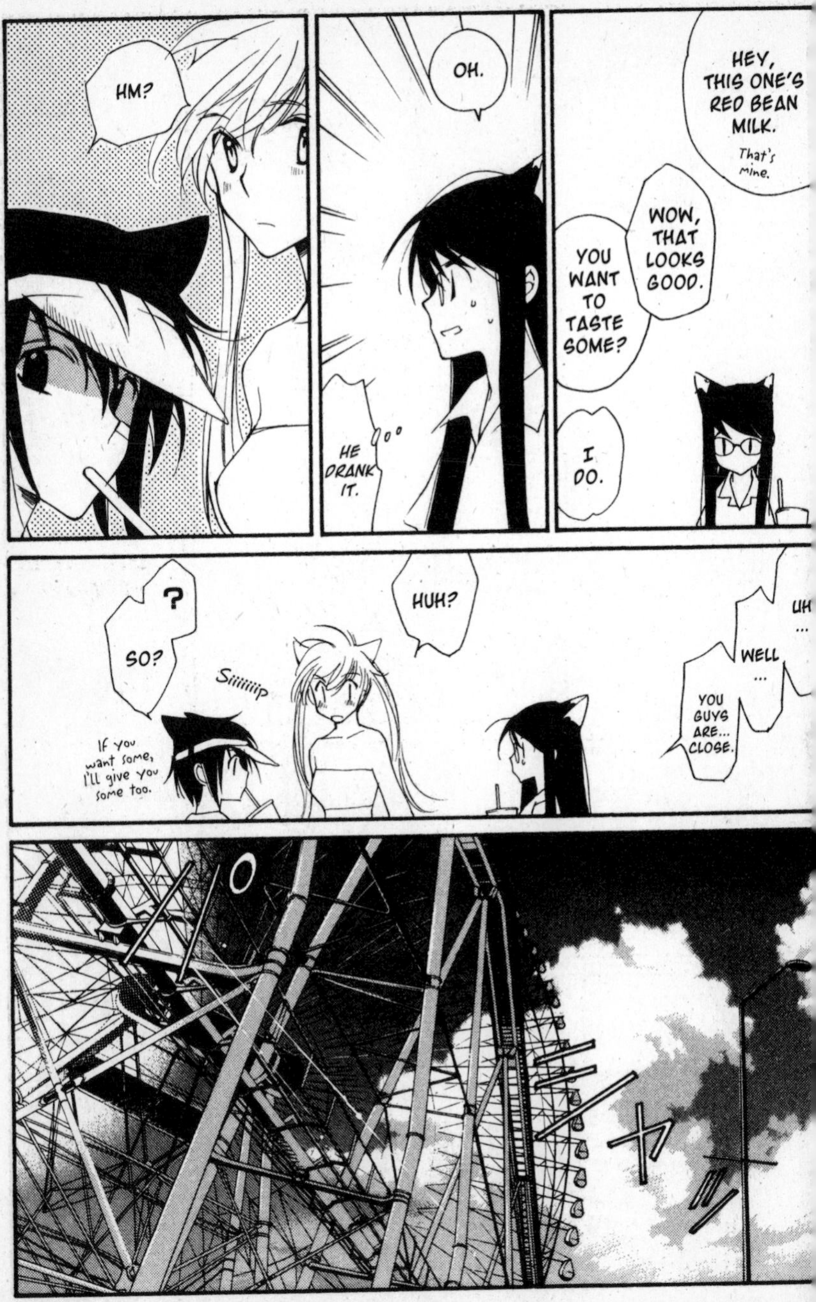
HEY, THIS ONE'S RED BEAN MILK.
That's mine.
WOW, THAT LOOKS GOOD.
YOU WANT TO TASTE SOME?
I DO.
OH.
HE DRANK IT.
HM?
UH... WELL...
YOU GUYS ARE... CLOSE.
HUH?
? SO?
Siiiiiiip
If you want some, I'll give you some too.

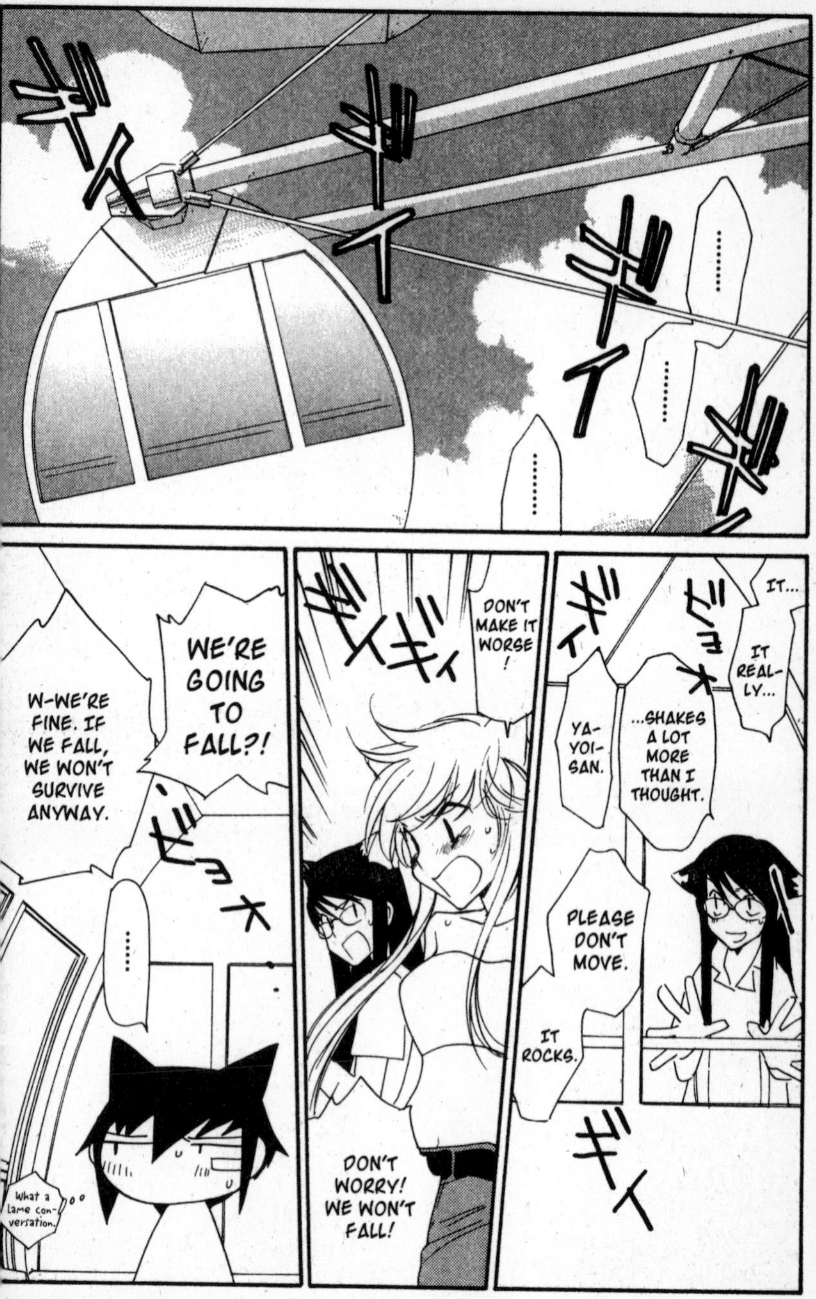
......
......
......
IT...
IT REALLY...
...SHAKES A LOT MORE THAN I THOUGHT.
YA-YOI-SAN.
PLEASE DON'T MOVE.
IT ROCKS.
DON'T MAKE IT WORSE!
DON'T WORRY! WE WON'T FALL!
WE'RE GOING TO FALL?!
W-WE'RE FINE. IF WE FALL, WE WON'T SURVIVE ANYWAY.
......
What a lame conversation.

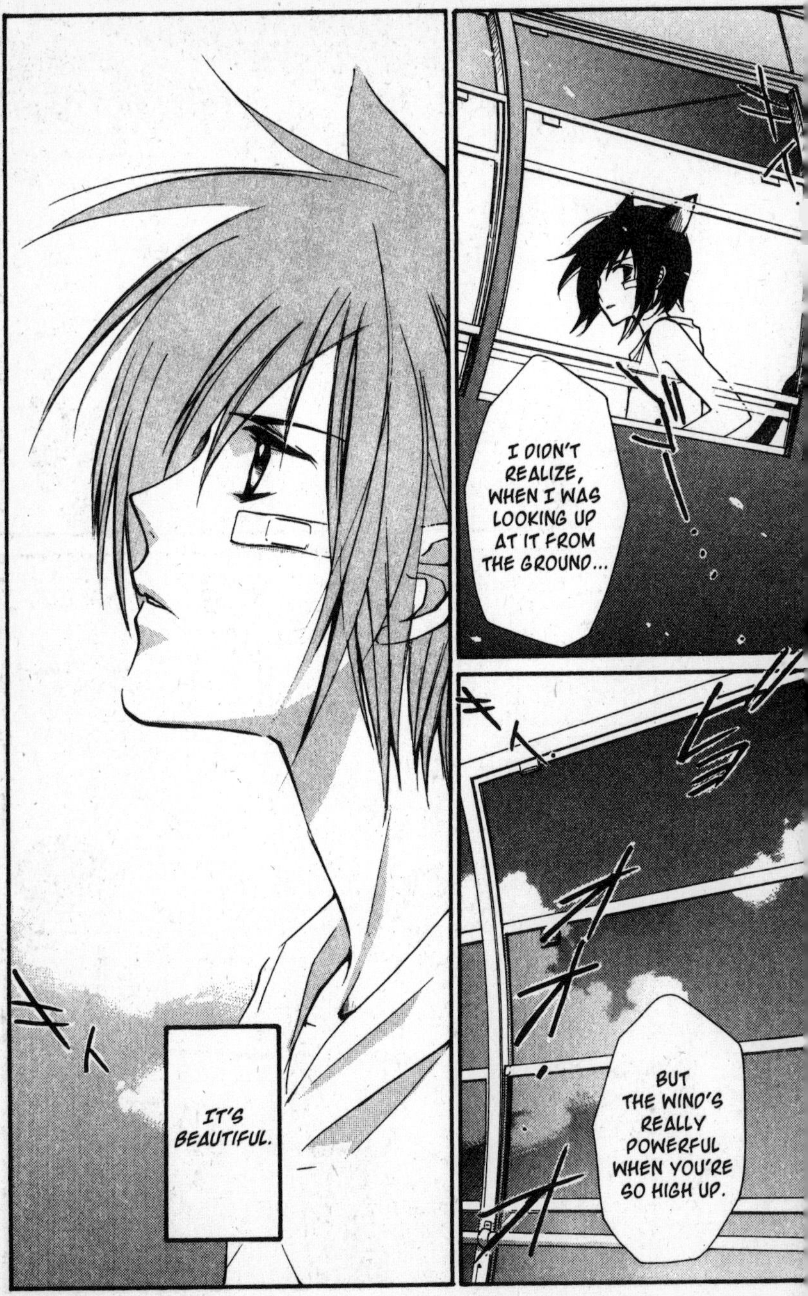
I DIDN'T REALIZE, WHEN I WAS LOOKING UP AT IT FROM THE GROUND...
BUT THE WIND'S REALLY POWERFUL WHEN YOU'RE SO HIGH UP.
IT'S BEAUTIFUL.

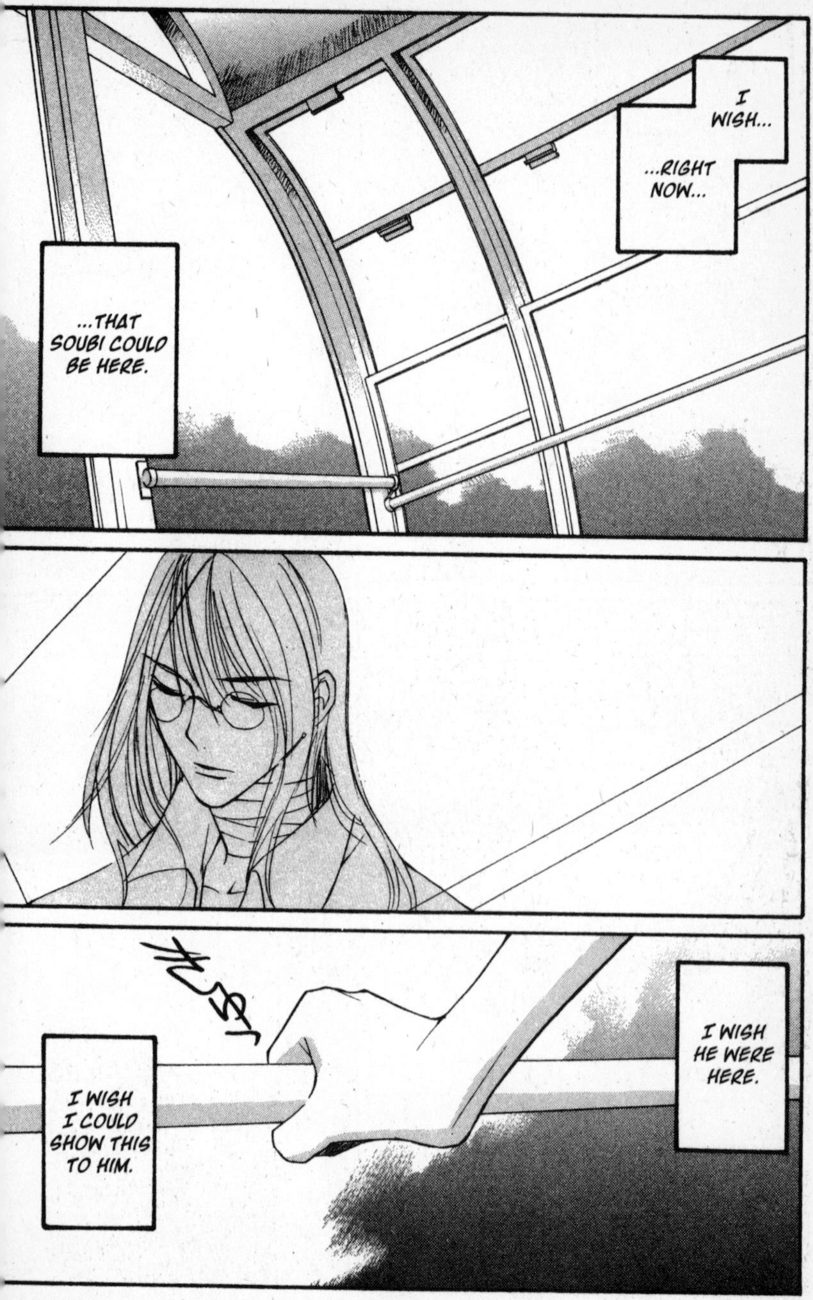
I WISH...
...RIGHT NOW...
...THAT SOUBI COULD BE HERE.
I WISH HE WERE HERE.
I WISH I COULD SHOW THIS TO HIM.

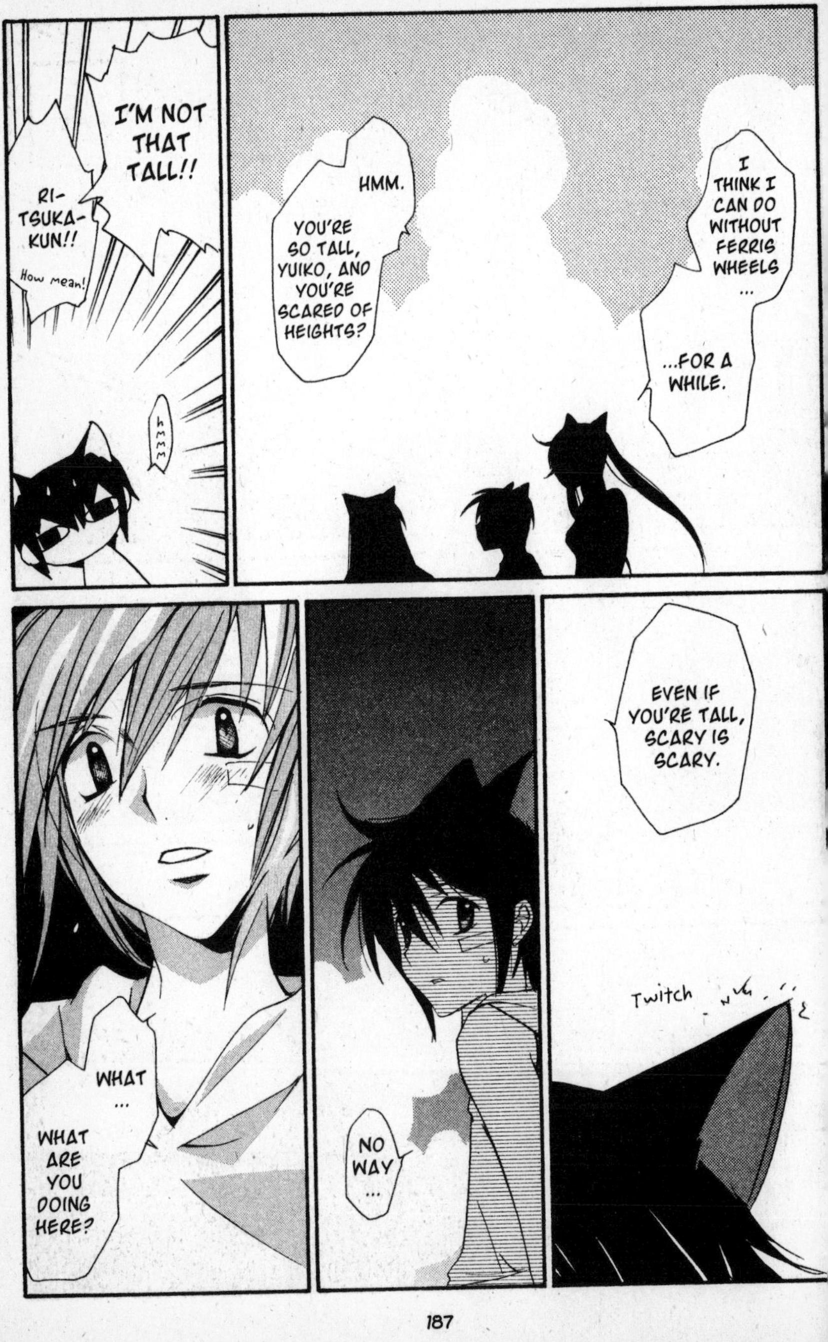
I THINK I CAN DO WITHOUT FERRIS WHEELS ...
...FOR A WHILE.
HMM.
YOU'RE SO TALL, YUIKO, AND YOU'RE SCARED OF HEIGHTS?
I'M NOT THAT TALL!!
RI-TSUKA-KUN!!
How mean!
hmmm
EVEN IF YOU'RE TALL, SCARY IS SCARY.
Twitch
NO WAY ...
WHAT ...
WHAT ARE YOU DOING HERE?

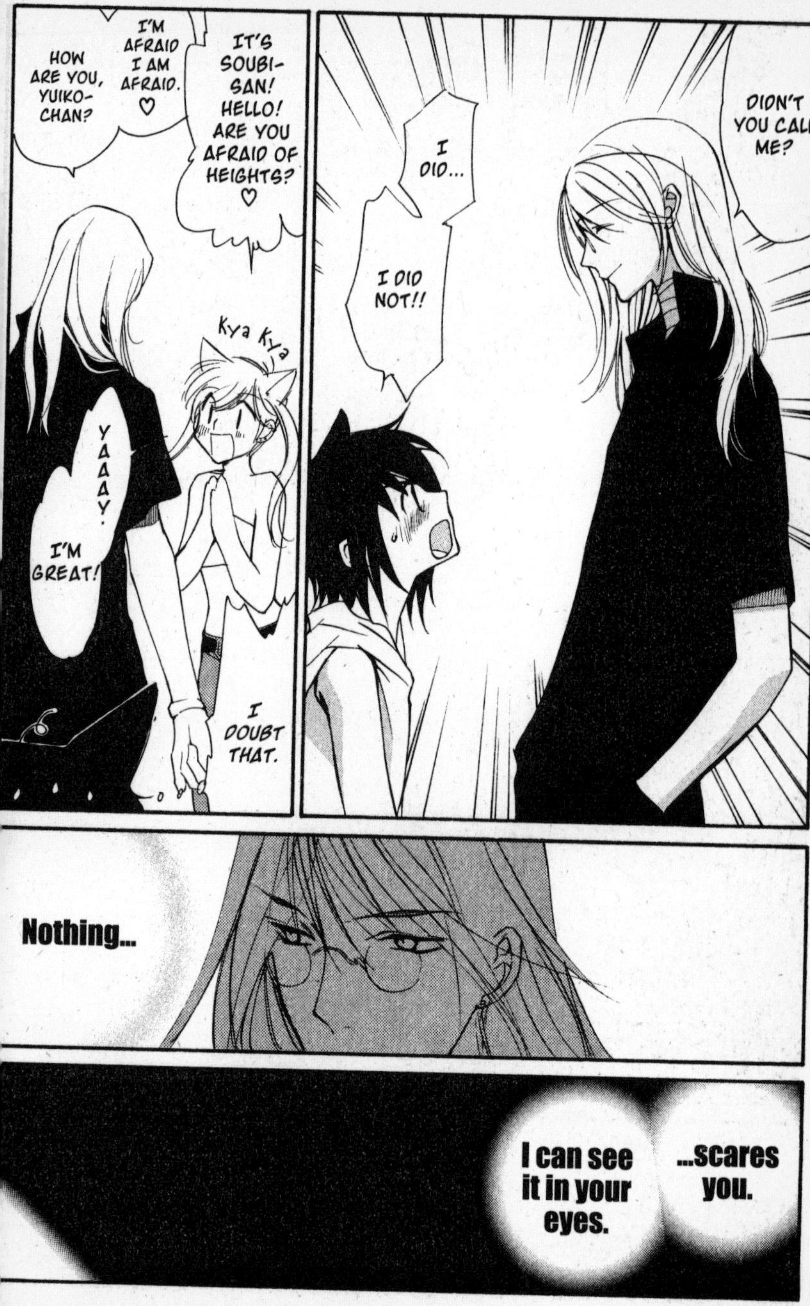
DIDN'T YOU CALL ME?
I DID...
I DID NOT!!
IT'S SOUBI-SAN! HELLO! ARE YOU AFRAID OF HEIGHTS? ♡
I'M AFRAID I AM AFRAID. ♡
HOW ARE YOU, YUIKO-CHAN?
Kya Kya
YAAAAY. I'M GREAT!
I DOUBT THAT.
Nothing...
...scares you.
I can see it in your eyes.

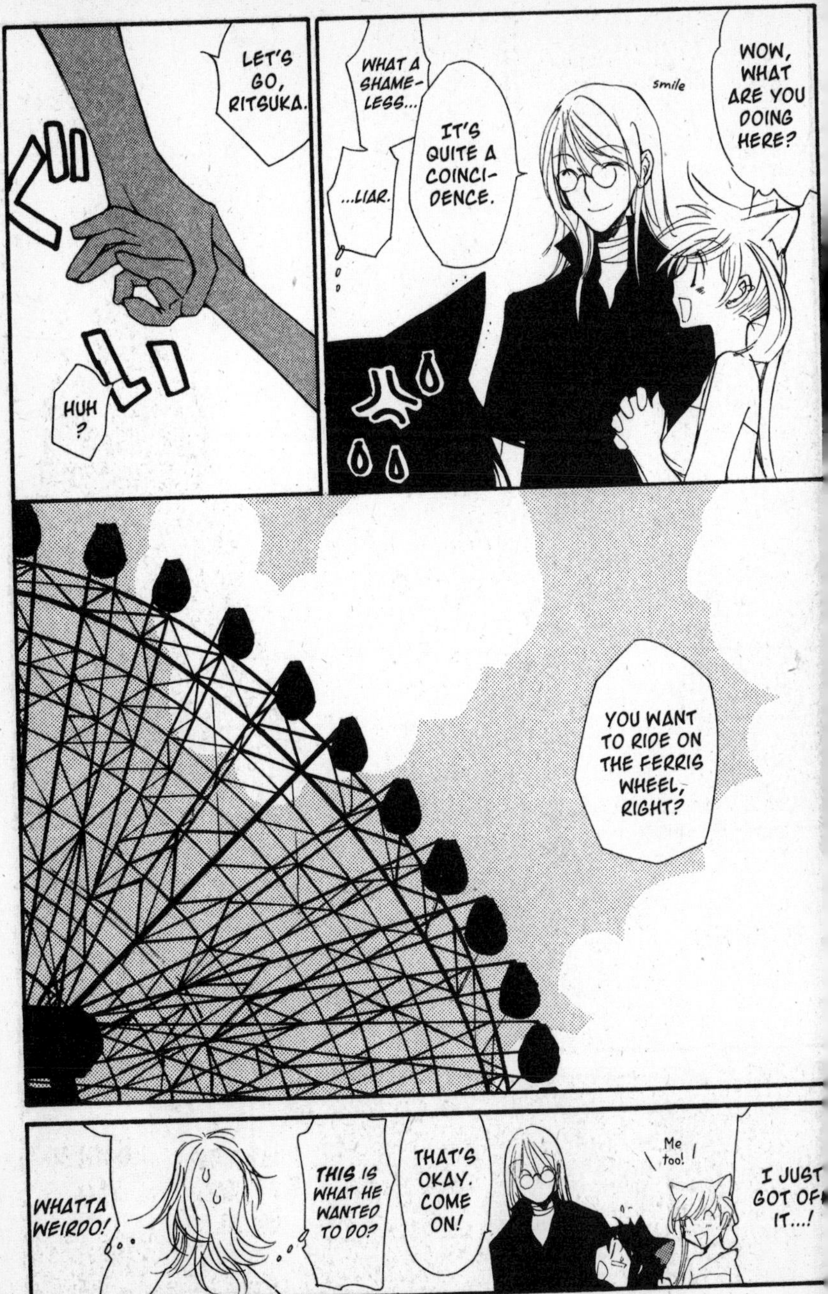

WOW, WHAT ARE YOU DOING HERE?
smile
IT'S QUITE A COINCIDENCE.
WHAT A SHAMELESS...
...LIAR.
LET'S GO, RITSUKA.
HUH?
YOU WANT TO RIDE ON THE FERRIS WHEEL, RIGHT?
I JUST GOT OF IT...!
Me too!
THAT'S OKAY. COME ON!
THIS IS WHAT HE WANTED TO DO?
WHATTA WEIRDO!

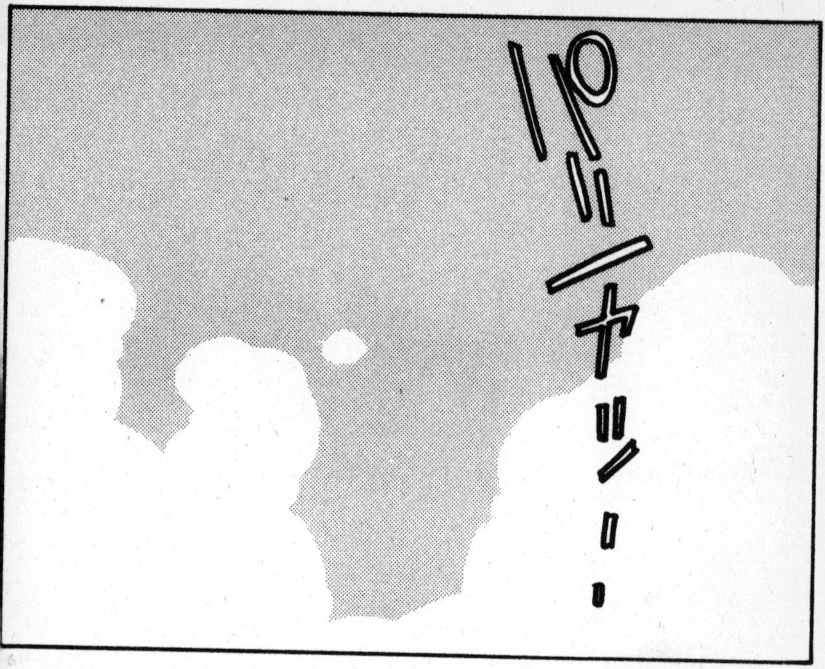

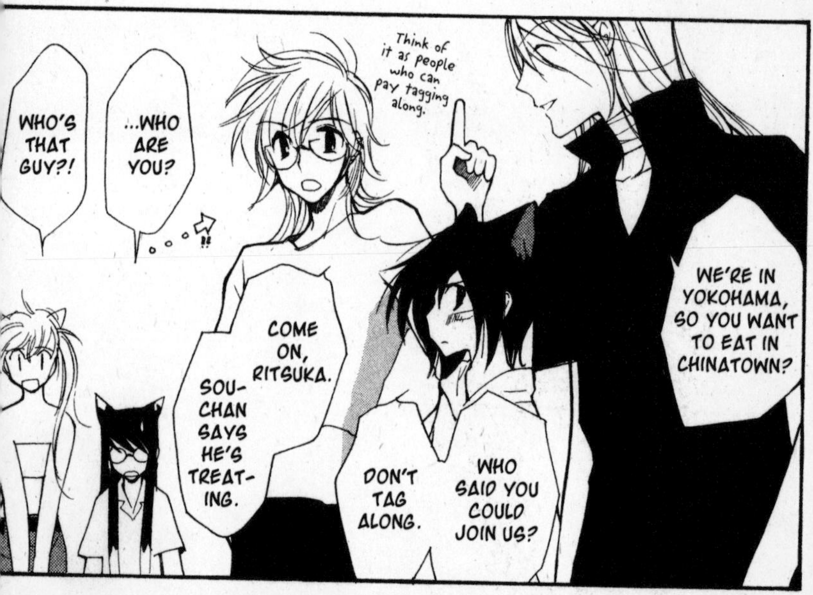

Think of it as people who can pay tagging along.
...WHO ARE YOU?
WHO'S THAT GUY?!
WE'RE IN YOKOHAMA, SO YOU WANT TO EAT IN CHINATOWN?
WHO SAID YOU COULD JOIN US?
DON'T TAG ALONG.
COME ON, RITSUKA.
SOU-CHAN SAYS HE'S TREAT-ING.

Loveless 2 The End

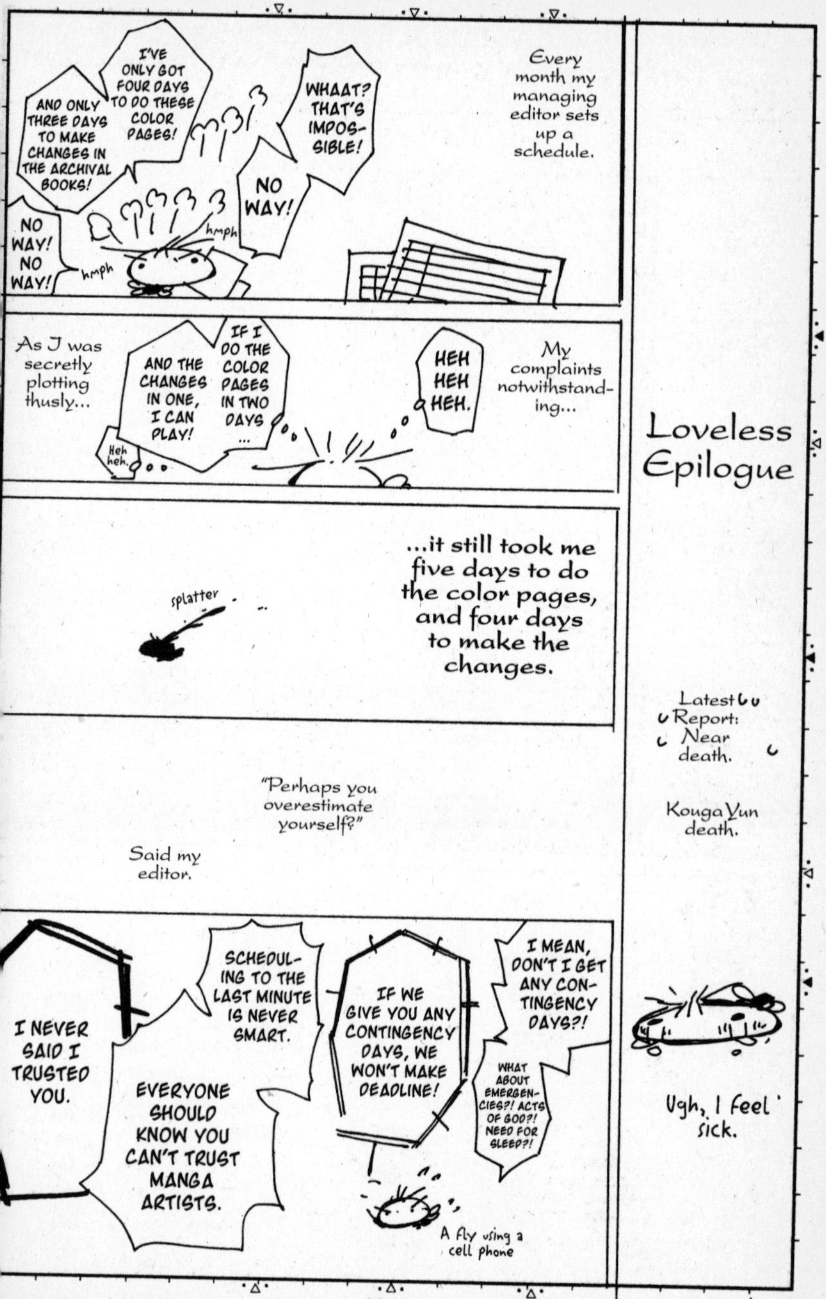
Loveless Epilogue
Latest Report: Near death.
Kouga Yun death.
Ugh, I feel sick.
Every month my managing editor sets up a schedule.
WHAAT? THAT'S IMPOSSIBLE!
NO WAY!
I'VE ONLY GOT FOUR DAYS TO DO THESE COLOR PAGES!
AND ONLY THREE DAYS TO MAKE CHANGES IN THE ARCHIVAL BOOKS!
hmph
NO WAY! NO WAY!
hmph
My complaints notwithstanding...
HEH HEH HEH.
IF I DO THE COLOR PAGES IN TWO DAYS...
AND THE CHANGES IN ONE, I CAN PLAY!
Heh heh.
As I was secretly plotting thusly...
...it still took me five days to do the color pages, and four days to make the changes.
splatter
"Perhaps you overestimate yourself?"
Said my editor.
I MEAN, DON'T I GET ANY CONTINGENCY DAYS?!
WHAT ABOUT EMERGENCIES?! ACTS OF GOD?! NEED FOR SLEEP?!
IF WE GIVE YOU ANY CONTINGENCY DAYS, WE WON'T MAKE DEADLINE!
SCHEDULING TO THE LAST MINUTE IS NEVER SMART.
A fly using a cell phone
EVERYONE SHOULD KNOW YOU CAN'T TRUST MANGA ARTISTS.
I NEVER SAID I TRUSTED YOU.

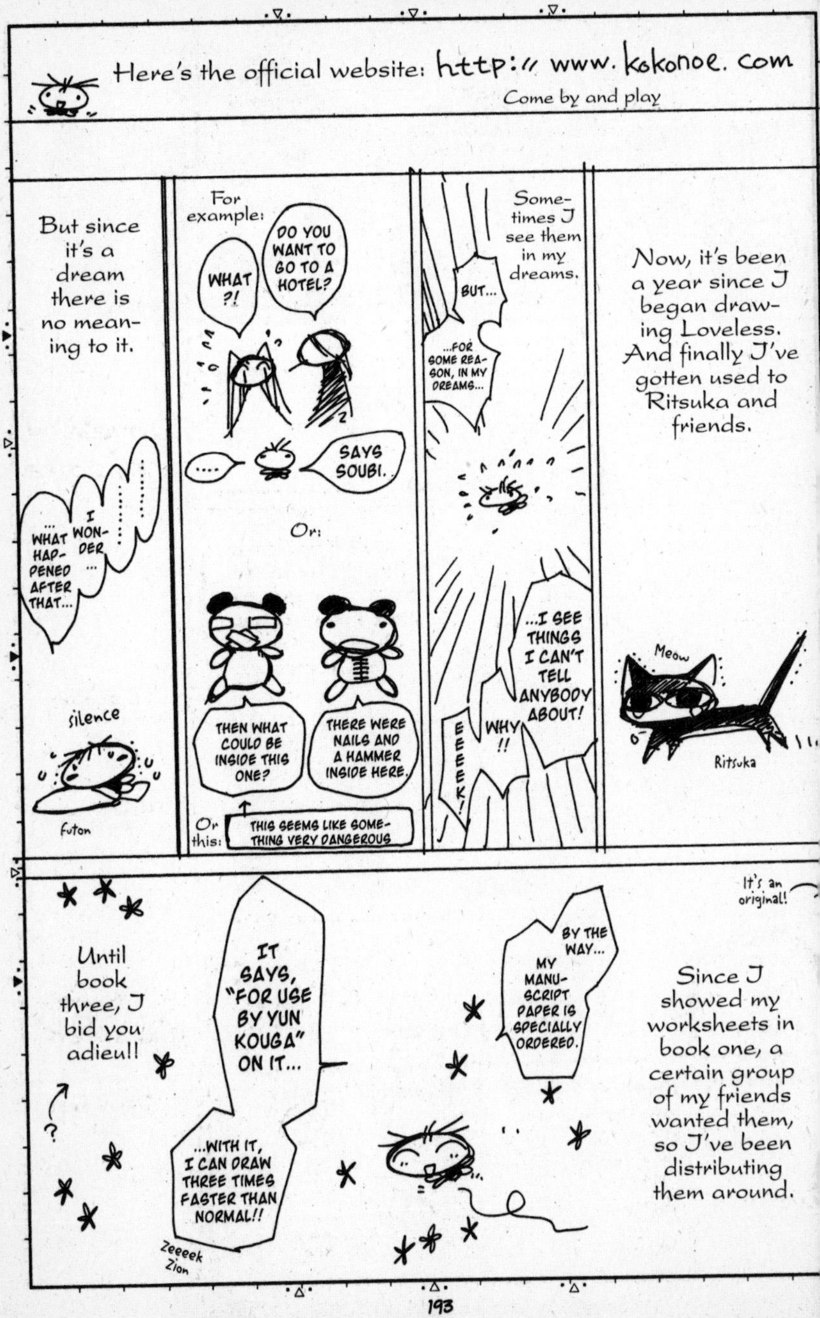
Here's the official website: http:// www.kokonoe.com
Come by and play
Now, it's been a year since I began drawing Loveless. And finally I've gotten used to Ritsuka and friends.
Meow
Ritsuka
Sometimes I see them in my dreams.
BUT...
...FOR SOME REASON, IN MY DREAMS...
...I SEE THINGS I CAN'T TELL ANYBODY ABOUT!
WHY!!
EEEEEK!
For example:
DO YOU WANT TO GO TO A HOTEL?
WHAT?!
SAYS SOUBI.
....
Or:
THERE WERE NAILS AND A HAMMER INSIDE HERE.
THEN WHAT COULD BE INSIDE THIS ONE?
Or this:
THIS SEEMS LIKE SOMETHING VERY DANGEROUS
But since it's a dream there is no meaning to it.
I WONDER...
...WHAT HAPPENED AFTER THAT...
silence
Futon
Since I showed my worksheets in book one, a certain group of my friends wanted them, so I've been distributing them around.
It's an original!
BY THE WAY... MY MANUSCRIPT PAPER IS SPECIALLY ORDERED.
IT SAYS, "FOR USE BY YUN KOUGA" ON IT...
...WITH IT, I CAN DRAW THREE TIMES FASTER THAN NORMAL!!
Zeeeek
Zion
Until book three, I bid you adieu!!
?

In The Next Volume of

LOVELESS

LOVELESS
by Yun Kouga

3

After a grueling battle against the powerful Zeros, Soubi is badly injured, and in spite of his training, the pain almost too much to bear. He goes to see Ritsuka, but Soubi's erratic behavior and unpredictable emotions take over, and he abruptly storms away before Ritsuka can care for him. Ritsuka is left tormented and confused...but the mystery behind the death of his older brother is about to take an unbelievable turn. Ritsuka finally decodes the message left by Sleepless and goes to meet one of the members of Septimal Moon!

Loveless Vol. 3 Available October 2006

EPILOGUE: EDITORIAL NOTES ON LOVELESS

In our last volume, Loveless rewriter Christine Boylan commented on Yun Kouga's use of language and the concept of words as power. Building off of that, this time around I'm going to talk a bit about Japanese honorifics and Japanese name order.

As noted in volume 1, this series maintains the Japanese name order, such that family name comes first (Aoyagi) and given name second (Ritsuka, Seimei). While many fans see the Japanese order as lending extra "authenticity" to a text, it can be initially very confusing to new readers who may not be as familiar with Asian naming conventions, and so editors often choose to reverse the name order when presenting a book to Western audiences. However, manga creators can be very particular, and frequently come up with unusual, highly evocative names for characters. In a book where words, and specifically names, are so weighted, I made the editorial decision to try and maintain the Japanese cadence.

Additionally, suffixes on names are also maintained in this version. Suffixes greatly aid Japanese manga authors in establishing character hierarchies linguistically. Some suffixes show a greater distance and/or respect, and changing an honorific suffix, or dropping the suffix altogether, could either show a closer, more casual relationship, or in some circumstances, an offensive level of familiarity! They can be used almost as short cuts to explaining status, and changing a suffix mid-story can demonstrate the evolution of a relationship in a very compact and clear way.

However, English is a very flexible language, and a good writer can capture the essence of character interaction without relying on borrowed terms. After all, in most cases, a "Mr." or "Mrs." serves just as well as a "-san." Nevertheless, there are situations where maintaining honorifics makes sense. For instance, Shinonome-sensei's decision to call the younger Soubi "Agatsuma-kun," rather than "-san," reflects her attempt to restore what she sees as the proper balance in their relationship, and is a stronger statement than simply dropping "Mr." would imply to an English speaker. She's a teacher, and a (slightly) older, respected member of society, but even though Soubi spoke politely to her, the content of his conversation is cold and cruel, to the point of being arrogant. She's too shy to confront him very directly about his impertinence, but reminding herself to use the suffix generally reserved for younger people (the same suffix she uses with her male students!) is her attempt at establishing her authority after being humiliated. Unfortunately, her polite instincts are stronger than her will, and even when they meet a second time, later in the volume, she automatically starts to use "-san," and has to remind herself of her resolve.

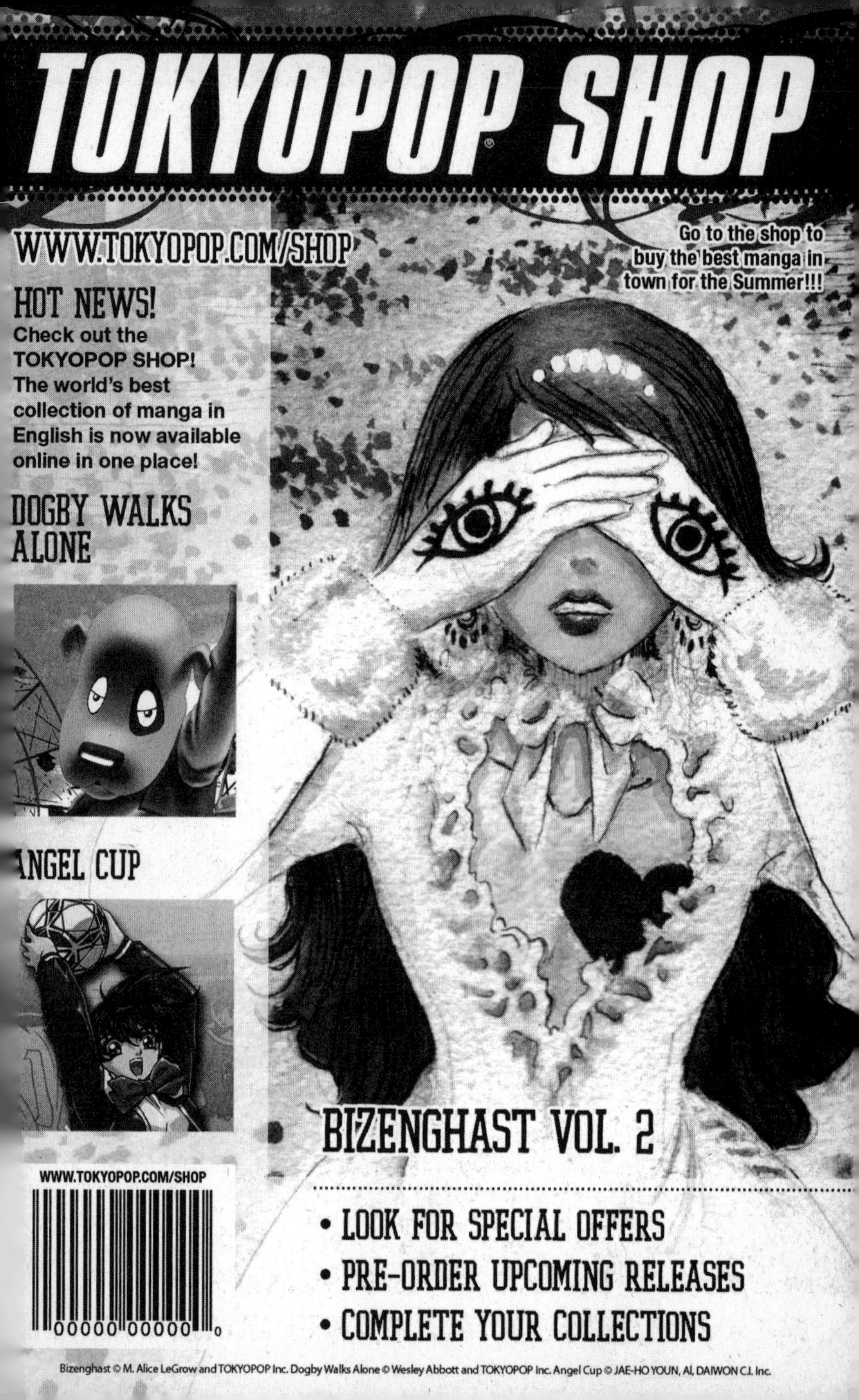

TOKYOPOP® SHOP
WWW.TOKYOPOP.COM/SHOP
Go to the shop to buy the best manga in town for the Summer!!!
HOT NEWS!
Check out the TOKYOPOP SHOP! The world's best collection of manga in English is now available online in one place!
DOGBY WALKS ALONE
ANGEL CUP
BIZENGHAST VOL. 2
• LOOK FOR SPECIAL OFFERS
• PRE-ORDER UPCOMING RELEASES
• COMPLETE YOUR COLLECTIONS
WWW.TOKYOPOP.COM/SHOP
00000 00000 0
Bizenghast © M. Alice LeGrow and TOKYOPOP Inc. Dogby Walks Alone © Wesley Abbott and TOKYOPOP Inc. Angel Cup © JAE-HO YOUN, AI, DAIWON C.I. Inc.

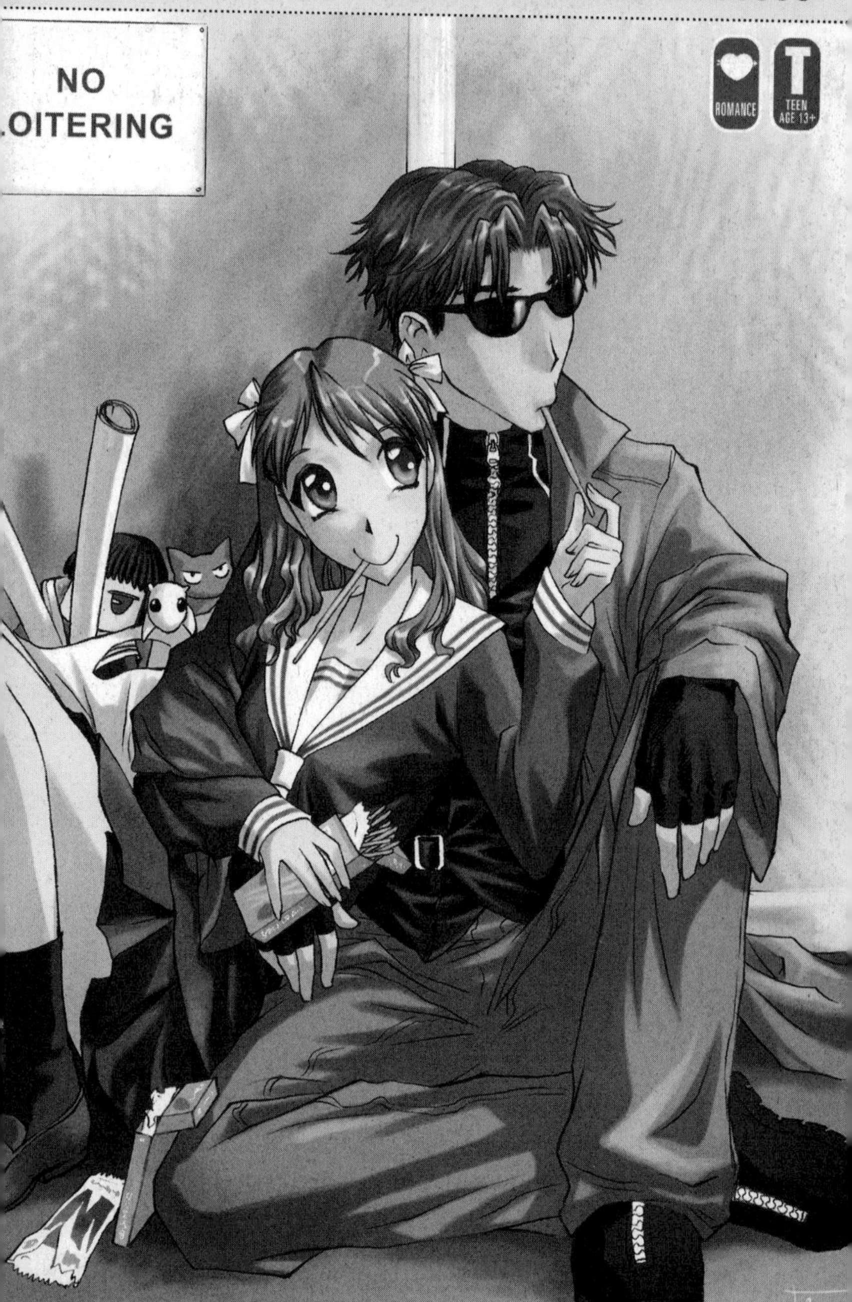
NO
OITERING
ROMANCE
T
TEEN
AGE 13+

STOP!

This is the back of the book.
You wouldn't want to spoil a great ending!

This book is printed "manga-style," in the authentic Japanese right-to-left format. Since none of the artwork has been flipped or altered, readers get to experience the story just as the creator intended. You've been asking for it, so TOKYOPOP® delivered: authentic, hot-off-the-press, and far more fun!

DIRECTIONS

If this is your first time reading manga-style, here's a quick guide to help you understand how it works.

It's easy... just start in the top right panel and follow the numbers. Have fun, and look for more 100% authentic manga from TOKYOPOP®!